PLASTICS
NOW

PLASTICS NOW

On Architecture's Relationship to
a Continuously Emerging Material

BILLIE FAIRCLOTH

Routledge
Taylor & Francis Group

LONDON AND NEW YORK

First published 2015
by Routledge
2 Park Square, Milton Park, Abingdon, Oxon OX14 4RN

and by Routledge
711 Third Avenue, New York, NY 10017

Routledge is an imprint of the Taylor & Francis Group, an informa business

British Library Cataloguing-in-Publication Data
A catalogue record for this book is available from the British Library

Library of Congress Cataloging-in-Publication Data
Faircloth, Billie.
Plastics now : on architecture's relationship to a continuously emerging material / Billie Faircloth.
    pages cm
Includes bibliographical references.
1. Plastics in building. 2. Architecture. I. Title.
    TA668.F35 2015
    691'.92—dc23
    2014029295

ISBN: 978-1-138-80450-0 (hbk)
ISBN: 978-1-138-80451-7 (pbk)

Typeset by Alex Lazarou

Printed and bound in the United States of America by Sheridan Books, Inc. (a Sheridan Group Company).

CONTENTS

ACKNOWLEDGMENTS

This collection was partially compiled during a time of transition, from academia into practice. "I acknowledge that plastics are difficult to decipher" was my first admission to anyone willing to engage the scope of this project, individuals from two distinct contexts: The University of Texas at Austin, Austin, Texas and the architectural practice of KieranTimberlake, Philadelphia, Pennsylvania.

At the University of Texas at Austin, I thank research assistant Robert Gay, a talented practitioner who worked alongside me while discovering historical gems that would ultimately lead to this project. I also thank colleagues Elizabeth Danze, Larry Doll, David Heymann, Larry Speck, Fritz Steiner, and Nichole Wiedemann, who listened and provided insight into my schemes.

At KieranTimberlake, I thank Stephen Kieran and James Timberlake, who provided considerable support and encouragement to finish this project and consistently asked, "Are you getting everything that you need?" Your support of querying inside our profession is one to be emulated. I thank Roderick Bates, Stephanie Carlisle, Peter Curry, and Eric Eisele, individuals with respective backgrounds in environmental management, lifecycle assessment, materials engineering, and fabrication, who deciphered and interpreted several technical aspects of this story. I thank Laura Buck, Andrea Calabretta, Laurent Hedquist, Crystal Peebles, Ryan Mellier, Carly Regn, Sarah Richendollar, and Hale Youngblood, who provided administrative, editorial, or illustrative support. I particularly thank Alex Cohn and Carin Whitney, who worked through several compiled and original data sets to help concoct original timelines and indices.

This book represents ten years of interaction with plastics across emerging and conventional paradigms. Working through plastics began in design studios taught at the University of Texas at Austin and in partnership with Cornerstone Research Group of Dayton, Ohio, in 2005 and 2006. At Cornerstone Research Group, I thank Patrick Hood, Ben Dietsch, and Tat Tong, who provided shadowing opportunities with their scientists and engineers which allowed me to understand the inherent design processes embedded in materials engineering and the considerable overlap between our professions. Tracking down plastics use in architecture began in December 2005 with work funded by the Association of Collegiate Schools of Architecture (ACSA) and the American Chemistry Council (ACC), work that provided the initial spark toward framing the position taken in this book. I thank ACSA Executive Director Michael Monti, ACC associates Rob Krebs and D'Lane Wisner for supporting the querying that ultimately led to this deeper investigation and for facilitating interaction with several in the plastics industry who might provide insight into chemistry, manufacturing, and processing. Finally, I thank the Graham Foundation who provided initial funding for this project and through their granting programs value and promote similar works of scholarship by architects and designers.

Along the way there have been noted presentations of the accumulated body of evidence alongside those individuals, designers, manufacturers, and chemists possessing a similar bent to dissect and sleuth materials in their context. The subject of "defining plastics" was presented at the fall 2009 symposium entitled *Plastics Modernities* organized by Jonathan Massey at Syracuse University's School of Architecture. Findings from this manuscript were delivered in the presentation "All. Plastics. In. Building.," at the spring 2011 symposium *Permanent Change* organized by Michael Bell and held at Columbia University's Graduate School of Architecture, Planning and Preservation. This presentation was subsequently formatted into the essay "All-Plastics (-in-Building)," and published in *Permanent Change: Plastics in Architecture and Engineering*, edited by Michael Bell and Craig Buckley (New York, NY: Princeton Architectural Press, 2014).

During the writing of this book I became convinced that plastics and the application in architecture was an inert proposition. Nowhere could I find a more effectual, yet problem-causing material, one capable of exciting much interest and debate simultaneously, yet willing to remain explicitly unnamed. This game of material "20 questions" that plastics are so prone to excite at times astounded, taxed, and overwhelmed.

In light of my admitted struggle, bordering on obsession with sleuthing why we use plastics the way that we do, and the fits and starts associated with many of these historical materials, I thank Jim and Calliope for your encouragement to do good work and to be patient. Finally, I dedicate this work to Julia, Bill, Ellen, Lynne, Holly, Jim, Lucas, and Calliope.

PROLOGUE
HOW SHOULD WE USE PLASTICS?

> The macromolecular compounds include the most important substances occurring in nature such as proteins, enzymes, the nucleic acids, besides the polysaccharides such as cellulose, starch and pectins, as well as rubber and lastly the large number of new, fully synthetic plastics and artificial fibers. Macromolecular chemistry is very important both for technology and for biology … In light of this new knowledge of macromolecular chemistry, the wonder of Life in its chemical aspect is revealed in the astounding abundance and masterly macromolecular architecture of living matter.[1]

> (Hermann Staudinger
> Chemist)

Plastics are defined by their complexity. They are products to be accounted for and processes to be described: a phenomena. Their sheer number and proliferation justifies the proclamation of a material ecosystem fully formed in a short 100 years.

Plastics' descriptive chatter is sometimes barely comprehensible, but offers certainty – the melting temperature of polycarbonate, additives for stability in ultraviolet light, and coefficients portending thermal expansion. But plastics' play is altogether different; in our minds it promises (tacit) knowing, comprehensibly worked out by the working of material in tune and step – moldable – "plastics" is synonymous with "plasticity." Plastics were never so easy to work with, never so easy to specify, never intended for architecture's physical and formal largeness – never so easy, but oh so alluring.

In the beginning, plastics' thermal transformation and mass manipulation was best understood, best controlled at the scale of the button, the hair comb, the snuffbox, the small and ornamental things. "How should we use plastics?" – a question with its origins in the profession of chemistry. Hermann Staudinger's persistence in describing the attributes and functionality of a macromolecular terrain in 1920 would only – could only – end with one word: application.[2] "How should we use plastics?!" – a question posed but unanswered by readers of *Modern Plastics* in 1926. "What we wanted, and are still looking for, is a really NEW use for the various plastic materials used in industry."[3] Momentary disappointment prevailed; not one idea merited a prize. The same comb, the same snuffbox, the same small things were suggested. "Plastics" or phenols were 15 years old; backer rod, rug underlayment, and skylights were just out of imagination's reach, along with the "all-plastic house." "How should we use plastics?" – an equally tired and boring question. Industry answered with "By the pound!"[4] Yet, multiple professions and popular culture claimed plastics, all rife with form, fashion, and function.

Who answered this question for architecture? And how was it answered?

NOTES

1   Hermann Staudinger. "Macromolecular Chemistry," in *Nobel Lectures, Chemistry 1942–1962* (Amsterdam: Elsevier Publishing Company, 1964), 397.

2   In the 1920s Hermann Staudinger hypothesized the existence and established the study of very large, long molecules with high molecular weight – cellulose, rubber, starch, sugars, those naturally occurring and those synthetically made. These are polymers. While working these types of materials began long before with others, Staudinger persisted in describing the attributes of such molecules, arguing that they were a class unto themselves and setting them apart from other molecular arrangements. He then dedicated his life's work to describing the attributes of "macromolecules." In 1953 he would receive a Nobel Prize for his work in the field. See his Nobel Lecture recounting this work delivered on December 11, 1953, titled "Macromolecular Chemistry."

3   *Modern Plastics*. 1926. "Ideas! Ideas!" 349.

4   Bruce Martin of *Architectural Review* likewise asked this question in the article titled "How Should We Use Plastics?" – a review of the first "all-plastics" house. See *Architectural Review*. 1956.

The emergence of plastics in architecture

Ninety-plus polymers listed by name and their phenomenal emergence over time. The first tick notes year of discovery (by accident or by intentional search), and the second notes year of commercial availability. Is 90 an important number? Not necessarily. There are hundreds if not thousands of polymers. Yet, these 90 plus have been "found" affiliated with architectural production as early as 1933 through direct mention in architectural journals, or direct use in prototypical experiments. Though synthetic polymers or "plastics" dominate, this list is inclusive of some naturally occurring ones such as keratin, and some recently emerged "smart" or "multifunctional" ones such as shape memory polymers. In aggregate this list suggests our implicit comprehension – materials in general and plastics specifically require much working as they continuously emerge.

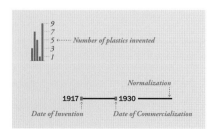

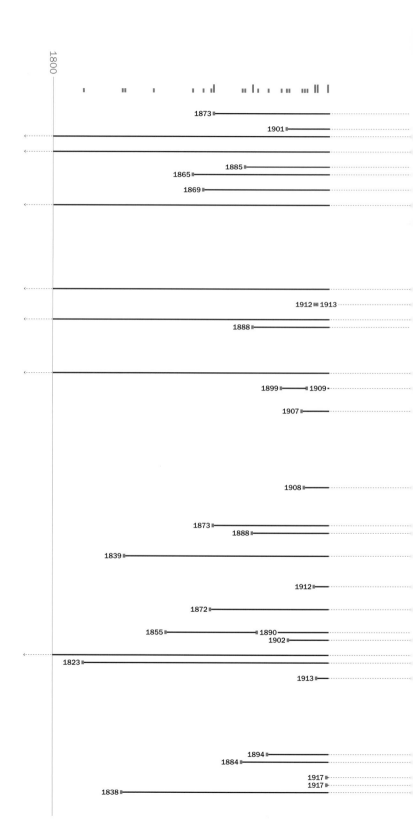

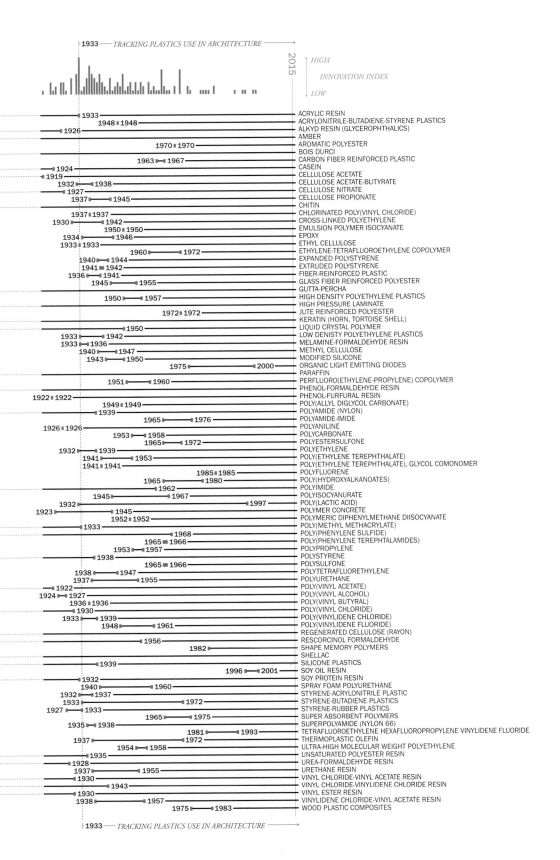

|1933 — *TRACKING PLASTICS USE IN ARCHITECTURE* ⟶

2015

HIGH

INNOVATION INDEX

LOW

|1933 — ACRYLIC RESIN
1948 ▪ 1948 — ACRYLONITRILE-BUTADIENE-STYRENE PLASTICS
◀ 1926 — ALKYD RESIN (GLYCEROPHTHALICS)
— AMBER
1970 ▪ 1970 — AROMATIC POLYESTER
— BOIS DURCI
1963 ▶—◀ 1967 — CARBON FIBER REINFORCED PLASTIC
◀ 1924 — CASEIN
◀ 1919 — CELLULOSE ACETATE
1932 ▶—◀ 1938 — CELLULOSE ACETATE-BUTYRATE
◀ 1927 — CELLULOSE NITRATE
1937 ▶—◀ 1945 — CELLULOSE PROPIONATE
— CHITIN
1937 ▪ 1937 — CHLORINATED POLY(VINYL CHLORIDE)
1930 ▶—◀ 1942 — CROSS-LINKED POLYETHYLENE
1950 ▪ 1950 — EMULSION POLYMER ISOCYANATE
1934 ▶—◀ 1946 — EPOXY
1933 ▪ 1933 — ETHYL CELLULOSE
1960 ▶————◀ 1972 — ETHYLENE-TETRAFLUOROETHYLENE COPOLYMER
1940 ▶—◀ 1944 — EXPANDED POLYSTYRENE
1941 ▪ 1942 — EXTRUDED POLYSTYRENE
1936 ▶—◀ 1941 — FIBER-REINFORCED PLASTIC
1945 ▶——◀ 1955 — GLASS FIBER REINFORCED POLYESTER
— GUTTA-PERCHA
1950 ▶—◀ 1957 — HIGH DENSITY POLYETHYLENE PLASTICS
— HIGH PRESSURE LAMINATE
1972 ▪ 1972 — JUTE REINFORCED POLYESTER
— KERATIN (HORN, TORTOISE SHELL)
◀ 1950 — LIQUID CRYSTAL POLYMER
1933 ▶—◀ 1942 — LOW DENISTY POLYETHYLENE PLASTICS
1933 ▶—◀ 1936 — MELAMINE-FORMALDEHYDE RESIN
1940 ▶—◀ 1947 — METHYL CELLULOSE
1943 ▶—◀ 1950 — MODIFIED SILICONE
1975 ▶————————◀ 2000 — ORGANIC LIGHT EMITTING DIODES
— PARAFFIN
1951 ▶——◀ 1960 — PERFLUORO(ETHYLENE-PROPYLENE) COPOLYMER
— PHENOL-FORMALDEHYDE RESIN
1922 ▪ 1922 — PHENOL-FURFURAL RESIN
1949 ▪ 1949 — POLY(ALLYL DIGLYCOL CARBONATE)
◀ 1939 — POLYAMIDE (NYLON)
1965 ▶——◀ 1976 — POLYAMIDE-IMIDE
1926 ▪ 1926 — POLYANILINE
1953 ▶—◀ 1958 — POLYCARBONATE
1965 ▶—◀ 1972 — POLYESTERSULFONE
1932 ▶—◀ 1939 — POLYETHYLENE
1941 ▶—◀ 1953 — POLY(ETHYLENE TEREPHTHALATE)
1941 ▪ 1941 — POLY(ETHYLENE TEREPHTHALATE), GLYCOL COMONOMER
1985 ▪ 1985 — POLYFLUORENE
1965 ▶—◀ 1980 — POLY(HYDROXYALKANOATES)
◀ 1962 — POLYIMIDE
1945 ▶——◀ 1967 — POLYISOCYANURATE
1932 ▶——————◀ 1997 — POLY(LACTIC ACID)
1923 ▶—◀ 1945 — POLYMER CONCRETE
1952 ▪ 1952 — POLYMERIC DIPHENYLMETHANE DIISOCYANATE
◀ 1933 — POLY(METHYL METHACRYLATE)
◀ 1968 — POLY(PHENYLENE SULFIDE)
1965 ▪ 1966 — POLY(PHENYLENE TEREPHTALAMIDES)
1953 ▶—◀ 1957 — POLYPROPYLENE
◀ 1938 — POLYSTYRENE
1965 ▪ 1966 — POLYSULFONE
1938 ▶—◀ 1947 — POLYTETRAFLUORETHYLENE
1937 ▶—◀ 1955 — POLYURETHANE
◀ 1922 — POLY(VINYL ACETATE)
1924 ▶—◀ 1927 — POLY(VINYL ALCOHOL)
1936 ▪ 1936 — POLY(VINYL BUTYRAL)
◀ 1930 — POLY(VINYL CHLORIDE)
1933 ▶—◀ 1939 — POLY(VINYLIDENE CHLORIDE)
1948 ▶——◀ 1961 — POLY(VINYLIDENE FLUORIDE)
— REGENERATED CELLULOSE (RAYON)
◀ 1956 — RESCORCINOL FORMALDEHYDE
1982 ◀ — SHAPE MEMORY POLYMERS
— SHELLAC
◀ 1939 — SILICONE PLASTICS
1996 ▶—◀ 2001 — SOY OIL RESIN
◀ 1932 — SOY PROTEIN RESIN
1940 ▶———◀ 1960 — SPRAY FOAM POLYURETHANE
1932 ▶—◀ 1937 — STYRENE-ACRYLONITRILE PLASTIC
1933 ▶—————◀ 1972 — STYRENE-BUTADIENE PLASTICS
1927 ▶—◀ 1933 — STYRENE-RUBBER PLASTICS
1965 ▶——◀ 1975 — SUPER ABSORBENT POLYMERS
1935 ▶—◀ 1938 — SUPERPOLYAMIDE (NYLON 66)
1981 ▶——◀ 1993 — TETRAFLUOROETHYLENE HEXAFLUOROPROPYLENE VINYLIDENE FLUORIDE
1937 ▶——————◀ 1972 — THERMOPLASTIC OLEFIN
1954 ▶—◀ 1958 — ULTRA-HIGH MOLECULAR WEIGHT POLYETHYLENE
◀ 1935 — UNSATURATED POLYESTER RESIN
◀ 1928 — UREA-FORMALDEHYDE RESIN
1937 ▶——◀ 1955 — URETHANE RESIN
◀ 1930 — VINYL CHLORIDE-VINYL ACETATE RESIN
◀ 1943 — VINYL CHLORIDE-VINYLIDENE CHLORIDE RESIN
◀ 1930 — VINYL ESTER RESIN
1938 ▶——◀ 1957 — VINYLIDENE CHLORIDE-VINYL ACETATE RESIN
1975 ▶——◀ 1983 — WOOD PLASTIC COMPOSITES

|1933 — *TRACKING PLASTICS USE IN ARCHITECTURE* ⟶

WRESTLING WITH THE EMERGENCE OF PLASTICS

METHODS

One might begin to determine who answered the question "How should we use plastics?" and the way it was answered by tracking plastics' architectural use with a simple experiment: Attempt to collect all architectural journal articles under the topical search "architecture and plastics."[1] This is precisely how this work began, although the initial motive for this undertaking was not an interest in plastics per se. Rather, it was a fascination extra to this material class. How do we talk to ourselves about emerging materials? Who does the talking? And does sufficient evidence remain amid one material's academic and industry chatter to discern the attributes and after-effects of its emergence?

Demand for "really NEW uses" now exists for a myriad of materials classed as emergent or smart. It is generally observed that production of architecture born out of the demand for "new uses" can fall into one of three categories: non-critical or applied research-driven material practices, political and entrepreneurial material practices, and critical or design-driven material practices.

One can reason that a "data set" describing the relationship between plastics and architecture over time is miniscule, a mere 80 years, compared to masonry's thousands. And one can reason that a data set can be found, making it a good candidate for this investigation. Plastics emerged alongside the maturing of popular architectural press, peer-reviewed press, and conference proceedings. Since 2000, architectural press documents more than 100 built works deploying plastics materials as large-scale totalizing elements – structures, façade systems, and building envelopes. But, simultaneously, we observe the day-to-day material practice of selecting plastics – insulation, rug backer, and baseboard. And presently we practice with plastics as building materials amidst the context of a debate regarding the material's general need for reinvention. Reinvention is present as chemical industries move polymerization practices toward green chemistry principles. These paired with the range of plastics building products, working of plastics, or literal plastics architecture should provide sufficient evidence to describe this material's trajectory as it engages the demands and desires of architecture over time.

And so, an initial hypothesis formed: The architectural journal cast as
a receptacle for popular architectural culture could provide significant
evidence regarding plastics' phenomenal emergence into architectural
application. It might contain enough evidence to suggest how plastics
normalized into the leading role of "bit part." Admittedly, attempting to
read our history this way is akin to being given a front row seat at a very
narrow venue.

Between 1934 and 2010, more than 200 articles can be found within the
following journals:

AD

Architecture

The Architectural Forum

The Architectural Review

AIA Journal

Architecture d' jour dui

Architect's Journal

Architecture Record

Association of Preservation of
    Technology

Architect

Bauen und Wohnen (Werk)

Casabella

Design Solutions

Detail

Harvard Design Magazine

House Beautiful

House and Home

Industrial Design

Interior Design and Decoration

L' Architettura

Metropolitan Home

Overseas Building Notes

Progressive Architecture

Techniques et Architecture

Urban Land

En-masse, this collection of articles functions as a quasi-history of the
relationship between plastics and architecture. This collection reveals
the designers who engaged plastics directly and tacitly, the experts who
would describe their mechanical properties and the societies and agencies
who would debate their proper application. The majority of articles occur
between 1940 and 1975. Fewer are available between 1975 and 1990. The
pace of references to plastics and architecture picks back up again around
the mid 1990s. It is no coincidence that this is the case.

Early articles on plastics attempt to transfer materials and fabrication
methods from World War II applications to building applications.[2] Efforts
are sustained through the 1950s and 1960s by the newly formed field
of materials science, where high-performing plastics gain mention and
transfer into popular culture. The oil crisis of 1973, lawsuits surrounding

foam plastics' burning characteristics in 1975, fatigue and failure of early plastics, and plastics' general normalization as building materials follow – hence, one can speculate, the offloading of the topic to "building"- and trade-related magazines rather than architectural journals. The engineering of high-performance, customized, multifunctional polymers and the continuous re-engineering of existing plastics provide the impetus for a second wave of enthusiasm.

The majority of publications occurring between 1955 and 1975 publish architectural projects, typically in survey style, and many of these projects are attributable to one plastic – polyester resin – and processes for producing composite stressed skin structures. However, a complete palette of architecturally affiliated plastics is likewise found, as are projects – houses, many of which are affiliated with prefabrication schemes, and structures – short- and long-span, all in prototypical form, and many that claim to be "all-plastic." Review of the publishing record of US journals *The Architectural Forum*, *Architectural Record*, and *Progressive Architecture* is enough to move our query forward by providing evidence of the several strategies used to describe and translate this new material to an architectural audience.

SOME EVIDENCE

Architectural Forum

Architectural Forum may be the first journal to publish a comprehensive survey of plastics products, and to use "survey style" as a didactic device with its article titled "Plastics in Building," appearing in the June issue of 1940. How to use plastics is summarized in four functional categories: molded products; cast, extruded, sheets, rods, and tubes; decorative laminates; and resin-bonded plywood. Plastics are proffered by name, including Bakelite, Lucite, Vinylite, Formica, Plexiglas, Marblette, Weldwood, and others. Applications for building products are amply demonstrated through arrays of photographs – a molded doorknob, an interior ceiling, and exterior siding. Here appears a complete kit of "plastics in building" alongside the promise of an "all-plastics" structure – a plane's fuselage made from resin-bonded plywood.

Forum's use of these photos in this way, which can now be interpreted as a critical juxtaposition of the conceptual positions "plastics in building," and "all-plastics," may have seemed as obvious at the time. On one hand, this article represents a thorough range of possibilities with a direct message: there is now a complete palette of building products made from plastics that can serve diverse functions. But there is also the potential to imagine a new kind of architecture, one that is based on a lightweight, stressed skin, all-plastics structure. *Architectural Forum*'s pairing appears, from our vantage point, laden with prescience and foreshadows the two dominant conceptual positions through which these materials would be worked out and worked on.

But the editor also presents plastics as an incomprehensible and unwieldy material class with the promise to supplant every known building material:

> Another purely mental handicap which holds back the application of plastics to building is their very multiplicity. In the first place, no one seems to know just where the field begins and ends. By any definition, rubber, glass and putty – to mention only a few "ordinary" plastic materials – are just as much plastics as cellulose acetate and acrylic resins. Secondly, even the new synthetic materials are so numerous and various that they defy generalization, and discoveries are being made every day which render yesterday's advances partially or wholly obsolete. Unfortunately for the builder, there is no "plastics store" where he may purchase any or all of the materials, and simply to decide which of the kinds on the market is most appropriate to a given purpose can be a man-sized job.
>
> What building professionals need, therefore, is not so much a smattering of Plastics chemistry as a guide to readily available products and their common applications, plus an estimate of the probable effect of present trends and developments on construction technique. To this end the material on the following pages has been broken-down according to functional rather than chemical classification.[3]

The problem with these series of statements is that architects still utter them. From our present-day perspective, our originality may be questioned; but more importantly it is observed that this kind of relationship between plastics and architecture – what amounts to gross materials mystification – persists.

Fourteen years later the editorial chairman published "In Architecture, Will Atomic Processes Create a New 'Plastic' Order?" It appears in the September issue of 1954 and begins with the image of a leaf, an egg, and a shell – a collection of natural structures that are simulacra for future architectures made from plastics. Here provocation is based as much on current "form types" by architects Saarinen, Corbusier, Breuer, and Nervi as it is on a technical breakthrough, which is the use of irradiation to change the physical properties of plastics.[4] The single shell, the monocoque, the "all-plastic" conceptual position is summarized thusly:

> Tomorrow's structure may be typically all "skin." Its skin may be formed to become its shell and its interior columns of cellular structure. Even its "windows" may be simply transparent patches of its skin. A single continuous envelope of a thin sandwich material may yield structure and enclosure; resistance to destructive forces from outside; solidity or porosity; control of light and view; insulation for heat and sound, color and finish – all the characteristics we now impose separately.[5]

Architectural Record

Architectural Record's first offering on plastics is as comprehensive as *Forum*'s but adopts a text-based approach instead of an image- and brand-based one. "Plastics … Practically Speaking," appearing in its April 1943 issue, is as its title suggests, a thorough and current description of methods for working plastics, and an itemization of the classes of plastics available. A supply chain diagram is provided to describe the "lines of flow" for building products made from plastics. The only diagram in the article, it supports the overall message that plastics are accessible. But from our perspective, this diagram is beguiling. It is inclusive of "manufacturing chemists," connected to "molders, extruders, laminators, fabricators, and manufacturers of surface finishes," connected to "dealers and distributors," connected to "ultimate consumers." And though the author means from the outset to set aside hyperbole, when he stretches designers across the entire supply chain, implying a relationship with all of its actors, he is making a bid, a proposal, a wish, for a kind of relationship with plastics that suggests what the optimal relationship to plastics should be.

In subsequent articles *Architectural Record* continues this thorough and direct strategy, though augmenting it by engaging an emerging

Architectural Engineering

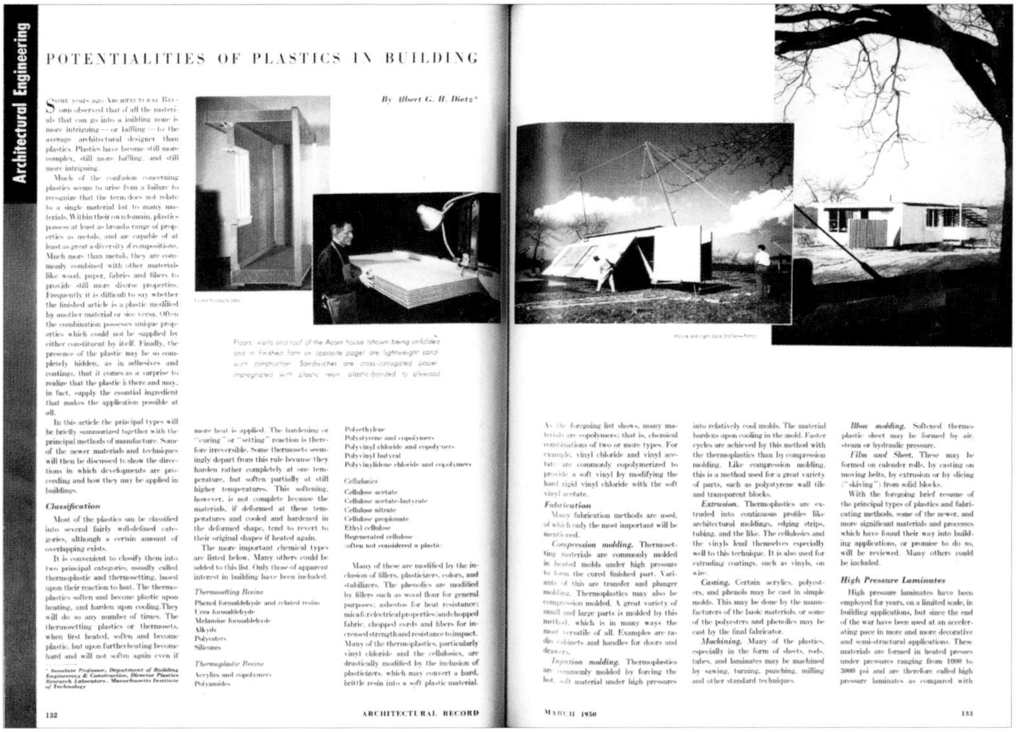

POTENTIALITIES OF PLASTICS IN BUILDING

By Albert G. H. Dietz*

Floors, walls and roof of the Acorn house (shown being unfolded and in finished form on opposite page) are lightweight sandwich construction. Sandwiches are cross-corrugated paper impregnated with plastic resin, plastic-bonded to plywood

132 ARCHITECTURAL RECORD MARCH 1950 133

ARCHITECTURAL ENGINEERING AE

SELECTING PLASTICS FOR BUILDING USES

By Albert G. H. Dietz*

Five years ago in this section Professor Dietz wrote that "The next five to ten years may be expected to bring out new materials, modifications of the old and further applications." While this has happened, perhaps more significant is the fact that architects are using plastics with much greater confidence and are more actively exploring new applications. To aid in the appraisal of plastics for building, present and future, this article discusses the physical properties of plastics, describes fabrication methods and outlines the types of plastics—all of this being related to actual and potential uses in buildings. The article also identifies the various building components that today are made of plastics

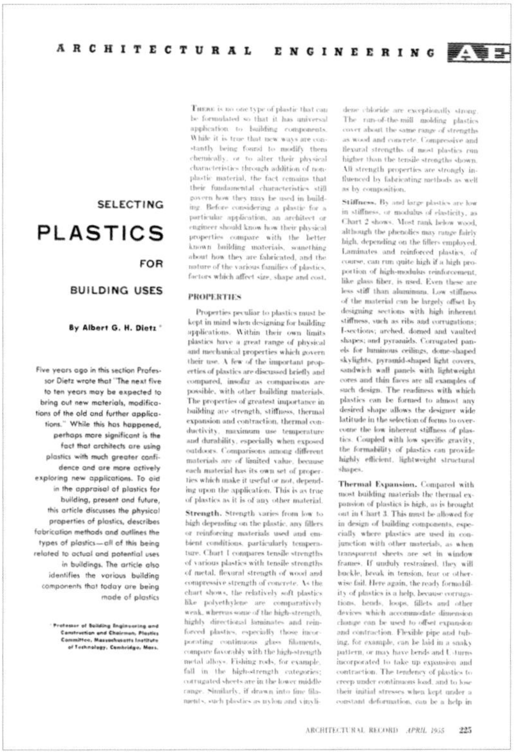

ARCHITECTURAL RECORD APRIL 1955 225

In *Architectural Record* Dr. Albert G.H. Dietz provides technical surveys on emerging plastics.

TOP
"The Potentialities of Plastics in Building," March 1950.

BOTTOM
"Selecting Plastics for Building Uses," March 1955.

Dow Chemical Company "Five Minute
Forum on Plastics," appearing in the
August 1944 issue of *Architectural
Record*.

plastics expert, Dr. Albert G.H. Dietz, a professor of civil engineering and
architecture at the Massachusetts Institute of Technology, to translate
this material class to architects. Dr. Dietz had previously authored
Materials of Construction: Wood, Plastics, Fabrics (1949), which provided a
comprehensive overview of new materials. *Architectural Record* published
"Potentialities of Plastics in Building" in March 1950. In it, Dr. Dietz reviews
classes of plastics and provides a comparative analysis between their
attributes. Unlike any previously published article, Dr. Dietz is intent on
conveying this information numerically. Plastics are simply described and
understood to be known, as other materials, numerically and therefore
capable of being engineered into structural shapes. "Selecting Plastics for
Building Uses," published in April 1955, is presented to the reader as an
update to these previously published tables.

Advertisements for building products made with plastics begin to appear
in the mid 1940s in several journals. The *Architectural Record*'s August 1944
issue includes advertisements for Formica, which directs architects to view
the film *The Formica Story*. In the same issue, Dow Chemical Company's
advertisement under the heading "Five Minute Forum on Plastics"
questions, "What have plastics in common with metals?" and reviews the
properties of its products "Styron," "Ethocel," and "Saran." Advertisements are
seemingly innocuous in the data set, yet recognizing when they emerge
corroborates the timing of commercially available off-the-shelf plastics
products, and the initiation of our practices with plastics such as procuring
them as "customers" in the building products supply chain, deciphering
them to specify them for buildings, and determining if they comply with
building code.

Progressive Architecture

Of all architectural journals, *Progressive Architecture* consistently addresses
plastics applications, successfully capturing their sobering normalization.
The first article, "Design Data for Acrylic Plastics," published in January
1946, begins simply but effectively to summarize the optical and light
conductance qualities of acrylics. The topic is addressed again with "Acrylic
Plastics in Architecture" in 1949, followed by "Vinyl Plastics and Resins in
Architecture" in 1951, and "Plastics for Interior Walls" in 1956. Up to this
point, the articles are direct, lacking hyperbolic speech. But in 1960, the
journal makes a significant decision: Devote an entire issue to plastics.

With the title "Plastics in Architecture," the editors provide the following agenda for its June 1960 issue:

> In the following review, [we] have attempted to reflect this whopping use of plastics components in contemporary architecture. Presentations of origins, definitions, and applications; foams; structural possibilities; residential potentials; decorative embedments; performance evaluations; related and interior design data; and the chemist's participation; may lead the designer to a better knowledge of plastics as now used, and open vistas of consideration for the future.[6]

The journal seems finally ready to declare plastics a legitimate material for architectural production: By its publishing date, 16 all-plastic houses had been prototyped, documented, and circulated. Two of them, All-Plastic House (France) and Monsanto Corporation's House of the Future (US), had made international headlines. A US model building code on plastics developed by the Society of the Plastics Industry (SPI) and the Manufacturing Chemists' Association (MCA) was put forth for adoption in 1955. The US National Research Council's Building Research Institute (NRC BRI) formed a Plastics Study Group, and by 1960 had held successive conferences. The proceedings from each nearly sold out. And though plastics building products were numerous, their taxonomy was clearly not of interest to *Progressive Architecture*. Instead, the journal emphasized a plastics architecture, both light-transmitting and plastically conceived, informed by material attributes. The June 1960 compilation is, at its best, a sleuthing exercise, and it is the most comprehensive up to that date, even to the point of engaging chemists and engineers as informants.

Given their rigor, *Progressive Architecture*'s decade of silence on plastics might seem misplaced, but in 1970 the journal again decided to devote an entire issue to the topic of plastics in architecture. For the issue's preparation, the journal consulted with Dr. Dietz, and Armand Winfield. Like Dietz, Winfield had committed himself to knowing plastics, and his activities were broad across the field – surveys of plastics use, materials research, and education on plastics.[7] The journal's editors addressed the topic of plastics use in architecture with the following admission:

Progressive Architecture **publishes its first whole issue dedicated to the subject of plastics in architecture, June 1960.**

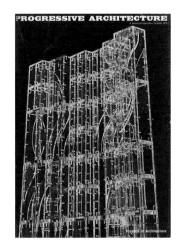

Progressive Architecture **publishes its second whole issue dedicated to the subject of plastics in architecture ten years later, October 1970.**

Ten years ago when the editors of P/A developed their last major review of the man-made plastic materials, they believed that architecture was about to enter the age of plastics. Although the volume of this material used annually in building construction has increased substantially we have not experienced the many exciting and innovative uses of plastics that were expected. However, there have been notable refinements in design and construction techniques, just as there continue to be misapplications and unabashedly obtuse designs.[8]

These introductory comments reflect that between 1960 and 1970, experimentation with plastics architecture continued – especially with glass fiber reinforced plastics – and resulted in an additional 40-plus all-plastic house prototypes and further characterization of plastics as structural materials. But experimentation was not normal practice. Architecture's structural, spatial, and phenomenal paradigms remained intact, undiluted by this material class. On the other hand, the pounds of plastics sold per year in the form of plastics products increased. The new normal, it seemed, was for plastics to completely and surreptitiously supplant building products made from other materials.

"Pandora's Plastics Box," published in the September 1975 issue of *Progressive Architecture*, bids adieu to "all-plastics" and gives the SPI the floor to tell architects what they believe we should know about plastics. SPI is direct: Stop experimenting and start paying attention to plastics' attributes. Sensibility is brought to the fore as the plastics industry finds itself in the atmosphere of "oil shock," and addressing life safety issues related to the actual rather than ASTM-tested burning characteristics of foam plastics.[9, 10]

Progressive Architecture finally retreated to the normalized realm of plastics products. "Update on Plastic Laminates" was published in August 1977. It was followed by "High-impact Material" in August 1979, again on the topic of plastic laminates. The "Light Heavyweights" is *Progressive Architecture*'s final offering on the topic in October 1981. Here, the subject of light-transmitting plastics, polycarbonate and acrylic, is covered, with the following introduction indicating the occurrence of a second "oil shock" in 1979, but also foreshadowing a future debate on resources for building materials:

It does seem a devilish fate that many of the same brainchildren that are so dependent on petroleum provide some of the best insulating materials and the most versatile energy-saving glazing. Further typifying the influence of human nature and man's incapacity to fully predict the ramifications of his inventions, the greatest weaknesses that plastics have are related to the health and safety problems for building occupants which can occur when such materials are incautiously used.[11]

PLASTICS INERTIA

There remains a problematic finding amidst the total collection of journal articles, one which compelled this work forward in an unpredicted direction. As a separate experiment, 16 articles from which to track mention of specific plastics over time were selected. The results of this experiment are provided in *Plastics in Architecture, a Slightly Unorthodox Bibliography*. Articles were selected to participate in this experiment for one of two reasons: Either they were the most comprehensive for their time, claiming to summarize plastics materials at a precise moment in architectural practice, or they were the most provocative of their time, suggesting a direction for this material class. While in the process of recording the mention of cellulose acetate butyrate here or polyvinyl chloride there, what comes to the fore are a series of statements, repeated regardless of decade or disposition of author:

> Plastics are (a/the/in our) future.

> Plastics are not substitute materials.

> Plastics are difficult to decipher.

We cannot seem to help, then or now, but utter these statements about plastics, indicating a curious material predicament: inertia.

Plastics in architecture, a slightly unorthodox bibliography

Plastics named in 16 articles appearing in architectural journals published between 1940 and 2008 are tracked to create this collection. Articles are either comprehensive for their time, as in "these are the plastics now used by architects," or provocative for their time, as in "these are the plastics that might yield new aesthetics and new architectures." Implicit in this collection is the author's choice to eschew the general identifier "plastics" for more precise and descriptive chemical identifiers such as "cellulose acetate," or "polyvinyl chloride," a choice that might indicate some tenacity. Which plastics are mentioned, how often and when, and might we discern a trend? Polymethyl methacrylate, also known as acrylic, has a sustained mention, as does glass fiber reinforced plastics and several in the polyvinyl family. Foam and adhesive chemistries are amply represented. The early plastics, the cellulosics, see mentions then and now. Somewhere in time, promise for use meets up with experimentation in prototypes for architecture (see pp. 172–3 and pp. 258–9).

1 Plastics in Building
The Architectural Forum
June 1940

2 Plastics…Practically Speaking
Rober F. Marshall, Architectural Record
June 1943

3 Potentialities of Plastics in Building
Albert G.H. Dietz, Architectural Record
April 1950

4 Potentialities of Plastics in Building
Albert G.H. Dietz, Architectural Record
April 1955

5 Look how many ways you can now use PLASTICS!"
House & Home
September 1956

6 BRI Reviews Plastics for Roof Construction
Journal of the AIA
December 1957

7 Plastics Permeate Specifications Sections
Progressive Architecture
October 1960

8 Structural Plastics in Europe
Z.S. Makowski, Arts and Architecture
August 1966

9 A Case Study: The Plastic House
Armand G. Winfield, Progressive Architecture
October 1970

10 Foam: The controversial new building material
House & Garden
May 1973

11 Pandora's Plastic Box
Progressive Architecture
September, 1975

12 The Light Heavyweights
Progressive Architecture
October 1981

13 Plastics, Past and Future
Forrest Wilson, Architecture
April 1988

14 Multi-Source Synthesis: Atomic Architecture
Battle and McCarthy, Architectural Design
January/February 1995

15 Mutant Materials: On plastics and other artifacts of material culture
Paola Antonelli, Harvard Design Magazine
Summer 1998

16 Plastics: Ethereal Materials or Trash Culture?
Simone Jeska, Detail Magazine
May 2008

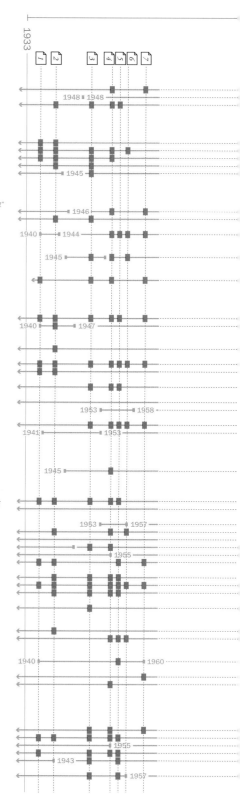

Instance of Plastics Found

TRACKING PLASTICS USE IN ARCHITECTURE

Plastics are (a/the/ in our) future

Again and again plastics embody a promise of something new; yes, new forms, new aesthetics, new performance, but also something newly desired, intuited as possible but yet to be known with descriptive thoroughness.

"Design Principles Applied to Plastics"   **Feb 1940**
Interior Design and Decoration

"Plastics in Building"   **Jun 1940**
The Architectural Forum

"The New World of Plastics"   **Jan 1943**
The New Pencil Points

"Plastics...Practically Speaking"   **Apr 1943**
Architectural Record

"Potentialities of Plastics in Building"   **Apr 1950**
Architectural Record

"Why Polyethylene?"   **Feb 1955**
Industrial Design

"How Should we Use Plastics?"   **Aug 1956**
Architectural Review

"Look how many ways you can now use PLASTICS!"   **Sep 1956**
House & Home

"Future: Role of the Chemist"   **Oct 1960**
Progressive Architecture

"The Structural Use of Foam Plastics"   **Aug 1966**
Arts and Architecture

"Structural Plastics in Europe"   **Aug 1966**
Arts and Architecture

"A Case Study: The Plastic House"   **Oct 1970**
Progressive Architecture

"Foam: The controversial new building material"   **May 1973**
House and Garden

"The Light Heavyweights"   **Oct 1981**
Progressive Architecture

"Plastics, Past and Future"   **Apr 1988**
Architecture

"Multi-Source Synthesis: Atomic Architecture"   **Jan 1995**
Architectural Design

"Mutant Materials: On plastics and other artifacts of material culture"   **Aug 1998**
Harvard Design Magazine

"Plastics: Ethereal Mateirals or Trash Culture?"   **May 2008**
Detail Magazine

"Plastics represent a very large part of the enormously expanded resources that we have at our command today for the building of a saner and better world." —Walter Dorwin Teage, pg. 44

"What building professionals need, therefore, is not so much a smattering of Plastics chemistry as a guide to readily available products and their common applications, plus an estimate of the probable effect of present trends and developments on construction technique." —pg. 412

"The future of plastics is exciting because of two things—availability and physical properties. They are made from everything. Wood waste, coal war chemicals, petroleum gases, brine, limestone, air, cotton, natural gas, skim milk, fat products and wastes, and plant oils. They will be cheap in the world of tomorrow." —Raymond R. Dickey, pg. 38

"There is a great opportunity for joining the skills of the architect and the plastics industry. Its realization waits upon a better understanding of their mutual needs and abilities." —Robert F. Marshall, pg. 54

"The entire industry is still developing fast, and the next five to ten years may be expected to bring out new materials, modifications of the old, and further applications." —Albert G.H. Dietz, pg. 137

"Last year there were only two major producers of polyethylene powder: Bakelite and Du Pont. This year their may be as many as nine: first of the new suppliers to get into production is Eastman Chemical. The increased tonnage on the market means two things to American industry: more possibilities for design in this material, and decreasing cost." —pg. 48

"In recent years the range of plastics has widened considerably so that the requirements of a particular building component may be satisfied by using the most suitable plastic material. But the concept of 'component' is itself relatively new, and it is clear that with new materials the form of a traditional component may change radically." —Bruce Martin, pg. 134

"Plastics have already found a big and growing market for some 50 uses in today's house. And almost every day brings out a new plastic or a new way to use a plastic." —pg. 119

"In the future, tailor-made plastics with specific built-in properties will undoubtedly become even more common as new families of plastics are discovered and new ways of making and handling them are developed." —James H. Krieger, pg. 202

"The main research goal can therefore be considered to be the development of total systems involving the design, production and marketing of foam plastic structures in which adjustments can be readily made to cover the widest possible range of housing requirements in each developing country." —pg. 10

"In the past, the use of plastics has been confined most exclusively to non-load bearing elements. However, during recent years considerable interest has been focused on semi-and even fully structural applications of plastics. Most of such applications are still largely of experimental nature, but with the great interest expressed in plastics materials and with the rapidly increasing volume of research on structural plastics now being carried out at many universities and government research establishments, one can expect with every confidence a real breakthrough in structural use of plastics during the next decade." —Z.S. Makowski, pg. 20

"What do plastics have to offer the building profession? Most important, they release the architect and builder from the conventional confines of modules, and from restrictions of the senior materials (wood, metals, concrete, etc.)." —Armand G. Winfield, pg. 81

"In the last few years, many architects and designers have been experimenting with sprayed urethane foam to change the shape of rooms or even to build whole houses." —pg. 58

"More than any other building material, plastics are a creation of the human mind. The vital link with the human thought process has accounted for the great variety of plastics available as well as the hundreds of products and applications plastics have in buildings. It does seem a devilish fate that many of the same brainchildren that are so dependent upon petroleum provide some of the best insulating materials and most versatile energy-saving glazing." —pg. 125

"He [Uwe S. Wascher] says plastic buildings are inevitable. The building and construction industry is the largest plastics market in the world, with packaging a distant second and car bodies third. A hundred times more plastic material is consumed in building and construction than in the automotive industry. Plastics is also the fastest growing material industry in the world, and it is the only proven, affordable material capable of meeting the increasingly crucial, constant demand for building, he continues." —Forrest Wilson, pg. 103–104

"In particular, the plastics industry and institutions...are investing huge resources into polymer research and development including being able to construct industrial components from small molecules without the necessity of melting and casting. The cloning of such a process will herald a new technical revolution in mass production of recycled atoms and molecular matrices." —Battle and McCarthy, pg. iii

"Plastic is, of course, one of the most important materials of our age—and perhaps the material of the 20th century." —Paola Antonelli, pg. 47

"As a result of the dissolution of the relationship between form and material and the attendant altered approach to design, plastics have now been re-established in experimental architecture." —Simone Jeska, pg. 12

Plastics are not substitute materials

Assiduous assertions of what plastics are not appear alongside assertions of what they are, revealing the resident tension that comes from lumping hundreds of materials into one material class whose chief property has and always will be "transmutation" – or shifting into a form previously occupied and known culturally to be inhabited by another material.

"Design Principles Applied to Plastics" ----- **Feb 1940**
Interior Design and Decoration

"The New World of Plastics" ----- **Jan 1943**
The New Pencil Points

"Plastics...Practically Speaking" ----- **Apr 1943**
Architectural Record

"Potentialities of Plastics in Building" ----- **Apr 1950**
Architectural Record

"Selecting Plastics for Buildng Uses" ----- **Apr 1955**
Architectural Record

"Look how many ways you can now use...PLASTICS!" ----- **Sep 1956**
House & Home

"BRI Reviews Plastics for Roof Construction" ----- **Dec 1957**
Journal of the AIA

"Future: Role of the Chemist" ----- **Oct 1960**
Progressive Architecture

"The Structural Use of Foam Plastics" ----- **Aug 1966**
Arts and Architecture

"Structural Plastics in Europe" ----- **Aug 1966**
Arts and Architecture

"Plastics and the Building Code" ----- **Oct 1970**
Progressive Architecture

"A Case Study: The Plastic House" ----- **Oct 1970**
Progressive Architecture

"Pandora's Plastic Box" ----- **Sep 1975**
Progressive Architecture

"The Light Heavyweights" ----- **Oct 1981**
Progressive Architecture

"Plastics, Past and Future" ----- **Apr 1988**
Architecture

"Mutant Materials: On plastics and other artifacts of material culture" ----- **Aug 1998**
Harvard Design Magazine

"Plastics: Ethereal Mateirals or Trash Culture?" ----- **May 2008**
Detail Magazine

"Plastics are not substitutes; they have virtues of their own. And those virtues must be realized and developed." —Walter Dorwin Teage, pg. 46

"In plastics, industry has magic things which can be altered to any need that the builders of the future may require. They can be transparent for windows that pass the ultraviolet light of the sun, or opaque, as you choose. They can be gaudy or somber, sound deadening or brassy loud, strong or fragile, smooth or rough, rigid or flexible—if you don't see what you want, ask. The only thing we haven't got is what hasn't been thought of yet." —Raymond R. Dickey, pg. 38

"One thing should be said at the outset. Plastics are not to be considered solely, or even chiefly, as substitutes for materials like glass, copper, aluminum, steel, wood and stone." —Rober F. Marshall, pg. 54

"Within their own domain, plastics possess at least as broad a range of properties as metals, and are capable of at least as great a diversity of compositions. Much more than metals, they are commonly combined with other materials like wood, paper, fabrics and fibers to provide still more diverse properties." —Albert G.H. Dietz, pg. 132

"There is no one type of plastic that can be formulated so that it has universal application to building components. While it is true that new ways are constantly being found to modify them chemically, or to alter their physical characteristics through addition of plastic material, the fact remains that their fundamental characteristics still govern how they may be used in building." —Albert G.H. Dietz, pg. 225

"Plastics are the result of man playing at being mother nature. They are more truly man-made than any other materials we use. Processes very like those found in the sun's rays, the earth's pressures and the waters of the world are used by man to make plastics. The huge chemical plants that turn out tons of plastics every year are simply mechanical simulation of nature's forces." —pg. 120

"At St. Louis, the maturing of plastics as materials of construction was much in evidence. Speakers got down to cases on costs and construction experiences with plastics in roofing, as compared to costs of conventional materials." —pg. 466

"...in today's plastics, the chemical industry has given the architect a group of materials that, as a whole, provide him with perhaps the widest range of properties of any of the building materials." —James H. Krieger, pg. 202

"Throughout this research the selected foam plastics have been explored for what they can do in their own right as structural materials, rather than as substitutes for other materials. They have been investigated as primary, secondary and contributing structural materials, but in each case the aim has been to discover what new or better solutions to structural problems can be realized through their use and to investigate as many different structural possibilities as were permissible within the limitations of time and resources." —pg. 10

"Plastics are a new class of materials and should not be treated as direct substitutes for steel, aluminum or timber. If used merely as a replacement for other materials, plastics may wall prove to be more expensive, but if applied in an intelligent way in shapes appropriate to their characteristics, the unique properties of plastics may lead to efficient and economical solutions." —Z.S. Makowski, pg. 20

"It is not surprising that when we approached building officials in those early days for approval of plastics we were asked, 'What are you talking about? Those war-time substitutes? Do you expect us to approve plastics for use in building? Do you really think it is possible to write a building code for plastics?' It is no good for us to assure building officials that in defining acrylic sheet we were not defining plastics in general but were talking about a specific product with its own properties and possibilities." —F.J. Rarig, pg. 97

"Most architects specify plastics only if these materials improve performance, meet existing codes, and lower costs. The architect who initiates a new, untried material and works it into a project is rare. Content to specify tested and approved materials regardless of the freedoms that plastics offer, he often fails to realize that plastics are acceptable in the locality where his structure is to be built." —Armand G. Winfield, pg. 81

"The SPI emphatically states that an all-plastics house is not an industry goal. There are situations for which plastics are most sensible, and those which are not." —pg. 86

"Plastic manufacturers lament that if plastic had been born before glass, it would have had a much easier time fending off glass replacements for plastic products than in the reverse situation offered by history." —pg. 125

"There are more than 10,000 different kinds of plastics marketed today, and their performance abilities span those of every other known material from soft rubber to steel. Mies would be proud. Where did plastics come from? Where are they going? Where is Mies now that we really need someone to design with the materials he searched for?" —Forrest Wilson, pg. 104

"To survive in our postindustrial world, plastic has had to abandon all ideology. And, in fact, new technology - manufacturing processes that allow for greater variation in appearance; more precise thermosetting techniques—has created a new family of plastics, plastics that are softer and more scratch-resistant; sturdier, more flexible, and hence more structural; and capable of holding truer and more subtle colors." —Paola Antonelli, pg. 50

"Plastic can take on virtually any form, and its transmutability ties this synthetic material to digitally animated architectural form. Due to its flexibility, efficiency and adaptability, it is almost predestined for bionic concepts, as well as for an architecture in which the main themes are metaphor, sensuousness, atmosphere, irritation and doing away with boundaries..." —Simone Jeska, pg. 12

Plastics are difficult to decipher

Equally assiduous assertions exist on the subject of plastics' indecipherability. These may be bound up in any number of knowledge practices that would cross methods and professions to allow architects to know all plastics.

"Plastics in Building" ----- **Jun 1940** ------------
The Architectural Forum

"Plastics...Practically Speaking" ----- **Apr 1943** ------------
Architectural Record

"Potentialities of Plastics in Building" ----- **Apr 1950** ------------
Architectural Record

"Selecting Plastics for Buildng Uses" ----- **Apr 1955** ------------
Architectural Record

"Look how many ways you can now use...PLASTICS!" ----- **Sep 1956** ------------
House & Home

"Plastics Permeate Specifications Sections" ----- **Oct 1960** ------------
Progressive Architecture

"The Structural Use of Foam Plastics" ----- **Aug 1966** ------------
Arts and Architecture

"Plastics and the Building Code" ----- **Oct 1970** ------------
Progressive Architecture

"A Case Study: The Plastic House" ----- **Oct 1970** ------------
Progressive Architecture

"Pandora's Plastic Box" ----- **Sep 1975** ------------
Progressive Architecture

"Plastics, Past and Future" ----- **Apr 1988** ------------
Architecture

"Mutant Materials: On plastics and other artifacts of material culture" ----- **Aug 1998** ------------
Harvard Design Magazine

"Another purely mental handicap which holds back the application of plastics to building is their very multiplicity. In the first place, no one seems to know just where the field begins and ends." —pg. 413

"Of all of the materials that can go into a building, there probably is none more intriguing to the designer than plastics. Also none more baffling. In the occasional contact with the subject, architects and engineers have been excited by glimpses of unthought-of possibilities for plastics in new building techniques, and confused by an array of strange laboratory labels and trade names. Much that has been published about plastics has been either so technical as to be discouraging, or too strictly 'inspirational,' full of romance and startling photography. As a result the average architect admits that apparently almost anything can be done with plastics, but he doesn't know where to go from there." —Rober F. Marshall, pg. 54

"Much of the confusion concerning plastics seems to arise form a failure to recognize that the term does not relate to a single material but to many materials." —Albert G.H. Dietz, pg. 132

"As is true of all materials, plastics must be applied with discretion to the solution of any given problem. Their physical and mechanical properties and methods of fabrication, as presented in these pages, have an important effect on their applications in building. Properly used, they can add greatly to the range of materials at the disposal of the architect, but improper use can lead to unhappy results." —Albert G.H. Dietz, pg. 228

"There is more confusion over the word 'plastic' than over almost any other word in the English language, because: Plastics are not always plastic." —pg. 120

"The introduction into building construction of materials made from plastics has taken a concerted effort by manufacturers, fabricators, architects, and engineers. It has required research, exploration, tests, and use by imaginative architects and owners to overcome the problems first associated with plastics in its various forms." —Harold J. Rosen, pg. 206

"Building codes are usually blamed by the plastics industry of the lack of acceptance of foam plastics in the building market. Up to a point it is true that codes have inhibited the use of plastics. Many codes are archaic and need revision, since they are usually based on materials and dimensional specifications rather than on desired performance standards." —pg. 10

"The architects made it clear that hey wanted plastic materials dealt with as plastics and indexed as plastics. They did not consider it practical to endeavor to establish in building codes separate provisions for individual classes of plastics that would be identified by esoteric generic terms identifying classes of polymers and copolymers." —F.J. Rarig, pg. 97

"More architects and contractors should utilize the services of plastics consulting organizations in order to obtain a view of plastics materials that is broader than that of manufacturer's literature." —Armand G. Winfield, pg. 86

"Does this oblige the architect to be an amateur chemical engineer? The plastics industry thinks not. Inasmuch as a designer can create steel structures without applying more than an elementary knowledge of steel metallurgy, SPI feels the same should apply to plastics. That is to say, architecture is more concerned with design of the configuration of standard building components than with original designs for these components. Materials engineering is not an architectural responsibility." —pg. 86

"Value judgments on plastics are more difficult. We cannot readily distinguish a difference between commodity plastic and high performance engineering plastic. The average consumer sees a plastic garbage bag and the space shuttle as the same material." —Forrest Wilson, pg. 107

"But if plastic has been reborn and found acceptance, it is only after a century of experiment and use. Some of today's new materials are challenging us, just as plastic once angered and perplexed us; some new materials have outstripped our ability to adapt to them, like computers that surpass the speed of our fingers on the keyboard." —Paola Antonelli, pg. 50

Evidence suggests that the relationship between plastics and architecture was and continues to be worked and described: Plastics for building applications were identified by several groups, including government, industry, and academic entities.[12] Plastics attributes appropriate for building applications were defined over a period of 50 years and continue to be monitored and redefined. Plastics, as a material class, are in a continuous state of emergence; materials scientists and engineers can customize polymers toward specific outcomes. Plastics' potential customization places them in the position to receive desired functionality.

We take leave to presently utter these statements when we come up against unresolved, sustained, and continuous tensions in the relationship between plastics and architecture. Smatterings of these are provided below:

1. We use one word, "plastics," to describe what are really hundreds of distinct, separately attributed and characterized materials.

2. We desire plasticity. We do not desire plastics. We desire the capacity to thermally treat any material to the point that it will flow. Resin, when introduced to a catalyst, will heat toward hardening, taking the form of a mold. Plastics embody plasticity in ways that concrete cannot. They provide a plasticity that is light, thin, insulating, or transparent. There is no doubt that what we are attempting to preserve is the option of plasticity, a formal option and construction logic. Hence, we confuse plastics with plasticity.[13]

3. Building products made from plastics achieved practical status. Plasticity did not. The weather strip, the window, the rug backer, the embedded and factory-produced things are practical and standardized. A business plan for "plasticity," dependent on composite technologies and single shell integrative forms, though attempted repeatedly, does not exist for architecture's largeness.[14]

4. Plastics products confound our inclination for part-to-whole relationships. The plastics industry makes parts. Architects make wholes. All-plastics architecture remains a task of accreting building products as the architect remains the customer of so many different manufacturers, rather than direct engagement of a research and development process that embodies the process to customize plastics.

5.   Plasticity confounds our inclination for part-to-whole relationships. Plasticity, concretized as one change in degree related to the next, may reach physical material and method limits, at which point "big" things become "small" things – challenging us to solve for part-ness.

6.   Plastics offer functionality, sometimes fictive, beyond other materials.

7.   Plastics require simple talk. Mold. Form. Resin. Heat. But plastics also require complex talk. They require an explicit understanding of chemistry, chemical constraints, materials engineering methods, and materials fabrication constraints (all depending on an understanding of chemistry).

Now, read this list again with the following two phrases fixed firmly in your mind:

Plastics in building.

All-plastics.

These are the two phrases that label the opposing poles of our conceptual or literal working-out and working-on plastics. By naming these poles we name the source of tension in the relationship between architecture and plastics as two dominant and opposing conceptual positions that may be assumed by engaging this material. It is a mistake to think of the phrases "plastics in building" and "all-plastics" as nonspecific and insignificant labels. As the numerical constraints of plastics became known, codified, and applied, as plastics use in architecture emerged, both phrases headline repeatedly, especially between the years 1933 and 1975, as titles for journal articles, books, conferences, and planned or built architectural prototypes. Material intentions are succinctly captured by these phrases. As intimated by the material state "plastics in building," plastics are parts to be specified, subtly embedded in systems of construction, never nearly reaching the status of componentry. Or, as intimated by the material state "all-plastics," plastics are wholes, or at least have the promise for providing a whole architecture. They are liquids to be cast or sheets to be formed. Both phrases have the potential to perpetrate conceptual miscues because we want to interpret them with a subtext in mind – a part-to-whole subtext – recognizing that our experience with these materials allows us to presume a "part"-driven position, or a "whole"-driven position. These phrases may lace our present thinking about plastics, as they implicitly resonate within the question "Why do we use plastics the way that we do?" One needs to know where he or she stands with plastics when using the phrase "plastics in building" and "all-plastics."[15]

Now, pair these three statements, repeated across time, which capture plastics inertia:

> Plastics are (a/the/in our) future.

> Plastics are not substitute materials.

> Plastics are difficult to decipher.

… with the two conceptual positions – material states – that headline repeatedly throughout the cumulative record:

> Plastics in building.

> All-plastics.

Pairing plastics inertia with our dominant conceptual positions more fully depicts the implicit schema for working plastics found in the record. We seem to continuously work plastics more toward one state or more toward the other – back and forth. Does this matter? To overcome plastics' seemingly inert state, should we jettison these dominant conceptual positions entirely?

Assembling Schein,
Magnant, and Coulon's
All-Plastics House,
March 1956, Paris.

1956, Paris

"Plastics in building" and "all-plastics," the dominant conceptual positions foreshadowed by the Architectural Forum *16 years earlier, now emerge as distinct pursuits. Articles such as* House & Home's "Look How Many Ways You Can Now Use … Plastics!" *photographically inventory plastics building products.*[16] *In Paris, architect Ionel Schein marshals plastics, mostly polyester resin, but also acrylics and vinyls, into the first full-scale house, and brands it the "All-Plastics House." Its exhibition marks the beginning of what would become architecture's engagement in full-scale prototyping with plastics – a prolific period of working plastics that will last for the next 17 years.*

PLASTICS NOW

As you are reading this, where do you stand? Are you for or against plastics? Are you for or against plasticity? Do you consciously track your use of plastics as they are explicitly part of the materials that you specify? Do you leverage plastics attributes and performance, seeking novel outcomes? Are you acutely aware of the numerous chemicals in current plastics materials that have found their way toward extinction? Are you seeking alternative plastics products because you desire plasticity without the same old plastics? Are you consciously or unconsciously working from the conceptual position "plastics in building" or "all-plastics?" Some architects desire a tacit understanding of plastics. Some architects desire the thorough description of plastics. How can architecture support a material that seemingly defies tacit interaction? And how can architecture specify a material whose attributes are so wholly conceived by another profession and a highly regulated industry?

Plastics Now: On Architecture's Relationship to a Continuously Emerging Material, could be a firsthand account of the perils of engaging plastics, or it could smack of the incredible optimism found in the molecular, rotomolded, vacuum-formed universe. Yet it takes a form not imagined at its outset: a sleuthing exercise. It seeks to describe, with as much possible evidence, the past, present, and future relationship between plastics and architecture. It presents evidence that such a relationship exists and that it has taken various forms as desires for this material have been articulated and rearticulated.

As a compilation, *Plastics Now* abandons comprehensive pretenses, instead proposing that a plastics ecosystem, and its unsolicited emergence and affiliation with architectural and building practices, can only be understood through the methodology of transection. A transect is a research path along which one records and counts occurrences of the phenomenon of study in order to understand scalar and non-scalar phenomena. The tool of transection, one may reason, is necessary in the face of plastics' unwieldy data set. Multiple paths through the relationship between plastics and architecture have been taken in hopes that the cumulative effect might be sufficient to answer the question, "Why do we build with plastics the way that we do"?[17] While there is the risk that an essential path has not been taken, there remains the need to stop and assess. Still, it is true that many of these transections through plastics floundered because of its inertia, its inability to define itself because of its ceaseless redefinition, commoditization, branding, and its sources.

There are six chapters in this book which incorporate "transections" through a collection of sources. Collection activities started with the exercise described above – to amass all journal articles under the topic "architecture and plastics" or "plastics in building." As the story unfolded from this initial collection, additional materials were found – pamphlets, conference proceedings, books, materials specifications. Transections take the form of timelines and collections, that attempt to juxtapose additional data sets (images and charts) to the overarching theme of the chapter. Periodically reprinted, in full, is text found along the way, excerpts of dialogue and full reprints, which have the capacity to summarize an aspect of this relationship in a timeless voice.

Chapter 01, *Defining Plastics* orients us to the task at hand by first challenging us to redefine "plastics." Terminological presentations are found throughout this history as a means to allay our unfamiliarity with this material class. Herein is provided one such collection, in overtly didactic rather than alphabetical order, from monomer to end of life. Thusly organized, this collection may be read as an alternative narrative on the differentiation of hydrocarbon sources into thermally treatable, moldable materials, and useable products.

Chapter 02, *Describing Plastics* searches through recorded transcripts and conference proceedings published between 1954 and 1976 to comprehend how the use of plastics in building became known and numerically described. Included here are the voices of architects, engineers, builders, industry representatives, government researchers, code officials, and lawyers, who met, talked out-loud, and formed a temporary community to work out plastics' use. The recurring vetting of codes and standards, burning characteristics, and structural use over this period is recounted in depth.

Chapter 03, *Plastics. In. Building.* explores the first of two dominant and opposing conceptual positions used to work plastics. It searches through a collection of books published by various authors and organizations between 1949 and 1973 that index building materials made from plastics, and their associated technical and detailing criteria. Though we engage these materials as consumers of building products, new material functionality continuously emerges through the manipulation of polymer chemistry. A collection of present-day building materials made from plastics is indexed alongside future polymers from the chemist's bench.

Chapter 04, *All-Plastics* explores the second of two dominant and opposing conceptual positions used to work plastics. It searches though the originating data set, which contains over 200 articles from popular architectural press, and represents photographic evidence of our repeated attempts to work plastics into whole prototypical architectures. Indexed are prototypes from the years 1928–1972, unbuilt and built, with an overtly domestic agenda, but also multiple interpretations of what it means to work from this conceptual position.

Chapter 05, *Why We Use Plastics the Way That We Do* reconciles the two dominant conceptual positions from the past with our present use of plastics by recounting the geopolitical and judicial events of 1973 which permitted plastics use in architecture to diverge from a presumed course. A collection of projects, built between 2000 and 2013, which address diverse structural and infrastructural, formal and phenomenal, logistical and performance-based agendas, and which exhibit the resident tenacity to work plastics, is found herein.

Chapter 06, *Professing Plastics* exhorts us to consider our individual positions on plastics in the present moment. In dialogue with Roland Barthes' 1957 essay entitled "Plastic," it compiles 22 think pieces by present-day voices from the fields of history, architectural theory, chemistry, engineering, design, fabrication, and construction. In so doing, it attempts to discern if there is room to establish a transdisciplinary dialogue for plastics in architecture.

Finally, the timeline provided at the outset of this introduction is the originating transect. After all is traversed, 90-plus plastics have been culled from the larger panoply of plastics affiliated with architectural and building production, through actual use, citation, or speculation.

It is ultimately in this spirit that *Plastics Now* is offered: Multiple transections may provide a way of thinking about architecture's relationship to a material that continues to emerge. While the boundaries of our profession inhibit us from understanding the material routines that exist within chemistry, architecture's specific and persistent mystification surrounding the working of plastics is not without consequence. A material should never require moral fortitude for comprehension, especially when we consider the very real relationship we might have to processes that transform matter into material: We are, after all, already complicit in this act.

October 1956,
Washington, DC

Perhaps all 500 attendees at the US NAS-NRC-sponsored conference Plastics in Building, *the first conference of its kind, are sitting in on the very last panel session entitled "The Future of Plastics in Building." The backgrounds of our panelists are sufficiently diverse. Two days of discourse on the question "How should we use plastics?" has included individuals across the chemical, building, and construction industries, and engineering and architectural professions. Thus, for our final series of speakers, one of them directs research for a major chemical company, another directs engineering for a company that produces plastics building materials, and four are practicing architects. Foamed-in-place walls, glass fiber reinforced plastics (GFRP) panel applications, and proposals for long-span structures – a cable-supported dome and a geodesic dome – will be presented. The last panelist to speak is Max Abramovitz, an architect very familiar with pioneering new uses for new materials. Moderator Johan Bjorksten cues Max, charging him with an important task – "represent all architects!" Max's comments number over 1,500 words, and between the beginning and the end, which is excerpted below, he reminds the audience that there is much, much more to architecture than new technologies. He cites people, inhabitation, climate, and performance over time, while he simultaneously wrestles with the problems and promise of working new technologies into architecture. His closing comments are as much a suggestion for a way to work as they are a need for numbers and assurances that might allow plastics to be used in buildings robustly.[18]*

DR. BJORKSTEN:

BJORKSTEN RESEARCH
LABORATORIES, INC.

Thank you very much, Mr. Clark. Now I would like to call on Mr. Max Abramovitz, who is a partner in the firm of Harrison & Abramovitz, Architects, in New York City. Mr. Abramovitz is going to tell us what the architects want, so that the chemists can be guided accordingly in future developments. Mr. Abramovitz.

MR. ABRAMOVITZ:

PARTNER,
HARRISON &
ABRAMOVITZ

I am afraid that statement is a little too inclusive. There is no question that the gentlemen who have been on this platform before me do not lack for imagination. I almost feel as if my feet are clay, when I recall what we have seen the last three-quarters of an hour. Actually, an architect, in a broad sense, wants to enclose space, with the least possible amount of limitation, and we concentrate always from an idealistic point of view of solving the world's problems, anyone's problems, whether they are practical, spiritual, playful, and we don't want to be hampered with any dream child we have got. We have our own theoretical esthetics about how to use materials and they, frankly, change every year. But, we may use any material we can get our hands on, as you well know. We get involved with steel, with glass, and now we are going to talk plastics.

… And, lastly, it is your industry that has to stick its neck out. You tell us, as architects, to lead you, but we are just small, little people with limited funds. If you have ideas, you should develop serious research programs to find out the qualities of your product, develop your standards, maintain an approach of integrity, and I think we will try to either catch up with you or hope to get ahead of you. Thank You.[19]

NOTES

1 The search began with the phrase "architecture and plastics," and then quickly became "plastics and building," or "building with plastics," and proceeded to become increasingly refined as people, projects, societies, and events were identified.

2 Transfer of plastics technology, composites, adhesives and acrylics that matured during World War II is suggested directly with photographic documentation found in *The Architectural Forum*. 1940. "Plastics in Building"; and in Albert G.H. Dietz, *Materials of Construction, Wood, Plastics, Fabrics* (New York: Van Nostrand and Company, 1949); and directly addressed in the report British Plastics Federation, *Plastics, Post-War Building Studies No. 3*. (London: HMSO, 1944), 20.

3 *The Architectural Forum*. 1940. "Plastics in Building," 421.

4 See also the companion article "Even With Small Doses of Irradiation Many Materials Undergo Dramatic Change," for a description of the science behind proposed irradiated plastics: Arthur Charlesby. 1954. *The Architectural Forum*, 102–103.

5 Douglas Haskell. 1954. *The Architectural Forum*. "In Architecture, Will Atomic Processes Create a New 'Plastic' Order?" 100.

6 *Progressive Architecture*. 1960. "Plastics in Architecture." Vol. 48 (June 1960), Introduction.

7 Syracuse University Libraries, "Armand G. Winfield Papers, Biographical History," http://library.syr.edu/digital/guides/w/winfield_ag.htm (accessed July 26, 2014).

8 *Progressive Architecture*. 1970. "Plastics: A Decade of Progress," 65.

9 Also known formally as "oil price shock" or "a sudden and drastic increase in the price of crude oil." See Jan Palmowski, "Oil price shock." In *A Dictionary of Contemporary World History* (Oxford: Oxford University Press, 2008). Precipitated by geopolitical events, the first oil price shock occurred in 1973, the second in 1979.

10 "The actual rather than the ASTM tested burning characteristics of foam plastics" refers to the US FTC lawsuit "In the Matter of The Society of the Plastics Industry, Inc., et al.," 1975. *Federal Trade Commission Decisions: Findings, Opinions, and Orders, July 1, 1974 to December 31, 1974*. A discussion of the implications of this lawsuit are found in this book's Chapter 05.

11 *Progressive Architecture*. 1981. "The Light Heavyweights," 125.

12 Sleuthing branched off significantly into proceedings from meetings, conferences, etc. based on the summary found in *Journal of the AIA*. 1957. "BRI Reviews Plastics for Roof Construction." Here is the first mention of the organization and efforts of the US focused Plastics Study Group of the US Building Research Institute, National Academy of Sciences – National Research Council.

13 To determine what is meant by uttering the word "plasticity," one might compare their position to the chapter titled "Plasticity" in Mark Rothko and Christopher Rothko, *The Artist's Reality: Philosophies of Art* (New Haven, CT: Yale University Press, 2004), 43–55.

14 It is true that some early "large" architectural cousins made in plastics – prefabricated bathroom modules and motor homes – were developed for mass production and have identifiable development trajectories. Consider, for instance, the bathroom modules developed for both the 1956 All-Plastics House (France), and the 1957 Monsanto House of the Future (US). Or refer to the table of contents of one of several published conference proceedings such as *Plastics in Building Construction, Realities and Challenges* (Stamford, CT: Society of the Plastics Engineers, 1972) for similar integrated products.

15 The thesis of the author's previously published essay "All Plastics in Building," in *Permanent Change: Plastics in Architecture and Engineering*, edited by Michael Bell and Craig Buckley (New York: Princeton Architectural Press, 2014).

16 *House & Home*. 1956. "Look How Many Ways You Can Now Use … Plastics!," 119–135. A photographically comprehensive and compelling compendium of building materials made from plastics, inclusive of finishes, coatings, sealants, hardware, foam, and piping, but also an array of insulated and translucent stressed skin panel products (pages 126, 129 and 132), prefabricated bathrooms (page 131), and whole building applications (pages 129, 131, 133–135).

17 Uruguayan structural engineer Eladio Dieste poses the question "Why do we build the way that we do?" in his essay titled "Architecture and Construction," which questions the dominance of specific construction logics, tools, and techniques. Dieste's question is applicable to a range of materials for construction, including plastics. See "Architecture and Construction" reprinted in Stanford Anderson, *Eladio Dieste: Innovation in Structural Art* (New York: Princeton Architectural Press, 2004).

18 Building Research Institute, *Plastics in Building* (Washington, DC: NAS-NRC, 1955), 111–121.

19 Ibid., 119–121.

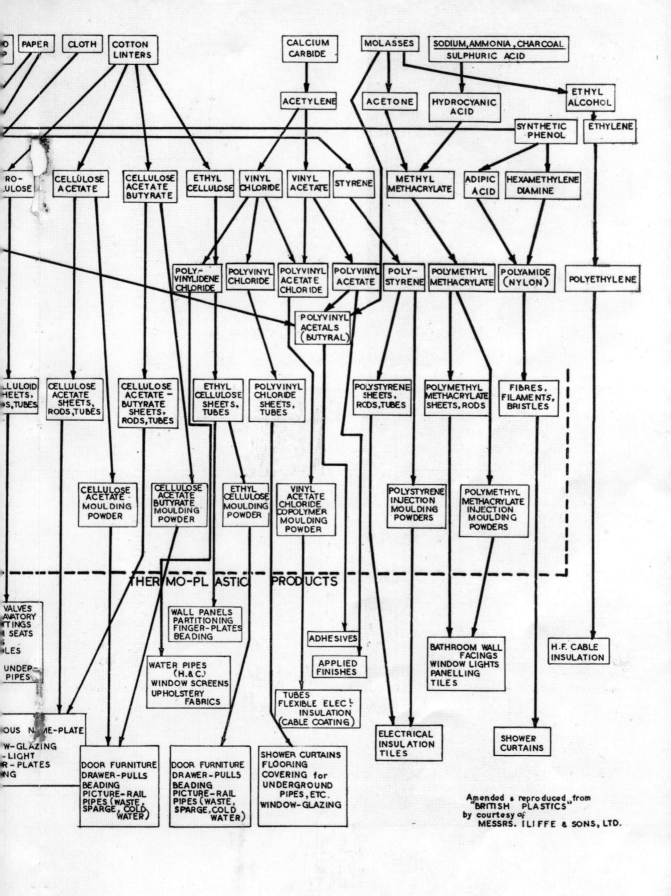

Amended & reproduced from
"BRITISH PLASTICS"
by courtesy of
MESSRS. ILIFFE & SONS, LTD.

CHAPTER 01

DEFINING PLASTICS

DEFINITIONS

Unraveling the multiple sets of evidence that might allow us to answer the question "Why do we use plastics the way that we do?" must begin with the definition of the subject at hand.[1] Not in a didactic sense, but rather as a means to become conscious of where we currently stand – to challenge our presumptions regarding this class of materials. So, to begin and toward this purpose, *one* definition of "plastics" may prove to be useful: "The commercial name of any of a class of substances, such as celluloid or viscose, which are *worked* into shape for use by molding or pressing when in a plastic condition."[2] Though circa 1925, it has currency.[3] Deciphering plastics from the outset assumed the notion "worked material." Contrast this definition to the admission that follows:

> While we shall attempt to keep the material appearing in our pages as free as possible from technical language, the exigencies arising from the fact that so much that enters into plastic products is of a chemical nature will no doubt necessitate considerable chemical terminology, and of this our lay readers, in the interest of our more technically trained friends, will pardon us.[4]

The initiated and the uninitiated; the chemist and the non-chemist; for my part, I understand a definition that includes "worked." "Worked into shape" does sound like clay, or iron, or glass; it does not sound like plastics circa 2014 – materials whose "working" is removed even more so from the visible expending of bodily energy.[5] I suspect that the notion of "worked" arises from plastic's origins – cellulose, horn, milk, cotton, materials with immediacy, and some immediately transformable into homogeneous fluid and formable resources. The problem with defining plastics is that its language is so wholly subject to another profession's actions and descriptions; and this is why I, as an architect, am decidedly for this 1925 definition. It causes us to let down our guard, and recast the present definition of "plastics" along other lines – lines where it might more currently belong – including *all* organic materials that might preserve heat- and pressure-induced plasticity: I refer to two classes of plastics: fossil fuel-based and biobased.

More of us know the origins of biobased plastics tacitly and perhaps in an instrumental sense, far better than the origins of fossil fuel-based plastics. We cannot pretend to oversimplify the difference between these two material classes. Each currently provides different functionality, especially in the context of architecture. But, suspend all artificial and time-eliding classifications and consider that the capacity to transform a field of corn, or soy beans (its proteins, polysaccharides, and oils), or a grove of sustainably forested hickory trees (its cellulose and lignin), a deposition of oil (its hydrocarbons), or the horn of Texas longhorn cattle (its keratin) is a technical capacity that has always been ours.

In order to answer the question "Why do we build with plastics the way that we do?" we must be willing to focus solely on a modern plastics industry, or roughly 100 years of very recent history. In the beginning we will find that directions for preparing horn from cattle or oxen as feedstock for products are similarly provided in *Modern Plastics*, the same issue that defines "plastic" as "worked into shape" to a then 15-year-old industry. The horn, made of keratin, a naturally occurring thermoplastic, will be received as stock:

> › It will be sorted (cattle in one pile, ox in another).
> › It will be sawn into sections – solid tip removed from a mostly hollow length.
> › Hollow lengths will be sliced lengthwise or spirally cut (depending on end use).
> › It will be washed.
> › It will be tumbled to remove roughness.
> › It will be soaked in a tub of water (from two hours to a day).
> › It will be heated in a kettle of hot water.
> › It will be heated in a kettle of hot oil (for four or five minutes).
> › It will be opened.
> › It will be pressed.
> › It will be squeezed under pressure.
> › It may be squeezed under pressure and with steam (depending on the type of press used).
> › It will be cooled.
> › It will be formed into a plate as feedstock for making a hair comb.[6]

In other words, it will be worked. But, so will crude oil.

> It will be pumped from the ground.
> It will be desalted (with heat) to remove contaminants.
> It will be heated again and fed into a distillation tower – a steel column roughly 120 feet high.
> In the column, under pressure and more heat, it will be separated (fractioned) into differently weighted hydrocarbons.
> The heaviest fractions are at the bottom of the tower.
> The lighter fractions turn to hot vapor and rise in the column.
> Fractions are considered products (heavy to light).
> Products may be oil, asphalt, lubricating oil, heating oil, kerosene, naphtha.
> Products will be separately removed and distributed through the requisite supply chain.[7]
> To make plastics the hydrocarbon naphtha will be shipped to a petrochemical manufacturer.
> It will be further separated (cracked) into more "products."
> With steam, naphtha will be pumped into a high-temperature furnace and vaporized.
> High-temperature vaporizing, or pyrolysis, initiates the cracking process.
> It will be pumped into several steel columns and fractioned into differently weighted products – known as ethylene and propylene.
> As a group, these are called "olefins," which are petrochemicals – feedstocks for some of the chemical reactions that result in the materials we call "plastics."[8]

The working of horn, or the natural polymer keratin, and the working of crude oil into olefins allow us to make two important but disjointed observations regarding the potential relationship between plastics and architecture. First, we can observe that the present disequilibrium that exists in sourcing very large organic molecules, from one source – oil – and the equipoise that might be gained with biomass, as well as the continued creation of a "smart" polymer class, only typifies plastics and therefore plasticity's condition – it has and always will be constantly emerging and requiring much "working."

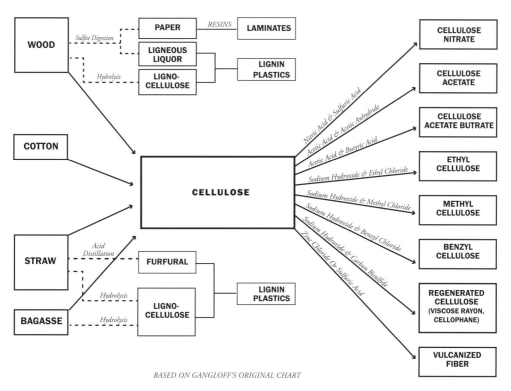

BASED ON GANGLOFF'S ORIGINAL CHART

The relationship between plastics and architecture started with cellulose, the abundant and naturally occurring polymer fiber found in plant life and sourced from wood, cotton, straw, bagasse, or jute. Plastics origination with cellulose likely had the residual effect of forever lumping wood with plastics in such places as the US Construction Specifications Institute (CSI) master format system. The plastics industry moved from cellulose and other biobased polymers to fossil fuel-based polymers. The relationship between plastics and architecture matured on the functionality – chiefly durability – afforded by hydrocarbons sourced from fossil fuels. We are in a period where biobased sources are once again regaining legitimacy and have the potential to transfer into architectural use.

The cellulosics are the first family of synthetic plastics. The cell wall material of vegetation, such as trees, cotton, or jute, yields cellulose – a naturally occurring macromolecule that can be transformed through chemical reaction into transparent or translucent plastic films.

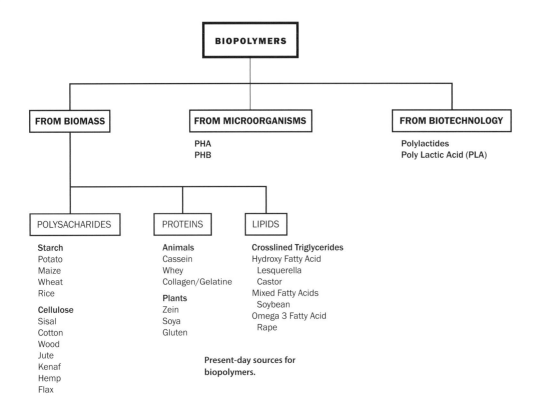

Present-day sources for biopolymers.

The second observation is this: Resources for plastics are worked at scales and in landscapes diverse and seemingly irreconcilable. The working of horn, once considered a vital part of the early plastics industry, might appeal to some because we can actually imagine a position of working, gaining the tacit understanding required to form a hair comb. However, the fractioning of crude oil into so many differently weighted hydrocarbons and cracking of naphtha into petrochemicals is monitored closely, but remotely, through a series of control rooms and across a landscape of equipment spanning hectares. Petrochemicals become feedstocks for chemical reactions that result in plastics resins or granulate – such as polycarbonate with a specific color, UV resistance, and mold release capacity – that is the end result and intended for a manufacturer who likewise has the capacity to add attributes before forming it into a building product. It is more "sensible," to borrow the Society of the Plastics Industry's term, to work these materials remotely and indirectly – communicating the multifunctionality desired of them.[9] But experimentation with plastics exists, in a material sense, because we have never been precluded from working a limited number of them directly. Cast in the role of "customers"

2003, Baytown, Texas

This false color image taken by the sensor ASTER on NASA's Terra satellite permits us to see the organization of Exxon Mobil's approximately 1,300-hectare petrochemical processing plant (beige and gray) amidst vegetation (red). Just off to the right of the image (not pictured) is Bayer MaterialScience Industrial Park at approximately half the size,

which processes chemicals into polycarbonate granulate. Plastics' untenable truth may be the scale of their production. Plastics for architecture, both fossil fuel-based and biobased, are worked across hectares of land in multistory chemistry sets. But does the scale of a process preclude us from admitting that we are complicit in working plastics here as well?

in a plastics products supply chain, we can buy and cast resin. We can machine acrylic. We can print polycarbonate.

How we define plastics is bound up in our perception of how we work them. Thus, acknowledging a literal multi-acre swampland site flourishing with flora, fauna, and control rooms might expand our definition of them, and our relationship to them – an important mental exercise when attempting to answer the question "Why do we use plastics the way that we do?" Such a site, such a space, such a place might reveal that we are all too comfortable with the role of "customer," in a linear building products supply chain. As "customers" we are permitted to operate as an isolated terminus, order and prescribe predetermined product specifications, and

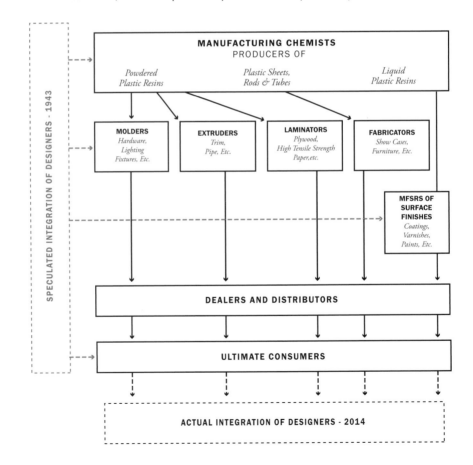

The nascent supply chain for plastics building products with designers stretched along its entirety based on the chart "Organization of the Plastics Industry" found in "Plastics … Practically Speaking" by Robert F. Marshall, *Architectural Record*, April 1943.

CHART OF CHIEF PLASTICS MATERIALS

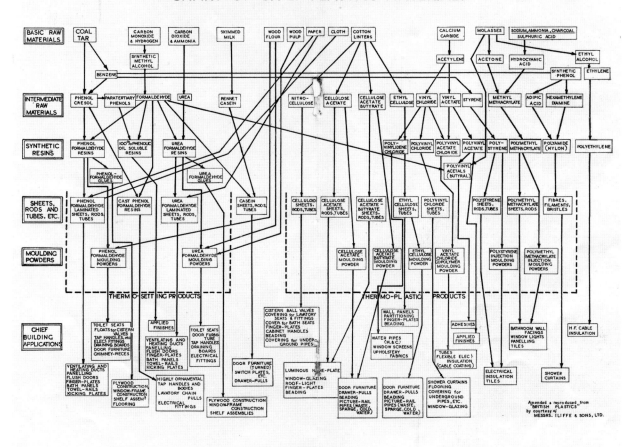

Circa 1940, Charting the transformation of feedstocks
into thermally treatable, moldable materials

Charting plastics, their origins, and chemical transformations, is a preoccupation throughout the found data set. This chart is exceptional for its time and purpose. Produced in the early 1940s, it documents the material state of "plastics in building." One may infer numerous applications, which is likely the reason that the British Plastics Federation chose to include it in their post-war report. The chart elucidates how basic raw materials may be transformed into synthetic resins which may be molded into many different bits of buildings (but not an "all-plastics" house, mind you). Choose a raw ingredient and track it through to its "chief building application." Coal tar transforms into ventilating and heating ducts, doors, and towel rails. Skimmed milk transforms into switch plates and drawer pulls. Molasses transforms into adhesives. It is all too easy to excise the intermediary steps in preference of the extreme termini – molasses > adhesive! Thus, even in the present day, it challenges our temptation to delimit our actions solely on the plastics building product.

2014, Inventorying the ingredients and impacts for the manufacture of a building material

Inventory diagrams, such as these ones for closed-cell polyurethane foam and soy polyurethane foam, arguably extend the work of charts such as the "Chart of Chief Plastic Materials." The inputs and processing steps for closed-cell polyurethane foam and soy polyurethane foam, which are comparable, are described across lifecycle stages, thereby re-presenting to us what we actually know – that the system boundary for a building product extends beyond point of sale and includes installation, use, and end of life. Lifecycle-type thinking aborts our predisposition to demarcate an exclusive boundary around a building product. It positions us to expand our working of plastics across time and scale. Furthermore, during the design of a building, we might wrap logistical thinking into the design process alongside the accounting of embodied environmental impacts. Then, how we define plastics may be more consciously aligned with how we actually work them.

Manufacturing

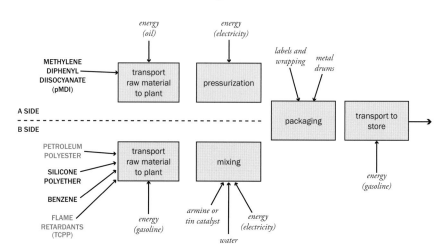

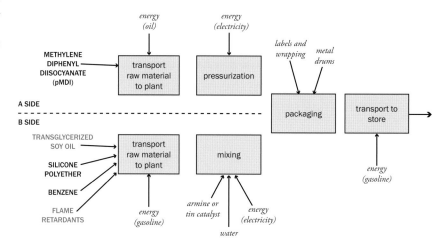

Point of Sale **Installation** **Use** **End of Life**

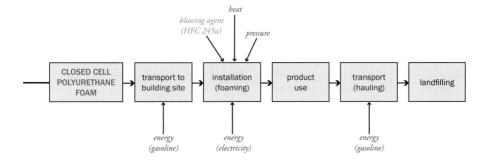

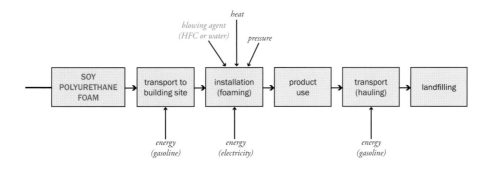

delimit our "working" to the point and time in which the product exists. Yet, in such a site, such a space, such a place resides the pre-existence of a building product. This acknowledgment yields to the admission that we, too, are complicit in the act of "arranging, disarranging and rearranging matter."[10] Our working of plastics is not delimited, therefore, to the product, the sheet of polycarbonate or the vinyl wall base, nor is it limited to the thrill of controlling resin. We work plastics (all industrially produced materials) far, far more pervasively than we have ever realized even as we specify them. Thus, our present definition of plastics may be far, far too small, too impotent and too mythical.

But, if we were to accept our position as pervasive workers, then we might begin to organize other supply chain structures; perhaps one where the linearly appointed and opposite terminus "raw materials," which is where much research and questioning happens, is wrapped around to be adjacent to us and our practices, permitting "talking" between the opposite ends. Or one where stretching us across the supply chain, as suggested by *Architectural Record* in 1943, imbues us with the agency to interact with all of its actors and to participate in the creation of materials for architecture. Our own working of plastics, and thus how we define them, may then become as powerful as the promise of their infinite customizability seems to be.

Yet, in light of our present approach to plastics – we know we specify them more than we know we work them – I offer one last provocation. It is curious that we are most likely to know the definitions of the terms "thermoplastic" and "thermoset." And if you are uninitiated, then I will add that it is curious that publications for architects on the subject of plastics are most likely to present this distinction first. Plastics classed as thermoplastics are continuously transformable by heat. That is, they can be heated and formed, heated and reformed, heated again and reformed again. They will continue to flow as long as heat is introduced. They will stop flowing and form when the heat is removed. Plastics classed as "thermosets" are set into place by heat. That is, they are first liquid and flowing. With the introduction of heat or a catalyst they change from liquid to solid. If heated again, they will likely burn. Beyond the technical necessity of classifying plastics as thermoplastic or thermoset, the persistent up-fronting of these two might contribute to our habit of falsely delimiting our working of plastics to the products in front of us, and is certainly the proverbial carrot for any architect who believes that plasticity, *not plastics*, and therefore "working," is not very far away.

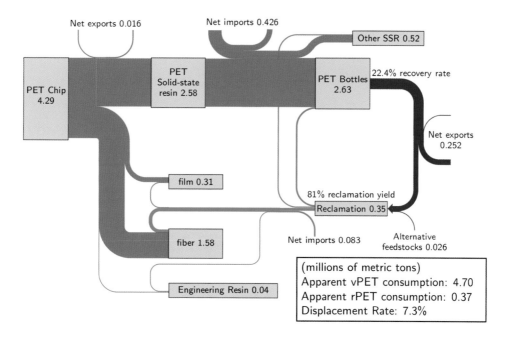

Net exports 0.016

Net imports 0.426

Other SSR 0.52

PET Chip 4.29

PET Solid-state resin 2.58

PET Bottles 2.63

22.4% recovery rate

Net exports 0.252

film 0.31

81% reclamation yield

Reclamation 0.35

fiber 1.58

Net imports 0.083

Alternative feedstocks 0.026

Engineering Resin 0.04

(millions of metric tons)
Apparent vPET consumption: 4.70
Apparent rPET consumption: 0.37
Displacement Rate: 7.3%

2006, Accounting for the massive flow of material commodities for a given economy

A Sankey diagram, such as the PET Material Flow, US (2006), might just extend the work of both of the preceding diagrams – The Chart of Chief Plastic Materials and Inventory Diagram – by challenging us to expand our definition of working materials to a national if not global scale.[11] Building products are made from commodity plastics. Both virgin (v) and reclaimed (r) types are used in manufacturing processes around the world, which means

they massively flow through global markets. The flow of plastics (all commodity industrial materials) is tracked on a regional and global basis using mass flow or material flow analysis methods, which are "a systematic assessment of the flows of stocks of materials within a system defined in space and time."[12] When we engage "mass flow or material thinking," we again expand our perception of how we work plastics and therefore how we define them.

PLASTICS

A report by a committee convened by
the British Plastics Federation

1944, London

*The British Plastics Federation
assesses with urgency the role
that plastics might have in
rebuilding Great Britain's cities,
left ruinous after repeated
bombing. They enumerate 213
points during their assessment.
But to begin, point numbers
1–10 must define what plastics
are because as newly emerged
materials for building they are
not really known like wood,
brick, and steel. They start by
describing a material shaped
by heat and pressure, one that
is decidedly not glass, nor is it
cementitious, but its origins
are very familiar – vegetation
and cows. They classify plastics
as either thermoplastic and
thermoset, thereby nuancing
the role of heat, pressure,
mold, and form. Plastics are
not substitute materials,
they caution. Though they
may take the form of many
things, they have limits that
must be understood – service
temperature for one, unique
failure profiles for another.
They remind that plastics and
processes for working them
are continuously emerging,
as are the size of objects
manufactureable – the limits
are unknown. Codes are
required to ensure quality.
Cooperation between the
building and plastics industry
is necessary. Is this 2014?
No. By point number 10,
where the volume of plastics
manufacturable is questioned,
we are decidedly back in 1944.*

INTRODUCTION

1. Definition of plastics. The term "plastics" is applied to a group of materials which, though stable in use at normal temperatures, are plastic at some stage in their manufacture and can be shaped by the application of heat and pressure.

2. Plastics are organic materials, mainly synthetic, but they include semi-synthetic materials derived from cellulose and casein, and also certain materials incorporating bitumen and shellac. Rubber, though organic and falling within the definition given, is, by common consent, not considered to be a "plastic," though synthetic, rubber-like materials are. Inorganic plastic materials, such as glass, ceramics, and Portland cement, are likewise excluded.

3. Thermoplastic and thermosetting plastics. Plastics fall into two broad classes, thermoplastic and thermosetting. Thermoplastics soften on heating and harden on cooling, and this softening on heating can be repeated as often as may be desired. Thermosetting plastics, on the other hand, can be prepared in a form in which they are initially thermoplastic, in which condition they can be moulded under appropriate conditions of temperature and pressure; further heating at quite moderate temperatures (260–350 °F.) causes them to set permanently. They cannot again be softened by heating, but, being organic materials, they char at a temperature of about 650 °F.

4. Merits and limitations. Although plastics have taken the place of metals, wood, and ceramics in many articles in common use, and quite properly can be looked upon as alternative materials, they are not to be regarded as substitutes in any derogatory sense, but rather as materials having certain properties by virtue of which they are capable of fulfilling particular functions or meeting particular demands. That is not to say that plastics are suitable for all purposes, or that a plastic can always be found to suit a particular purpose. Like all other materials, they have their merits and their limitations. Their uses should be chosen accordingly.

5. Among their merits are their good dielectric properties, their wide range of colour, and their clean finish, which, for indoor use at all events, is not subject to corrosion and does not need protection with paint or lacquer. Plastics lend themselves to mass production, and, being manufactured products subject to technical control throughout the various processes, can be produced in a degree of uniformity difficult to attain in a natural material. To all intents and purposes they leave the machine in a condition in which they are ready for use; polishing and furnishing operations are not always required. The equipment is expensive, and the cost must necessarily be spread over a large number of articles if the process is to be economic. A valuable feature of plastics is their adaptability. They lend themselves to a variety of manufacturing operations, yielding products that cover a wide range of uses.

6. Plastics are not suitable for use at high temperatures; some can be used up to 200 °F. and others up to 450 °F. Some plastics are not suitable for use out of doors, though materials of improved durability have become available and further improvement can be expected. Again, some plastics tend to creep under sustained loads, and some are subject to a brittle type of fracture with no pronounced yield-point. These features impose certain limitations on their use as building materials.

7. Historical development. Although bitumen has been known and used from ancient times, and some of the materials employed have long been known to chemistry, the plastics industry may be said to date from the discovery and applications in 1865 of a method of plasticising cellulose nitrate. Since then there has been a phenomenal development of new materials, the result of chemical achievement, and a continual adaptation of the processes of manufacture, leading to the production of plastics in new forms and with new uses. A large number of the plastics in use today have been introduced within the past twenty years, many within the last two or three years. Objects are now being moulded in

sizes that would have been considered quite impracticable a short while ago. The pace of development makes it very difficult to forecast future trends or to say categorically that plastics are unsuitable for this purpose or for that; today's outlook may be quite changed by the advent of a new material or new process.

8. Specifications and hall-mark of quality. Some applications of plastics to buildings are already well established, and materials have been manufactured to fairly definite standards of material and design. Sometimes, however, plastics mouldings for building and other uses have been designed to a price rather than with proper regard to functional requirements, and have proved unsatisfactory in service. The standards of the materials used are maintained by specification (see Appendix III). Design is much more difficult to control, and design plays a large part in determining the efficiency of a moulded plastic. It was with the intention of ensuring the production of well-designed, efficient products that the British Plastics Federation in collaboration with the British Standards Institution took steps in 1938–9 to initiate a hall-mark scheme. Completion of this scheme has been delayed by war conditions, but is now being reconsidered.

9. Consultation between building and plastics industries. Besides the established uses of plastics in building, there are others, notably for plumbing, which have yet to prove their practical worth. Other applications for which plastics would be suitable, such as the manufacture of composite wall linings of good thermal insulation value and pleasing appearance, have yet to be studied in detail. Guidance from the building industry on the properties and sizes desired in a material of this kind would greatly assist the plastics industry in formulating its plans. Where a new proposal involves no more than the fabrication of materials already in production or the simple modification of existing processes, experiments and trials can be undertaken without much difficulty, providing the materials and plant can be released for the purpose. But where a

new proposal involves the production of a moulded article – a window frame, for instance – the manufacture of prototypes for trial cannot be lightly embarked upon. The moulds are expensive. Their design, the choice of moulding material, and every aspect bearing on the production of a satisfactory article at a reasonable cost must first be given the most careful consideration. The cost of moulded plastics cannot be discussed in general terms because so much depends on the numbers over which the cost of the moulds can be distributed. Some articles can be produced in plastics with greater efficiency and at less cost than in other materials. Some may be more expensive. In the post-war period choice may need to be guided by the relative availability of the various alternatives, irrespective of their relative cost.

10. Post-war production of plastics will depend on supplies of materials and on plant capacity. And it must be borne in mind that the output of plastics materials will be limited by the availability of raw materials, and that, in some cases, raw materials are limited by factors outside the control of the industry; many of them depend on products of the chemical industry. While there has been an expansion in production to meet demands for war equipment, an expansion which, incidentally, has been accompanied in some instances by notable reductions in the cost of manufacture, plastics are not produced in such large quantities as to compare with the basic industries in building, such as steel, cement, and brick. The total production of plastics in Great Britain represents but a small fraction of the volume of building materials likely to be required in the immediate post-war period. Not all this production will be of materials suitable for application to building use, and some of the post-war supplies will be needed for other purposes. While there will undoubtedly be wide scope for the use of plastics in the post-war programme, it will be important to select applications that will make the best use of the plant and materials available and give the greatest satisfaction in service.[13]

Front and back cover of *Plastics, Post-War Building Studies No. 3*, the British Plastics Federation, 1944.

PLASTICS TERMINOLOGY ORGANIZED FROM MONOMER TO END OF USEFUL LIFE

Plastics terminology collected and defined are found throughout the aggregated data set of journal articles. Some are simply lists of words, some are lists with diagrams and images, some are taxonomic matrices, and some propose to set terms aside in favor of collecting images of plastics as a means to demonstrate what they do. Curiously, *The Architectural Forum*'s "Plastics in Building" from 1940 chooses the last of these tactics, proposing to suspend the use of terminology, stating, "Most discussions of plastics are peppered with words like 'polymerization' and 'hydrophobic' whose meanings are fairly simple, but not very important to the building industry."[14] They proceed to "define" plastics by grouping plastics products into function classes rather than chemical classes. Conversely, *The Architectural Record*'s two contributions by Dr. Albert G.H. Dietz occurring in 1950 and 1955 are rigorous terminological collections, narrative-driven rather than itemized. The first of these provides a sustained narrative outlining classifications of plastics and fabrication techniques, and then reviews each available class and their potential to be worked. *Progressive Architecture*'s 1960 and 1970 issues dedicated solely to the topic of plastics both contain glossaries but also diagrams that compare types of plastics to each other across selected attributes. Common to all attempts is the need to be selective regarding which terms to offer the architect.

Our use of plastics, whether aligned more closely with the conceptual positions "plastics in building" or "all-plastics," whether hands-on or hands-off, relies on the practices of sourcing, selecting and specifying products – building products. This collection of terms implicitly and simultaneously acknowledges our practices with building products and challenges it. Terms are organized from monomer to end of life, a pairing with lifecycle thinking yes, but also a bid to continue the mental exercise of acknowledging that we work plastics pervasively. We might think of this collection as framing a product's working, use, disuse, and submergence. We might think of it as a narrative on the differentiation of hydrocarbon sources into thermally treatable materials, and normalization routes for plastic products. And then there is the simple usefulness of such a list applied to a sleuthing exercise that seeks to answer the question "Why do we use plastics the way that we do?" as it provides a current reference for unraveling a material class that we have defined as inert but constantly emerging.

Still, we must recognize the limitations of such a list. A definition comes into being because consensus is reached around its meaning. Some definitions are not as useful as they first appear because they cannot embody an inherent trajectory, whether cultural or technical, of attempts to both work and describe a subject. To know a material is both to work it and describe it. In this regard we might wish the medium of delivering the written word that intends to help us agree on what plastics are to be as mutable as plastics themselves.

Pairing design with lifecycle stage thinking

A building product's lifecycle, this one diagrammed for a structural insulated panel, may be understood as a system of processes and actions that requires inputs and produces outputs across the stages of raw materials extraction and processing, manufacturing and construction, use and end of life. The potential to impact the environment happens throughout all stages – energy is continuously required as an input, certain processes produce emissions such as carbon or nitrous dioxide. Local, regional, and global phenomena are the result. For instance, water bodies turn more acidic, disrupting food webs (acidification); water bodies become choked with plant life, decreasing the available amount of oxygen for animal life (eutrophication); greenhouse gases disperse into the atmosphere, decreasing the amount of solar radiation reflected back into space, thus increasing the amount absorbed by Earth's surfaces (global warming potential). When we expand the system boundary from one exclusively encircling a (plastics) building product to one inclusively encircling it and its lifecycle, we do more than acknowledge environmental impacts. We expand the potential of design. Now we might be poised to proactively ask what kind of phenomena we want a building material to produce? This question suggests that we might begin to participate in the design of materials for architecture.

SIPS PANEL
LCA LIFE CYCLE STAGES (ISO 14040)

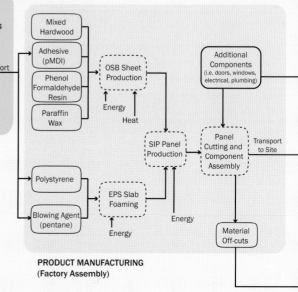

RAW MATERIALS EXTRACTION AND PROCESSING

1.1 Building Blocks
Monomers
Hydrocarbons
Fossil Fuels
Coal
Crude Oil
Natural Gas
Biomass
Biomass Derived Monomer
Polysaccharide
Proteins
Lipids
Organism Derived Monomer

1.2 Processing
Fossil Fuel Distillation
Biomass Distillation
Bio-derived Monomer Distillation
Organism Derived Distillation
Polymerization
Polyaddition
Polycondensation
Off-site_Refinery Production
Off-site_Factory Processes
Off-site_Factory Synthesis
Off-site_Factory Compounding
Off-site_Factory Formulation
Off-site_Factory Forming
On-site_Mixing and Casting
Additives
Fillers
Inhibitors
Stabilizers
Pigments
Plastic Resins

1.3 Plastics Defined
Polymer
Natural Polymers
Plastics
Bioplastics

1.4 Polymer Attributes
Thermoset
Thermoplastic

PRODUCT MANUFACTURING
(Factory Assembly)

MANUFACTURING & CONSTRUCTION

1.5 Manufacturing
Blow Molding
Calendaring
Casting
Compression Molding
Contact Molding
Digital Fabrication
Extrusion
Filament Winding
Foam Molding
Injection Molding
Laminating
Machining
Pultrusion
Roto Molding
Spunbond
Thermoforming
Transfer Molding
Welding

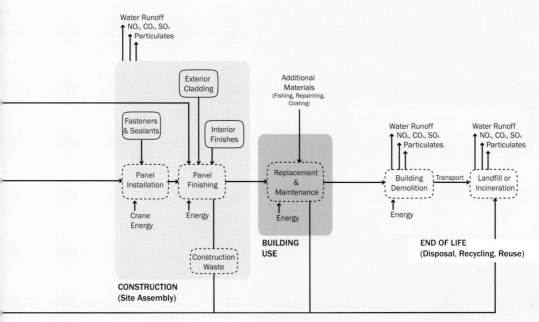

Water Runoff
NO$_x$, CO$_x$, SO$_4$
Particulates

Exterior
Cladding

Additional
Materials
(Fishing, Repainting,
Coating)

Fasteners
& Sealants

Interior
Finishes

Water Runoff
NO$_x$, CO$_x$, SO$_4$
Particulates

Water Runoff
NO$_x$, CO$_x$, SO$_4$
Particulates

Panel
Installation

Panel
Finishing

Replacement
&
Maintenance

Building
Demolition

Transport

Landfill or
Incineration

Crane
Energy

Energy

Energy

Energy

Construction
Waste

BUILDING
USE

END OF LIFE
(Disposal, Recycling, Reuse)

CONSTRUCTION
(Site Assembly)

1.6 Material Specification
Naming Conventions
International Building Code Reference
CSI Master Format Number
Flame Spread Index, FSI
Smoke Development Index, SDI

1.7 Properties
Uv Resistance
Light Transmittance
Chemical Resistance
Scratch Resistance,
Wear Resistance Index
R-value (Thermal Resistance)
Thermal Coefficient of Expansion
Maximum Service Temperature
Heat Sensitive Adhesion
Pressure Rating
Water Vapor Transmission
Water Absorption
Modulus of Elasticity
Flexural Strength
Compressive Strength
Tensile Strength
Tear Strength
Peel Strength
Pressure Rating
Puncture Strength
Burning Characteristics
Creep

1.8 Options
Biodegradable Plastics
Photodegradation
Hydrolytic Degradation
Compost
Microbial Digestion
Recycle
Pre-consumer Waste
Post-consumer Waste
Resin Identification Code
Pre-consumer Waste
Post-consumer Waste
Incineration
Landfill
Reuse
Useful Life

RAW MATERIALS, EXTRACTION, AND PROCESSING

1.1
Building Blocks

What are the fundamental building blocks of this material class?

monomers
A monomer is a simple set of molecules of low molecular weight that can combine or react with like or unlike molecules to form polymers.

What is the origin of a monomer?

hydrocarbons
Monomers may originate from hydrocarbons, a group of organic chemical compounds of hydrogen and carbon in either a gaseous, liquid, or solid state.

Where do hydrocarbons come from?

fossil fuels
Any hydrocarbon containing compound found below the surface of the earth which is of finite supply within the human timescale. Fossil fuels include coal, crude oil, peat, and natural gas. All fossil fuels contain high levels of hydrocarbons and burn if ignited in the presence of oxygen. Fossil fuels can also be converted into a variety of chemicals useful as raw materials in manufacturing. The conversion process depends upon the type of fossil fuel, but the ease of conversion is largely dependent upon how pure the hydrocarbons are within the fossil fuel, which is frequently a mix of desirable hydrocarbons along with numerous other less desirable compounds.

coal
A heterogeneous metamorphic rock formed through the aggregation of plant matter in a moist location, such as a swamp. The low oxygen levels present in such stagnant water prevents aerobic decomposition creating, through a process known as coalification series, peat, then lignite, subbituminous and bituminous coal, and eventually anthracite. These metamorphic stages occur at sequentially greater depths and under increasing pressure and temperatures. To transform coal into a usable form, mined coal undergoes preparation where it is cleaned and crushed to create a homogenous mixture. The chemicals necessary for creating plastics are created by subjecting the prepared coal to one of two processes: direct liquefaction and pyrolysis.

crude oil
Crude oil applies to any organic (carbon-based) compound which is liquid in its underground storage state. This liquid may become a solid or a gas at surface temperature and pressure. Oils may contain a number of compounds, the precise combination of which vary from source to source, but the primary components are hydrocarbons. As the cycle of oil creation occurs over a period significantly longer than the human scale, oil is not considered a renewable resource despite being organic in origin. The hydrocarbon-rich content of oil make it well suited as a fuel and combustion releases carbon dioxide into the atmosphere.

The hydrocarbons contained in oil can be extracted through exposure to high heat and pressure, which stratifies the various hydrocarbons by density. Once separated the various components of oil can be used as fuel or converted into the raw materials for production, including plastics.

natural gas
Gas, predominantly methane and to lesser degrees other gases such as propane, ethane, and pentanes, found below the earth's surface in deposits typically coinciding with the presence of crude oil. Deposits vary in depth from several hundred feet to multiple miles and are either mixed with crude oil or trapped between oil deposits and impermeable rock formations. Drilled and extracted natural gas is processed to remove unwanted gases and to separate out the marketable gases. Natural gas can either be transported as a gas or alternatively liquefied for non-pipeline distribution. Through the Fischer–Tropsch

process the various gases found within natural gas can be converted into synthetic fuels, allowing conversion into a variety of other raw materials for industrial processes, including plastics.

biomass

Plant, microbe, and animal-derived organic matter not directly used in food or consumer products, which would traditionally be considered waste products. This includes leaves, roots, seed husks, manure, and municipal waste. Biomass typically contains a mixture of fats, proteins, minerals, and carbohydrates, with the ratio of components depending upon the origin of the biomass.

Biomass, being primarily plant-derived or derived from organisms which feed on plants, is considered a renewable resource. This is not only because the mass is replaced within a timescale far shorter than that required to generate oil or coal, but also because the carbon emitted in processing and combusting biomass is sequestered when the biomass is regenerated.

biomass-derived monomer

Monomers distilled from one of three organic sources: polysaccharides, proteins, and lipids.

polysaccharide

Typically referred to as a sugar, a group of ten or more monosaccharide molecules linked together with glycosidic bonds, created through the elimination of water. The compounds formed by linking the monosaccharides serves the biological function of either energy storage as glycogen and insulin or for structural elements as chitin and cellulose. As an energy source polysaccharides are amorphous, while assuming more orderly, crystalline form when structural, such as in the case of cellulose and chitin. A common polysaccharide-based resin is PLA, which is refined from corn starch; other plant starches are becoming increasingly common as raw materials for bioplastics.

proteins

Proteins are chains of more than 100 amino acids which are found in various quantities in biomass. The proteins, despite assuming a large variety of functions and characteristics, consist entirely of the same 20 amino acids. By varying the type of amino acids, the bond structure between acids, and the composite patterning, proteins assume different characteristics as evinced by keratin, which is the base material for both hair and claws.

lipids

The oils or fats found in plants. Soybean and corn oil are the primary source of raw materials for lipid-based bioplastics.

organism-derived monomer

The use of bacteria, fed on a food source that is typically an inexpensive waste product, which convert and store food as energy within their cells in the form of polyhydroxyalkanoates (PHAs). The PHAs are a form of polysaccharides and can be converted into plastics in the same manner as other polysaccharides.

1.2
Processing

How are monomers processed into plastics and bioplastics?

▼

fossil fuel distillation
A refining process whereby crude oil is separated into a wide variety of hydrocarbon products based on molecular weight (chain length). The process is driven by heat and gravity, and produces materials such as natural gas, liquid fuels (by grade and type inclusive of kerosene, jet fuel, and gasoline), oils, waxes, and bitumen.

biomass distillation
The extraction of raw materials – polysaccharides, proteins, and lipids – which are suitable for conversion into bioplastics that vary by type. An example of polysaccharide biomass distillation is chitin, which is derived from the shell of arthropods. Polysaccharides can be extracted from chitin by dissolving the calcium carbonate of the shell in acid and then using alkaline extraction to remove the protein. The remaining polysaccharide can then be used as a raw material in industrial processes. Chicken feathers are an example of a biomass which can be distilled to yield protein polymers suitable as raw materials in industrial processes. Feathers consist predominantly of the protein keratin, which can be extracted by grinding clean feather and mixing them with glycerol and reduction agent. The mixture can then be extruded either into pellets for use as a raw material in plastic manufacturing, or directly into usable bioplastic products.

bio-derived monomer distillation
Conversion of the monomer chains, or polymers, found within biomass into a plastic or raw materials suitable for conversion into a plastic. Processes vary depending on the component of the biomass being distilled (polysaccharide, protein, or lipid), but most involve the application of heat and a catalyst to break chemical bonds and form new ones necessary to achieve the desired material properties.

organism-derived distillation
To harvest PHAs, bacteria are exposed to an enzyme which breaks apart the cell membrane and then placed in solution which allows the PHAs to be separated out from the other components of the bacteria. PHAs derived from bacteria represent a renewable resource and can be produced when fed inexpensive waste products. The feed can be altered to change the characteristics of the PHAs produced and in turn the plastic generated. The plastics produced from PHAs also have the benefit of being biodegradable. Plants may also be used to generate PHAs, increasing carbon sequestration potential and PHA yield. The genetic engineering required to create plants which serve as hosts for the bacteria has occurred alongside the genetic engineering of bacteria, with *E. coli*, among others, manipulated to produce and store large quantities of PHA.

How are monomers added together to become polymers?

▼

polymerization
A process in which monomers, or short hydrocarbon chains, react to form larger more complex polymer chains. Many different types of polymerization exist, marked by the mechanisms by which active sites are introduced on the monomer to induce chain growth. The objective of any modern polymerization process is to control the resulting chain length (also known as molecular weight) and chain branching structure in a predictable manner to produce polymers with specific properties.

polyaddition
A type of polymerization reaction whereby monomer molecules join a polymer chain without forming any byproducts.

polycondensation
A type of polymerization reaction in which byproduct molecules are split off from chain ends as monomer molecules join together. These byproducts are often water molecules and are removed from the polymer reaction by heat or a combination of heat and vacuum.

Where are polymers processed?

▼

refinery production

Many polymers are manufactured at such great quantity that the monomers are reacted into various polymers shortly after being isolated from oil or natural gas. Such is the case for polyethylene and polypropylene, which respectively require gaseous ethylene and propylene monomers. Monomers such as ethylene and propylene are manufactured by "cracking" longer-chain gaseous or liquid hydrocarbons at high temperatures into the shorter monomer chains. After reacting these monomers into polymers, they leave the refinery site in the form of solid pellets.

factory processes

Most polymer products are either wholly manufactured or partially processed in factories before being manufactured into end products. Various manufacturers are involved in the synthesis, compounding, formulation, and forming steps of polymer products.

factory synthesis

Polymer manufacturers most often create intermediate products such as liquid resins and solid polymer pellets for other manufacturers to process into products. Some polymer manufacturers are also involved in polymer compounding and end-product manufacturing as well.

factory compounding

Polymer compounding involves melting a solid polymer and blending the polymer melt with other polymers or additives, most often using a twin-screw pellet extruder. Polymers are most often compounded with pigments, fillers such as fibers and powders, and additives such as UV inhibitors, plasticizers, or fire retardants. Compounding results in differentiated polymer products for many thousands of applications. The compounding step is often done after synthesis; however, an extruder or injection molder will often complete compounding within their facility. Alternatively, some manufacturers specialize solely in polymer compounding.

factory formulation

Formulation of polymer products occurs when a manufacturer blends polymer products with other ingredients to create paints, adhesives, coatings, resins, and other products for intermediate and end products.

factory forming

Includes polymer extrusion, film blowing and extrusion, fiber spinning, and molding of intermediate and end products.

on-site mixing and casting

Many polymer products are formulated with unreacted monomers so the end user can complete the final polymerization steps. Such is the case for two-part epoxies, two-part polyurethanes, and air-cured adhesives which may be reacted and thus polymerized right before our eyes on a construction site.

What is added prior to thermal treatment of resins?

▼

additives

A material added to a plastic or resin used to affect its attributes. Examples include fillers, inhibitors, stabilizers, and pigments.

fillers

An additive used to vary general material properties like processability, optical qualities, thermal conductivity, flame retardancy, hardness, and tear resistance. Often they are used to increase volume in order to decrease final material cost.

inhibitors

An additive to resin, often polyester or styrene, used to slow the chemical reaction that causes curing.

stabilizers

An additive used to improve material resistance to degradation, typically from UV radiation.

pigments

An additive to a resin used to affect material color. Also known as a colorant.

What are the products of processing?

▼

plastic resins

Any processed product of a polymerization reaction that can take several forms: liquid, semi solid, and solid resin in granule or pellet form.

An example of polymerization processes using polyethylene (PE)

PE is manufactured though a process called slurry polymerization. Monomer, ethylene gas sourced from crude oil or natural gas, is injected at pressure into a dilutant (isobutane), which causes droplets of the monomer to form which are not soluble in the dilutant. A small amount of catalyst material is pre-dissolved in dilutant and added to the slurry of monomer and dilutant, initiating the reaction. Solid product (PE) forms in the slurry and sinks to the bottom of the reaction vessel. The product is then separated from the dilutant and extruded into pellets; the dilutant is recycled and used again. Modern PE manufacturing plants utilize massive loop reactors to continuously manufacture PE products at great scale. The loop reactor is driven by the rate of adding feedstock and circulation pumps which control the residence time of the slurry in the loop reactor, influencing the molecular weight. Carefully engineered catalysts can also help control the resulting molecular weight. Many modern PE products such as MDPE, HDPE, HMWPE, and UHMWPE exhibit a bimodal molecular weight distribution, which means that the polymer structure is dominated by two distinct molecular weight products which enhance the mechanical properties of the polymer. The bimodal molecular weight and further differentiation in the various PE polymer products is achieved by either using two connected loop reactors or by using two catalysts.

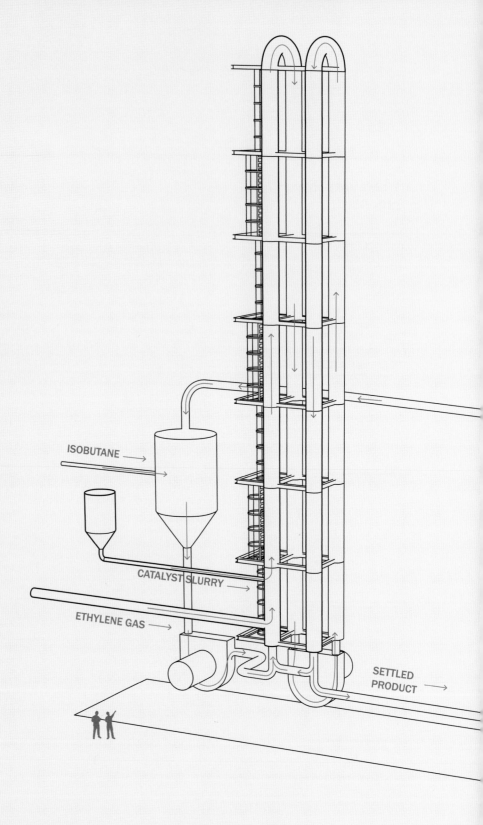

ISOBUTANE

CATALYST SLURRY

ETHYLENE GAS

SETTLED PRODUCT

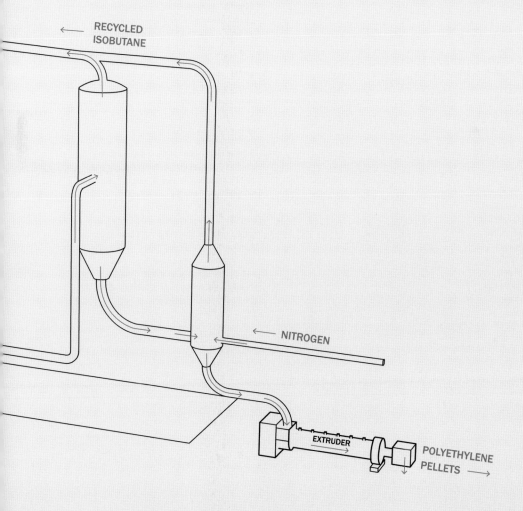

RECYCLED
ISOBUTANE

NITROGEN

EXTRUDER

POLYETHYLENE
PELLETS

1.3
Plastics defined

What is the fundamental definition of this material class?

polymer
A material – synthetic or natural – consisting of molecules that are characterized by the repetition of monomeric units instead of ends, junctions, and other irregularities.

natural polymers
A polymer made from raw monomers found in nature. Examples of natural polymers include silk, keratin, hair, natural rubber (gutta percha), natural starch, celluloses, chitin, shellac, horn, and even DNA and RNA.

plastics
Synthetic, as opposed to naturally occurring polymers. They are described as macro or very large molecules resulting from the addition of monomers into large chains. Saying that something is made from plastics is typically too general. There are literally hundreds of synthetic polymers all resulting from one of three processes: polymerization, polyaddition, or polycondensation. Also, they mostly result from one of five monomers: methane, ethylene, propylene, butylene, or benzene. The diversity of synthetic polymers is then largely dependent on processes of differentiation by manipulating time, pressure, and temperature, both at the scale of a chemist's workbench and the scale of a petrochemical processing facility.

bioplastics
Bioplastics, also known as organic plastics, are plastics derived by sourcing monomers from a renewable biomass source like trees, crab shells, or potatoes. Given these monomeric origins, the carbon they contain can be described as "contemporary," when compared to the age of carbon found in fossil fuels. In order to achieve functionality, chiefly durability, bioplastics may contain a ratio of biomass and fossil fuel-sourced monomers.

1.4
Polymer attributes

What are the primary working attributes of plastics?

thermoset
Thermoset is a term used to describe plastics that become permanently hardened when heated or cured. The curing process of thermosets causes a chemical reaction that creates permanent connections between the material's molecular chains. Due to their molecular bond, thermoset plastics have superior durability and will not change shape due to extreme thermal and chemical conditions, thus often outperforming other building materials.

thermoplastic
Thermoplastic is a term used to describe plastics that become soft and pliable, but do not set when heated. Thermoplastics have the ability to harden into a particular mold, but because there is no chemical change that occurs during the curing process, the material is able to be reprocessed numerous times. The major advantage of thermoplastic materials is their ability to be recycled, though continual recycling may adversely affect the quality of the polymer.

MANUFACTURING
▼

1.5
Manufacturing
techniques

How are plastics or bioplastics worked? How are plastics or bioplastics products manufactured?
▼

blow molding

Blow molding is the process by which a molten plastic tube is inserted inside a closed mold and inflated with air, forcing it to conform to the mold surface. Injection, extrusion, and stretch are three major types of blow molding; each presents a different method for introducing the plastic material (parison) into a mold cavity. *Injection blow molding* uses a preformed injection-molded tube which is placed and heated inside a mold cavity and then inflated into shape. *Stretch blow molding* utilizes similar procedures to the injection process, but the heated tube (parison) is stretched linearly with the blow tube before it is inflated. *Extrusion blow molding* utilizes a plastics extruder with a cylindrical die to extrude a preformed parison between two mold halves which are closed, securing the form before it is inflated. Thermoset plastics such as polypropylene, polyethylene, PVC, and commonly PET are used for this process, which is largely employed in the production of bottles.

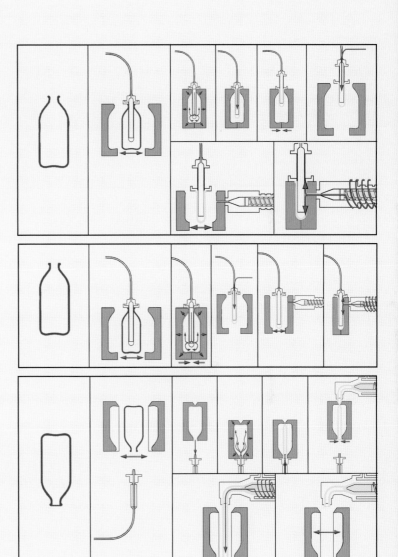

calendaring

Calendaring involves feeding molten plastic through heated rollers which form the polymer into film material. The finished material is gradually produced by processing the film through multiple sets of rollers that reduce its thickness until the final gauge has been achieved.

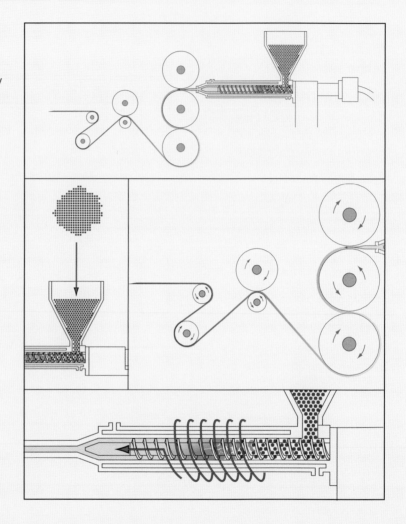

casting

Casting is the process of producing objects by pouring a liquid or molten material into a mold cavity. Solidification is enabled via the physical properties of material with plastic; thermoset resins produce an exothermic reaction which cures the material. In hot-melt casting of plastics, the materials are allowed to cool in the mold. Different from molding, the material in casting is not forced into shape; rather, it is a result of gravity, air pressure, and the material's plastic state that it is able to fully consolidate within the mold cavity.

Thermoset resins are the most commonly cast plastic materials; these include acrylic, epoxy, polyester, and urethane. Resins typically comprise a two-component mixture: the base material and the catalyst which accelerates the curing process.

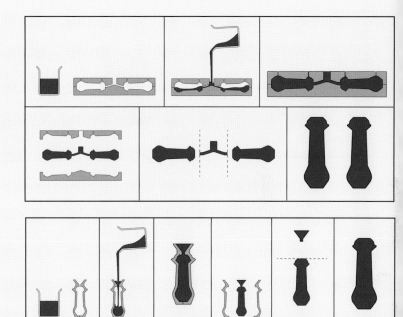

compression molding

Compression molding is in principal a simple process that utilizes a two-piece mold, male and female components, that work in compression to mold heated material into a shape by force. In molding plastic, granulated or sheet material is placed into an open mold cavity which is heated, either melting or rendering the material pliable, before fully closing together the two mold halves to form the finished part.

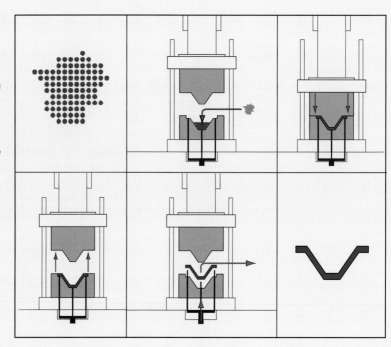

contact molding

Contact molding involves building up a form over a mold by "laying up" layers of fiber reinforcement through impregnating them with resin. This is an open mold process similar to drape forming (VaRTM) and involves thermoset resins infused with a dense matrix of fiber strand or fiber cloth, curing onto a mold surface replicating its form and texture. The vacuum bagging process is used for the creation of higher-performance parts that require tighter tolerances of form and strength. Composite forms using carbon fiber and Kevlar are typically produced with this process. Carbon and Kevlar are typically used in fabric form and are laid-up much the same as glass fiber cloth over a mold. The vacuum bagging process eliminates surface defects by sucking the composite material into close contact with the mold surface and by drawing out excess resin content into the vacuum bag fabric. Pre-impregnated fabrics are commonly used and require the use of a curing oven to activate the embodied resin.

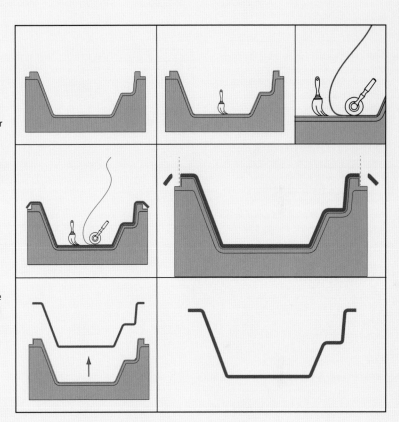

digital fabrication
Digital fabrication in the context of this description includes rapid prototyping and direct digital manufacturing processes. These are additive fabrication processes that build objects directly from digital solids (3D models) by layering and laser-curing thermoset and photopolymer resins. Objects are literally built from the bottom up, much in the same way cardboard and plywood laminate forms are created.

Direct digital manufacturing (DDM) is the use of this technology to produce functional products for distribution and real use. FDM (fused deposition modeling) is commonly used for the DDM process and can be employed to create fully functional pieces of furniture and industrial products such as automotive components. FDM builds objects with premium-grade polymers such as ABS plastic and polycarbonate, which enables the creation of production-grade objects that can be hot-air welded to form assemblies and fully finished.

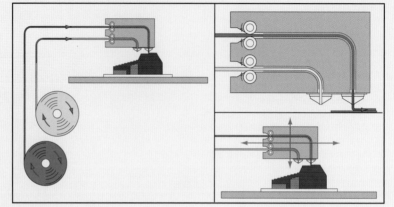

extrusion

The extrusion process is used for the production of linear shapes and generates continuous spans of formed plastic by forcing molten polymer through a die. There are three major types of extrusion: profile extrusion, tube extrusion, and sheet extrusion. Profile extrusion produces linear parts such as structural shapes – channels, angles, etc. Tubular extrusion or pipe extrusion is different from profile extrusion in that the die contains an inner component which produces and shapes the interior of the extruded product. Sheet products are extruded in a similar manner as profiles; however, after extrusion the material is processed through a set of rollers which gauge its thickness and provide a finished surface.

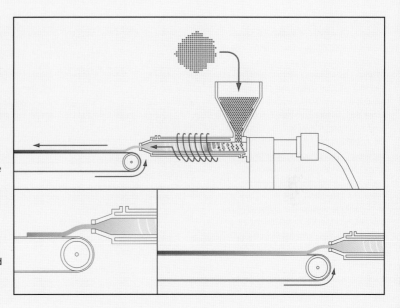

filament winding
Filament winding is used to fabricate
high-strength composite structures by
winding fiber reinforcement around
a mold. The process entails winding
variably tensioned filament strands
around a positive form, called a mandrel,
in various patterns designed to optimize
structural integrity based on high-stress
areas within the form. The filament can
be applied wet or pre-impregnated.
In wet winding, filament strands are
continuously drawn through a resin bath,
much the same as the pultrusion process,
while simultaneously being tensioned
around the mandrel form. The method
utilizing pre-impregnated fiber is much
the same, but the material must be heat
cured.

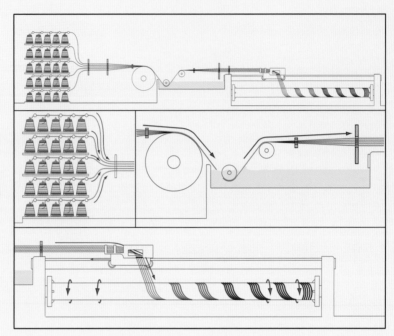

foam molding

(Foam) steam chest molding is a process commonly used to manufacture strong, lightweight, and highly insulative products from EPE, EPP, and EPS foam beads. The process involves injecting steam into a metal mold filled with foam beads which causes the individual particles to expand and fuse together under heat and pressure. Prior to molding, the foam beads are preprocessed through two steps which include pre-expansion and stabilization. In pre-expansion, raw plastic pellets are "foamed" and converted into cellular plastic through steam treatment. Stabilization is the process that follows pre-expansion, whereby the foam beads are cooled prior to being transported into the mold.

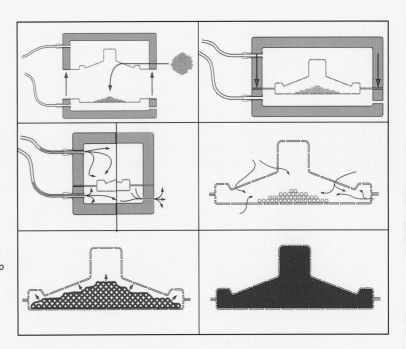

injection molding

Injection molding is a manufacturing process in which a molten (plastic) material is injected under high-pressure into a mold to produce a formed object. The process utilizes most thermoplastics in granular form, which are fed into a heated chamber that churns and melts the material. The churning mechanism or screw feeds the material through a chamber where it is pressure injected into the mold. After the part has cooled it is ejected and the process resumes.

Gas-assisted injection molding, a variant process, is typically used to manufacture large objects with hollow sections such as furniture. In this process, gas is injected into the mold cavity with the molten polymer and forces the material into contact with the mold surface.

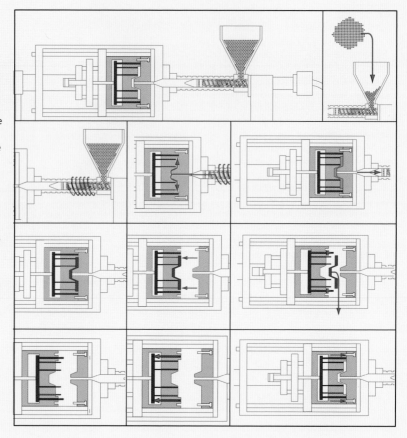

laminating

Laminating is the process of layering materials to form a unified structure. In architectural plastics, two major types of lamination produce composite structures; high-pressure laminates (HPLs), which are panel goods that are manufactured from sheets of paper infused with phenolic resin; and structural core laminates such as honeycomb panels. More industrial are fiberglass and carbon fiber composite sandwich panels that are manufactured and utilized for their superior strength-to-weight ratio. Honeycomb structures, of which aluminum is very common, provide a structural core that can be cut and shaped prior to laminating a fiber composite to its surface. Honeycomb and fiber composites in laminated form make for a material that has superior impact resistance while retaining high tensile strengths. Other materials used in sandwich applications include Kraft paper, polycarbonate, and polypropylene honeycomb. Balsa wood end blocks and vinyl foam are also common.

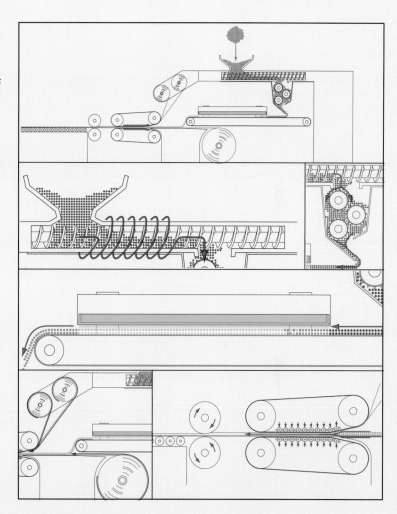

machining

Machining implies cutting a material to produce a part. It is a reductive process that begins with a mass of material that is physically altered by methods including milling, drilling, and abrasive shaping – which are all cutting operations. Three common types of cutting used in plastic fabrication are die cutting, laser cutting, and water-jet cutting.

Die cutting utilizes a sharp profiled blade, like a cookie cutter, which is mechanically pressed into a sheet material, cutting out a shape.

Laser cutting is an automated process that uses a focused laser beam to cut material. Laser cutting can also be used to engrave, etch, and score sheet goods. The intensity of the laser beam can be focused to give almost complete control over cutting depth and is a very clean method for producing shapes.

Water-jet cutting is similar to laser cutting in that it is a CNC-driven process; however, it uses a blend of water and abrasive powder to cut through materials. Whereas laser cutting is limited by the thickness at which it can cut, theoretically water-jet technology has no thickness restraints. It can cut virtually any material including stone, glass, and titanium at thicknesses up to roughly 24 inches. By filtering the blend of water and abrasive through a fine spray nozzle at pressures ranging from 55,000 to roughly 90,000 psi this technology is capable of cutting incredibly detailed patterns in very dense, hard materials with the utmost precision and cleanliness. Because it is not a hot process, the cuts produced are very clean and usually require little to no post-finishing work.

CNC milling is used to cut and shape solid materials and encompasses a diverse range of machinery that can be used to produce complex three-dimensional geometries in virtually any media by reductively modifying a formal mass. Milling machines use a rotary-driven cutting tool to gradually shape matter in up to five axes. Whereas laser cutting operates by locating points within a two-dimensional plane, CNC milling works by locating points in real space.

pultrusion

Different from the extrusion process where molten polymer is forced through a die producing a shape, pultrusion utilizes continuous strands of resin-impregnated fiber to produce composite profiles. Fiber is continuously fed from reels into a resin bath, where it passes into a preformed die that bunches and guides the material into a heat-curing die which produces the formed product. After curing, the material is cut and the process goes on.

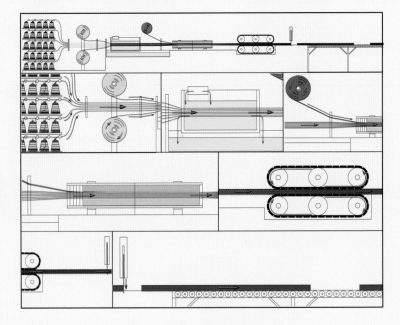

roto molding

Roto molding is a process for creating hollow parts from plastic materials such as polyethylene and polypropylene. The process includes heating a powdered material to the point of liquidation and rotating it in a biaxial manner within a mold. The rotation of the mold causes the material to coat the mold walls with thin layers of polymer which gradually build up, forming the object. After the mold walls have been evenly coated, the mold is cooled and the part removed.

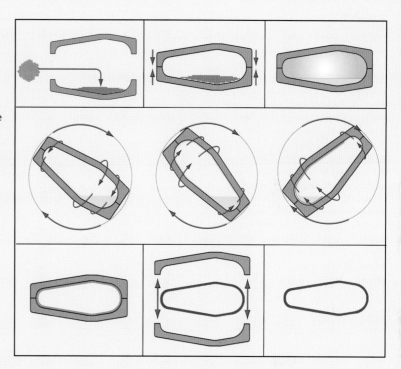

spunbond

Spunbond describes the two-part process of spinning fibers and bonding them together. The spunbond process is used to produce fibrous fabric materials, termed non-woven textiles, by dispersing individual fiber filaments onto a surface, usually flat, and bonding them through diverse methods such as heat rolling and chemical bonding. A spinneret is used to extrude molten polymer in the form of fiber onto the production surface, which continuously feeds the depositions through the bonding system. Materials commonly used in this process include: polypropylene, polyethylene, polyurethane and nylon. Spunbonding is often used to produce materials such as geo-textiles and products such as Tyvek.

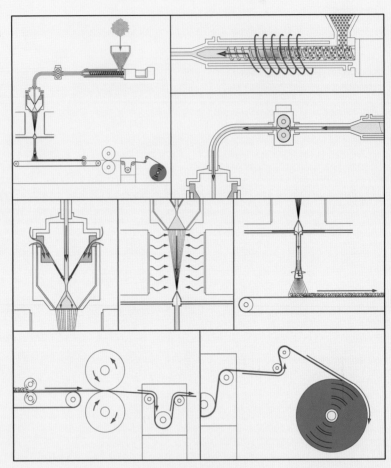

thermoforming

The principals of thermoforming include heating a plastic sheet material until it is pliable and forcing it to conform over a mold surface by using mechanical or vacuum pressure or simply the force of gravity alone. Drape forming – the simplest of thermoforming techniques – relies on the principles of heat, gravity, and elasticity to form a plastic sheet material. Whereas in vacuum forming, vacuum pressure is utilized to draw a pliable material into shape, in drape forming pressure is applied mechanically, by hand and through gravitational pull, thus enabling a pliable sheet material to literally fall into shape. Thermoforming is well suited for one-off and mass production runs, and relatively complex forms with three-dimensional curves are attainable.

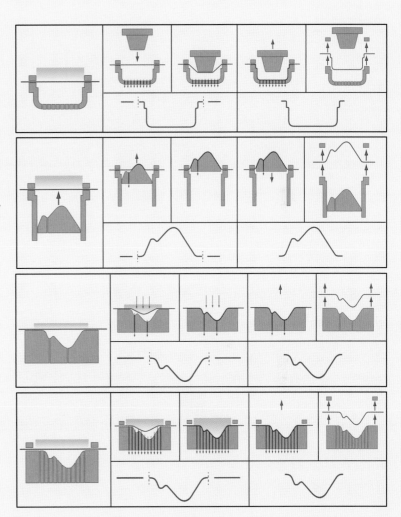

transfer molding

Transfer molding is a process that combines the principals of both injection and compression molding, through using force to compress a molten polymer into a closed mold by way of an injection chamber.

Resin transfer molding is used for the manufacture of composite/fiber reinforced parts. This process employs the resin injection method to impregnate dry fiber reinforcement contained in a closed mold cavity.

Vacuum-assisted resin transfer molding (VaRTM) is an open-mold process, meaning the part produced will only have one finish face. Dry fiber reinforcement is "laid up" in a mold cavity and the assembly is enclosed in a vacuum bag. Vacuum pressure is introduced and draws resin into the mold and through the preformed fiber.

Both transfer mold and resin transfer molding are high-production processes that include expensive set-up costs. VaRTM is better suited for low production runs due to the relative simplicity of the process; however, it is extremely labor intensive.

All three processes are suited for producing large parts, VaRTM especially so. With this process, objects up to the size of boat hulls can be fabricated.

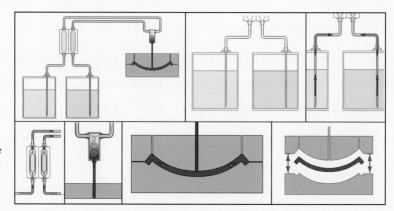

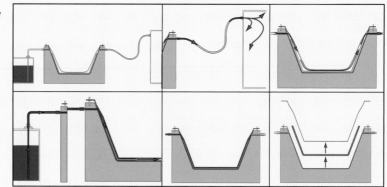

welding

Within the plastics industry welding facilitates a principal function in joining materials and represents a diverse array of processes from simple solvent bonding to sophisticated techniques such as ultrasonic welding. Welding technologies for plastic are application-specific and are designed for use with particular materials at different scales of production. Three common technologies used for large-scale fabrication include high-frequency, heated-tool, and hot-air welding.

High-frequency welding is used to join thin-sheet films or fabrics and utilizes radio frequency waves to melt and join contacting materials. This process is also referred to as the heat sealing of plastics. The weld is created by overlapping edges of film or sheet materials and applying pressure on the joint with a metal die which transmits radio waves through a table surface that welds the materials through heat and compression. Typical materials used in this process include vinyl, PVC, polyurethane, PET, and nylon.

Heated-tool welding is commonly used to edge-bond plastic sheets. Through heating opposing edges of sheet material with a heated metal plate a weld is created when the edges are converged.

Hot-air and hot-air extrusion welding are manual processes that enable the fabrication of plastic components using stock materials – much in the same manner as fabricating with sheet and structural metals. Handheld hot-air welding is a simple process akin to oxyacetylene and TIG welding – a welding torch is used to heat the surface of two pieces of material, and through the introduction of filler material, a permanent bond is fashioned. The tool consists of a torch with an air supply which provides a stream of hot gas that continuously heats both substrates and filler materials.

USE AND MAINTENANCE

1.6
Material Specification

What is the convention for communicating these materials?

naming conventions
Given their long chemical names such as polydiphenylmethanediisocyanate, plastics are typically recognized by an acronym such as pMDI. ASTM publishes an official list of polymer abbreviations to be used in the building and construction industry.

international building code reference
The IBC is mostly concerned with a plastics Flame Spread Index (FSI), Smoke Developed Index (SDI), and combustibility. The FSI indicates the ability of a flame to travel across the surface of a material in a given amount of time. The SDI indicates how much smoke is created when a material is burned. A low SDI number corresponds to a smaller volume of smoke. The combustibility of a plastic, or its ability to contribute to the fuel load of a fire, varies significantly across the range of plastics available. Some plastics are highly flammable and combustible; others cannot sustain flaming once the source of the flame is removed. Some plastics, and the compounds they contain, will produce toxic gases when burned. Chapter 26, "Plastics," of the IBC is organized to address both types of plastic (insulating or light transmitting) and their location in the building (interior finish, exterior wall, glazing, and roof). Chapter 26 must be used in conjunction with other IBC chapters, most notably chapter 8 which addresses interior finishes.

CSI master format number
The Construction Specifications Institute is largely a volunteer organization which promotes technical communication within the construction industry. It publishes Master Format, a numbering system organizing the technical data or specifications for all building materials and systems. Specifications for materials and their methods are organized into three parts: general, products, and execution. Plastics are specified under Division 06 along with wood and composites. But plastics can actually be specified in multiple divisions because they are functional companions to multiple materials. For instance, in Division 03: Concrete, one might find polyethylene listed under Part II products as a vapor barrier in a concrete slab assembly.

Flame Spread Index, FSI
A rating describing the distance and speed by which flames spread across a material surface. Ratings are given relative to red oak, with an arbitrary rating of 100, and reinforced cement board, with a rating of 0. A rating can also be described by three classes: class A is rated 0–25, class B is 26–75, class C is 76–200.

Smoke Developed Index, SDI
A rating describing the amount of visibility, or lack of smoke, permitted by a material burning. It is often a two-part rating, describing the rate of smoke development in flaming and non-flaming conditions. It can also be derived from the Steiner tunnel test (class A, B, and C are rated 0–450).

1.7
properties

What are the potential properties of polymers?

▼

UV resistance (UV)
A rating describing the ability of a material to resist deterioration due to ultraviolet light (poor, fair, good, or excellent).

light transmittance (LT)
A ratio of light transmitted through a material to the total amount of light exposed to the material. Typically pertains to light transmitters and textiles. (Light Transmitted)/(Total Light Exposure).

chemical resistance (CR)
A rating describing the ability of a material to resist deterioration when exposed to a variety of chemicals under standard conditions (poor, fair, good, or excellent).

scratch resistance (SR)
A measure of resistance to scratching or marring of a material surface (poor, fair, good, or excellent).

wear resistance (index) (WRI)
A rating describing the ability of a material to resist surface damage or deterioration from abrasion or friction (poor, fair, good, or excellent).

r-value (thermal resistance), r
A measure of resistance to the passage of heat through a material of a stated thickness; the reciprocal of conductance. Typically pertains to insulators.

thermal coefficient of expansion (coefficient of thermal expansion, CTE)
A factor describing the dimensional response of a mass to temperature change. Typically heating results in expansion and cooling results in contraction. (Change in Length)/(Original Length × Change in Temperature).

maximum service temperature (MST)
The maximum service temperature of a material is the measure of the highest temperature, in °F, a material can withstand before thermal degradation renders it unfit for service.

heat-sensitive adhesion
A method by which a material uses pressure to adhere to another material. Typically pertains to adhesives.

pressure rating
A rating describing the ultimate internal pressure allowed by a vessel, tank, or piping before failure. Typically pertains to conductors like piping.

water vapor transmission (WVT)
Water vapor transmission is a measure, in perms, of the amount of water vapor that will pass through a material over time.

water absorption
A ratio of the weight of water absorbed by a material to the weight of a material when immersed for a standard period of time. (Water Absorbed Weight)/(Material Weight).

Young's modulus (modulus of elasticity) (E/YM/ME)
The ratio, in psi or pounds of force per square inch, of stress over strain for a material with linear elastic behavior. It can be determined and represented by a stress–strain curve. (Tensile Stress)/(Tensile Strain).

flexural strength (modulus of rupture, MR)
A measure, in psi or pounds of force per square inch, of the ultimate stress a material can withstand before failure (rupture).

compressive strength (CS)
A measure, in psi or pounds of force per square inch, of the ultimate amount of axially applied forces a material can withstand before failure.

tensile strength (break strength, TS)
A measure, in psi or pounds of force per square inch, of the ultimate tensile stress a material can receive before failure.

tear strength (TS)
A measure, in psi or pounds of force per square inch, of the ultimate tensile stress a textile can receive before it tears. Typically pertains to air/moisture barriers.

peel strength (PS)
A measure of the force needed to peel a length of material off a surface at a specific angle, in a variety of standard ways. Typically pertains to adhesives. Averaged (Load)/(Width).

END OF LIFE

1.8
End-of-life options

What are the end-of-life options for plastics and bioplastics?

biodegradable plastic
Plastics which can be broken down through aerobic decomposition. ASTM has created standard ASTM D6868-03 Standard Specification for Biodegradable Plastics Used as Coatings on Paper and Other Compostable Substrates which defines plastic biodegradability. The standard dictates plastics, in order to be referred to as biodegradable, must be compostable, or susceptible to aerobic degradation equivalent to other readily compostable materials, such as leaf litter. In aerobic decomposition, bacteria – in the presence of oxygen – feed upon the bioplastic. The bacteria gain energy from consuming the plastic and produce, as a waste product, predominantly carbon dioxide and water, along with smaller quantities of other compounds.

photodegradation
The chemical transformation of a compound into smaller compounds caused by the destabilization of internal bonds through the absorption of photons, most commonly ultraviolet, visible, or infrared radiation. Polymers are particularly sensitive to photodegradation, either within the polymer structure itself or through impurities contained within the polymer. Typically degradation occurs through an oxidative reaction, where the polymer is destabilized through the loss of an electron. The loss of an electron creates a polymer radical which bonds with

atmospheric oxygen, leading to further degradation. The area of greatest photodegradation is typically on the surface of a material as most photons are absorbed before striking the back of the polymer and the internal areas are effectively separated from oxygen, preventing oxidation. Various additives have been developed which are added to polymers during the manufacturing process to limit the extent of UV degradation.

hydrolytic degradation
A chemical process in which the bonds of a compound are broken by separating water into hydrogen and hydroxyl in the presence of the compound, causing the compound to degrade into two separate components: one bonded to the hydrogen and the other to the hydroxyl. This reaction can also occur without water, instead using acids or bases in various combinations, usually accompanied by high-temperature conditions. A wide variety of industrial products can be created from biomass through the application of hydrolytic degradation, as can manufactured polymers be similarly degraded into their constituent monomers.

compost
Compost is the byproduct of biodegradation where organisms such as bacteria, small insects, and fungi break-down organic matter. The primary activity is conducted by bacteria and fungi, which consume biomass and excrete waste in a process referred to as aerobic decomposition. The byproduct of this aerobic biodegradation is carbon dioxide, water, a soil-like substance, and various other compounds including nitrogen. The nitrogen content in particular makes

---

pressure rating (PR)
A rating describing the ultimate internal pressure allowed by a vessel, tank, or piping before failure. Typically pertains to conductors like piping.

puncture strength (PS)
A measure of the ultimate amount of standardized, concentrated force a material can withstand before failing. Failing can be characterized as a puncture or rupture, or when an elongation limit is reached. Typically pertains to light and air/moisture barriers.

burning characteristics
The attributes of a material when exposed to flame. Attributes vary based on the types of plastics. For instance, a flame might cause a plastic to melt and drip, vaporize, combust, or produce smoke with toxic particulates. Burning characteristics for plastics are both studied closely in an experimental sense and tested rigorously according to ASTM protocols. The Flame Spread Index (FSI) and Smoke Developed Index (SDI) are indices which directly communicate and numerically translate the burning characteristics of plastics.

creep
Under stress, exposed to high temperatures, and over time, plastics may slowly but permanently deform. This requires designers to account for the rate of creep, or the rate of deformation when designing with plastics. For instance, the tensioning components of a single-layer plastic membrane structure should also incorporate a strategy for re-tensioning. Due to the phenomena of "creep," the tensioned membrane will appear to "slack" over time, which in turn presents the risk of membrane failure.

compost appropriate as a soil additive to promote growth. The nature of the chemical bonds within a polymer dictate microbial digestibility, with certain bioplastics and fossil fuel-derived plastics capable of being composted.

microbial digestion

The decomposition of biomass with bacteria in either an environment with oxygen (aerobic) or without oxygen (anaerobic) resulting from bacteria consuming the biomass as a food source and excreting waste byproducts. The waste generated in aerobic digestion is carbon dioxide and water, while anaerobic digestion produces methane and fatty acids. Aerobic digestion is the process involved in composting, while aerobic processes are found within landfills. The susceptibility of plastics to microbial digestion varies depending on the nature of the chemical bonds within the polymer, with some being highly susceptible and others extremely resistant.

recycle

Recycling is the appropriation of waste products as raw materials in industrial processes or the reuse of products for either the original purpose or a new application. In construction, plastics are primarily used in piping, conduits, cladding, insulation, and seals, which can all be recycled at the end of their useful lives. There is also the recycling of waste plastic generated during the construction process, which can include vinyl siding scraps, conduit, and sections of piping.

Various efforts have been made to expand recycling of plastic waste generated during the manufacturing and construction period, or pre-consumer

waste, and for plastics which have served out their useful life for the end consumer, or post-consumer waste.

pre-consumer waste

Industrial waste product which can be recovered and reincorporated into the production process as a raw material. PVC manufacturers have engaged in pre-consumer recycling by grinding and reintroducing PVC scrap into the production. Other companies have explored the recovery of PVC from construction sites, which is reground and sold to manufacturers as a raw material. Within pre-consumer construction-related plastic recycling, PVC is the most prevalent; both due to the ease of recycling and the ubiquity of its presence within buildings.

post-consumer waste

Recycling streams are for construction materials that have served out their useful deployed life. Much of the construction-related post-consumer plastic recycling has focused on vinyl products due to their ubiquity, particularly roofing, siding, and window frames. Sika Sarnafil has been able to establish a successful vinyl roof recovery and recycling program where vinyl roofs, at the end of their useful lives, are recovered and reprocessed as raw materials in new roof construction. Other, smaller, independent plastic recyclers accept vinyl siding, window frames, and piping and actively recover it from construction sites without fees. The market for consumers to sell back used plastics as well as no-cost recovery reduced landfill fees. These smaller companies grind the recovered vinyl and sell it back to manufacturers as a raw material.

resin identification code

A coding system originally developed in 1988 by the Society of the Plastics Industry, Inc. (SPI) to identify the resin type in bottles and containers commonly found in residential waste streams. The coding system is used by consumers and waste sorters to determine the eligibility for recycling of different plastics. ASTM assumed responsibility for the resin ID system to regulate the definition of the code, as well as the manner of its presentation on containers.

The coding system accounts for seven different resin categories:

> › PET
> › HDPE
> › PVC
> › LDPE
> › PP
> › PS
> › Other.

pre-consumer waste

Waste generated during manufacturing processes that is not normally reincorporated into the same production process from which it originated.

post-consumer waste

Waste generated by households or other end users of a given product which is no longer of use to the consumer.

incineration

The combustion of waste products producing heat, ash, and waste gases as byproducts. Incineration can occur on the municipal scale, with large facilities incinerating household waste, using the heat produced to generate electricity.

The waste gases can contain high levels of pollutants, requiring removal before release into the atmosphere. The energy potential of plastic, reflective of its fossil fuel source, is quite high. This energy intensity makes it desirable to combust relative to other, less energy-intensive waste products.

landfill
Site for the disposal of waste through compaction and burial under layers of soil. Once buried, the waste undergoes anaerobic decomposition, producing methane, among other byproducts. The methane produced by landfills has been captured and used for power generation, the degree of utility dependant upon the size of the landfill, amount of moisture within the landfill, and temperature, with less decomposition occurring in cooler, drier conditions. Most landfills are lined to prevent the leaching of pollutants into groundwater and once full are capped to prevent water penetration, which can encourage more leaching. The degradation of plastics within landfill conditions is expected to take several hundred years. Concerns have been raised about landfilled plastics, with certain plastic additives exhibiting the potential to leach out, placing even greater emphasis on the engineering of landfill liners and caps.

reuse
The use or salvaging for use a product that would otherwise be discarded, recycled, or downcycled. Reuse requires no industrial energy inputs, unlike recycling, and thus is considered the more preferable option. There exists a limited market for reused plastic construction materials, primarily due to the degradation plastics suffer over the course of deployment and the relative low cost of virgin plastic construction materials versus that of appropriating used materials.

useful life
Plastics can degrade over time through chemical change initiated by several environmental factors, including UV light, pollutants, moisture, and microbial activity. Detailing of assemblies with weather-exposed plastics should account for weathering characteristics and the manufacturers stated useful life of the plastic.

"Research in the plastics industry,"

H.M. Richardson, Chief Engineer, General Electric Plastics
Division, Pittsburgh, Massachusetts

1940, New York

The occasion is The National
Conference on Plastics
*sponsored by the monthly
digest* Interior Design and
Decoration.[15] *Could this be
one of the earliest organized
gatherings on the topic of
plastics and architecture? Here,
designers will talk new goods
– furniture, lighting, and wall
coverings – made from the new
materials vinyls and acrylic.*

*H.M. Richardson's address
takes a slightly different tone.
He describes to the audience
challenges ahead – cost,
fabrication, and durability
– and proposes research
as the process for moving
forward. We can imagine that
Richardson inhabits a moment
of uncertainty dosed with the
certainty of potential: Will
plastics normalize? Of course.
But how? Will plastics become
durable? Will plastics become
affordable?*

*As we begin to discern why we
use plastics the way that we do,
his ruminations have an entirely
other effect. In his search of
"molding materials" he does not
discriminate between biobased
or fossil fuel-based monomers.
Here, soybeans exist alongside
benzene, evincing the capacity
that has always been ours – to
source materials to become
treatable, moldable masses.*

Research is a word which has a multitude of
meanings, depending on what the many users
of it have in mind. To some it connotes the
search for, development, and perfection of new
substances, methods, or devices. To others it
may be the inquiry into the how, the why, and
the wherefore of existing things. And to others
it means enlightened, scientific exploration into
new fields in search of things which man never
knew before and the evaluation of the discov-
eries in terms of economic needs. In my own
thinking I confine research to the limits of this
last definition but for the purpose of this talk,
perhaps it should be broadened to include also
the development of the products of research up
to a point where they become useful articles of
commerce.

In order to do effective research, we must first
of all know what to look for, what objective
to reach. Let us ask ourselves these questions:
What are the future needs of the plastics industry? What have been the trends of the past, and
do they lead to the satisfaction of the needs of
the future? What fundamental conditions must
be met in order to satisfy the future needs?

Let us start by reviewing the past: I think it is
safe to say that plastics have not created many,
if anything entirely new but have been used
to make articles which have been, or could be
made of other structural materials, and make
them better, cheaper, more attractive, more durable, lighter or stronger so a greater demand is
created for the articles using plastics than using
the previous materials. If these are the reasons
for the success of plastics so far, the extension
of these factors to a higher degree, either by
refinement of present materials, methods, and
processes, or by discovering and development
of new and better plastics should bring more
success to the industry.

In the field of interior design the properties
of plastics which have *promoted* their use are:
color, texture of surface finish, translucency or
transparency, lightness, strength, warmth to
touch, versatility of form, and permanence of
finish.

The factors which have *hindered* the use of
plastic in this field are: high unit cost of
plastic materials. Difficulty of fabrication when

only a small number of pieces is made. Low
softening point of thermoplastic materials.
Low scratch-hardness of glass-like plastics.
Susceptibility of certain plastics to cold-flow
under pressure and of certain others to change
in shape on absorbing and giving up moisture.

Plastics research is concerned with both lists –
to improve the good properties of the present
available plastics or discover new ones which are
better; and to remove the obstacles in the same
way. Probably the removal of the obstacles is the
more direct way to increase the use of plastics.

What is research doing to bring this about? Let's
take the obstacles one by one: *Cost* is probably
the most important factor in the expansion of
plastics in interior design. Cost is made up of
material, labor, and expense.

Our search for lower cost materials is for those
which come from abundant sources and which
can be developed into usable form with a
minimum of expenditure. Most of our present
organic plastics come from abundant raw materials such as coal, air, water, salt, and energy.
From these we get the elements from which
organic plastics are built. These sources of material are abundant and cheap, so our problem
is to improve the economy of synthesis. This
usually calls for large-volume production; and
large volume production of the intermediates of
which plastics are made means that there must
be other large uses aside from plastics.

Now let us consider some of the existing plastics from this viewpoint. The best example of
this is urea-formaldehyde resin, such as Beetle
and Plaskon. Urea is made from ammonia and
carbon dioxide – both easily made, and abundant. And urea is widely used in agriculture as
a fertilizer material – so it must be low priced
(about $100 a ton). Formaldehyde is made by
the catalytic oxidation of methanol (wood alcohol), which is used in tremendous quantities
as an anti-freeze liquid for automobile cooling
systems. Potentially, urea-formaldehyde resins
are among the lowest in cost, as far as raw
materials are concerned. Research on the urea
resins, therefore, should be directed to improving and simplifying the process of manufacture
and control so the finished product can be sold
profitably at lower and lower prices.

The phenolic plastics such as Bakelite and Durez are obtained as a by-product of coal tar or by synthesis starting with benzene. There isn't half enough phenol in coal tar to supply the plastics industry, so the remainder must be synthetic phenol. Benzene is plentiful and cheap enough so that most of what is produced in the United States is blended with gasoline for motor fuel, but the process of making phenol from benzene is rather difficult, and furthermore the other uses for phenol outside the plastics industry are relatively smaller than the uses of urea, so the price of phenol is about $240 a ton – compared to $100 for urea. The formaldehyde is the same. Actually phenolic compounds are lower in price than urea compounds because of greater volume and lower processing cost. Thus, in order that phenolic resins be still lower in cost the research should be directed toward cheaper ways of making phenol.

To cite another example, take the cellulose plastics – cellulose acetate, such as Lumarith and Tenite, and ethylcellulose – the cellulose is cheap and abundant, but the processing needs to be more economical to lower their cost. Also other esters of cellulose with improved properties have been developed and are coming into general use.

Polystyrene is made of abundant materials, but the high purity necessary to make a satisfactory plastic requires expensive processing. Here the research should be directed toward more economical processes or toward ways of stabilizing styrene so the high degree of purity is not necessary. Methyl methacrylate starts with acetone, which is relatively cheap, but the processing is expensive, involving several steps. Research, toward improving the process, should bring good results. Plastics based on vinyl chloride and vinyl acetate are potentially low in cost if made in sufficient quantity.

New lower cost resins and compounds from abundant sources of raw material are the object of wide research, and we can expect to add more new names to the list of plastics each year. Some of these may be derived from farm products. For example, surplus skim milk is a source of casein from which "Lani-

tal" or synthetic wool can be made – and also of lactic acid, from which may be derived ethyl acrylate. Much work has also been done on the development of ligno-cellulose plastics from wood chips, or from the woody portion of sugar-cane stalks (bagasse). Ligno-cellulose as a plastic is getting much attention from the paper industry. Another field of research is in fermentation of sugars.

Proteins from corn or soybeans have been studied and commercial plastics developed which are tough and horn-like, but which have a rather high moisture-absorption.

The Department of Agriculture has recently established four large Research Laboratories devoting their time to the development of industrial uses for farm products, and plastics are scheduled for considerable attention in their program. The petroleum industry also has shown that crude oil and natural gas are sources of raw material for making formaldehyde, phenol, butadiene for synthetic rubber, glycerine for alkyd resins.

The primary value of all these researches to the plastics industry, is to provide it eventually with lower-cost molding materials. Other work is also being done with the molding processes and the molds to bring about lower costs. New automatic molding machines with high output have been developed for injection molding of thermoplastics and compression molding of thermo-setting materials.

Improved methods of making molds are being developed. For individual castings of plastics, some advance has been made in the use of molds made of rubber or of rubber-like plastics, such as plasticized polyvinyl chloride. This has allowed the casting of complicated shapes which would never be removed from rigid molds and shortens the step from the clay model to the cast plastic reproduction of it. Thermoplastic transparent materials, like cellulose acetate or methyl methacrylate, are made in sheet, tube, and rod form. These may be softened, formed, and cemented together. This is an attractive way to make custom-built pieces. I mentioned that the low softening point of the thermo-plastic materials was a handicap. Those in commercial use all soften

at temperatures around or below 100 degrees, Centigrade, but considerable research effort is being spent to raise the softening point to 125 or 150 degrees, Centigrade, and eliminate "cold-flow." Beyond this, I cannot predict just when such a material will appear commercially.

In general, the thermo-plastic materials have low scratch-hardness. On the other hand, the thermo-setting plastics like the phenolics and ureas are quite hard and abrasion resistant, particularly the ureas. What we need is something which is formed as readily as thermoplastic, but which has the surface hardness of a urea-formaldehyde resin and is as clear as methyl methacrylate. So far, such a material has not shown itself, but we will not say it is impossible – although we may end up by getting the abrasion resistance by making the surface tough like rubber, instead of hard like glass.

In the past, there have been some objections to urea resins for their absorption of moisture, but this is being overcome and their stability greatly increased. Also, there are under development new light colored plastics with almost the range of color possibilities of the ureas but with the moisture stability of the phenolics.

Earlier I spoke of the fundamental properties of plastics which have promoted their use in interiors. Many plastics have been mentioned and all have combinations of several of these desirable properties.

While I have spoken mainly of plastics, this talk would not be complete without mention of resin-bonded plywood and synthetic resin finishes, because the same names are becoming common to all three of the fields. Phenolic and urea resins have been developed for hot and cold pressed plywood and the molding or forming of plywood structures will be developed and advanced strongly in the next few months. This combination is attractive and can be extended in the furniture field.[16]

NOTES

1 Our query dissects the relationship between plastics and architecture. A definition of architecture is assumed, even as we begin by defining "plastic." Later in the query, the definition of "architecture" may be challenged by the arrival of the conceptual position "plastics in building" which will be found repeatedly throughout the data set.

2 *Modern Plastics.* 1925. "Plastics: A Definition." 1, 20.

3 The definition is circa 1925, and is presented by the editors of *Modern Plastics* to their readers for usage in this particular issue. However, the editors also note that they have referenced it from the *Century Dictionary*, and they have approved of the definition with the exception that it might make broader mention of synthetic plastics and natural resins.

4 *Modern Plastics.* 1925. "Plastics: A Definition." 1, 20.

5 Ibid. Clay is definitively excluded from the definition.

6 Paraphrased from L.B. Kavanagh, *Modern Plastics.* 1925. "Preparing Horn Stock for Combs." 1, 23.

7 For a description of crude oil refining processes "desalting" and "fractionation," refer to United States Department of Labor. "Section IV: Chapter 2, Petroleum Refining Processes," *OSHA Technical Manual*, accessed July 24, 2014, www.osha.gov/dts/osta/otm/otm_iv/otm_iv_2.html#4

8 Donald L. Burdick and William L. Leffler, "Chapter 5, Olefin Plants, Ethylene, and Propylene." In *Petrochemicals in Nontechnical Language* (4th edition) (Tulsa, OK: PennWell Corporation, 2010), 59–61.

9 The quotation marks around the word "sensible" makes reference to The Society of the Plastics Industry's position on the use of plastics in architecture as published in *Progressive Architecture*. 1975. "Pandora's Plastic Box," 86–91.

10 Paraphrased from Alfred Marshal. *Principles of Economics*, 3rd edn. (London: Macmillan and Co, 1895), 133. The full quote reads: "But as his production of material products is really nothing more than a rearrangement of matter which gives it new utilities; so his consumption of them is nothing more than a disarrangement of matter, which diminishes or destroys its utilities."

11 *Resources, Conservation and Recycling*. 2010. "Material Flow Analysis of Polyethylene Terephthalate in the US, 1996–2007," 54(12), 1161–1169.

12 Paul H. Brunner and Helmut Rechberger, *Practical Handbook of Material Flow Analysis* (Boca Raton, FL: CRC Press, 2004). 3.

13 British Plastics Federation. 1944. *Plastics, Post-War Building Studies No. 3*. London: HMSO, 6–8.

14 *The Architectural Forum*. 1940. "Plastics in Building," 413.

15 Richardson's address and other speakers' addresses at the National Conference on Plastics were reprinted as abridged versions: *Interior Design and Decoration*. 1940. "A Portfolio of Addresses at the National Conference on Plastics Sponsored by Interior Design and Decoration." 14 (2), 43.

16 H.M. Richardson. 1940. *Interior Design and Decoration*. "Research in the Plastics Industry." 14 (2), 68, 74, 76, 78, 80, 82.

BUILDING
RESEARCH
INSTITUTE

Plastics

IN BUILDING

National Academy of Sciences-
National Research Council

PUBLICATION 337

CHAPTER 02

DESCRIBING PLASTICS

The formation of societies, federations, and associations

Alongside the phenomenal emergence of plastics over time is the phenomenal business of using plastics. Societies, federations, and associations, country by country, form to represent to publics and governments the plastics industry – as plastics are commodities and are competitive with other material-focused industries such as wood and metal. Such entities form (reform and rename over time) and represent, on the behalf and in the interest of "members" such as companies producing chemicals or resins, companies manufacturing equipment – injection-molding machines and extruders, and individuals specifying plastics. Annual activities include quantifying the amount and types of plastics used across sectors – transportation, packaging, electronics, and construction – on an annual (country by country) basis. "Plastics in building" is then represented as a use sector amid a myriad of uses for plastics.

Formation of these groups lags the rate at which plastics are discovered – which seems normal for invention-to-commercialization cycles. However, for some, this lag may also be attributed to changing government regimes, for instance, where a state-controlled plastics industry transitions to a free-market endeavor. One might also note the re-emerged business of green chemistry and bioplastics, which presently results in the formation of separate representative boards.

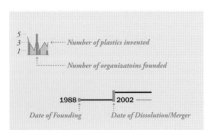

1800

1852

1884

1917

1872
1876

1898

1863

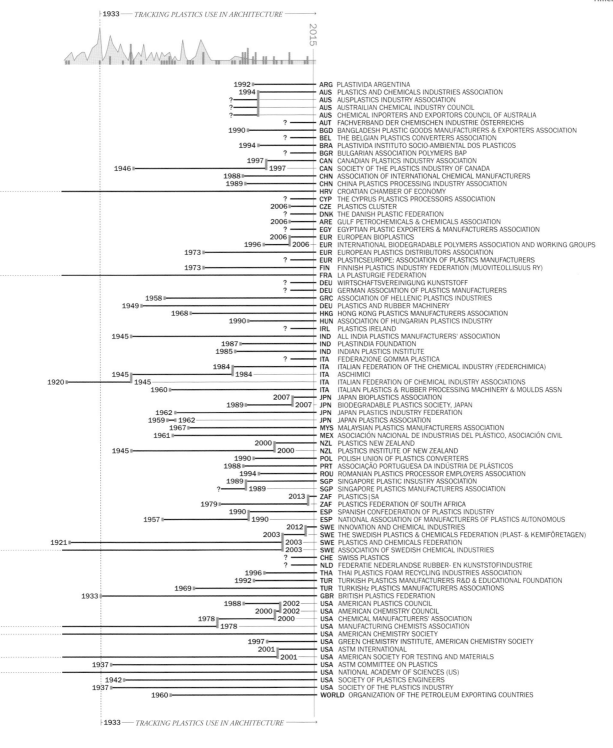

1933 — TRACKING PLASTICS USE IN ARCHITECTURE

2015

Year	Code	Organisation
1992	ARG	PLASTIVIDA ARGENTINA
1994	AUS	PLASTICS AND CHEMICALS INDUSTRIES ASSOCIATION
?	AUS	AUSPLASTICS INDUSTRY ASSOCIATION
?	AUS	AUSTRAILIAN CHEMICAL INDUSTRY COUNCIL
?	AUS	CHEMICAL INPORTERS AND EXPORTERS COUNCIL OF AUSTRALIA
?	AUT	FACHVERBAND DER CHEMISCHEN INDUSTRIE ÖSTERREICHS
1990	BGD	BANGLADESH PLASTIC GOODS MANUFACTURERS & EXPORTERS ASSOCIATION
?	BEL	THE BELGIAN PLASTICS CONVERTERS ASSOCIATION
1994	BRA	PLASTIVIDA INSTITUTO SOCIO-AMBIENTAL DOS PLASTICOS
?	BGR	BULGARIAN ASSOCIATION POLYMERS BAP
1997	CAN	CANADIAN PLASTICS INDUSTRY ASSOCIATION
1946 · 1997	CAN	SOCIETY OF THE PLASTICS INDUSTRY OF CANADA
1988	CHN	ASSOCIATION OF INTERNATIONAL CHEMICAL MANUFACTURERS
1989	CHN	CHINA PLASTICS PROCESSING INDUSTRY ASSOCIATION
	HRV	CROATIAN CHAMBER OF ECONOMY
?	CYP	THE CYPRUS PLASTICS PROCESSORS ASSOCIATION
2006	CZE	PLASTICS CLUSTER
?	DNK	THE DANISH PLASTIC FEDERATION
2006	ARE	GULF PETROCHEMICALS & CHEMICALS ASSOCIATION
?	EGY	EGYPTIAN PLASTIC EXPORTERS & MANUFACTURERS ASSOCIATION
2006	EUR	EUROPEAN BIOPLASTICS
1996 · 2006	EUR	INTERNATIONAL BIODEGRADABLE POLYMERS ASSOCIATION AND WORKING GROUPS
1973	EUR	EUROPEAN PLASTICS DISTRIBUTORS ASSOCIATION
?	EUR	PLASTICSEUROPE: ASSOCIATION OF PLASTICS MANUFACTURERS
1973	FIN	FINNISH PLASTICS INDUSTRY FEDERATION (MUOVITEOLLISUUS RY)
	FRA	LA PLASTURGIE FEDERATION
?	DEU	WIRTSCHAFTSVEREINIGUNG KUNSTSTOFF
?	DEU	GERMAN ASSOCIATION OF PLASTICS MANUFACTURERS
1958	GRC	ASSOCIATION OF HELLENIC PLASTICS INDUSTRIES
1949	DEU	PLASTICS AND RUBBER MACHINERY
1968	HKG	HONG KONG PLASTICS MANUFACTURERS ASSOCIATION
1990	HUN	ASSOCIATION OF HUNGARIAN PLASTICS INDUSTRY
?	IRL	PLASTICS IRELAND
1945	IND	ALL INDIA PLASTICS MANUFACTURERS' ASSOCIATION
1987	IND	PLASTINDIA FOUNDATION
1985	IND	INDIAN PLASTICS INSTITUTE
?	ITA	FEDERAZIONE GOMMA PLASTICA
1984	ITA	ITALIAN FEDERATION OF THE CHEMICAL INDUSTRY (FEDERCHIMICA)
1945 · 1984	ITA	ASCHIMICI
1920 · 1945	ITA	ITALIAN FEDERATION OF CHEMICAL INDUSTRY ASSOCIATIONS
1960	ITA	ITALIAN PLASTICS & RUBBER PROCESSING MACHINERY & MOULDS ASSN
2007	JPN	JAPAN BIOPLASTICS ASSOCIATION
1989 · 2007	JPN	BIODEGRADABLE PLASTICS SOCIETY, JAPAN
1962	JPN	JAPAN PLASTICS INDUSTRY FEDERATION
1959 · 1962	JPN	JAPAN PLASTICS ASSOCIATION
1967	MYS	MALAYSIAN PLASTICS MANUFACTURERS ASSOCIATION
1961	MEX	ASOCIACIÓN NACIONAL DE INDUSTRIAS DEL PLÁSTICO, ASOCIACIÓN CIVIL
2000	NZL	PLASTICS NEW ZEALAND
1945 · 2000	NZL	PLASTICS INSTITUTE OF NEW ZEALAND
1990	POL	POLISH UNION OF PLASTICS CONVERTERS
1988	PRT	ASSOCIAÇÃO PORTUGUESA DA INDÚSTRIA DE PLÁSTICOS
1994	ROU	ROMANIAN PLASTICS PROCESSOR EMPLOYERS ASSOCIATION
1989	SGP	SINGAPORE PLASTIC INSURTRY ASSOCIATION
? · 1989	SGP	SINGAPORE PLASTICS MANUFACTURERS ASSOCIATION
2013	ZAF	PLASTICS|SA
1979	ZAF	PLASTICS FEDERATION OF SOUTH AFRICA
1990	ESP	SPANISH CONFEDERATION OF PLASTICS INDUSTRY
1957 · 1990	ESP	NATIONAL ASSOCIATION OF MANUFACTURERS OF PLASTICS AUTONOMOUS
2012	SWE	INNOVATION AND CHEMICAL INDUSTRIES
2003	SWE	THE SWEDISH PLASTICS & CHEMICALS FEDERATION (PLAST- & KEMIFÖRETAGEN)
1921 · 2003	SWE	PLASTICS AND CHEMICALS FEDERATION
· 2003	SWE	ASSOCIATION OF SWEDISH CHEMICAL INDUSTRIES
?	CHE	SWISS PLASTICS
?	NLD	FEDERATIE NEDERLANDSE RUBBER- EN KUNSTSTOFINDUSTRIE
1996	THA	THAI PLASTICS FOAM RECYCLING INDUSTRIES ASSOCIATION
1992	TUR	TURKISH PLASTICS MANUFACTURERS R&D & EDUCATIONAL FOUNDATION
1969	TUR	TURKISHz PLASTICS MANUFACTURERS ASSOCIATIONS
1933	GBR	BRITISH PLASTICS FEDERATION
1988 · 2002	USA	AMERICAN PLASTICS COUNCIL
2000 · 2002	USA	AMERICAN CHEMISTRY COUNCIL
1978 · 2000	USA	CHEMICAL MANUFACTURERS' ASSOCIATION
1978	USA	MANUFACTURING CHEMISTS ASSOCIATION
	USA	AMERICAN CHEMISTRY SOCIETY
1997	USA	GREEN CHEMISTRY INSTITUTE, AMERICAN CHEMISTRY SOCIETY
2001	USA	ASTM INTERNATIONAL
· 2001	USA	AMERICAN SOCIETY FOR TESTING AND MATERIALS
1937	USA	ASTM COMMITTEE ON PLASTICS
	USA	NATIONAL ACADEMY OF SCIENCES (US)
1942	USA	SOCIETY OF PLASTICS ENGINEERS
1937	USA	SOCIETY OF THE PLASTICS INDUSTRY
1960	WORLD	ORGANIZATION OF THE PETROLEUM EXPORTING COUNTRIES

1933 — TRACKING PLASTICS USE IN ARCHITECTURE

DESCRIPTIONS

If defining plastics by working them directly – natural, bio, or synthetic – is momentarily accepted as mere material fantasy – for instance, we do not work injection-molding machines – plastics' real definition in architecture is quantitatively "described." The attributes of keratin plastics and polycarbonate may be provided numerically. All materials used in building and construction – wood, steel, masonry, and concrete – are subject to numeric description. The habit of describing is related to consensus around meaning and consensus around use. Numerical descriptions are essential. They are pragmatically and legally essential.

The process of describing plastics was then and still is an accretive task to be accomplished by engineers and chemists who acknowledge a specific use context – buildings. This use context has required and will continue to require the working out of plastics' mechanical properties, weathering characteristics, burning characteristics, and the working in of fillers to increase toughness and impact resistance, and plasticizers to increase flexibility. Presently it requires the accounting of volatile organic compounds, toxins, embodied environmental impacts, lifecycle analysis, and end-of-life optioning.

While several classes of synthetic plastics figure prominently in this early act of describing plastics, such as the light transmission properties of acrylics and the burning characteristics of foams, why we build with plastics the way that we do is likely more a result of how such describing endeavors organize. Research, or searching and searching again, is the catalyzing agent. Plastics description efforts organize through a scientific process and through basic and applied research. How plastics are described, the actual language used to define them, reflects the cultural and technical practices affiliated with bench science and engineering.

Plastics identified as applicable to building are "worked" by researchers in the service of being "described" or fundamentally known. They are polymerized and then burned, heated, cooled, melted, scratched, and fatigued. Polymer construction logic, the addition of one monomer to another and another and another, is just enough of a description to imagine how much work could possibly be done. Funded by chemical manufacturers and government agencies, early polymer scientists and engineers, whether affiliated with industry or academy, did something that they still do in the presence of an emerging material technology. They formed a community and talked, out loud, and quite publicly, about what was known and not known, and about what was working and not working.

When architect Max Abromovitz challenged the plastics industry to "stick its neck out" in 1954 (p. 28) at the US NAS NRC-sponsored conference *Plastics in Building*, he was alluding to this essential task of describing plastics for use in buildings, which is also the task that H.M. Richardson, Chief Engineer of General Electric Plastics Division, described to a room full of designers 14 years earlier in 1940 (p. 80). "Describing plastics" is a task that our originating data set, 200 plus articles from popular architectural press, hints existed, but it preferred instead to mostly publish outputs – building products made from plastics and projects using plastics. The significant exception – significant because it leads us directly to this "history" of describing plastics, specifically in the United States – is found in the *Journal of the AIA*'s December 1957 issue and is curiously titled "BRI Reviews Plastics for Roof Construction." The article begins by summarizing the past meetings sponsored by the Building Research Institute. It makes references to the existence of the "BRI Plastics Study Group." It indicates that hundreds have attended these meetings inclusive of architects, engineers, plastics industry representatives and contractors. And it indicates that proceedings were published for each of these meetings. In light of our task, which is to answer the question: "Why do we use plastics the way that we do?", one's response can only be to find(!) these proceedings and read them.[1]

1954, On working to describe plastics numerically

With the emergence of plastics comes the collection of numbers that index their usefulness for certain applications.

MR. PHILLIP H. DEWEY:

INTERCHEMICAL
CORPORATION

DR. DIETZ:

PROFESSOR,
MASSACHUSETTS
INSTITUTE OF
TECHNOLOGY

To Dr. Dietz. Do you have any figures or do you know where there are any figures on fatigue of plastic materials? I understand polyesters particularly are subject to fatigue.

I do not have such figures from our laboratory, since we have not gone into fatigue work. Some fatigue values have been published from time to time in publications of the American Society for Testing Materials and especially of the American Society of Mechanical Engineers. I would suggest that you refer to the publications of ASME and of ASTM and other publications on the subject of modern plastics as the best place to go for information of this type. I think you will just have to go through the literature and find it. I do not know of any place where this has all been compiled. I think you will find it is incomplete.[2]

1954, On working to assure plastics performance

With the emergence of plastics come watchful and measured appraisals of their performance over time.

MR. WALTER A. TAYLOR:

AMERICAN INSTITUTE OF ARCHITECTS

In our clinic service we have had claims about colorfastness of this plastic material in exterior use, and the dissent from colorfastness. Is there any reassurance today?

MR. BERKSON:

PRESIDENT, ALSYNITE COMPANY OF AMERICA

There are standards being set up within the industry. I am sorry to say the standards have not been completed to date. The product is not entirely colorfast, but it is approaching that condition. It is fade resistant, to a point. Let's put it this way – where a known or standardized product is involved, you can expect reasonable colorfastness; where unknown or unestablished products are involved, it is very difficult to say, very difficult to know the pigments and the resins that were used.[3]

The interchange between Mr. Dewey and Dr. Dietz and Mr. Taylor and Mr. Berkson typifies several hundred public exchanges transcribed and published along with papers and summaries of presentations in the conference proceedings of the US NAS-NRC BRI between the mid 1950s and into the 1960s. The Manufacturing Chemists Association (MCA), the Society of Plastics Engineers (SPE), and the Society of the Plastics Industry (SPI) helped to organize these nationally sponsored conferences. These societies likewise held their own national and regional meetings annually and published proceedings accordingly.

Conferences held during this period permitted an industry-wide vetting on the first use of plastics in building. In these proceedings and reports one finds evidence of sustained activities – those that facilitated an exchange of information between the emerging plastics industry, construction industry, academia, architect, and engineer, one that formed to describe a model building code for plastics, and one that formed by a mandate to re-describe the burning characteristics of foam plastics. Accounts of each permit the accumulation of insights into why we define, describe, and hence build with plastics the way that we do.

THE BRI PLASTICS STUDY GROUP

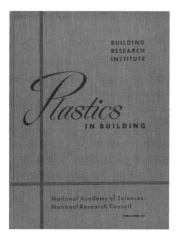

US NAS-NRC publication, *Plastics in Building*, proceedings from the conference held in 1954.

The Building Research Institute (BRI), jointly formed by the US National Academy of Sciences (NAS) and the National Research Council (NRC) was founded as a unit of the Division of Engineering and Industrial Research. Its stated primary purpose was to facilitate interaction toward "improving the design and construction of buildings." The BRI first facilitated cross-industry exchange on porcelain enamel in 1952. In 1954 it held its first conference on plastics, titled *Plastics in Building*. It was jointly sponsored by the SPI and the MCA, and it was attended by chemists, engineers, and architects from industry, professional practice, and academia, collectively totaling 500 individuals. As a result of this conference, the BRI formally convened the Plastics Study Group.

The Plastics Study Group's activities began in 1955. Its first meeting was held at the University of Michigan. Plastics in housing, plastics in the building skin, and plastic building products were discussed. It convened again in July of 1956 at the Massachusetts Institute of Technology (MIT).

Monsanto's House of the Future, designed in partnership with MIT, figured prominently in these discussions, as did plastics for insulating, gasketing, and sealing, the weathering of plastics, and the impact of plastics on community development. During that same year, in December, it convened at the Illinois Institute of Technology to discuss the model building code for plastics, directions for work, and the interior use of plastics. It convened in September of 1957 at Washington University, St. Louis, to discuss the topic of plastics for roof construction, also addressing the spanning capacity of plastics. Three hundred individuals attended, again representing a cross section of chemists, engineers, and architects from industry and academy. "BRI Reviews Plastics for Roof Construction" summarizes the meetings' technical content to readers of the *Journal of the AIA* and provides a general introduction to the presence and sustained activities of the BRI Plastics Study Group (PSG). In 1958, the fifth meeting of the Plastics Study Group, the topic focused exclusively on the subject of building illumination.

Five conferences covered a large body of plastics knowledge and potential plastics applications – and, in many respects, evidence that the BRI's mission through the PSG was being fulfilled. However, the report *Information Requirements for Selection of Plastics for Use in Building*, published in 1960 by a separate task group of the BRI's Plastics Study Group, reveals that unaccounted factors were hampering the integration of plastics into buildings.

> About two years ago several of us became concerned by the fact that plastics were not being used to their fullest extent in building. Designers were steering clear of plastics, just as they tend to with any new material, but here the language was confusing them and they were being misled by advertising claims. We decided among ourselves that there could be a simplified standard method – a thumbnail sketch reporting of plastics information, and that we could develop a format which, if universally accepted, could go a long way in furthering the use of plastics. We felt that just as the Steel Handbook, the lumber data books, etc., have become acceptable standards for reporting information on these well-known materials, we could start on a similar project for plastics.[4]

Talking out-loud about the potential use of plastics in building

Determining an answer to the question "How should we use plastics in building?" is pressing. In 1954 the US NAS-NRC's BRI teams with the US Society of the Plastics Industry and the US Manufacturing Chemists' Association to organize a conference in Washington, DC across industry and profession. In so doing, they mark the beginning of a sustained 20-year period of conferencing involving multiple organizing entities who would gather together chemists, engineers, architects, builders, and code authorities to wrestle with this question. Research findings were shared, numbers vetted, successful and unsuccessful applications demonstrated.

A selection of 17 conferences yielded roughly 180 papers. Indexing these papers per conference, per author affiliation, and per use allows us to discern the range of applications discussed, when, and how frequently across time. Some conferences were themed on exploring a particular use, such as "plastics and interior lighting" or "plastics and the building code." The "talking out loud" transcribed and published as part of most conferences' proceedings (e.g., Mr. Dewey to Dr. Dietz) captures the tone of uncertainty across these various topics – the "I don't know, but I want to know" feeling that comes with the continuous emergence of plastics. Left unmapped, but certainly resident in this collection, is the network of relationships between people that would become the community of individuals (Dietz, Makowski, Rarig, Winfield, etc.) working plastics, that emerged over time.

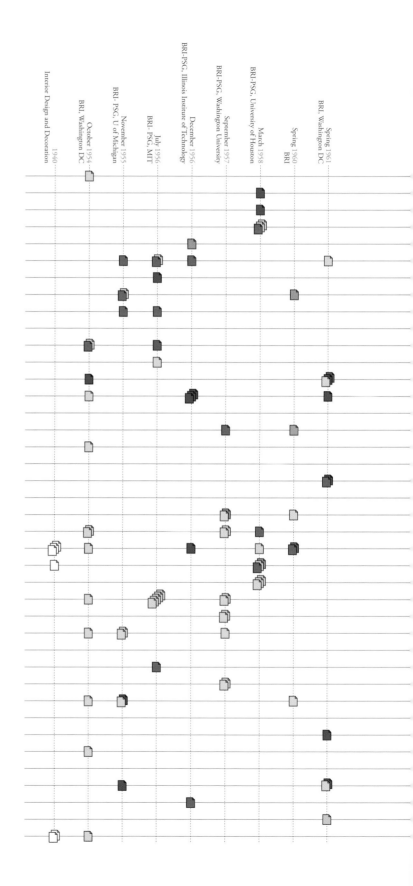

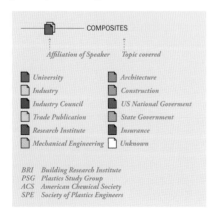

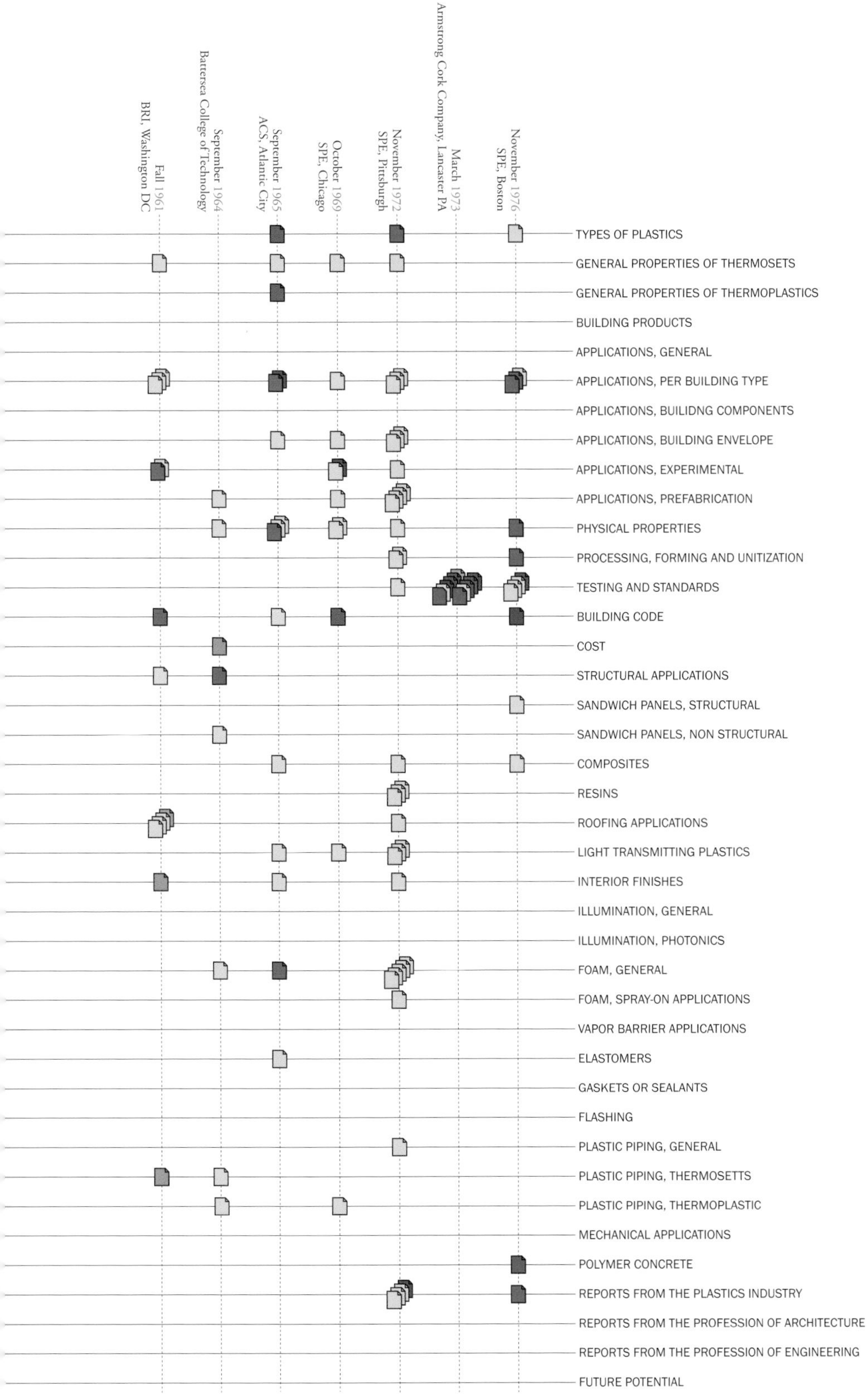
Fall 1961
BRI, Washington DC
September 1964
Battersea College of Technology
September 1965
ACS, Atlantic City
October 1969
SPE, Chicago
November 1972
SPE, Pittsburgh
March 1973
Armstrong Cork Company, Lancaster PA
November 1976
SPE, Boston
TYPES OF PLASTICS
GENERAL PROPERTIES OF THERMOSETS
GENERAL PROPERTIES OF THERMOPLASTICS
BUILDING PRODUCTS
APPLICATIONS, GENERAL
APPLICATIONS, PER BUILDING TYPE
APPLICATIONS, BUILIDNG COMPONENTS
APPLICATIONS, BUILDING ENVELOPE
APPLICATIONS, EXPERIMENTAL
APPLICATIONS, PREFABRICATION
PHYSICAL PROPERTIES
PROCESSING, FORMING AND UNITIZATION
TESTING AND STANDARDS
BUILDING CODE
COST
STRUCTURAL APPLICATIONS
SANDWICH PANELS, STRUCTURAL
SANDWICH PANELS, NON STRUCTURAL
COMPOSITES
RESINS
ROOFING APPLICATIONS
LIGHT TRANSMITTING PLASTICS
INTERIOR FINISHES
ILLUMINATION, GENERAL
ILLUMINATION, PHOTONICS
FOAM, GENERAL
FOAM, SPRAY-ON APPLICATIONS
VAPOR BARRIER APPLICATIONS
ELASTOMERS
GASKETS OR SEALANTS
FLASHING
PLASTIC PIPING, GENERAL
PLASTIC PIPING, THERMOSETTS
PLASTIC PIPING, THERMOPLASTIC
MECHANICAL APPLICATIONS
POLYMER CONCRETE
REPORTS FROM THE PLASTICS INDUSTRY
REPORTS FROM THE PROFESSION OF ARCHITECTURE
REPORTS FROM THE PROFESSION OF ENGINEERING
FUTURE POTENTIAL

US NAS-NRC publication, *Performance of Plastics in Building*, 1963.

The solution to plastics' indecipherability was to organize a standard format for reporting a given plastic's attributes, one that was applicable to all plastics types and would permit "reading" across this material class.[5] "General Information Format for Plastics Used in Building," the name given to the proposed standard outline, included seven sections: "Description of Product"; "Physical Properties"; "Design Criteria"; "Installation"; "Maintenance"; "Economics"; and "Case Histories." There were 33 subsections.

In 1961 the Plastics Study Group reformed into The BRI Planning Committee on Plastics in Building. The committee no longer felt the need to study plastics, but rather the need to intervene as an objective intermediary, a translator of sorts, defining how plastics should and could be used, and it considered these its responsibilities:

> To bring to light better information on the characteristics and properties of plastics materials as they apply to building products.

> To develop criteria for the selection, design and application of plastics in building.

> To transmit to the plastics industry a better concept of building functions, operations and performance requirements to guide the development and application of plastics building products and materials.

> To serve as a central agency for dissemination of information on industry activities pertaining to the use of plastics in building construction.[6]

Intersociety Reports on Plastics in Building Activities documents a meeting of the taskforce in 1961 convened because disparate research groups, seemingly making progress on the topic, were not communicating. The societies brought together for this meeting include:

> The Plastics in Building Professional Activity Group of the International Society of Plastics Engineers, Inc.;

> Fiberglass Reinforced Panel Council of the Society of the Plastics Industry;

> The Thermoplastic Pipe Division of the Society of the Plastics Industry;

> The Plastics in Building Committee of the Manufacturing Chemists' Association;

The Rubber and Plastics Divisions of the American Society of Mechanical Engineers;

The Plastics Laboratory at the Massachusetts Institute of Technology;

The Building Code Advisory Committee of the Society of the Plastics Industry;

ASTM Committee #5 on Fire Tests of Materials and Constructions;

The Flammability Committee, Cellular Plastics division, Society of the Plastics Industry;

ASTM Committee E-6 on Methods of Testing Building Construction;

Plastics and the Home Manufacturers Association.

Two years later "Proposal for the Compilation of a Design Handbook of Plastics in Building" was presented at the BRI's fall conference on *New Building Research*.[7] And years later, the Society of the Plastics Industry makes reference to the general need for such a project in *Progressive Architecture*, commenting, "Architects have relied on 'bibles' of design data for steel, wood, and concrete construction for years, but there is no 'plastics bible.' In the absence of a single authoritative source of information on plastics engineering and design detailing, the architect is obliged to seek third party help. There is no equivalent body in this industry to perform the design services of an American Iron and Steel Institute."[8]

The Plastics Study Group, though unable to coalesce a single guiding source of technical information, did facilitate a national conversation surrounding the use of plastics in building. Plastics succeeded in coalescing into describable building products without the universal format deemed essential. Conference presenters, regardless of affiliation, were working out the requisite building system for which plastics may be applied – roof, structural, interiors, utilities, and building envelope systems – and attempting to agree on the essential engineering criteria for each system. Presenters were likewise working out the performance of discreet plastics products such as pipes, tiles, light-fixture lenses, panels, wall coverings, trim, skylights, windows, and bathroom fixtures. Thus we witness parts becoming standardized products as described through efforts of individual companies, indicating that while the leadership of the Plastics Study Group desired a universal format, one which communicated individual plastics' attributes, participating entities, specifically industry, were answerable for the technical specifications of plastics chemistries and building products.

The Plastics Study Group's unswerving emphasis on defining building applications for plastics indicates trending from product experimentation toward product standardization, which fixes the relationship between material, form, and technique. For instance, the record solidly evidences the degree to which extruding thermally treatable materials becomes essential to realizing profitable plastic building products, which in turn engenders a die to form relationship and fixes the scale at which plastics in architecture are tenable. This fixing of unit and scale is corroborated by the Society of Plastics Engineers' regional and national conference proceedings from the mid 1970s, only further confirming why we presently cast plastics' relationship to architecture as "bit part." Finally, this group was not charged with working out whole prototypical architectures. They were not wrestling with the relationship between prototypical plastic "parts" to the prototypical plastic "wholes." The group's focus on the Monsanto House of the Future and composites research conducted by the MIT Plastics Laboratory in 1956 are exceptions to this part-driven discourse. No – again, architecture's largeness is broken down into discrete and separate routes of plastic parts standardization, a plastics and architecture strategy that is tenable given numerous and separate plastic materials and the parts they may become.

"We have fallen blindly in love with the word 'plastics,'" Frederick J. McGarry, Associate Professor of Building, Engineering and Construction of Massachusetts Institute of Technology, would state at the third meeting of the Plastics Study Group. His continuation of this statement summarizes the opposing poles of our working-out and working-on plastics – "plastics in builidng" and "all-plastics" precisely:

> We believe that in plastics we can find answers to all our problems. Our major difficulty is scale – the transition between little things and big, structural things. The impetus is there – manufacturers like the building market – architects like the physical properties. But let's be more candid – let's tell architects not to make the units too large, as yet. Let's back off for a while and express plasticity in terms of flat sandwich panels and workable things until we can control additional uses more adequately. The plastics industry just hasn't the experience and equipment for the large units that the architect desires.[9]

1954, On attributes of future plastics

With the emergence of plastics comes the recognition that new and unprecedented attributes may be found by applying novel processing steps to polymer chemistries.

MR. BOYER:

DIRECTOR, POLYMER
RESEARCH, DOW
CHEMICAL COMPANY

This article in [the] *Architectural Forum* was claiming, among other things, that treatment of plastic with atomic radiation could build the strength up equal to that of steel.[10]

You may have realized from Professor Dietz's charts yesterday that there already exists a number of plastics that have the tensile strength of piled steel, particularly in the form of oriented materials. A textile fiber or stretched sample of plastic already has the tensile strength of mild steel of up to 50,000 to 100,000 pounds per square inch, so I can believe that some plastics treated in certain ways in atomic radiation could have the tensile strength of steel. However, if you take just a simple molding of plastic – an ordinary tensile bar of any sort of molding – and treat that with atomic radiation, the data I have seen does not indicate that you can build the strength up anywhere near that of steel: perhaps a 25 percent increase of tensile strength. However, Mr. Read from *Architectural Forum* assures me that he has *the straight dope* on that story.

**MR. VERNON
READ:**

ARCHITECTURAL FORUM

Yes, the fact is that our information is that tests have shown that the strength property of certain plastics, anyway, is improved by certain irradiation processes. The thing that is controversial is precisely the strength of the plastics. The tensile strength, for instance, is improved by irradiation. The *Forum* article did not get into the question of degree so much. That was an imaginative article intended to stimulate thinking of what might be done.[11]

The collection of conference proceedings indicate a period of discourse on plastics use as lighting, piping, roofing – or as building products made from plastics, augmented by sustained discourse on two topics, the adoption of plastics in US building code, and characterization of how plastics burn through repeated testing. Because experimentation with plastics in the form of whole, "all-plastics" architectures was initiated and occurred concurrently with this period, a third topic may be inferred from this collection of proceedings – the structural use of plastics. Reviews of discourse on these three subjects, summarized from various conference proceedings, provide further evidence that may allow us to understand our present practice position with plastics.

CODES AND STANDARDS FOR PLASTICS

In the US, plastics' legal definition for building may first be found in "A Model Chapter on Plastics for Inclusion in a Building Code," a booklet drafted jointly by the Society of the Plastics Industry (SPI) and the Manufacturing Chemists' Association (MCA) in 1956.[12] Here, plastics are defined as "A material that contains as an essential ingredient organic substance of large molecular weight, is solid in its finished state, and at some stage in its manufacture or in its processing into finished articles that can be shaped by flow."[13] This definition is listed as point number four in a booklet whose purpose is stated thusly:

> This recommendation represents an effort by the Plastics Industry to discharge its responsibility to assist Building Officials by furnishing information and appropriate regulations to permit the use of plastics material in building construction.[14]

The number of plastics in buildings did begin to increase, as did the number manufacturing them, making their legal definition essential to their use. Frederick J. Rarig, the assistant secretary and attorney for Rohm & Haas Company of Philadelphia, addressed the subject of plastics' safe use at the BRI's inaugural 1954 conference, providing an account of how his company first sought official approval for the use of light-transmitting acrylic plastics as glass substitutes. Rarig's description of these efforts invokes his affiliation with broader industry efforts – those which would result in the Model Chapter booklet. Rarig clarifies:

My own company was brought into the building field by architects and designers who dreamed up uses for our materials which never occurred to the chemists who invented them and, as you might expect, architect's drawings were our letters of introduction to building inspectors.[15]

Plastics attributes, their burning characteristics, methods of identification, and maximum allowable area per building element per construction type, are drafted on behalf of multiple interests, delimiting the sections of the Model Chapter, and foreshadowing "Chapter 26 Plastics" of the current International Building Code. Simultaneously standards for plastics use were being developed by the National Bureau of Statistics (NBS/NIST), along with individual standards per product type, which might inform the Model Chapter.[16]

The Model Chapter defined an initial barrier for a plastic's approved use in building: Plastic materials used in products must be sufficiently standardized such that they appear in the MCA's *Technical Data on Plastics*. The 1952 edition of *Technical Data on Plastics* lists 26 standardized plastics:

Technical Data on Plastics, the 1948 issue.

1. urea-formaldehyde molding materials

2. melamine-formaldehyde molding materials

3. phenolic molding materials

4. alkyd molding materials

5. silicone molding materials

6. epoxy resins

7. cast phenolic resins

8. laminated melamine products

9. laminated thermosetting products

10. allyl and polyester plastics

11. acrylic plastics

12. polyethylene plastics

13. polytetrafluoroethylene

14. polyvinyl formal and butyral plastics

15. vinyl chloride polymer and copolymer plastics

16. vinylidene chloride plastics

17. styrene plastics

18. cellulose acetate sheets

19. cellulose acetate molding compositions

20. cellulose acetate butyrate molding compositions

21. cellulose propionate molding compositions

22. ethyl cellulose plastics

23. cellulose nitrate plastics

24. nylon

25. foamed plastic

26. plastic films.

As the founding dictionary upon which plastics building and construction use is legitimized, the data found in *Technical Data on Plastics* was derived based on tests conducted by each MCA member manufacturer on their own products. In Section XI "Acrylic Plastics," data are presented courtesy of E.I. du Pont de Nemours & Co. and Rohm & Haas Company. Tables associated with acrylics' attributes include a series of values and associated ASTM tests related to fabrication methods and durability, and results from electrical conductivity tests, mechanical tests, and miscellaneous tests including light transmittance, water absorption, and thermal coefficient of expansion. Graphs are presented to summarize acrylics' impact strength, compressive and flexural strength, tensile strength, modulus of elasticity, and spectral transmittance. For each of 26 plastics, this information is provided. Here it may be said that architects have a route, albeit a numerical one, to a handbook on plastics.

But rather than mete out plastics based on individual attributes, the Model Chapter would coalesce these 26 materials into one word – plastics. As Rarig would reflect in the pages of *Progressive Architecture* in 1970,

The architects made it clear that they wanted plastics dealt with as plastics and indexed as plastics. They did not consider it practical to endeavor to establish in building codes separate provisions for individual classes of plastics that would be identified by esoteric generic terms identifying classes of polymers and copolymers.[17]

The Model Chapter would proceed to categorize plastics use per maximum allowable area, per use group and construction type based on building component: interior finish and trim, wall panels, roof panels, skylights, light-transmitting panels in monitors and sawtooth roofs, light-diffusing systems in ceilings, partitions, exterior veneer, awnings and canopies, greenhouses, and signs, fences, and similar structures.[18]

A performance-based all-plastics code indicates, then and now, how difficult it is to be visually and tacitly certain when granting building use approval for "an organic substance of large molecular weight, solid in its finished state." Plastics are solid, appear solid – appear thoroughly and undoubtedly homogeneous. Color, pattern and texture are not identifying markers. No singular characteristics differentiate one species of plastics from another. Wood and steel are likewise coalesced as "wood" and "steel" by a performance code. However, it can be said that wood species support visual acknowledgment based on differentiation of color, pattern and texture, one species to the next. Steel suffers the same homogeneous fate as plastics, but its use is meted out as a strong material per rolled form attribute in steel construction manuals. The form of plastics – light-transmitting, foam, or laminate – is the closest we come to declaring visual differentiation between plastics materials' applications to parts – which is exactly how the Model Chapter handled difference between plastic types. However, plastics use in building would play out as a deciphering game, as on-site visual inspection was the method officials used to enforce the building code.

The Model Chapter proposed a method for on-site plastics identification – a place to start when attempting to decipher the safe and unsafe use of a plastic material – a place to start when attempting to define plastics. It was proposed that each plastic material be identified by the manufacturer with a trademark name, generic name, and ASTM abbreviation. Based on this requirement, one might assume that a light-transmitting plastic sheet material made by Rohm & Haas could be found on a jobsite labeled as Plexiglas®, Acrylic, PMMA.[19] Yet later versions of the code removed this manufacturing requirement entirely, and by 1969 it appears that this requirement was voluntary.[20]

Plastics' correct or incorrect identification were and still are undoubtedly confused, and further complicated by the fact that light-transmitting plastics have a fourth name. The acronym PMMA most closely resembles its true name – poly(methylmethacrylate). By 1956 multiple trade names were circulated by competing chemical companies.[21] And, plastics' acronymical shorthand was in circulation. The Model Chapter refers to the use of acronyms two years prior to their official recognition. ASTM Committee D-20 through standard D1600-58T titled *Tentative Abbreviations of Terms Relating to Plastics* establishes 31 abbreviations for plastics and resins, and 14 abbreviations for plastic and resin additives. The document makes this sobering statement regarding acronym endorsement:

> The abbreviations now in use have grown naturally out of the need for convenient, readily comprehended shorthand for long chemical names. This process can be expected to continue along natural lines of least resistance and will serve as a basis for further standardization as the need arises.[22]

Featureless and nameless, but in forms immediately recognizable as building products, plastics use and building did normalize through measures that ensured life safety. Regional code authorities reviewed, adopted, or adapted the Model Chapter. And committee members responsible for its authoring delivered reports, updating constituents on its status of comprehension. In 1961, five years after the Model Chapter's dissemination, Frank Ambrose, reporting for the Building Code Advisory Committee of the SPI, addressed the BRI Planning

Commission of Plastics in Building at its spring conference titled *Intersociety Reports on Plastics in Building Activities*. He relayed some opposition to the plastics industries' building code efforts by the American Iron and Steel Institute, who in 1957 circulated a "lengthy document attacking the Model Chapter."[23] He indicated continued testing of plastics, both small scale and in situ, at the request of building code officials. He reported adoption of the code by three major regional codes – Basic Building Code, the Southern Building Code, and the Uniform Building Code. And he referenced plastic parts – the increasing number of standardized plastic products – and adjustments that the code would need to make to address "core panels with plastic facings" which may include aluminum or foamed plastics cores, and plastics veneers.

At the same conference Russell B. Akin, on behalf of the Plastics in Building Committee of the MCA, reported on several initiatives, all of which were aimed at increasing literacy on plastics materials. He referenced the MCA's own efforts to publish a plastics handbook – a primer for building officials – and referenced a second primer addressing plastic processing methodology for standardized plastic building products. Relaying the MCA-sponsored research titled "A Study of Fire Safety Aspects of Plastics in Building Construction," conducted by the Southwest Research Institute, Akin summarized the first five years of the Model Chapter's introduction thusly:

1. Broad expansion of plastics building materials is possible within modern building codes.

2. Many building officials lack understanding of the nature of plastics, and are hesitant to apply normal performance criteria.

3. Many within the plastics industry are not familiar with building codes, their terminology and administration. Occasional inept or incorrect use of terms (e.g., "fire resistance") has delayed adoption of plastics materials which might otherwise have been satisfactory.

4. Variations in code requirements penalize building design and construction.

1958–2008, The emergence of acronyms for plastics

Acronyms such as UF, PMMA, PVA – paths of linguistic least resistance – have emerged, and are circulating and becoming essential shorthand for talking plastics. Yet, even these must also be agreed upon, written down, and codified. That's where standard ASTM D1600 ("Tentative Abbreviations of Terms Relating to Plastics") comes in handy. Published first in 1958, seven updates have been made to the standard in the years 1964, 1971, 1975, 1986, 1991, 1999, and 2008. Plotting our "list of plastics found affiliated with architectural production" against each issuance of ASTM D1600 reveals which of these have acronyms and the year officially recognized. Which plastics acronyms do you deploy most often? Are you aware of the long chemical version of a plastic's name? Does such reflexive naming matter to how you practice with plastics?

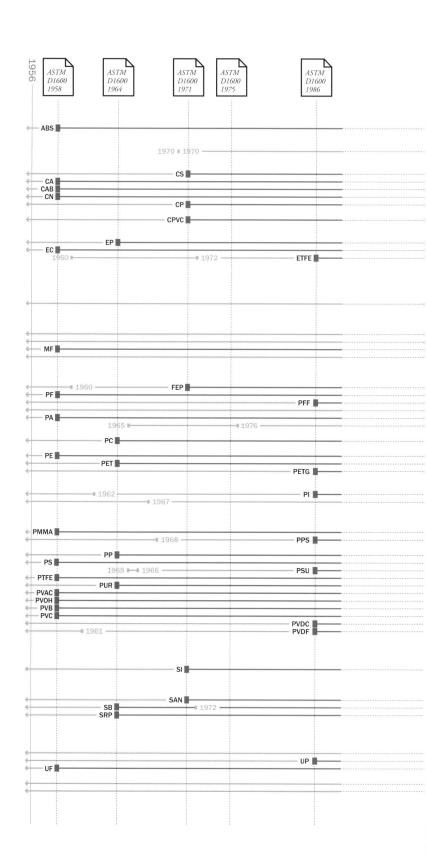

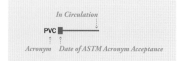

5. Plastics building materials should continue to be subject to the same fire safety regulations as traditional materials. Where transition from specifications to performance type codes is incomplete, plastics materials should seek acceptance under demonstrated equivalent basis.

6. Concise primers should be developed to speed cooperation between the building and the plastics industries.[24]

In 1965, nine years after the Model Chapter's introduction, Akin, addressing the Division of Petroleum Chemistry of the American Chemical Society, cited lack of credible information, hyperbolic claims, and misuse of terminology as primarily hindering the discussion between the architect, contractor, and code official, and ultimately use of plastic building products. Indicating barriers, regardless of the Model Chapter's adoption into major regional codes, he described how code officials work and their resources, and summarized five barriers to be addressed post-haste by the plastics industry, inclusive of "prejudice" against plastics, indecipherability of trade names, exaggeration of durability and "misuse" of terminology related to burning characteristics, performance history inclusive of numerics and assurances of quality, and "vague uneasiness" with regards to how plastics behave in a fire.[25]

CHARACTERIZING HOW PLASTICS BURN

The Model Chapter stated that plastic building components must have an acceptable burning rate, required in addition to their sufficient standardization in the MCA's *Technical Data on Plastics*. It required components made from plastics to pass ASTM D635, which sets burning rate limits for horizontal plastic materials; and ASTM D568, which sets burning rate limits for vertical plastic materials. Burning rates were affiliated with component locations – interior, exterior, or overhead locations – and their dimension. In comparison, the current version of the International Building Code (IBC) provides "Chapter 26: Plastic." In addition, plastic materials are referenced in several chapters: "Types of Construction," "Fire-Resistance Rated Construction," "Interior Finished," "Exterior Walls," "Roof Assemblies and Rooftop Structures," "Soils and Foundations," "Glass and Glazing," and "Special Construction." The IBC

1961, On working plastics into the building code

With the emergence of plastics comes the reckoning of their use across separate regions by independent code-reviewing authorities.

R.T. BUSKO:

AVISUN CORPORATION

Please discuss the building code aspects of the PVC pipe installation in Key West.

MR. GILLER:

NORMAN M. GILLER & ASSOCIATES, ARCHITECTS AND ENGINEERS

This is a relatively new use for this type of piping, and many of our building codes, in Florida and in other places throughout the country, have not yet accepted plastic piping. There hasn't been enough experience background and, probably, there hasn't been a good enough selling job done on the building officials to show them what the product can do. In the Key West area, of course, we were not particularly concerned with the local code. This particular project happened to be a Government reservation and, therefore, as long as it met the approval of the Federal authorities, which it did, there was no objection to it. I think it also met the Key West officials' approval.[26]

classifies materials, plastics included, as either class A, B, or C per two metrics – their flame-spread rating and Smoke-Developed Index.

> Class A: flame spread 0–25; smoke developed 0–450.
>
> Class B: flame spread 26–75; smoke developed 0–450.
>
> Class C: flame spread 76–200; smoke developed 0–450.

Numerical constraints related to flame and smoke, rather than plastics' definition, are arguably the primary shapers of plastics' relationship to architecture. Coupled with the code's component-based use groups, plastics' burning characteristic emerges as the most contentious subject in this data set. Two sources, one prior to the model building code and one published two plus decades after the model building code, adequately describe the research arc sustained to ensure life safety for an emerging material class.

The first source is Frederick J. Rarig's narrative which recounts Rohm & Haas' efforts to meet code official's criteria in 1954 – a narrative which hinges on ensuring fire safety: The City of New York, once convinced based on test results that acrylic (and other plastics) would not shatter under conditions of "atomic explosion", now requested that Rarig's employer, Rohm & Haas Company, address acrylic's combustibility and produce results which ensured fire safety. The request required Rarig to determine existing or original data for acrylic's application.

> Having defined the subject, we were asked by the building officials how we proposed to classify plastics according to their fire hazard. We turned to the basic classification of plastics according to their fire hazard published by the National Board of Fire Underwriters in its Research Report No. 1 – "Fire Hazards of the Plastics Industry" and we developed test procedures based on ASTM test procedures which eliminate rapid-burning plastics and classify slow-burning and self-extinguishing plastic material.[27]

Rarig's testing methodologies remain unclear from the information provided in *Progressive Architecture*. However, it is certain that phrases such as "slow-burning" and "self-extinguishing," affiliated with ASTM D1692, are in circulation, as plastics construction logic requires both technical and cultural engagement.[28] Debate, and hence contention, surrounds the testing methodologies themselves, and the use of terminology: Are the ASTM-adapted testing procedures correct? And which plastics are correctly represented as "slow-burning" and "self-extinguishing"?

The second source, *Fire Research on Cellular Plastics: The Final Report of the Products Research Committee*, published in 1980, summarizes the results of a five-year, five million dollar research program governed by the Products Research Committee (PRC). The committee, a freestanding charitable research trust, was established in 1974 via an agreement between the United States Federal Trade Commission (FTC), 26 plastics manufacturers, ASTM, and the Society of the Plastics Industry (SPI). The report recounts that the US FTC

Fire Research on Cellular Plastics, 1980.

> alleged that a broad class of cellular plastics contributed substantially to fire hazards in the United States, that methods of testing for the fire behavior of such cellular plastics were inadequate, and the fire resistance of such products was often misrepresented by the manufacturers in their trade literature and advertising.[29]

Hence, the settlement supported research which would permit the safe use of these materials, and the determination of the proper terminology to describe the burning characteristics of plastics. The PRC admits that at the outset of their work, "The proposed complaint went to the heart of the problem confronting the fire research community. The question was, and still is, how to represent the infinite number of exposure conditions possible in real fires by a controlled laboratory test."[30] The report reviews the accuracy of testing methodologies and small-scale and large-scale tests. The committee affirms the SPI's 1975 guidelines – a half-inch thick gypsum sheet over cellular plastics is the best practice. Exceptions to this assembly may only be given in the event that an assembly passes a full-scale test.[31]

1961, On tests for toxicity

With the emergence of plastics comes the working out of rigorous testing methods to ensure that we actually know them.

LEO GOLDSTEIN:

DEPARTMENT OF
LICENSES & INSPECTIONS,
PHILADELPHIA

Are there standard tests or references for determining the degree of toxicity of products of combustion? I haven't been able to find any.

MR. YUILL:

SOUTHWEST RESEARCH
INSTITUTE

There are standard laboratory procedures for analyzing combustion gases. While the material is burning, you can pump out gases through water, and dissolve them in the water. Then you can break that water up into 20 different samples, and analyze them to see if they contain oxides of nitrogen, hydrogen, cyanide, etc. But, you have to run a separate test for each and you have to have a separate sample. This makes it very expensive. And, when you wind up, you may have isolated 20 gases. However, there may be a gas that is more lethal and more toxic than any of those, but you haven't analyzed for it because you didn't suspect it was there. So, our analyses aren't necessarily complete. There is much to be learned about this matter of gas analysis.

We think that possibly the best approach is to work from the other way around. Through the chemical formula of most materials, we can get a fairly good idea of what combustion gases will be produced. To check yourself, we could then run animal tests. If we find that the gas is safe in the normal analysis, but is still lethal, then we know that we've missed something and go to other analytical methods. One of our big weaknesses in terms of this gas problem is that a great deal of work has been done under dissimilar circumstances, so we can't compare the results of one program with another.[32]

CHARACTERIZING THE STRUCTURAL USE OF PLASTICS

The model code did not address plastics use as structural materials, nor did it distinctly address GFRP, denying the legitimization of the conceptual approach "all-plastics" as realizable, as intimated by *The Architectural Forum*, as stressed skins. Yet, as the efforts of the BRI PSG were just gaining momentum, so too were the efforts to prototype plastics structurally, efforts that would take the form of shells, folded plates, systems of pyramidal components, hyperbolic paraboloids, and air-supported structures.[33] All of these aspired to achieve long spans. Z.S. Makowski recounts this collection of work in the article "Structural Plastics in Europe," appearing in *Arts and Architecture*'s August 1966 issue. Structural efforts did originate with smaller-scale prototypes such as the "all-plastics" house prototypes of 1956 and 1957. These small-scale efforts contrast the singular effort to "clear span," as noted by the ample photographic evidence provided by Makowksi. This "describing" record does not reference the bulk of "all-plastics" prototypes attempted to date – houses, holiday cabins and disaster relief shelters – with the exception of the Monsanto House of the Future. And, it is not clear how the search for robust structural systems factored into the clear direction established by US code efforts. What is certain is that the topic of the structural use of plastics was taken up separately by other communities of engineers during this period. Fifty-two years after the introduction of the Model Chapter, in 2008, the American Composite Manufacturers Association (ACMA) announced that it was working to introduce fiber reinforced plastics (FRP) composites into the International Building Code. A year later the new edition of the code did include a separate section on FRP, which addresses FRP sandwich panels with foam cores, and light-transmitting panels.

1954, On the structural use of plastics

With the emergence of plastics comes the desire to codify them as structural materials.

MR. DAVID RUBENSTEIN:

CHEM-STRESS
STRUCTURES COMPANY

Mr. Rarig, have you any knowledge of the acceptance of reinforced fiberglass in any building code in places where steel is commonly used as a structural wall-bearing material, either alone or as reinforced concrete or in combination with steel as a multi-structural material? And, if you have, how long would it take the building code people to give us a code?

MR. RARIG:

LEGAL COUNSEL, ROHM
& HAAS COMPANY

I don't know of any code which would explicitly, in so many words, permit this material in a structural member, although it is obvious that the conventional use of reinforced polyester sheet in light steel building is in part structural. As for predicting how long it would take regulatory officials to do anything, I would not venture into that realm of speculation. One might say, I suppose, that one could develop a built-up section that would perform equally with an accepted material. Many, many building codes permit the substitution of a new material for an established material if you can demonstrate equivalent performance. So you might, on a case by case basis, very well get a wall section or honey-comb section approved, but there is no legislative program at the moment which provides for that eventuality.[34]

PLASTICS WORKED AND DESCRIBED

A definition comes into being because consensus is reached around its meaning. Definitions are not as useful as they first appear because they cannot embody an inherent trajectory, whether cultural or technical, of attempts to both work and describe a subject. To know a material is both to work it and describe it.

Between 1954 and 1980, the preponderance of activities by science and industry describing plastics use in building coincides with the preponderance of activities by architects and designers working plastics into whole prototypical architectures.[35] Thus, plastics were worked and described across multiple bodies of knowledge, and regardless of the methodology employed by individuals owning a specific body of knowledge, be they chemists or architects, all were connected by the subset "atmosphere of experimentation." It might be a stretch to say that architects affected describing activities. The remaining evidence defies measurement. But consider that research-based conference proceedings from this period are littered with the experiments of both academic and professional architects. And consider that architectural journals are littered with translations on the subject of plastics to us. We were talking. Plastics terminology emerged with modern architecture. It is incorrect to assume that we had no say in defining this material class.

Architects need descriptions of plastics in order to tacitly work them. Chemists and manufacturers still need to work them in order to describe them. These motivations to work and describe are simply at odds – we are not solving the same problem. They appear to be less at odds if it is believed that consensus can be reached through technical data.

To understand the early relationship between architecture and plastics, we have to lose our current material paradigm, which has the creation of materials for architecture separate from us – at the extreme end of the supply chain terminus. Instead, when contemplating why we use plastics the way that we do, we find that two potential material cultures bloomed simultaneously. One is evident through efforts such as the Plastics Study Group, and is a culture of interdisciplinary working and experimentation. The other has an interior that is private, less known, and it is the interior of research efforts by chemical companies who would create plastics for buildings.

More scrappy and experimental, less rote and codified, though seeking codification to the point of near extinction, "plastics worked" in architecture is now rare, but so too are "plastics described." Plastics' mostly inert relationship to architecture may result from our lack of consensus regarding the value of extending working and describing activities beyond the discrete boundaries of the chemical industry to the architectural industry. Or, if "plastics worked" is supported, it is done so through building products made from plastics.

The folded-plate structural system experiments of Professor Z.S. Makowski appearing in a Shell Oil advertisement.

June 1965, London

Z.S. Makowski and B.S. Benjamin present "The Analysis of Folded-Plate Structures in Plastics," one of 35 plus papers searching for the structural use of plastics delivered at the conference Plastics in Building Structures. *Paper topics range from loading specific types of plastics, to fire resistance, to components such as sandwich panels, beams and columns, to whole structures with plastics. Shell Chemical's placement of an advertisement in the published conference proceedings congratulating Professor Makowski captures a moment of interdependency, producing the effect of coalescing the relationship between architecture and plastics into one image.*

1964, On how to get plastics into the building industry

With the emergence of plastics comes the confession that inertia may be imminent.

MR. T.L. BIRRELL:

DIRECTORY, YARSLEY
RESEARCH LABORATORIES
LTD.

I have been in the plastics industry since 1928, with the British Xylonite Group, and, two years ago on retirement, joined Yarsley Research Laboratories, Limited.

In 1937, I visited the first Plastics Exhibition ever held, at Dusseldorf, where PVC and polystyrene were in commercial production and building applications, such as pipes and floor coverings, were already known, so that our problems are not new.

We have had excellent papers and useful discussion, but I would like to have heard much more from the members of the building industry in the audience, and I fear that it is going to be a long and difficult task to get plastics introduced into the building industry. I would like to ask the authors their views as to the best methods of achieving this.

**PROFESSOR
Z.S. MAKOWSKI:**

HEAD OF THE
DEPARTMENT OF
CIVIL ENGINEERING,
BATTERSEA COLLEGE OF
TECHNOLOGY

I think that Mr. Birrell has touched on a very important point, on the problem of communication, or rather the lack of communication, between different professions. This morning a colleague of mine said "This conference is one of the very few occasions when plastics technologists, civil engineers and architects meet together. I hope that they will find a common language."

Have we succeeded in doing this? The plastics industry knows so much about plastics, but still finds it difficult to put this knowledge across to the user. The architects and engineers, even those who seem to be genuinely interested in this material, know so very little about its properties. Some architects, especially the younger ones, are over-enthusiastic – they underestimate the practical limitations of plastics. They like to think that plastics are the panacea to all their problems; on the other hand, many civil engineers are too cautions, too conservative, they are not bold enough to experiment. Should we blame them for this? I do not think so.

Plastics manufacturers are impatient – they would like to see a much greater acceleration of the use of plastics in building applications. Many factors slow it down – the cost, the fire resistance and, last but not least, the outdated building regulations. However, the picture is not so black as some of us may think. We witness great changes in the rate of acceptance of plastics by the general public, and by professional people. We can still speed up the whole process by making the architects and engineers aware of the potential of plastics, not by glossy publicity leaflets, but by factual publications, drawing attention not only to the advantages of plastics, but also showing clearly their limitations and disadvantages.[36]

NOTES

1 From here, the narrative becomes US-based. Because the record led me to a trove of information on US conference proceedings, I am able to recount the US efforts to describe plastics. There may be similar nation- or company-specific acts of description available. For instance, the HMSO document points to this.

2 Building Research Institute, *Plastics in Building* (Washington, DC: NAS-NRC, 1955), 25.

3 Ibid., 45.

4 Building Research Institute, "Introduction," in *Information Requirements for Selection of Plastics for Use in Building* (Washington, DC: NAS-NRC, 1960), 4.

5 Building Research Institute, "General Information Format for Plastics Used in Buildings," in *Information Requirements for Selection of Plastics for Use in Building* (Washington, DC: NAS-NRC, 1960), 2.

6 Building Research Institute, "Introduction," in *Intersociety Reports on Plastics in Building Activities* (Washington, DC: NAS-NRC, 1962), 1.

7 C.S. Grove Jr., "Proposal for the Compilation of a Design Handbook of Plastics in Building," in *Plastics Performance in Building* (Washington, DC: Building Research Institute, 1963), 163.

8 *Progressive Architecture*. 1975. "Pandora's Plastic Box," 86.

9 Building Research Institute. *Plastics Study Group of the Building Research Institute, Report of a Meeting at the Illinois Institute of Technology* (Washington, DC: NAS-NRC, 1957), 11.

10 Douglas Haskell. *The Architectural Forum*. 1957. "Does Atomic Radiation Promise a Building Revolution," 131.

11 Building Research Institute, *Plastics in Building* (Washington, DC: NAS-NRC, 1955), 122–123.

12 You can find the original six-page booklet bound inside the report documenting the Plastics Study Group's third meeting at the Illinois Institute of Technology, which is on file at the National Academy of Sciences Archives.

13 Harold Perrine, "Chapter 3: Building Codes and Regulations," in *Plastics in Building*, ed. Irving Skeist (New York: Reinhold Publishing Corporation,1966), 34–37. See herein "Appendix D," which is a reprint of the SPI and MCA pamphlet "A Model Chapter on Plastics for Inclusion in a Building Code," a draft of a building code distributed and discussed at the first meeting of the Plastics Study Group occurring on November 14–15, 1955 at the University of Michigan, Ann Arbor.

14 Ibid.

15 Building Research Institute, *Plastics in Building* (Washington, DC: NAS-NRC, 1955), 97.

16 Ibid., 94.

17 F.J. Rarig, *Progressive Architecture*. 1970. "Plastics and the Building Codes," 51, 96–99. Rarig is acting as the Secretary and Legal Counsel for Rohm & Haas Company. The result of the decision to refer to plastics as "plastics," especially in the context of the building code, is that we refer to classes of plastics such as "light-transmitting plastics" and "foamed plastics."

18 From "A Model Chapter on Plastics for Inclusion in a Building Code," reprinted as "Appendix D" by Harold Perrine, "Building Codes and Regulations," in *Plastics in Building*, ed. Irving Skeist (New York: Reinhold Publishing Corporation,1966), 34–37.

19 Russell B. Akin, "Building Codes and Durability as Factors in Marketing Plastics for Construction," in *Technical Papers, Regional Technical Conference "Plastics in Building"* (Washington, DC: American Chemical Society, 1965), A-51.

20 Russell B. Akin, "Fire Testing and Acceptance of Plastics in Building Codes," in *Technical Papers, Regional Technical Conference* "Plastics in Building," ed. John Hyden (Stamford, CT: Society of Plastics Engineers, 1969), 51.

21 For a helpful listing of trade names for plastics *c.*1950, see the "Glossary of Trade Names," in Joseph B. Singer, *Plastics in Building* (London: The Architectural Press, 1952), 161–169.

22 ASTM. *Tentative Abbreviations of Terms Relating to Plastics, D 1600-58T* (Philadelphia, PA: ASTM, 1958).

23 Frank Ambrose, "The Building Code Advisory Committee of the Society of the Plastics Industry," in *Intersociety Reports on Plastics in Building Activities* (Washington, DC: NAS-NRC, 1962), 40.

24 Russell B. Akin, "The Plastics in Building Committee of the Manufacturing Chemists' Association," in *Intersociety Reports on Plastics in Building Activities* (Washington, DC: NAS-NRC, 1962), 26.

25 Russell B. Akin, "Building Codes and Durability as Factors in Marketing Plastics for Construction," in *Technical Papers, Regional Technical Conference "Plastics in Building"* (Washington, DC: American Chemical Society, 1965), A-51.

26 Building Research Institute, *Performance of Plastics in Building* (Washington, DC: Building Research Institute Inc., 1963), 101.

27 F.J. Rarig. *Progressive Architecture*. 1954. "Plastics and the Building Codes," 51, 96–99.

28 *Progressive Architecture.*1975. "Pandora's Plastic Box," 90.

29 Products Research Committee, *Fire Research on Cellular Plastics: The Final Report of the Products Research Committee* (Washington, DC: PRC, 1980), 6.

30 Ibid., 6.

31 Ibid., 131.

32 Building Research Institute, *Performance of Plastics in Building* (Washington, DC: Building Research Institute Inc., 1963), 62.

33 A collection of all structural logics attempted with plastics does exist. There are ample projects and serial reviews found throughout the data set which solely address structural systems.

34 Building Research Institute, *Plastics in Building* (Washington, DC: NAS-NRC, 1955), 102.

35 The majority of all-plastics houses, pavilions, and experimental prototypes will be found published in architectural journals during this period.

36 R.M. Davies, *Plastics in Building Construction* (London: Blackie & Son LTD, 1965), 145.

· LUMINOUS CEILINGS ·

CHAPTER 03

PLASTICS IN BUILDING

PLASTICS. IN. BUILDING.

When we begin to dissect the record to understand the use and origin of this dominant conceptual position, this opposing pole of "all-plastics," we find three words – a phrase – authors, editors, and organizations choose to repeatedly title conferences, conference proceedings, books, and journal articles on plastics. "Plastics" is a noun. "Building" may be a noun or a verb. Interposing one article of speech – "in" – may force the grammatical hand. Shall we mean "plastics in building," noun and noun? As in "Are there plastics in that building?" Or, shall we mean "plastics in building," noun and verb? As in "Did you build this house out of plastics?"

Plastics. In. Building. Fact or process?

In 1940, when the editors of *Architectural Forum* published their first (the first?) comprehensive article on plastics and titled it "Plastics in Building," they may have given a title to a materials movement – a multi-decade defining and describing effort to parse plastics into several use categories toward the goal of becoming discrete building products. But, based on *Forum*'s article alone, we can observe that use categories were sufficiently identified by 1940 and that early plastics – acrylics, cellulosics, formaldehydes, and vinyls – served a multitude of uses such as doorknobs, grills, partitions, lighting, wall covering, and flooring. Somewhere between 1926 and 1940, or the year that the editor of *Modern Plastics* challenged its readers to invent "new uses" for plastics and the year *Forum* offered "Plastics in Building," the building and construction sector became a market reality for the plastics industry.[1] By 1960 Harold J. Rosen could offer a "specifications clinic" to readers of *Progressive Architecture*'s June issue where he proceeds to track for the architect the functions that plastics perform throughout 11 specification sections.[2] For instance, under "concrete work" he lists the functions vapor barrier, form-board, perimeter insulation, waterstops, and expansion joint material – each one based on a separate polymer chemistry. "Plastics in building" was a fact. It was not a process, and the title "Plastics in Building" kept on appearing because it was comprehensive and comprehensible, formalizing McGarry's pitch to architects in 1956 at the third Plastics Study Group (PSG) to focus on the "flat sandwich panels and workable things."

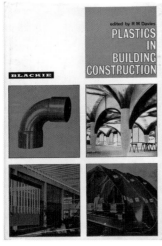

Plastics in Building Construction,
Davies, 1965.

Plastics in Building,
Skeist, 1966.

The Use of Plastics Materials in Building,
EEUA, 1973.

Publications titled or nearly titled "Plastics in Building"

"Plastics. In. Building." An all-inclusive phrase in circulation in publications for decades, indicating that plastics, in the form of building products, may be found anywhere in a building and serve several disparate uses. It also implies the multi-decade "becoming" of discrete building products made from plastics alongside the emergence of new polymer chemistries. Right now "Plastics in Building," and not "all-plastics" is the present and dominant state for using these materials – as it aligns perfectly with the architectural practice of sourcing, selecting, and specifying building products.

Conferences/conference proceedings:

> *Plastics in Building*, NAS-NRC, 1954
> *Plastics in Building*, NAS-NRC, 1955
> *Information Requirements for Selection of Plastics for Use in Building*, NAS-NRC, 1960
> *Performance of Plastics in Building*, BRI, 1963
> *Plastics in Building Construction*, Davies, 1965

Books:

> *Plastics in Building*, Singer, 1952
> *Plastics and Building*, Mactaggart and Chambers, 1955
> *Plastics-in-Building, Handbook*, W.S. Penn, 1964
> *Plastics in Building*, Skeist, 1966
> *Plastics in the Building Industry*, Reboul and Mitchell, 1968
> *The Use of Plastics Materials in Building*, EEUA, 1973

Singer's *Plastics in Building* (1952) organizes subject matter thusly:

› Introduction
› Plastics for exterior work
  – Walls
  – Sheet plastics
  – Windows
  – Glazing
› Plastics for interior work
  – Partitions
  – Wall coverings
  – Floor coverings
  – Heat and sound insulation
  – Furniture and miscellaneous applications
  – Electrical equipment and lighting
  – Applied finishes
› Future possibilities.

Reboul and Mitchell's *Plastics in the Building Industry* (1968) provides the following chapters:

› Plastics for all-weather protection
› Plastics for concreting and brickwork
› Plastics for insulation
› Plastics for plumbing
› Plastics in floor finishes
› Plastics in fixtures and fittings
› Plastics in decorative finishes and linings
› Plastics in lighting, heating and ventilating
› Adhesives, mastics and joint fillers.

Focusing on 11 publications, books, and conference proceedings titled or nearly titled "plastics in building," each publication in this minor collection attempts mostly the same thing: to communicate to architects and builders that plastics building products are emerging and that there are routes for their adoption. Market research on plastics in the building and construction industry for 1960 supports such bibliographic redundancy. "Plastics are making inroads in the field of building," Armand G. Winfield relayed to those who assembled in 1961. Indicating that annual expenditure figures for plastics are quite minimal when compared to the overall annual expenditure in the construction sector, he points out that this figure represents 15–18 percent of the total annual output of plastics. He follows, "It is, however, still quite small because of resistance by the architects, builders and code writers."[3] Winfield further intimates other essential market research most indicative of plastics' future – decreasing costs and manufacturing automation.[4] Application, adoption, and education are reoccurring themes in each publication, and emphasis is placed first and foremost on describing plastics use rather than its chemistry.

Use-driven organization, use-driven research and discourse as evidenced by the collection *Talking Out-Loud About the Potential Use of Plastics in Building* remind us that plastics may be worked into a myriad of mass-produced building products previously manufactured from other materials. Plastics have and will continue to supplant materials – wood, metal, and fabrics – even though "plastics are not substitute materials." Such pragmatic organization supports plastics' systematic embedment with other building technologies, and comparatively small and discrete deployments. Plastics are laid down, adhered, and sequenced in with other materials. For instance, under Reboul and Mitchell's chapter, "Plastics for Concrete and Brickwork," the authors provide detailing of a PVC waterstop for proper installation in a foundation. They provide a detail for layering expanded polystyrene insulation into both solid masonry walls and masonry cavity walls. Thus, plastics are nearly never whole buildings in this collection – though Singer does provide a brief historical overview of "all-plastics" residential building systems, and the Monsanto House of the Future is mentioned in more than one. Such a small, redundant collection may be useful when determining why we build with plastics the way that we do, because it captures plastics movement as explicit and tacit knowledge, hence technical and cultural adoption increase over time.

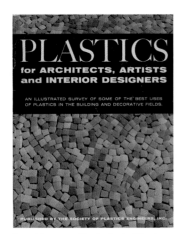

Pamphlet cover, *Plastics for Architects, Artists and Interior Designers, 1961.*

Exhibition advertisement,
Plastics, A New Dimension in Buildings,
1961.

FACING PAGE
"Light Transmitting Panels,"
from the exhibition *Plastics,*
A New Dimension in Buildings.

PLASTICS, A NEW DIMENSION IN BUILDING

A twelfth item, dissimilar in form but not content, may be added to this collection – an exhibition. *Plastics, A New Dimension in Building,*[5] sponsored by the Society of Plastics Engineers and financially underwritten by 22 companies, was scheduled for 16 US cities between 1961 and 1963. Equally use-driven in its organization, 21 of 30 display units organized plastics per the following: structural glazing, skylights, luminous ceilings, lighting fixtures, sandwich panels, structures, roofs, interior wall surfacing, floor covering, slab on ground construction, insulation, piping, plumbing fixtures, electrical equipment, hardware and drawers, ducts, and counter tops. Winfield, as exhibition chairman, distinguished its purpose by stating, "This is not a traveling commercial trade show, and does not contain booths assigned to specific companies."[6] As an educational exhibition, the intention was to describe through text, material sample, and full-scale mock-up, plastics' present and future diversity – making exhibition photos read as a tactile version of any one of the 11 aforementioned publications. The exhibition's audience, as reported by the Society of Plastics Engineers, was the professional architect, contractor, builder, and student. Some newspapers would add "artists" and "homemakers" to this list.[7] Artists because several plastics sculptures were included such as *Perspex Sculpture* by William P. Reimann, which is featured in the exhibition's advertisement or Harold Krissel's "Laminate" series, which was likewise featured on the June 1960 issue of *Progressive Architecture.* Organizers planned outreach to professionals in each city, declaring the exhibition a "demonstration laboratory" for the working out of plastics use.[8]

Yet, this small collection of conference proceedings and books, exhibition included, has entirely another effect – it renders the current impetus for plastics use unoriginal; in the world of building products made from plastics, especially translucent, paneled, or structurally insulated paneled ones, it seemingly has all been done before. Skeist's, whose offering is decidedly the most rigorous, provides an essay by Z.S. Makowski titled "Plastics Abroad," which in turn provides an image of choice cross sections for the solid foam core or honeycomb core plastics sandwich panels developed at Battersea College.[9] These are the ones integral to Makowski's explorations of folded-plate- and polyhedral-based stressed skin structures. Davies provides invitingly translucent complex extrusions.[10]

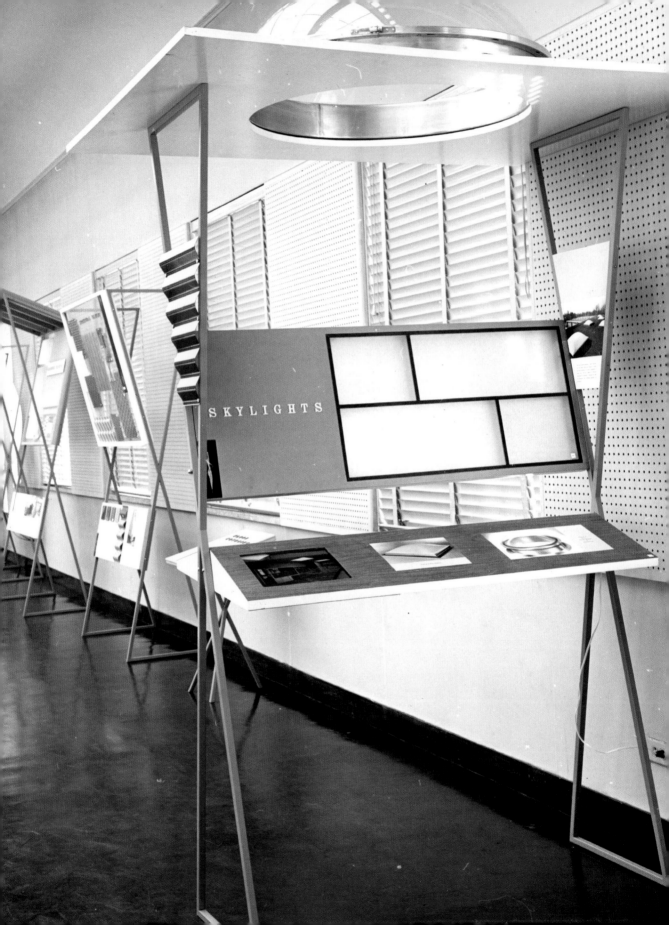

SKYLIGHTS

A display unit from Winfield's exhibition arrays potential translucent screen patterns adjacent to veneer plywood and stressed skin panels. Perhaps the most illustrative and stunning find amid this data set is the research conducted on translucent insulation. Under the title "The Capillary Structure – A New System for Producing Sandwich Panels," researcher G. Peters introduces bundled acrylic capillary tubes, capable of insulating and transmitting light.[11] Architectural journals and other conference proceedings corroborate our present unoriginality, likewise documenting similar plastic building products. Translucent resin panels, phenolic-coated paper honeycomb cores, and foam structural panels are found amply represented, such that one could conduct a product development transect for light-transmitting plastics and structurally insulated panels between the years 1933–1975.[12]

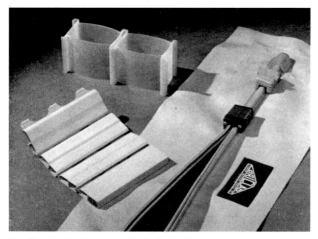

Translucent extrusions, appearing in *Plastics in Building Construction* by Davies, 1965.

FACING PAGE
"Skylights," from the exhibition
Plastics, A New Dimension in Buildings.

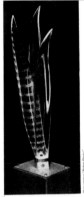

Lucite sculpture by Nishan Toor, mounted on wood base which conceals a light source; surface decoration is emphasised by light conductance of the plastic.

DESIGN DATA FOR
ACRYLIC PLASTICS ... PART I

This is the first of a series of brief presentations on methods of employing the great family of plastics architecturally. "Acrylics" are technically methyl methacrylate resins, available in several forms, sold under the trade names Lucite and Plexiglas, although there is a heat-resistant type which will withstand high temperatures. They are thermoplastic; that is, they soften at temperatures from to 200° F, although there is a heat-resistant type which will withstand higher temperatures. They are tough and rigid, highly resistant to water and most exposure, and to most household chemicals and solvents (but paint removers and very strong alcohol should be avoided). They are available in a wide range of colors, possess great brilliance whether colored or clear, and are essentially transparent. Their dielectric and impact strength, and optical properties, are remarkable. Sources for further information include publications of the Society of the Plastics Industry, the magazine, "Modern Plastics," and the manufacturers, Rohm and Haas Co. (Plexiglas) and du Pont (Lucite).

LIGHT CONTROL with acrylics: LEFT, new star-studded ceiling, Grand Central Station, New York City; CENTER, Lucite light conductors of different sizes used in the core to transmit light from a single source to many store. RIGHT, acrylic torch for interiors of shell parts.

FABRICATED ACRYLICS: LEFT, Plexiglas cabinet shelves, transparent, shatterproof, rounded, easily cleaned corners. CENTER, surface-engraved Plexiglas. RIGHT, shape formed by air pressure; material is a laminate of Lucite and another plastic imparts certain properties to the product.

OPTICAL CONSIDERATIONS GOVERN "SEE-THROUGH" APPLICATIONS

LIGHT CONDUCTANCE ALSO OBEYS OPTICAL LAWS

Plastics in Building
as documented
by *Progressive
Architecture*:

TOP
"Design Data for
Acrylic Plastics,"
1949

BOTTOM
"Vinyl Plastics
and Resins in
Architecture," 1951

FACING PAGE
"Plastics for Interior
Walls," 1956.

p/a materials and methods

Vinyl Plastics and Resins in Architecture

Plastics, in general, provide qualities of durability and versatility and are vastly more suited to modern mass production methods of manufacture than many older materials; vinyl plastics, which can be applied and kept clean with ease and are economical and colorful, have many architectural applications. To more thoroughly understand the advantages and limitations of this material, one should have at least a small understanding of its chemical properties.

what are vinyl plastics and resins?

Vinyl resins in their primary state are exceedingly fine colorless powders formed by the polymerization of organic chemical molecules containing the vinyl groupings. Polymerization is a process in which molecules are linked together in long chains—a process which can be regulated so that the number of these molecules can range from hundreds to hundreds of thousands. The various vinyl compounds that lend themselves to polymerization and co-polymerization include vinyl acetate, vinyl chloride, and vinylidene chloride. With the variations that can be made in molecular weight, together with other variations that may be obtained in the basic vinyl molecule itself, the number of possible vinyl resins, theoretically possible, is infinite.

The vinyl chloride type resins, which include the vinyl chloride-acetate copolymers, account for the largest portion of these materials. Not only are they free from color, odor, and toxicity, but also they have the advantage that they can be made to any degree of flexibility by the addition of plasticizers. These characteristics make them suitable for the formulation of film and sheeting, tile, surface coatings, molded articles, and wire and cable insulation.

In preparing the flexible plastics the basic vinyl resin is mixed with small amounts of stabilizers (to minimize deterioration under exposure to heat, oxygen, and light), lubricants, and colorants, and from 25 to 45 percent by weight of plasticizer. Plasticizers, which are usually high boiling esters, convert the hard plastic into soft, flexible materials. This mixture is converted into usable forms by mixing and fusing; it can then be processed into film and sheeting of various thicknesses by means of a calendering operation. It can also be extruded as rods or tubes, or to coat wire, and it can be molded into almost any shape.

wall and window covering

Flexible film (the Society of Plastics Industry defines film as any continuous material not over 10 mils in thickness) and sheeting made from vinyl plastics can be manufactured in any thickness, although they are commercially available only in thicknesses of .003, .004, .006, .008, .010, .012, .020, .030, and .040, in continuous rolls of varying widths. The color range is unlimited and many textures are possible. Both film and sheeting are flexible, resilient, and highly resistant to tearing, abrasion, scuffing, flexing, and may be compounded so that they are resistant to fire. Because of its exceptional durability vinyl sheeting serves effectively as a wall covering material in hospital and hotel corridors, schools, restaurants, buildings and apartment lobbies, elevator cabs, railroad terminal public spaces, and department store walls. Recommended wall surface backgrounds for the application of this plastic include plaster, plywood, and sheet rock.

A relatively new vinyl material has been made by coating reinforced cellulose fibers to produce a sheeting that is flexible, crackproof, and stainproof. Used as a wall covering it can be cleaned with soap and water; for installation purposes it can be cut, stitched, or pasted with ease. Some of the uses for flexible vinyl film which may be described as adjuncts

Right—woven vinyl plastic fabric used for organ screen in church balcony. Fabric which can be cleaned without removal was applied to rough framing before the screen installation was erected in place. It is claimed that this type of screening material helps to maintain high quality of tone transmission. Architects, Saarinen, Saarinen and Associates. Photo courtesy of Lumite Division, Chicopee Manufacturing Corporation.

Far right—sheeting of vinyl plastic was specified for walls of this bathroom at Levittown, Long Island. Photo by Ben Schnall.

materials and methods

plastics for interior walls

by Michael F. X. Gigliotti*

Plastic building materials have gained an increasingly prominent role in the construction field and are beginning to play an important part in interior-wall construction. If an architect is to use a plastic properly in any segment of construction, he must be familiar with the composition of the material, its characteristics, its advantages, and its limitations.

It would require volumes to cover all of the technical aspects of plastics—what they are, how they are formed, and how they are varied. There are hundreds of different plastics, each suited to a particular set of requirements. Broadly speaking, however, plastics are organic compounds of carbon mixed with other elements, such as hydrogen, oxygen, and nitrogen. Some of the mixtures form thermoplastic materials which have long, chain-like molecules that will soften under application of heat and harden when cooled. Other mixtures form thermosetting materials, which have long-chained molecules cross-linked to form large net-like molecular assemblies. Most thermosetting plastics are prepared originally in thermoplastic form, but are molded under pressure and high temperature so that they set permanently—thereby becoming infusible and insoluble. Thus the thermosets show greater strength characteristic and will hold up under higher temperatures.

Though there are hundreds of different formulations of plastics, there are only five basic groups which need be considered for interior-wall use. In the thermoset category, phenolics, aminos, and polyesters are used in interior walls, while in the thermoplastic category, styrenes and vinyls are used.

design characteristics

Design characteristics that should be kept in mind when using plastics in any form of construction are: load factor, thermal expansion, resistance to moisture, shaping, and temperature range.

The coefficient of expansion of many plastics is high (*Figure 1*), ranging anywhere from that of steel to about 19 times that of steel, for certain phenolics. Therefore, when used in conjunction with steel or glass, the coefficient of the plastic should be checked and allowance made for expansion in joints.

Load factor is important in that an adequate safety factor should be included in all designs. Primary fact here is that thermosetting plastics are, in most cases, stronger than the thermoplastics.

Where possible, materials that absorb moisture should be avoided in wall panels, because the resultant swelling and contraction will cause crazing in the plastic. Although long-term studies of plastics under all weather conditions have not yet been completed, so far most plastic materials have shown fairly good resistance to the elements.

Plastic materials are not fireproof as they stand, but they can be treated or combined with fire-resistant materials. For the plastics used most commonly in wall panels, the maximum-use temperatures range from 160F up to 300F (*Figure 2*). The thermosets show the best fire-resistant qualities.

A minimum number of changes in thickness of the plastic material should be strived for in any one unit. Sharp edges and V-notches should be avoided where possible, because of the stress they place on the material. Uneven thicknesses cause poor curing.

interior-wall requirements

After considering the characteristics of the plastic materials available, it is well to consider the functional requirements of the unit in which the plastic will be used—in this case the interior wall.

The purpose of an interior wall or partition is to divide space so that privacy, satisfactory viewing, and acoustical comfort are provided. In addition to functional requirements, the interior wall must be relatively easy to install, and must have low maintenance cost, or be simply and inexpensively replaced. In the case of plastics, the interior wall might even offer mobility. It may be used to control light effects through use of plastics which have transparent, translucent, opaque, or luminescent qualities.

An esthetic requirement of the wall is to provide decoration and the plastic wall's adaptibility to color, texture, and application of ornamentation is extremely wide.

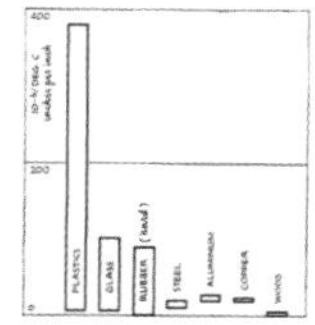

Figure 1—thermal coefficients of expansion, inches per inch, for plastics and various other familiar building materials (left). Relatively large amount of expansion in plastics demands careful consideration of joint details.

Figure 2—average maximum-use temperatures of different plastics (right).

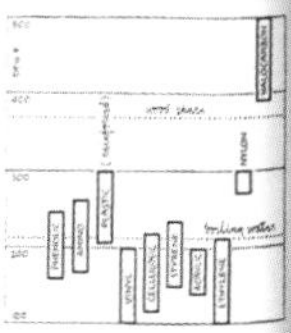

Although interior partitions are frequently nonloadbearing, when the interior wall is an important structural component of a building certain plastics can be used successfully by taking advantage of their high strength-to-weight ratio.

Plastic walls also should be considered as possible outlets for radiant heat, heating ducts, and air-conditioning equipment.

acoustical characteristics

Acoustical characteristics of plastics in interior walls vary. Generally, vinyls range from good to excellent in terms of sound absorption, but styrenes and melamines range from fair to poor. Current experimentation in various plastic formulations and combinations should increase the variety of panels offering greater sound absorption.

For instance, sandwich panels have been made combining a honeycomb core of phenolic-impregnated kraft paper, surfaces of reinforced plastic, and various types and amounts of core fillers, such as sand and finely divided silica.

In tests, an unfilled panel had a sound-transmission loss of five db. By filling the core with the silica, a transmission loss of 30 db was obtained without adding unreasonably to the weight of the panel. Commercially available "lightweight" partitions had a transmission loss of 20 to 25 db. Tests of these panels were conducted for a one-octave band (600-10,000 cycles or approximately the frequency range of average household noise).

core applications

Perhaps the greatest contribution that plastics will make to the building industry is in the curtain-wall field where exterior and interior surfaces, as well as core material, can be of plastics. The combination of strength, light weight, ease of fabrication, good insulation, and moisture resistance adds up to plastic curtain walls being suited for wide use in framed buildings and in loadbearing structural units for frameless structures.

There have been recent examples of partition and curtain-wall panels using both a plastic core material and the plastic skin. Sandwich panels designed to be mounted on a light aluminum frame have been as large as 4'0" x 9'4" and ½" thick. The core materials used in these panels have been low-density vermiculite, grain balsa wood, foamed cellulose acetate, or honeycomb paper bonded with phenolic resin.

An experimental building at the University of Michigan now utilizes a plastic sandwich panel which is composed of a self-extinguishing foamed-styrene core between glass-fiber-reinforced polyester skins.

When used as the core material for a wall panel, a plastic can offer many advantages. Most plastics are good insulators and are ranked as "exceptional" when used in an expanded foam. The foaming is done mostly with the styrenes (*Figure 3*) and the isocyanates. These materials have a low K factor (0.25), are light in weight (approximately 1.3 to 4 lb per cu ft), have good compressive strength (30-35 psi), and have good water resistance and negligible vapor transmission.

In addition to styrenes and isocyanates, other plastics which can be foamed and used as core materials are cellulose acetates, acrylics, phenolics, and polyesters. Certain foams can be formulated to have isolated or interlinked cell structures to provide considerable variation in insulation and other properties. Isocyanates, for example, can be controlled for insulation, density, and rigidity.

All of the foamable materials can either be preformed into large sheets or foamed in place between the skins of the wall at the construction site. A variation of the latter method consists of setting up wall forms, pouring the foam into the form, and applying the wall skins to the foamed core. Because of the extensive machinery required for foaming plastics, however, foaming in place is suitable only for mass-construction operations involving at least 10 homes.

The phenolics and styrenes are the most economical of the plastic core materials. The isocyanates give the best rigidity and strength, and the acrylics, though high in cost, are the best for use in translucent panels which might be exposed to the sun.

*Manager, Structural Plastics Engineering Group, Monsanto Chemical Company, Springfield, Mass.

Figure 3—typical assembly details of laminated sandwich panels composed of glass-fiber-cloth polyester faces and foamed-styrene cores: (1) joint with batten strips; (2 and 3) mitered and rabbeted corner joints with plastic angles; (4) fixed window with channel; (5) cutout or exposed-edge corner joint.
Details: Bakelite Manufacturing Corp.

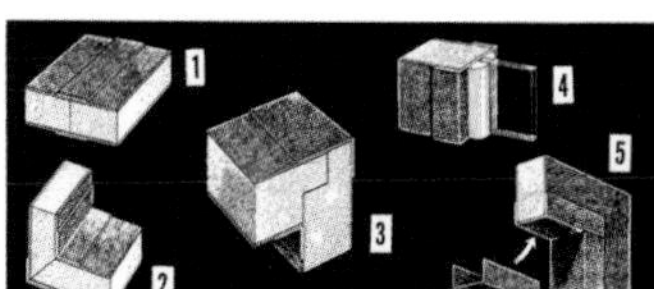

138 Progressive Architecture

February 1956 139

materials and methods

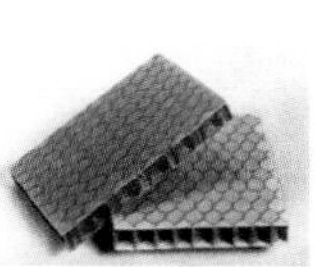

Figure 4—one-half inch sandwich panels of translucent-plastic skins and phenolic-impregnated paper cores (left) can be used for interior partitions; larger panels can also be used for exteriors. Synagogue (below), designed by Fishman Alschuler Associates, uses this translucent material in façade adorned by Star of David.
Photo and rendering: The Englander Co., Inc.

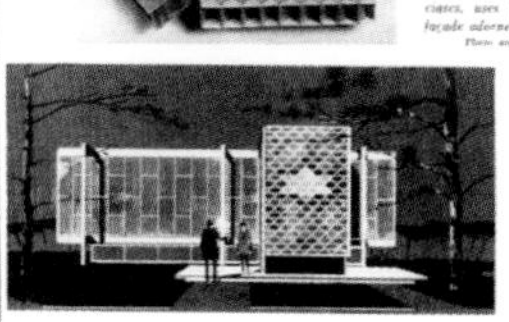

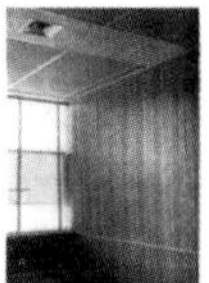

Figure 5—striations on new styrene wallboard are formed during extrusion of panel.
Photo: Monsanto Chemical Co.

Another wall-panel core utilizing plastic materials is the phenolic-impregnated paper honeycomb. This particular material is available in any desired thickness and provides good strength when bonded to the wall skins. It is extremely light and allows large panels to be used. Phenolic-impregnated paper honeycomb offers excellent visual possibilities if used with translucent surfaces (*Figure 4*). It has high sound- and heat-transmission qualities when used without filler—and is used to best advantage when these are not factors in the panel function, since filler adds to cost and weight.

Phenolic-impregnated wood chips also are used as a core material. These add exceptionally high strength to the panel. They are nondirectional, heavy, and are dimensionally more stable than an equivalent thickness of soft wood.

Phenolic-impregnated wood chips are produced on a continuously moving belt and are available in eight-ft widths in any length desired. This is a relatively inexpensive material since it is made primarily of granulated wood. Phenolic-impregnated wood chips permit factory fabrication of custom partitions with unlimited strength. The structure of this core is rigid and no skin, or only a very thin nonstructural skin, is required. If no skin is used an interesting textural effect can be obtained. This panel core has fair acoustical characteristics and has good fire resistance.

The principal problem encountered in the use of plastic materials as wall-panel cores is that a suitable method of standard jointing for the panels still needs to be developed. This is especially true when the plastic is used in conjunction with other building materials, such as steel or aluminum. The differences in coefficient of expansion might result in buckling of the panel or cracking around bolts unless adequate allowance is made for movement between the panel and supports. One suggestion that has been advanced to overcome this handicap is that an extruded-plastic edging strip, which also serves as a joint, with gasketing for soundproofing, might be incorporated with the panel during manufacture.

special effects

Where borrowed light is required or where special spatial effects are desired, a translucent or transparent plastic panel is ideally suited. This type of panel is usually made of acrylic, polyester, or glass-butyral-glass material.

A translucent or transparent plastic wall-panel surface can be metalized so that light can penetrate from both sides but vision is just one way. In the laminated type of panel, any pattern can be printed or sandwiched into the panel. The acrylic, which has poor surface scratch resistance, can be improved by an integral silical face. Polyester, reinforced with glass fiber with a corrugated or molded core offers extremely high strength in thin, translucent panels.

Polyester, combined with glass, and decorative safety glass also are utilized for decorative purposes in wall paneling. Though both are extremely durable and offer advantages in cases where light transmission is desired, they are limited because of the cost factor.

The sandwich panels offer unlimited combinations of materials to give desired mechanical and visual qualities. Because plastic panels are extremely light in weight and can be produced simply, it is feasible to manufacture them in large sizes, reducing labor costs and cutting erection time on the job.

140 Progressive Architecture

plastics for interior walls

surfaces

From a functional point of view, plastics offer the architect a variety of materials which present an easily cleaned, attractive, and durable surface on any wall panel. An almost infinite variety of textures and colors can be achieved with plastic materials. Because of these factors, the widest current use of plastics in relation to wall panels is for surfacing.

Decorative melamine and polyester are very similar in their characteristics. They both offer wide color range, but melamine is limited texturally. Polyester is slightly lower in initial cost, but the higher mar resistance of the melamine results in lower maintenance costs.

For both new and existing construction in areas outside of the bathroom and kitchen, it is felt that the vinyl covering or surfacing offers the most suitable and adaptable characteristics. It has a very tough, abrasion-resistant surface, will not support combustion, and is available in a broad range of colors and textures. Another important favorable characteristic of vinyl is the ease with which it can be installed.

The durability of stryrene as a wall-surface material has been well established in the bathroom area in the form of wall tile. A completely new style development in the wall-tile field was announced recently. This styrene tile makes it possible to obtain an unique textured effect in various colors, which incorporates a suggestion of a stippled second color. The result is a dramatic change from conventional wall-tile color effects since the illusion of a granite-patterned surface is achieved.

A striated, styrene wall panel for improved surface texturing of plastic sheeting is now being marketed (*Figure 5*). The striations—formed during the styrene panel's extrusion—add depth to wall surfaces, thereby lending an added character to institutional and residential interiors.

A new development gaining wide usage is the plastic-coated cinder block (*Figure 6*). A polyester glass-fiber or sand-filled resin containing a styrene monomer is laminated to the cinder blocks to provide a structural unit which is durably predecorated and requires no further finishing treatment during or after construction.

In terms of total construction costs, these special blocks compare favorably with conventional cinder units and, therefore, it is expected that the building industry will continue to expand its application of them. For instance, it is foreseen that realtors will offer residential home buyers an added inducement in the form of a prefinished cellar den with little or no extra construction costs involved.

The use of plastic materials in construction of interior walls adds to the design freedom of the architect. Flexible use of space is made possible by movable partitions and by free-standing storage units serving as space dividers. When using these flexible partitions, the architect is faced with the problem of providing visual appeal, light weight, sound and thermal insulation, and movability—all at low cost. Plastics satisfy all of these considerations.

The plastic materials offer the architect and builder an attractive design and engineering medium which can be used in ever increasing amounts for more functional and attractive structures.

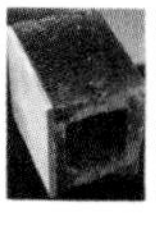

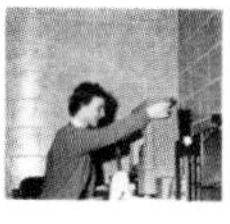

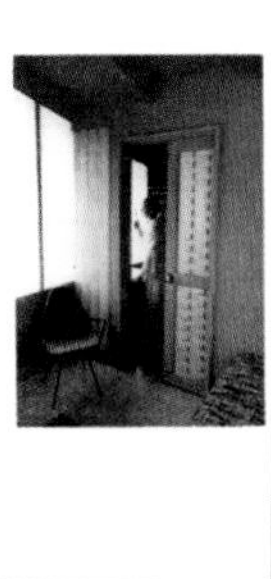

Figure 6—polyester-glass-fiber surface laminated to cinder block (above left) provides extremely durable finish.

Figure 7—for industrial laboratory (above right) cinder blocks are surfaced with a color-impregnated, reinforced-plastic facing that is only 1/32" thick. This skin material is still in the experimental stages.

Figure 8—louver-type partitions and grill-work on door are of reinforced plastic.
Photos: Monsanto Chemical Co., U. S. Rubber Co., Russell Plastics Corp.

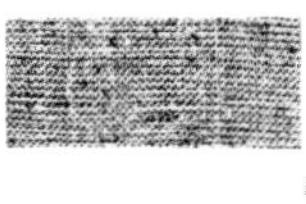

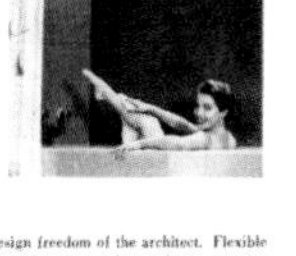

Figure 9—these bathroom walls are covered with vinyl-plastic-coated metal sheet. Plastic applied by patented process is waterproof and scuff resistant. Detail (above) shows three-dimensional pattern which is formed after plastic has been bonded to metal sheet.
Photo: Clad-Rex Steel Co.

February 1956 141

Plastics in Building
as documented by
Progressive Architecture:

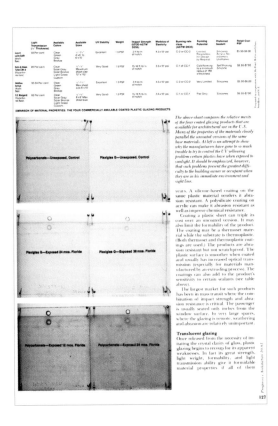

PLASTICS LITERACY ONE NUMBER AT A TIME

However, a thirteenth item not titled "plastics in building" but on the subject nonetheless contrasts the use-driven taxonomic approach and replaces it with a property-driven, numerical approach. It is actually the first comprehensive book on the subject, titled *Materials of Construction: Wood, Plastics, Fabrics*, published in 1949 and authored by Dr. Albert G.H. Dietz, then Associate Professor at the Department of Building Engineering and Construction, MIT.

Dietz would make a career on a direct, numerically driven approach to determine appropriate and inappropriate uses of plastics. His scholarship on the subject was communicated broadly – for instance, through two decades of committee work with the National Research Council of the National Academy of Sciences (NAS-NRC), and through committee work with the American Society for Testing and Materials (now known as ASTM).[13] He likewise consulted directly with the Manufacturing Chemists' Association (MCA) to determine which engineering metrics were needed by architects, fabricators, and buildings in the MCA's *Technical Data Book on Plastics*.[14] Dr. Dietz's academic career began in 1934. His plastics research spanned from the Forest Products Laboratory to the Plastics Laboratory at MIT. His engineering scholarship was applied directly to the plastics composites system executed for the Monsanto House of the Future. Given his approach toward the subject of "plastics in building," he made comparatively sobering communication with architects via popular architectural press. His scholarship and expertise is repeatedly encountered in this selected record:

Books:

> *Materials for Construction: Wood, Plastics and Fabrics*, 1949
> *Plastics for Architects and Builders*, 1969
> *Composite Engineering Laminates*, 1969.

Book chapters:

> "Design Theory of Reinforced Plastics" in Sonneborn's *Fiberglas Reinforced Plastics*, 1954.

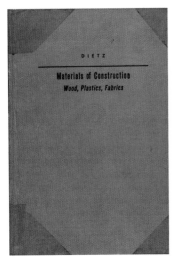

*Materials for Construction:
Wood, Plastics, Fabrics,* 1949.

Conference proceedings:

> "Physical and Engineering Properties of Plastics," Building Research Institute, 1955
> "Engineering the Monsanto House of the Future," Building Research Institute, 1956
> "The Plastics Laboratory at the Massachusetts Institute of Technology," Building Research Institute, 1962
> "Engineering with Plastics," American Chemical Society, 1965.

Popular architectural press:

> "Potentialities of Plastics in Building," *Architectural Record*, March 1950
> "Selecting Plastics for Building Uses," *Architectural Record*, April 1955
> "Plastics: The Next Decade," *Progressive Architecture*, April 1970.

Associations and Societies:

> "Designing Plastics for Strength," Technical Data on Plastics MCA, 1957
> *Composite Materials, Edgar Marburg Lecture ASTM*, 1965.

Materials of Construction: Wood, Plastics, Fabrics provides a brief introduction, not to "building with plastics," but to their chemistry, defining plastics and their three basic tenants: thermoplastic, thermoset, and polymerization. On the definition of plastics, he states, "There is, at present, no adequate definition of plastic. The field is young and continually growing, so there is little chance for a concise definition until more settled conditions prevail."[15] Chapters on plastics include "Chemistry of Plastics and Resins," "Plasticizers, Fillers, Colors, Film and Sheet, Coatings," "Molds and Molding Methods," "Plastics-Based Laminates, Vulcanized Fiber, Resin-Wood Combinations," "Properties of Plastics," and "Building Boards, Structural Sandwiches, Timber-Concrete." Images span from cellulose packaging to a polyvinyl chloride shower curtain, to cellulose acetate film winterizing a building under construction, to single shell acrylic turret molding, to the Celotex House employing stressed skin panels.

In this early publication Dr. Dietz identifies 12 types of plastics in the context of construction.[16] Per plastic, he describes numerically their mechanical properties – tension, compression, and flexure. And he numerically describes their electrical conductivity, light transmittance, color, thermal coefficient of expansion and conductivity, heat distortion point, flammability, water absorption, effect of light (UV resistance), service temperature and chemical resistance to attack. For instance, regarding PMMA he notes that clear resin discolors slightly if exposed to Florida's climate for one year.[17] He surrounds each plastic type with numerical information primarily sourced from *Technical Data on Plastics; Modern Plastics Encyclopedia*, and a chart produced by the Chemical Division of the Koppers Company.

This first book makes apparent Dr. Dietz's real interest, the engineering of novel composites, and foreshadows his continued trajectory. "The inclusion of wood, plastics and fabrics in one volume is a logical consequence of their growing use in combination, in addition to their separate uses," Dietz explains in the book's introduction.

> For many purposes the best adhesives for wood are based upon plastics. Plastics also furnish a large group of saturates, impregnates, and coatings for wood and fabrics. Wood and fabrics in turn reinforce plastics, and in the plastics-based laminates the combination of paper fabric, wood and plastics results in essentially new material saving properties not to be found in any of the constituents.[18]

Chapter ten addresses wood veneers and associated adhesives which include animal glues, blood albumin, casein, vegetable glues – naturally occurring plastics – alongside the synthetics resorcinol, urea, and melamine formaldehyde. Molded plywood applications are addressed and images of monocoque constructions include a plane fuselage, station wagon roof, and aircraft ducts. "Design Theory of Reinforced Plastics," his contribution to *Fiberglas Reinforced Plastics* (Reinhold Publishing Corporation, 1954), presents structural calculations for several fiberglass reinforced plastics forms, including plain reinforced plates, composite plates, bending of beams and plates, plate and rib constructions, and sandwich constructions, noting that "data respecting properties, and experience in design with these materials are accumulating."[19]

*Plastics for Architects
and Builders*, 1969.

Dr. Dietz was committed to aggregating and representing to architects data on plastics that could make them known and worked pervasively across the building products supply chain. His numerical approach seems impartial to the intended material states – impartial to "plastics in building" and "all-plastics." And his work continues to suggest that there is a way to think critically about both states, but particularly about "plastics in building" as he demonstrates that plastics may be known and understood as individual materials rather than lumped into use categories. In his final book on the subject, titled *Plastics for Architects and Builders*, he summarizes his approach and, one may infer, two-plus decades of work to present information on plastics thusly:

> This book attempts to acquaint the designer sufficiently with plastics so that he may have some realization of their potential in building … Though the reader will not be an expert when he finishes this book, he should have obtained some notion of what plastics are and what they can and cannot do. Many promising applications are missed because of ignorance, but it is equally true that uninformed uses leads to disappointment and disillusionment. If this book helps to correct such situations, it will have fulfilled the aim of its author.[20]

PLASTICS. ONE WORD.

One word can be used to describe thousands of differently functional materials. Up to this point I have only used one word – "Plastics." "Plastics" is a technically acceptable description. Furthermore, evidence suggests that, as Fredrick J. Rarig recounted when explaining the position of the Model Chapter, this is what architects wanted:

> The architects made it clear that they wanted plastics dealt with as plastics and indexed as plastics. They did not consider it practical to endeavor to establish in building codes separate provisions for individual classes of plastics that would be identified by esoteric generic terms identifying classes of polymers and copolymers." [21]

The success of this early decision may affront some who, like Dr. Dietz, are more determined to mine plastics for their attributes. But how should we classify plastics? Should we classify them based on use, or property, and does it matter based on what we want to do with them?

1961, On the future of plastics in building

With the quick, emphatic, emergence of plastics – not one but hundreds of materials that shapeshift into known and novel forms – comes our desire to know from experts just where all of this is heading.

E.S. COLEMAN:
U.S. RUBBER CO.

What is the future of plastics in building?

DR. DIETZ:
PROFESSOR, MIT

Cloudy. I do not believe that plastics are going to push other building materials out of the picture. They are going to find their place along with the other materials that we have, both in their own right and also as composites. We haven't begun to do the work in the field of composites, employing plastics along with other materials, that could be done. Plastics are going to be a group of materials which will enrich the field of materials we can use in the building industry, but they are certainly not going to take the place of concrete and timber.[22]

Describe a plastic as thermoset or a thermoplastic. The mass of plastics in architecture bifurcates along strategies for working. Describe a plastic as foam plastic insulation, interior finish and trim, plastic veneer, or light-transmitting. The mass of plastics are grouped into use as in chapter 26 of the 2006 International Building Code. Describe a plastic as belonging to the acrylics, vinyls, phenols, or polyesters. The mass of plastics will be grouped according to originating monomer. Describe a plastic as a light-transmitter, load resistor, reinforcer, binder, barrier, adherer, sealer, coater, or insulator. The mass of plastics will divide perceivably by how they are used. Describe a plastic's UV resistance, light transmittance, weather resistance, chemical resistance, scratch resistance, wear resistance, R-value, coefficient of thermal expansion, service temperature, heat/pressure adhesion, water vapor transmission and water absorption. The mass of plastics no longer exists. Each individual material is described as it encounters flow of light, use, temperature, and water.

The context for these materials is much more subtle and sometimes depends on one's willingness to *see* it apart from a structural dilemma. This context is a dynamic milieu of light, wind, water, vapor, inhabitation, breath, and scent. This is a constant, four-dimensional milieu, construed and misconstrued as evasive, erosive, corrosive – an aging agent. Yet, it is the context of all architecture and all material practices.

It is most useful to use the term plastics to mean thermally treatable, homogenous materials. This description embodies the notion "worked into shape." It embodies construction logic. And, it is most useful to describe thermally treatable, homogenous, and capable of being worked into shape materials numerically, and therefore individually, as they encounter the dynamic milieu of light, use, temperature, water, stress and energy. Again, such descriptive rigor anticipates "worked into shape," but it also anticipates rigorous assembly. Any description between "mass" and "individual" is merely a taxonomic and therefore didactic device which is distracting and indecipherable chatter.

That these materials then must be called by name – e.g., polyethylene terephthalate – is residue of their chemical heritage. If this is off-putting, then the public relations campaign that allowed plastics to be sanctioned by their acronym – e.g., PET – may be much more appealing. However, describing "plastics in building" was rarely attempted agnostically. Rather, describing plastics, and therefore "reasonably" working them, was more likely to be affiliated with building products. And plastics products were never intended to flow, but to stay fixed and perform.

A collection of plastics attributes organized per use and environmental flow

A categorization schema that attempts to eliminate the mass of materials that we call "plastics" in favor of describing them individually and numerically as they encounter the flow of light, atmosphere, heat, water, and force. Major use categories – light-transmitter, load resistor, reinforcer, binder, barrier, adherer, sealer, coater, or insulator – are indexed to those specific attributes that, when measured, indicates something about how it interacts with this dynamic milieu. Not all attributes are typically applicable or measured for all use categories, but they could be. For instance, "UV resistance" reported as a rating – excellent, good, fair, poor – is an attribute that can be understood for all plastics; "puncture strength," measured in psi, is typically reported for films and membranes but, depending how one might want to use plastics, might be necessary to understand; while "peel strength" is an exclusive attribute measured for adhesives.

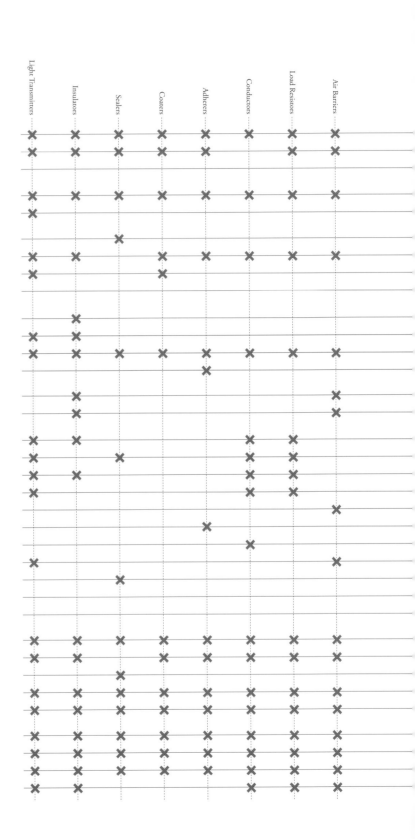

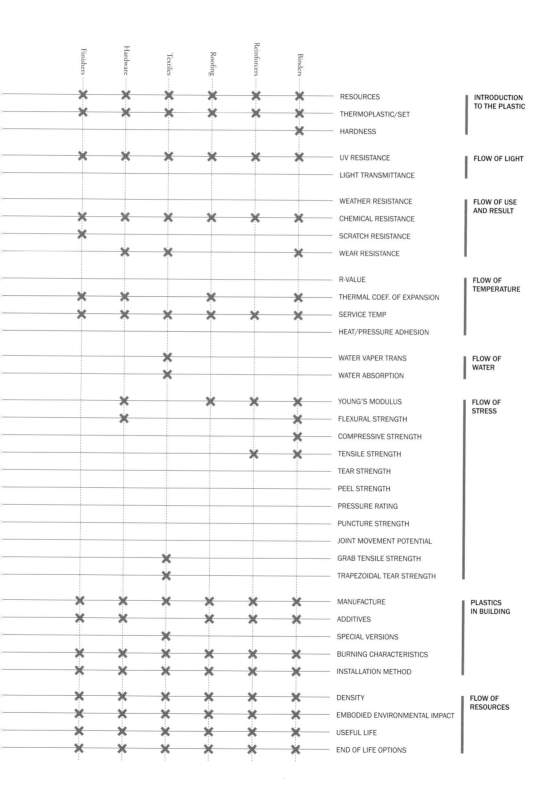

Finishers | Hardware | Textiles | Roofing | Reinforcers | Binders

RESOURCES — INTRODUCTION TO THE PLASTIC
THERMOPLASTIC/SET
HARDNESS

UV RESISTANCE — FLOW OF LIGHT
LIGHT TRANSMITTANCE

WEATHER RESISTANCE — FLOW OF USE AND RESULT
CHEMICAL RESISTANCE
SCRATCH RESISTANCE
WEAR RESISTANCE

R-VALUE — FLOW OF TEMPERATURE
THERMAL COEF. OF EXPANSION
SERVICE TEMP
HEAT/PRESSURE ADHESION

WATER VAPER TRANS — FLOW OF WATER
WATER ABSORPTION

YOUNG'S MODULUS — FLOW OF STRESS
FLEXURAL STRENGTH
COMPRESSIVE STRENGTH
TENSILE STRENGTH
TEAR STRENGTH
PEEL STRENGTH
PRESSURE RATING
PUNCTURE STRENGTH
JOINT MOVEMENT POTENTIAL
GRAB TENSILE STRENGTH
TRAPEZOIDAL TEAR STRENGTH

MANUFACTURE — PLASTICS IN BUILDING
ADDITIVES
SPECIAL VERSIONS
BURNING CHARACTERISTICS
INSTALLATION METHOD

DENSITY — FLOW OF RESOURCES
EMBODIED ENVIRONMENTAL IMPACT
USEFUL LIFE
END OF LIFE OPTIONS

BUILDING MATERIALS MADE FROM PLASTICS DESCRIBED NUMERICALLY

Building products made from plastics are "collected" and represented, arrayed as palettes of materials throughout the aggregated data set of journal articles, conference proceedings, and books. Most collections, as evidenced by the organization of books titled *Plastics in Building* and the exhibition *Plastics, A New Dimension in Building*, are use-driven, and demonstrate at a glance the capacity for products made from plastics to "permeate" throughout a building.

This collection, like the terminology collection, implicitly and simultaneously acknowledges our practices with building products and challenges it.[23] Implementing the metadata schema proposed by our plastics attributes diagram takes up the challenge to know plastics individually by name and attribute. But, before wrestling with how to know these plastics individually, wrestle first with knowing and comprehending the dynamic milieu – the flow of light, atmosphere, heat, water, and force that is the context for all materials. Look back at the proposed metadata schema with comprehension in mind. Such a milieu is specific to climate, microclimate, region, and culture; and it changes over time. Numerics and terms of use on technical data sheets provided by manufacturers of building products implicitly represent this milieu. Each material put to use – and yes there are thousands of plastics, but there are also thousands of species of wood, concrete mix designs, steel alloys, clays, etc. – interacts with this milieu in a different and specific way.

With such a precept in mind, and recognizing that the representation of plastics through exclusively use-driven categorization neutralizes this milieu, commit to breaking down the mass of materials that we refer to simply as "plastics" into individual materials. Ask: How does such a material interact with light, atmosphere, heat, water, force, etc.? Choose to begin to define "use" here. This is precisely what Dr. Dietz's approach demands of us when he describes multiple attributes of plastics materials numerically and why it is applicable right now. Rather than cast his as an engineer's perspective, cast it for what it is, an epistemic pursuit – to know (all) plastics. And be prepared to add to your numerical knowledge a rigorous working of plastics.

If we dare to do this then we expand the system boundary of the product during its "use." We literally have the means to redefine "use" and rephrase it as "use over time" which simultaneously recasts our definition of the "use and maintenance" stage nested in the building products lifecycle. Once again, we expand the potential of design. Once again, we might be poised to proactively ask what kind of phenomena – impacts, effects, affects – do we want a building material to produce when it is both manufactured and when it is used over time? This question, again, suggests that we might begin to participate in the design of materials for architecture.

MATERIAL NAME

PC

Polycarbonate

As a light-transmitting sheet material – solid, extruded, honeycomb, and corrugated.

DESCRIPTION

Polycarbonate plastics are available in sheets from 2 mm to 20 mm thick that offer high impact strength, toughness, and high heat deflection temperatures. PCs are manipulated into films, sheets, and panels; pigments can be added to modify the clarity of the plastic, ranging from opaque to clear with high optical qualities. PCs are exceptional engineering thermoplastics, but they should not be exposed to hot water for long periods of time and are prone to stress cracking if proper tolerances are not provided. Sheets of PC are used for windows, skylights, and translucent wall panels.

RESOURCES
Petroleum

THERMOPLASTIC/SET
Thermoplastic

UV RESISTANCE
Good

LIGHT TRANSMITTANCE
90 percent (translucent sheet product)

CHEMICAL RESISTANCE
Very good: fresh water, salt water, weak acids, and strong acids
Good: weak alkalis
Average: organic solvents
Poor: strong alkalis

SCRATCH RESISTANCE
Average

COEFFICIENT OF THERMAL EXPANSION
0.000036 in/°F

SERVICE TEMPERATURE
Maximum: 219–246 °F.
Minimum: −52.6–34.6 °F

YOUNG'S MODULUS
$0.3316–0.03344 \times 10^6$ psi

FLEXURAL STRENGTH
$8.65–8.8 \times 10^3$ psi

COMPRESSIVE STRENGTH
$10.4–10.6 \times 10^3$ psi

TENSILE STRENGTH
$9.09–10.5 \times 10^3$ psi

MANUFACTURE
Extrusion, thermoforming, injection molding, blow molding, gas-assisted injection molding, injection molding

ADDITIVES
Carbon, glass and PTFE, glass and silicone, glass, graphite, stainless steel, ABS, PBT

BURNING CHARACTERISTICS
Self-extinguishing (UL94; V2, V0, or 5V)

INSTALLATION METHOD
PC sheets can be sawn, laser cut, or drilled. For sawing and drilling, appropriate blade and bit types must be used to prevent crazing and cracking. Attachment details must take into account significant thermal expansion.

END-OF-LIFE OPTIONS
PC can be recycled if unreinforced

MATERIAL NAME

PET

Polyesters (PET) (PETG)

As a light-transmitting sheet material – solid, extruded, honeycomb, and corrugated.

PET solid sheet.

DESCRIPTION

Poly(ethylene terephthalate) (PET) and poly(ethylene terephthalate) glycol comonomer (PETG) are both saturated polyesters; a large group of plastics derived from a combination of "polymerization" and "esterification" that can be optimized for a range of uses. These plastics have excellent mechanical properties – they are tough, strong, and easy to shape. PET and PETG can be modified to reach high levels of clarity and can be easily colored with pigments. In addition, PET and PETG are resilient plastics that do not absorb water and are easy to recycle. Saturated polyesters are available as sheets, composite panels, and films that are up to 48" wide by 96" long.

RESOURCES
Petroleum

THERMOPLASTIC/SET
Thermoplastic

UV RESISTANCE
Good

LIGHT TRANSMITTANCE
PET film 93 percent; PETG 88 percent

CHEMICAL RESISTANCE
Very good: fresh water, salt water
Good: weak acids, weak alkalis
Average: strong alkalis, organic solvents
Poor: strong acids

SCRATCH RESISTANCE
Average

COEFFICIENT OF THERMAL EXPANSION
0.000069 in/°F

SERVICE TEMPERATURE
Maximum: 239–248 °F
Minimum: −72.4–36.4 °F

YOUNG'S MODULUS
$0.292–0.306 \times 10^6$ psi

FLEXURAL STRENGTH
9,720–10,700 psi

COMPRESSIVE STRENGTH
8,340–9,210 psi

TENSILE STRENGTH
8,700–9,570 psi

MANUFACTURE
Blow molding, injection molding, casting, extruding

BURNING CHARACTERISTICS
Flammable (ULp4: unrated)

INSTALLATION METHOD
Polyester sheets can be saw-cut with a conventional reciprocating or circular saw and shaped with machining tools used for plastics, wood, or metal. Cutting tools should be operated at speeds that will not melt the polyesters and must be sharp at all times. Sheets may be bound with mechanical fasteners or adhesives.

END-OF-LIFE OPTIONS
Good recyclability

MATERIAL NAME
ETFE

Ethylene-tetrafluoroethylene copolymer
As a light-transmitting film

DESCRIPTION
Ethylene-tetrafluoroethylene copolymer (ETFE) is a self-cleaning, chemically resistant plastic, applicable as transparent, pneumatically pre-tensioned pillows in roofs and façades. ETFE cushions, when pressurized, have increased thermal efficiency approaching an R-value of 4.9 for a five-layer/four-chamber assembly. Rolls of ETFE can be purchased in nominal thicknesses from 0.0005" to 0.0200". ETFE is used for wall assemblies, roof assemblies, and whole-building envelopes.

RESOURCES
Petroleum–olefin–naphtha–ethylene

THERMOPLASTIC/SET
Thermoplastic

UV RESISTANCE
Good

LIGHT TRANSMITTANCE
95 percent (translucent sheet product)

CHEMICAL RESISTANCE
Very good: fresh water, salt water, weak acids, strong acids, weak alkalis, strong alkalis, organic solvents

SCRATCH RESISTANCE
Average

COEFFICIENT OF THERMAL EXPANSION
7.0–7.4 in/°F

SERVICE TEMPERATURE
Maximum: 287.6–316.4 °F
Minimum: –328 °F

YOUNG'S MODULUS
0.117–0.123×10^6 psi

FLEXURAL STRENGTH
5,240–5,770 psi

COMPRESSIVE STRENGTH
6,760–7,450 psi

TENSILE STRENGTH
6,190–6,830 psi

MANUFACTURE
Polymerization, granulation, extrusion, preparation-welding, polymerization; method of manufacture changes the embodied energy associated with ETFE.

BURNING CHARACTERISTICS
Low flammability B1, tested in DIN 4102; ETFE self-vents the products of combustion to the atmosphere and does not drip material when enflamed, giving it a higher fire rating; self-extinguishing (UL94: V2, V0, or 5V)

INSTALLATION METHOD
ETFE sheeting is cut into the desired shape from a flattened cushion pattern. Cushions are fabricated with 2–5 layers of material. The edges of the cushion are seamed or "welded" around a beading material creating a formed edge which "locks" into a specially fitted aluminum extrusion, securing the cushion into its orientation. Firms specializing in ETFE installations typically have a range of proprietary extrusions.

USEFUL LIFE
25 years and counting

END-OF-LIFE OPTIONS
Good recyclability

MATERIAL NAME
PA

Polyamide
As a non-woven textile

▼

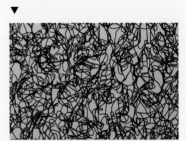

Non-woven geo-textile.

DESCRIPTION
Polyamide (PA), also known as nylon, is a non-woven three-dimensional polymer "textile" primarily produced for fortifying soil in erosion control applications. These products are also used for drainage control in building/construction and are typically installed as components in green roofs, roof underlayment and foundation wall protection. These products create a cavity between two substrates and enable airflow in the space which aids in evaporating moisture and prevents structural damage. Three-dimensional non-wovens are available in rolls up to 40" in width by 200' in length.

THERMOPLASTIC/SET
Thermoplastic

UV RESISTANCE
Good

CHEMICAL RESISTANCE
Very good

TRAPEZOIDAL TEAR STRENGTH
40 lbs/ft

GRAB TENSILE STRENGTH
125 lbs/ft

SPECIAL VERSIONS
Available bonded to non-woven
fabric such as polyester for drainage
applications

MANUFACTURE
Spunlaid, heat bonded?

BURNING CHARACTERISTICS
Flame Spread Index (25),
Smoke Developed Index (30)

INSTALLATION METHOD
Non-woven, three-dimensional
polyamide textiles can be nailed, stapled,
and/or adhered.

END-OF-LIFE OPTIONS
Recyclable

MATERIAL NAME
CFRP

Carbon fiber reinforced plastic
As a composite shell, slab, or profile

▼

CFRP composite.

DESCRIPTION
Carbon fiber reinforced plastic (CFRP) is
one of the highest performing composite
materials and offers extreme strength-
to-weight benefits in its mechanical
properties, exceeding most metals and
other composites. It is a very lightweight
material that is often used to supplement
metal in ultra-high-performance
applications, especially in the aerospace
and automotive industries where it is
used to create everything from body
panels to fuselages. Due to its high price
point, it tends to be cost prohibitive for
use in architecture and construction and
is relatively unexplored for such uses.
However, several CFRP products are
available within the industry including a
lightweight "woven" grid used instead of
rebar or wire mesh in concrete.

THERMOPLASTIC/SET
Thermoset resin (epoxy)

UV RESISTANCE
Good

CHEMICAL RESISTANCE
Good

TENSILE STRENGTH
40,000–200,000 psi

SERVICE TEMPERATURE
Maximum: 280–400 °F

MANUFACTURE
Contact molding (vacuum infusion),
compression molding, resin transfer
molding, filament winding, pultrusion

BURNING CHARACTERISTICS
Non-flammable (self-extinguishing)

CSI MASTER FORMAT NUMBER
067000: structural composite
068000: composites fabrication
068200: GFRP

INSTALLATION METHOD
Concrete reinforcement, custom
fabrications

DENSITY
0.05 lbs/in³

ADDITIVES
Hybrid fabrics (carbon/Kevlar® blends),
pigments, fillers (fibrous, metallic, glass)

FLEXURAL STRENGTH
75,000–200,000 psi

THERMAL COEFFICIENT OF EXPANSION
0.05–2 ustrain/°F

YOUNG'S MODULUS
68–144 gpa

END-OF-LIFE OPTIONS
Not recyclable

MATERIAL NAME
WPC

Wood plastic composite
As a composite board, plank, or sheet

▼

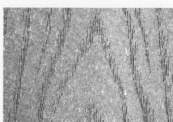

WPC board.

DESCRIPTION
Wood plastic composite (WPC) is a fully
recycled/recyclable composite material
manufactured from recovered plastic
blended with recycled natural wood fiber
in the form of sawdust or wood chips.
It is widely known as plastic lumber
and decking. WPC products pertinent
to building construction are typically
available in extruded forms such as
planks, sheets, structural panels, and
tubular profiles. They are also available
for wider industrial use as specialized
compounds for various manufacturing
processes. WPC extruded profiles are
available in both solid and tubular forms
in lengths up to 20' and nominal sizes up

to 12" × 16". It can be used to construct exterior decking, landscape components, furniture, trim work, and cladding.

RESOURCES
Polyethylene (PE) or polypropylene (PP), natural wood fiber blend

THERMOPLASTIC/SET
Thermoplastic

UV RESISTANCE
Good

CHEMICAL RESISTANCE
Very good

SERVICE TEMPERATURE
Maximum: 185 °F
Flash point: 750 °F

MANUFACTURE
Extrusion, thermoforming, injection molding

BURNING CHARACTERISTICS
Flame Spread Index 80, Smoke Developed Index ASTM E84

INSTALLATION METHOD
WPC products can be cut and installed using standard woodworking tools, glued using PVC adhesives, and painted with latex-based paints.

ADDITIVES
Pigments, natural fibers (including rice shell, straw, bamboo)

COMPRESSIVE STRENGTH
>4,500 psi

FLEXURAL STRENGTH
2,000–9,000 psi

THERMAL COEFFICIENT OF EXPANSION
0.0064 in/100°F

YOUNG'S MODULUS
100,000–500,000 psi

USEFUL LIFE
25–50 years

END-OF-LIFE OPTIONS
Recyclability: excellent; incinerated: no
Biodegradability: some versions available

MATERIAL NAME
LDPE

Low-density polyethylene
As a barrier to air and moisture

LDPE film.

DESCRIPTION
Low-density polyethylene (LDPE) can be a flexible, translucent film that has a high impact resistance and is resilient to a wide range of chemicals. LDPE can be used as an excellent, inexpensive air and moisture barrier in buildings due to its low cost and water absorption. Sheets of LDPE are typically sold from 0.001" to 0.030" thicknesses and are used in walls, foundations, basements, and crawl spaces.

RESOURCES
Petroleum

THERMOPLASTIC/SET
Thermoplastic

UV RESISTANCE
Good

CHEMICAL RESISTANCE
Very good: fresh water, salt water, weak acids, weak alkalis, strong alkalis
Good: strong acids, weak alkalis, strong alkalis
Average: organic solvents

TEAR STRENGTH
Elmendorf tear strength, MD: 348 g/mil;
Elmendorf tear strength, TD: 211 g/mil

MANUFACTURE
Blown film extrusion, cast film extrusion, extrusion coating, co-extrusion

BURNING CHARACTERISTICS
Flammable (UL94; unrated)

INSTALLATION METHOD
LDPE films are typically cut with a knife and mechanically fastened with nails or staples. Seams are taped to prevent air/ moisture from penetrating the barrier.

ADDITIVES
Anti-static, ultraviolet, flame retardant

YOUNG'S MODULUS
3.06 Air and Moisture Barriers

END-OF-LIFE OPTIONS
Good recyclability; recycle mark 4

MATERIAL NAME
PIR

Polysiocyanurate
As an insulator

DESCRIPTION
Polyisocyanurate (PIR) is available in the form of rigid sheets and sandwich panel cores. It is similar to PUR and can be used in many of the same locations. PIR rigid sheets are distinguished by a higher service temperature, increased fire performance, and reduced combustibility. Extruded sheets of insulation are available in sizes as large as 4' wide by 10' long and can be anywhere from 0.5" to 4" thick. Typical applications for PIR/PUR include wall, floor, and roof assemblies.

RESOURCES
Petroleum

THERMOPLASTIC/SET
Thermoplastic

UV RESISTANCE
Good

CHEMICAL RESISTANCE
Very good: fresh water, salt water, strong alkalis
Poor: weak acids, weak alkalis, organic solvents
Very poor: strong acids, strong alkalis

COMPRESSIVE STRENGTH
0.139–25 psi

MANUFACTURE
Extruded, foam molded

BURNING CHARACTERISTICS
Flammable (UL94: unrated)

INSTALLATION METHOD
Rigid PIR can be cut, drilled, and shaped with conventional woodworking tools. Adhesives and mechanical fasteners are used to position the insulation panels/sheets.

DENSITY
0.00116 lb/in³

WATER ABSORPTION
1–3.5 percent

WATER VAPOR TRANSMISSION
<1.5 perm

R-VALUE
Between R-7 to R-8 per inch

SERVICE TEMPERATURE
100 °F to 200 °F, average range

YOUNG'S MODULUS
3.07 insulators

EMBODIED ENERGY
1.105e4–1.213e4 kcal/lb

USEFUL LIFE
50 years with constant thermal performance

MATERIAL NAME

XPS

Extruded polystyrene
As an insulator

▼

XPS foam.

DESCRIPTION
Extruded polystyrene (XPS) is a closed-cell rigid insulating plastic that is available in the form of sandwich panels and extruded sheets. XPS sheets are typically identified by their pink, blue, or green pigments. As an insulator, XPS is noted for its good compressive strength, moisture resistance, and excellent thermal conductivity. Polystyrenes are applicable to most conditions where thermal insulators are necessary, including: wall, floor, roof, and foundation systems. XPS is available in sheets as large as 4′ × 9′ and up to 3″ thick.

RESOURCES
Petroleum

THERMOPLASTIC/SET
Thermoset

UV RESISTANCE
Average

CHEMICAL RESISTANCE
Very good: fresh water, salt water, weak acids, weak alkalis
Good: strong alkalis
Average: strong acids
Poor: organic solvents

COMPRESSIVE STRENGTH
116–145 psi

MANUFACTURE
Extruded, foam molded; sheets and rolls may be cut down from large foam blocks

BURNING CHARACTERISTICS
Flammable (UL94: unrated);
Flame Spread Index: <25;
Smoke Developed Index: <450

INSTALLATION METHOD
XPS insulations are cut, hot wired, sawn, and/or drilled to modify their size and shape. Once cut, the sheets can be adhered or mechanically fastened into position.

DENSITY
0.0017–0.00191 lb/in³

THERMAL COEFFICIENT OF EXPANSION
0.000035 in/°F

WATER ABSORPTION
1–3 percent water absorption at 24 hours

R-VALUE
3.5–5.0 hr ft² °F/Btu (per inch of thickness)

SERVICE TEMPERATURE
Maximum: 180–189 °F
Minimum: –112–76 °F

END-OF-LIFE OPTIONS
Recyclable

MATERIAL NAME

Biobased spray foam

Biobased spray foam
As an insulator

▼

Biobased spray foam.

DESCRIPTION

Biobased spray foam insulations are non-fibrous, non toxic foams derived from soy or vegetable oils. Bio foams are available as open-celled, semi-rigid and closed-celled, rigid spray foams. Once applied, the resin will expand to 30 times its original size filling and sealing cracks, voids, and gaps. Bio foams exhibit a high R-value, will not settle in walls or cavities, and are unaffected by moisture. In addition, soy-based insulations will not support mold growth and/or offer sustenance to insects or rodents. Biobased insulations can be used as sealants for HVAC systems and in wall, floor, ceiling, and roofing assemblies.

RESOURCES
Petroleum

THERMOPLASTIC/SET
Thermoset

CHEMICAL RESISTANCE
Good: fresh water

COMPRESSIVE STRENGTH
23 psi

BURNING CHARACTERISTICS
Flammable; Flame Spread Index 18 (ASTM E84-04); Smoke Developed Index 350 (ASTM E84-04)

INSTALLATION METHOD
The soy or vegetable oil resin is sprayed onto the substrate. After the foam has fully expanded and dried, the excess foam may be trimmed with saws or a knife.

DENSITY
0.000289–0.000984 lb/in^3

WATER ABSORPTION
0.2 percent (ASTM D 2842-01)

WATER VAPOR TRANSMISSION
0.8–1.8 perms (ASTM C-177)

R-VALUE
R-value: 3.8–6.8 °F h ft^2/Btu (per inch–ASTM C-155); R-values vary depending upon the cell type (open or closed) and the insulation densities.

USEFUL LIFE
Lifetime warranty

MATERIAL NAME

PMMA

Poly(methyl methacrylate)
As an insulator

PMMA insulation.

DESCRIPTION
Poly(methyl methacrylate) (PMMA) can be manipulated into a translucent capillary panel comprising tubes connected with a glass fiber tissue. The translucent insulators reduce heat transfer, improve building acoustics, and allow for light transmission with excellent color rendering. PMMA insulator panels are used to line windows and transparent wall systems – filling the building's interior with natural light while reducing thermal transfer. PMMA insulation panels are available in sizes as large as 3,500 mm in length and can range in thickness from 12 mm to 40 mm.

RESOURCES
Petroleum

THERMOPLASTIC/SET
Thermoplastic

UV RESISTANCE
Good

CHEMICAL RESISTANCE
Very good: fresh water, salt water, weak alkalis, strong alkalis
Good: weak acids
Poor: strong acids, organic solvents

COMPRESSIVE STRENGTH
14,900–17,000 psi

BURNING CHARACTERISTICS
PMMA is combustible and flammable but is increasingly being tested and produced with self-extinguishing additives; ASTM D1929 (determines ignition temp); ASTM E84 (determines surface burning characteristics); ASTM D2843 (determines the density of smoke)

INSTALLATION METHOD
PMMA translucent insulation panels should be preassembled in a controlled environment. If the insulating panels need to be trimmed, score the back of the panel with a knife. Once scored, fold the panel back and use a knife to score along the crease.

DENSITY
0.0011 lb/in^3

WATER ABSORPTION
0.2–0.3 percent water absorption at 24 hours

WATER VAPOR TRANSMISSION
1.62–1.79 g mm/(m^2 day)

R-VALUE
The R-value of PMMA insulations typically ranges from 2.86 to 4; R-value with 12 mm insulation and 44 mm air: 2.86; R-value with 40 mm insulation and 16 mm air: 4

SERVICE TEMPERATURE
Maximum: 194–212 °F; 176 °F is the maximum temperature for continuous use
Minimum: –103 to –85 °F

END-OF-LIFE OPTIONS
Recyclable; recycle mark #7

MATERIAL NAME

PVC

Poly(vinyl chloride)
As a sealer

DESCRIPTION
Poly(vinyl chloride) (PVC) waterstops are
extruded lengths of plastic profile that
are poured into the joints of a concrete
structure to prevent water leakage
by bridging any degree of separation
at the point of juncture. The profiles
of waterstop are tailored for specific
applications and are based on the type
of joint that will be created. The design of
these profiles is meant to accommodate
differing degrees of movement that occur
in concrete structures, mostly as a result of
thermal fluctuation. The joints themselves
provide the function of controlling
thermal expansion and contraction while
the waterstop serves only as a seal in
the joint that must be able to work in
motion with the structure. PVC waterstop
is available in widths of up to ten inches
wide and is packaged as fifty foot rolls.

THERMOPLASTIC/SET
Thermoplastic

JOINT MOVEMENT POTENTIAL
Elongation%: >350 psi

MANUFACTURE
Extruded, heat welded

INSTALLATION METHOD
PVC waterstops are placed in concrete
as control joints, expansion joints, and
construction joints.

SERVICE TEMPERATURE
Maximum: >180 °F
Minimum: −35 °F

SPECIAL VERSIONS
Profiles are application specific and
account for degrees of joint movement

USEFUL LIFE
Life of concrete

MATERIAL NAME

PMMA

Poly(methyl methacrylate)
As a finished solid surface

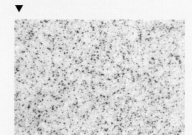

PMMA surfacing.

DESCRIPTION
Poly(methyl methacrylate) (PMMA)
is available as a thermoplastic and
thermoset. They can be manipulated
into an extensive range of finishes. As
a finisher, PMMAs can have a variety
of optical properties spanning from
transparent to opaque. These finishes
have excellent color stability in both
interior and exterior applications and
have superb resistance to UV radiation.
In addition, PMMA finishers have high
strength and durability with good
dimensional stability. PMMA's are
integrated into buildings as furniture,
countertops, and panels for walls, floors,
and ceilings.

RESOURCES
Petroleum–naphtha–olefin–benzene

THERMOPLASTIC/SET
Thermoplastic and/or thermoset

UV RESISTANCE
Good

CHEMICAL RESISTANCE
Very good: fresh water, salt water, weak
alkalis, strong alkalis
Good: weak acids
Poor: strong acids, organic solvents

MANUFACTURE
Blow molding, casting, extrusion, cell
casting, gas-assisted injection molding,
injection molding, rotational molding,
thermoforming

At the start of each process the PMMA
ingredients may be fully or partially
polymerized

BURNING CHARACTERISTICS
Flammable; Flame Spread Index <25
(ASTM E84); Smoke Developed Index <25
(ASTM E84)

PMMA is flammable but can be modified
with self-extinguishing additives

SCRATCH RESISTANCE
Average

THERMAL COEFFICIENT OF EXPANSION
0.0038 in/°F

INSTALLATION METHOD
Tooling, adhesives, induction bonding,
mechanical fastening, solvent welding,
spin welding, ultrasonic welding. Acrylic
sheets can be sawn, laser cut, or drilled.
For sawing and drilling appropriate
blade and bit types must be used to
prevent crazing and cracking. Attachment
details must take into account significant
thermal expansion. (1/32 of an inch for
each 20 °F change).

DENSITY
0.0401–0.0441 lb/in³

SERVICE TEMPERATURE
Maximum: 111.2–132.8 °F
Minimum: −103°F to −85 °F

USEFUL LIFE
25 years

END-OF-LIFE OPTIONS
Fair recyclability

SEARCHING MANUFACTURING REGIMES FOR CUSTOMIZATION POTENTIAL

Polymer construction logic, the addition of one monomer to the next, may yield the possibility of highly custom chemistries at the scale of bench science. However, building products made from plastics use stable and well-known polymer chemistries matched to constraints of manufacturing equipment. For building products, customization is more likely to occur during manufacturing steps, but to what degree do normal manufacturing regimes support customization or alteration to attributes like color, form, UV stability, porosity, or density, etc.? Answering this question might be instructive when one considers operating across the supply chain.

The manufacturing processes for PC cellular sheet, ETFE film, PIR foam insulation and PVC waterstop are considered in the following pages, and searched to reveal manufacturing constraints and customization opportunities. Each one of these presents differently – where PC cellular sheet uses PC pellets imbued with attributes during synthesis steps conducted by a raw materials supplier, PVC waterstop may be imbued with a range of attributes afforded by the arrangement of a manufacturer's extrusion equipment with hoppers for additives. Where the customization of ETFE film is limited mostly to thickness achieved during calendaring, plastic foams may be highly varied in their properties, mechanical and insulative, through the use of different chemical inputs – "part A, part B and a blowing agent" – the ratio of these inputs mixed, and control of speed and pressure at their point of mixing.

PC sheet, cellular.

PC cellular sheet

Cellular polycarbonate sheet is coextruded using two different polycarbonate resins. The bulk of the resin used for cellular polycarbonate is a UV-stabilized grade of polycarbonate. The outside face of cellular polycarbonate is often composed of a polycarbonate blended with a high-performance UV stabilizer to afford the panel enhanced weathering performance. Both types of polycarbonate resins are supplied as pellets to manufacturers of cellular sheet products. They may incorporate release agents and fire retardants, and are generally synthesized to have high melt viscosity suitable for extruding the delicate cellular features. The polycarbonate extruder can further blend pigmented polycarbonate into both polymer melts to change the color and opacity of the panel.

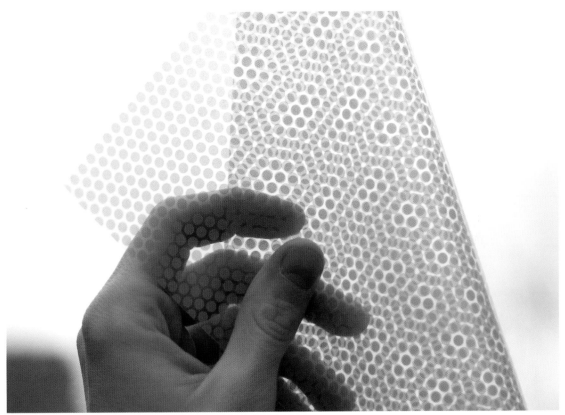

ETFE film.

ETFE film

ETFE is manufactured by copolymerizing ethylene and TFE gases through a pressurized water-based emulsification polymerization process aided by fluorosurfactants and catalysts. The molecular weight of the ETFE is controlled in this process to achieve a melt viscosity suitable for molding and forming of the isolated polymer. The result of this process is a colloidal mixture of 15–30 percent ETFE and water; the ETFE particles are then separated and melted into larger pellets, which are supplied to film extruders. This polymerization process is highly controlled with very little variability. Film extruders who source ETFE resins have the ability to modify the color or opacity of ETFE by compounding ETFE with pigments (resulting in highly pigmented pellets called masterbatches), and adding some of the pigmented masterbatch pellets to plain ETFE in the film extrusion process. Film extruders also have the ability to modify the thickness and surface finish of the ETFE film.[24]

PIR foam sheet.

PIR sheet

Polyisocyanurate foam is manufactured by injecting polyol prepolymer, diisocyanate, and a blowing agent between two sheets of foil on a continuous-sheet manufacturing line. These liquid raw ingredients are mixed and heated at the dispensing nozzles, resulting in a rapid exothermic polymerization reaction; the process heat and latent heat of polymerization quickly evaporate the blowing agent,

resulting in a foamed polymer. The mechanical properties of the polymer are influenced by formulation of the polyol prepolymer and selection of diisocyanate; the blowing agent selection, blowing agent concentration, process temperature, panel thickness, and manufacturing line speed all influence the resulting foam density, insulation properties, and further mechanical properties.

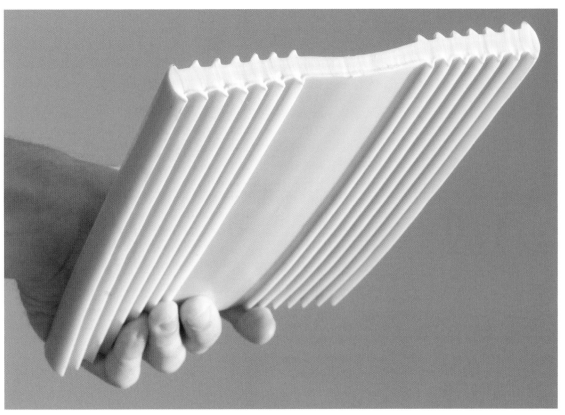

PVC waterstop.

PVC waterstop

PVC is an economical choice for extruding many different flexible, low-cost products due to its ease of processing and versatility. Most PVC products are extruded from raw polymers blended with fillers such as minerals or wood flour, as well as additives. Modern PVC extrusion equipment is typically customized for the product being manufactured, and can blend fillers, additives, and the raw polymer adequately in one step using twin-screw designs.

In the case of a typical PVC waterstop, the manufacturer is able to tailor the final product's mechanical properties through polymer choice, addition of additives, and filler selection and ratio. Further customization is possible by adding specialty additives, such as granular blowing agents to introduce porosity, UV stabilizers to protect against UV-induced discoloration, or pigmented masterbatches to add color to the product. Such extrusion lines can readily accept customized dies for different designs. Other products might utilize coextrusion to cap the exterior of the profile with a higher-performance material.

EMERGING POLYMERS DESCRIBED
FROM THE CHEMIST'S BENCH

Polymers found in building products originated as chemistries synthesized by chemists at their bench. Polymers emerge at a point in time, may be discovered by a team of chemists through intentional searching, accident, or trial and error. These searching efforts are inclusive of repeated batch synthesis and testing as a means to "characterize" the range of possible properties and the chemical structure that supports those properties. When a polymer's synthesis is sufficiently understood, "scaling up" production may occur which trends toward commercial availability of the resin. The mass production of resin follows that may be sourced for a myriad of commercial sectors and applications like backer rod, rug underlayment, and skylights. And … polymers *continue* to emerge at the chemist's bench – new types with new, never-before-seen functionality, and old types with new chemistries and improved functionality.

This collection of 26 selected emerging polymers typifies plastics and therefore plasticity's condition – it has and always will be constantly emerging and require much "working." What should be our response to this condition? Should we remain consumers and procurers of building products made from plastics, or might we respond by producing plastics for architecture alongside those with intimate knowledge of the macromolecular terrain? This collection does evidence the resident human tenacity to keep on working, testing, and knowing the limits of this terrain. Polymers found here emerge based on the human intuition that they can either do more and be made differently – they can self-heal, self-clean, move, and become super strong; and they can be made from feathers, and by microbes. While building products made from plastics challenge us to work pervasively across the supply chain, this collection might challenge us to halt the current supply chain altogether. Hyperbole? Perhaps. But, when we consider the direct relationship between materials performance and building performance we collapse the distance and discord across the supply chain and find the potential to design materials for architecture through chemical synthesis.

SMART POLYMERS

MOVER
Veritex™ fiber reinforced heat-activated shape memory polymer (SMP)

MATERIALS ENGINEER
Cornerstone Research Group Inc.

SUMMARY
Veritex is a fiber-reinforced composite that uses a shape memory polymer, Veriflex, as the matrix. This allows Veritex to easily change shape above its activation temperature. At lower temperatures, the material maintains high strength and high stiffness. When heated, Veritex will temporarily soften. It can then be reshaped and will harden in seconds, maintaining the new configuration. When reheated, Veritex will return to its original cured shape. This versatility allows for the design of structures that are stored and later deployed to the operational shape. Veritex can be manufactured with a variety of fiber reinforcements and shape memory polymer formulations.

CURRENT OR INTENDED APPLICATION(S)
Repair patches, reconfigurable tooling/molding, deployable structures, healable structures, reconfigurable (morphing) structures.

TESTING PROTOCOL(S)
Tensile strain below and above activation temperature, glass transition temperature, tensile and shear strength.

MOVER
Veriflex ® heat-activated shape memory polymer (SMP)

MATERIALS ENGINEER
Tat Tong, Cornerstone Research Group Inc.

SUMMARY
Veriflex is a fully formable thermoset shape memory polymer (SMP) resin system.

Cured Veriflex has unique "shape memory" properties. When heated above its activation temperature, Veriflex changes from a rigid plastic to a flexible elastomer. In its elastic state it can be twisted, pulled, bent, and stretched, reaching up to 200 percent elongation. If cooled and constrained in this new shape, the polymer hardens and can maintain its new shape. When heated unconstrained above its activation temperature, this polymer returns to the shape in which it was cured. This process can be repeated without loss of memory shape or degradation of the material.

CURRENT OR INTENDED APPLICATION(S)
Repair patches, reconfigurable tooling/molding, deployable structures, passive environmental sensors, healable structures, reconfigurable (morphing) structures, clothing, orthodontic devices.

TESTING PROTOCOL(S)
Tensile strain below and above activation temperature, glass transition temperature, tensile and shear strength

MOVER
heat-activated biodegradable shape memory polymer (SMP)

MATERIALS ENGINEER
Andreas Lendlein, Center for Biomaterial Development, mnemoScience

SUMMARY
Biodegradable heat-activated SMP adds the functional attribute of degradation to a polymer that can be deformed up to four times larger or smaller than its original, permanent shape, and can "learn" a second permanent shape. Its shapeshifting, which is induced by heat, and its biodegradability are attributes compatible with medical materials.

CURRENT OR INTENDED APPLICATION(S)
As a suture material for medical keyhole surgery or stents; other uses could be carrier systems for cosmetic and beauty care products, optical, electronic, and mechanical parts for control systems and recycling concepts, and the repair of accident damage of cars.

TESTING PROTOCOL(S)
The material was heated, stretched, then cooled. Loose sutures were put on a rat, heated, and then the pressure of the strand was measured.

MOVER
light-activated "photo mobile" shape memory polymer (SMP)

MATERIALS ENGINEER
Tomiki Ikeda, Tokyo Institute of Technology

SUMMARY
Light-activated, or "photo mobile" shape memory polymer, is a lamination of two polymer films that can change shape and move due to different types of light exposure. The lamination consists of a cross-linked azobenzene liquid-crystalline (CLCP) layer thermal compression bonded to a flexible polymer film, typically low-density polyethylene (LDPE). The CLCP contracts when exposed to UV light and expands again when exposed to visible light. A "walking" polymer is the result, where "gait" is controlled by changing the position and the intensity of the light. The movements can be large and rapid-responsive.

CURRENT OR INTENDED APPLICATION(S)
As the dynamic element in a variety of simple, photo-activated devices. For any number of applications based on CLCP composites converting light energy directly into mechanical work, moving without batteries or electric wires.

TESTING PROTOCOL(S)
Through physical measurements, video, and photography.

MOVER
programmable/water active shape memory polymer (SMP)

MATERIALS ENGINEER
Drs. Wei Min Huang, Bin Yang, and Chuan Li, School of Mechanical and Aerospace Engineering Nanyang Technological University, Singapore

SUMMARY
Shape memory polymers may be synthesized with functionally gradient transition temperature at different parts and can be actuated by water in addition to some other convenient means, e.g., heat. A functionally gradient SMP is fabricated to be actuated by the absorption of water. This technique provides an approach for recovery of shape memory polymers inside, e.g., a human body, without any heating system and in a programmable manner following a prescribed sequence.

CURRENT OR INTENDED APPLICATION(S)
Biomedical devices like self-tightening suture in minimally invasive surgery, retractable stent, etc.; micro-/nano-machines for surgery, e.g., inside living cells; micro-/nano-surface patterning to alter surface characteristics, such as surface tension, surface reflection, drag, etc.

TESTING PROTOCOL(S)
Shape recovery ratio, activating stress, transition temperature, etc.

SELF
self-cleaning plastic surfaces

MATERIALS ENGINEER
Max Groenendijk, Applied Laser Technology Group, University of Twente

SUMMARY
Self-cleaning plastic surfaces are highly hydrophobic due to a rippling micro- and nano-scale surface structure. Repelled fluid carries foreign particles with it, as neither fluid nor particles have the chance to cling to the surface. The texture is injection molded with a two-step laser material removal process that utilizes a self-organizing effect inherent in most materials. The result is a field of perpendicular grooves and resulting pillars that repel water more cheaply than a process-intensive topical coating.

CURRENT OR INTENDED APPLICATION(S)
As a surface for any material where a clean, hydrophobic surface is desired, e.g., frost-free glass, boat hulls, solar energy panels. Also, wherever an extremely tactile-smooth surface is desired, as the microscopic air pockets created by the texture make it silky smooth to the touch.

HIGH-PERFORMANCE POLYMERS

SELF
microvascular self-healing composite

MATERIALS ENGINEER
Kathleen Toohey, Nancy Sottos, Scott White, Jennifer Lewis, and Jeffrey Moore, University of Illinois at Urbana-Champaign, the Beckman Institute for Advanced Science and Technology

SUMMARY
Microvascular self-healing composite is a polymer material with an embedded three-dimensional, pervasive network of channels carrying chemically reactive components to repair repeated damage. It can successfully be used to heal a crack in a coating up to 16 times. Healing can be accomplished with a single fluid network of healing agent among a solid catalyst incorporated into the coating, or with both healing agent and catalyst in two separate fluid networks.

CURRENT OR INTENDED APPLICATION(S)
Possible applications include microelectronics, composites, and coatings.

TESTING PROTOCOL(S)
The restoration of fracture toughness (resistance to crack growth) is used to quantify the amount of healing. The "healing efficiency" is defined as the fracture toughness after healing divided by the fracture toughness of the initial damage. Also, to determine when cracks occur, an acoustic emission sensor is placed on the specimen to detect acoustic events that correspond to crack formation or opening.

SUPER
electrically conductive polymer

MATERIALS ENGINEER
Lynn Loo, PhD, Associate Professor, Organic and Polymer Electronics Laboratory, Princeton University

SUMMARY
Polymers that conduct electricity have been in existence since the 1960s, but only recently have they become easy to process while maintaining a relatively high conductivity. While they do not have the conducting capacity of some metals, they can be less expensive and more flexible in terms of processing than metals. Lynn Loo's research is currently focused on water-dispersible, conductive polyaniline and several p-type solution-processable anthradithiophenes.

CURRENT OR INTENDED APPLICATION(S)
Though less conductive than their metal counterparts, the low cost and ease of processing make electrically conductive polymer potentially useful in low-end, large-area, lightweight specialty thin-film applications.

SUPER
graphene reinforced polymer nanocomposites

MATERIALS ENGINEER
Cate Brinson, Jerome B. Cohen Professor of Mechanical Engineering, Northwestern University

SUMMARY
Acrylic, poly(methyl methacrylate), or PMMA, is reinforced with graphene sheets forming a "nano-composite," which conducts electricity and exhibits superior thermal and mechanical properties. As a "reinforcer" in the PMMA matrix, exfoliated graphene is less rigid and has a larger surface area, better enabling it to affect the matrix structure.

CURRENT OR INTENDED APPLICATION(S)
Electrical or structural uses, especially where resilience to moisture or gas is required: aircraft, sports equipment, solar cells.

TESTING PROTOCOL(S)
Electroconductivity, levels of permeability, transparency, thermomechanic qualities.

SUPER
ultra-high molecular weight polyethylene (UHMWPE), or Spectra® Fiber

MATERIALS ENGINEER
Honeywell

SUMMARY
Ultra-high molecular weight polyethylene (UHMWPE) has extremely long molecular chains, making it very tough with the highest impact strength of any thermoplastic presently made. UHMWPE can be processed in several ways, including gel spinning to form oriented-strand fibers. The resulting fibers are 20 times stronger than steel and lighter and more durable than Kevlar, but have a lower melting point than nylon. It has a long history as a biomaterial.

CURRENT OR INTENDED APPLICATION(S)
Biomedical implants, ballistic equipment, climbing gear, bow strings, fishing line, high-performance sails, suspension for parachutes, kites, and water sports lines.

TESTING PROTOCOL(S)
Impact strength, tensile strength.

SUPER, MIMIC
aluminum oxide reinforced chitosan

MATERIALS ENGINEER
Ludwig Gauckler, Swiss Federal Institute of Technology (ETH) Zurich

SUMMARY
Aluminum oxide reinforced chitosan is a strong yet stretchy film composite inspired by nano structures found in natural shells, bone, and tooth enamel. It is made from alternating layers of chitosan and aluminum oxide platelets dispersed in ethanol. It is stronger than aluminum foil and can be stretched to expand by 25 percent of its size, while aluminum foil can expand by only 2 percent before breaking. The process for making the material is time and labor intensive, and will have to be evolved before becoming a commercial product.

CURRENT OR INTENDED APPLICATION(S)
Dental and bone implants, automotive industries, airplanes, bendable electronic devices, anywhere a strong, flexible foil is desired.

TESTING PROTOCOL(S)
Modulus of elasticity, tensile strength.

SUPER, MIMIC
plastic steel, or ultra-strong and stiff, optically transparent plastic nanocomposites

MATERIALS ENGINEER
Paul Podsiadlo, University of Michigan and Center for Nanoscale Materials (CNM) at Argonne National Laboratory

SUMMARY
Plastic steel, or ultra-strong and stiff, optically transparent plastic is a composite of montmorillonite clay nanotube sheets and poly(diallyldimethyl ammonium chloride) (PDDA) polymer. Inspired by nacre, the iridescent material produced by some mollusks, the structure is made through a layer-by-layer assembly technique to alternately deposit nanometer-thin layers of clay nanosheets and polymer. The final sheet material is composed of hundreds of layers. It has achieved record high stiffness and strength test results.

CURRENT OR INTENDED APPLICATION(S)
Optical, automotive, military (body armor), aviation, biomedical (coatings), and energy applications.

TESTING PROTOCOL(S)
Young's modulus, ultimate tensile strength.

BIOPOLYMERS

PROTEIN, MIMIC
marine bioadhesive

MATERIALS ENGINEER
**Paul Gatenholm, Chalmers University
of Technology, Sweden**

SUMMARY
The proteins involved in barnacle
adhesion can be used to create high-
strength, protein-based adhesives
that are able to cure while submerged
in water. As a biopolymer, it has an
extracellular matrix (ECM) similar to other
biological materials and is chemically
versatile. The bioadhesive adheres more
strongly to poly(methylmethacrylate)
(PMMA) than poly(dimethylsiloxane)
(PDMS).

CURRENT OR INTENDED APPLICATION(S)
Underwater applications and medical
applications like coatings for prosthetic
implants to serve as an interface between
the prosthetic and the bone or other
tissue.

TESTING PROTOCOL(S)
Dynamic contact angle (DCA)
measurements at different temperatures,
differential scanning calorimetry
(DSC), force vs. displacement, dynamic
mechanical analysis (DMA) as a
function of temperature, quartz crystal
microbalance with dissipation monitoring
(QCM-D) method.

PROTEIN
feather keratin polymers (FKP)

MATERIALS ENGINEER
**Justin Barone, PhD, Virginia
Polytechnic**

SUMMARY
Feather keratin polymer (FKP) is a
100 percent biobased polymer made
through reactive processing of poultry
feathers and glycerol. It is designed to
be performance and price competitive
with petroleum-derived polyolefins.
Therefore, its applications are widespread.
Feather keratin polymer can be designed
to degrade based on its application's
lifetime.

CURRENT OR INTENDED APPLICATION(S)
As a direct replacement for petroleum-
derived polyolefins such as polyethylene
(PE) and polypropylene (PP).

TESTING PROTOCOL(S)
Elastic modulus, stress at break, strain at
break comparable to polyolefin for similar
application. Degradation/stability tailor-
made for application.

LIPID
soybean oil foam (SIPS)

MATERIALS ENGINEER
**Dr. Richard Wool, ACRES, University of
Delaware and Cara Plastics**

SUMMARY
Soybean oil foam is a foamed polymer
made from modified soy-based resin.
The insulating foam can be made
from 100 percent soybean oil using a
CO_2 blowing agent. Mechanical and
thermal properties of the foam can be
controlled with chemicals additives or
the genetic engineering of the soybean
plants themselves. Cellulose fiber (from
waste paper), cardboard, and chicken
feathers have been used as structural
reinforcement. The foam is biocompatible
but not biodegradable.

CURRENT OR INTENDED APPLICATION(S)
Foam applications would be in
construction, appliances, packaging tank
pipe insulation, automotive seating and
insulation, sports shoes, and emergency
housing in situations of hurricanes,
tsunamis, etc. As building material it is
estimated to last at least 25 years.

TESTING PROTOCOL(S)
Biodegradability, water solubility.

LIPID
soybean oil plastic with carbon nanotubes

MATERIALS ENGINEER
Dr. Richard Wool, ACRES, University of Delaware and Cara Plastics

SUMMARY
Soybean oil plastic with carbon nanotubes (CNTs) is a composite that combines acrylated epoxidized soy oil (AESO) with CNTs for reinforcement. A comonomer of methacrylate (MMA) is used as a dispersing agent. The CNT reinforcement increases the composite's viscosity and rubbery modulus relative to pure AESO.

TESTING PROTOCOL(S)
Dynamic mechanical analysis, visual with SEM and optical microscopy.

LIPID
soybean oil polymer: Soy45-St32-Dvb15-(Nfo5-Bfe3)

MATERIALS ENGINEER
Professor Richard C. Larock and Dr. Yongshang Lu, Department of Chemistry, Iowa State University

SUMMARY
This soybean oil polymer has a composition of 45 wt. % soybean oils, 32 wt. % styrene, 15 wt. % divinylbenzene, 5 wt. % Norway fish oil ethyl ester and 3 wt. % boron trifluoride diethyl ether. It is a biobased thermoset plastic with an overall toughness resembling polyethylene or polystyrene. The vegetable oils have been used to replace petroleum-based monomers in today's plastics. Their properties are competitive with those of petroleum-based polymers, and the vegetable oil starting materials are significantly less expensive. Using vegetable oils in the synthesis of bioplastics can add value to agricultural products, which is economically important for agriculture and overall economy. Furthermore, these plastics exhibit outstanding damping and shape memory properties generally not available in petroleum-based plastics, which the market is often willing to pay a premium for.

CURRENT OR INTENDED APPLICATION(S)
These vegetable oil-based plastics can be used as alternatives to petroleum-based polymers such as polyethylene (PE) and polypropylene (PP) and unsaturated polyester resins.

TESTING PROTOCOL(S)
Young's modulus, break strength, elongation at break, glass transition temperatures (temperature at which material starts to flow), cross-link densities, temperature at the maximum degradation rate.

POLYSACCHARIDE
Solanyl® potato starch plastic

MATERIALS ENGINEER
Rodenburg Biopolymers B.V.

SUMMARY
Potato starch plastic is a biobased plastic that uses starch resulting from the potato processing industry. Production of Solanyl uses 65 percent less energy than polyethylene. It is fully colorable and can be used in combination with natural fibers and other biopolymers to create biocomposites. Solanyl is suitable for use in conventional injection molding machines, and has excellent flow properties enabling thin wall thicknesses. It can be used with a variety of controlled release mechanisms like diffusion, dissolving, biodegradation, photo degradation, etc.

CURRENT OR INTENDED APPLICATION(S)
It can be used as a direct replacement for polyethylene or polystyrene. It can be used in horticulture, agriculture, aquaculture, packing/transport, building and construction, promotional, and automotive industries. For example, in flower pots, tomato clips, cultivation tubes, promotional items, various clips for horticulture, CD- and DVD-trays, protection corners for packaging, cup holders, plant stakes/plant labels, brushes for street cleaning, bank protection, golf tees, golf balls (one-hitters).

POLYLACTATE
poly(lactic acid), Ingeo® biopolymer

MATERIALS ENGINEER
Waggener Edstrom, NatureWorks, LLC

SUMMARY
Ingeo biopolymer is a poly(lactic acid) (PLA). PLA is made from lactic acid derived from the starch of corn, wheat, sugarbeets, or sugar cane. It is strong, dimensionally stable, resilient, and more resistant to UV light than most other synthetics. It can be extruded, thermoformed, and turned into coatings and films. When spun or extruded into fibers it is called Ingeo™. Relative to polyethylene, it requires half the energy to produce and emits half the greenhouse gases.

CURRENT OR INTENDED APPLICATION(S)
Packaging, utensils, coatings, and textiles for apparel and furnishings.

TESTING PROTOCOL(S)
Strength, dimensional stability.

BACTERIA
poly(hydroxyalkanoates), Mirel®

MATERIALS ENGINEER
Brian Ruby, Metabolix

SUMMARY
Mirel poly(hydroxyalkanoates) (PHA) is a bioplastic produced in the leaf tissue of switchgrass. Mirel PHA is resistant to moisture and liquids, but is biodegradable, breaking down in the presence of naturally occurring microorganisms like bacteria, fungi, or algae. It has a high heat resistance and good impact strength and toughness. It is suitable for injection molding, extrusion coating, cast film, sheet, blown film, and thermoforming.

CURRENT OR INTENDED APPLICATION(S)
Food service and single-serve disposables (hot cups, lids, containers, caps and closures, food containers, beverage cartons), consumer goods (personal care, cosmetic packaging, razors, brushes, applicators, cell phones, pens, and office supplies), film (compostable bags, agricultural films, and netting), agriculture (mulch film, sod stakes, erosion-control netting, plant pots, and plant clips).

TESTING PROTOCOL(S)
Strength, temperature, water solubility, biodegradability, composting, etc.

BACTERIA
poly(Hydroxyalkanoates), styrene feedstock (PHA)

MATERIALS ENGINEER
Kevin O'Connor, University College, Dublin, Ireland

SUMMARY
Poly(hydroxyalkanoates) (PHA) is a biodegradable plastic made from fatty acids produced by a soil bacteria called *Pseudomonas putida*. The bacteria can consume styrene oil derived from heating existing polystyrene plastic in the absence of oxygen. The result is a process that converts petroleum-based plastic into a biodegradable form, and demands less energy than traditional recycling. Thirty-five percent of the feedstock polystyrene is converted into PHA, as the microorganisms use some of the styrene oil to live and grow. PHA will degrade in soil, water, septic systems, and backyard composts, but can be designed to have a long shelf life. PHA could potentially be made from other plastics besides polystyrene.

CURRENT OR INTENDED APPLICATION(S)
As a disposable material for medical uses, kitchenware, packaging film, etc. Can be used in heat-resistant and cold-resistant situations.

TESTING PROTOCOL(S)
Glass transition test, a heating test, biodegradability tests.

Collection:
Emerging
polymers

BIOCOMPOSITES

POLYSACCHARIDE, MIMIC
cellulose whisker reinforced plastic

MATERIALS ENGINEER
Stuart Rowan, PhD, Dustin Tyler, PhD, and Dr. Jeff Capadona, Case Western Reserve University and Advanced Platform Technology (APT) Center at Louis Stokes Cleveland, VA Medical Center

SUMMARY
Cellulose whisker reinforced plastic is a plastic with a dynamic modulus of elasticity. It is rigid when dry, but becomes floppy when wet. Inspired by sea cucumbers, the material consists of an elastic polymer infused with microscopic cellulose fibers from a trunicate. Hydrogen bonds form between the fibers, keeping the material rigid when dry; but when wet, the fibers bond to the water instead of each other, making the material more flexible. Another version under development is electronically activated.

CURRENT OR INTENDED APPLICATION(S)
Brain implants, clothing that transforms between flexible and rigid, drug delivery.

TESTING PROTOCOL(S)
Modulus of elasticity, water absorption

POLYSACCHARIDE, MIMIC
loofah fiber reinforced recycled plastic

MATERIALS ENGINEER
Elsa Zaldívar and Pedro Padrós, Base ECTA

SUMMARY
Loofah fiber reinforced recycled plastic is a composite made from dried natural fibers and recycled plastic. Dried loofah fibers constitute most of the fiber reinforcement, with other vegetable fibers including cotton netting and chopped corn husks. The recycled plastic is burnable and comes from discarded plastic waste. A specially designed machine acts as a meting unit, mixer, extruder, and cutting unit to produce a panel 0.5 meters wide and 120 meters long in one hour. Different mixes and thicknesses can be produced, creating different levels of flexibility, insulating qualities, and weight. Coloring occurs in the manufacturing process, negating the need for paint once used. Worn-out panels can be remade into panels until there is too high a vegetable fiber concentration, at which point they can be burned as a high-energy fuel.

CURRENT OR INTENDED APPLICATION(S)
Used for inexpensive panels as walls and roofing in building and construction. Panels can be used in a sandwich system with honeycomb or earthen filler for more substantial panels. The source materials are either recycled or renewable, making this is an important option in ecologically sensitive areas. Also, the panels are lighter and more resilient than traditional building materials, making them better for earthquakes or other natural catastrophes.

POLYSACCHARIDE
Cellulose nanopaper

MATERIALS ENGINEER
Lars Berglund, Biocomposites, Fibre and Polymer Technology, Swedish Royal Institute of Technology

SUMMARY
Cellulose nanopaper is a paper made of gently processed cellulose which retains much of its original structural integrity. Instead of subjecting wood feedstock to mechanical pulping, wood pulp is digested with enzymes and fragmented with a beater, keeping the nano-sized cellulose fiber structures intact. The nano fibers, about 1,000 times smaller than typical paper fibers, meet and connect more often, making a tough nanofibrillar network structure with high mechanical nanofibril performance. It is 214 times stronger than the average sheet of writing paper, and can withstand more force before breaking than cast iron.

CURRENT OR INTENDED APPLICATION(S)
Used to reinforce paper or tape, or to help create tougher replacements for biological tissue.

TESTING PROTOCOL(S)
Strength, flexural.

LIPID
**Glass fiber reinforced soybean oil
plastic(45) + styrene(45) + fishoil(8)**

MATERIALS ENGINEER
Richard Larock, Iowa State University

SUMMARY
This polymer is a biobased thermoset
plastic made from soybean oil, styrene,
and fish oil. Glass fibers can be added
to increase tensile and flexural strength.
A portion of 46 percent glass fibers has
been developed.

CURRENT OR INTENDED APPLICATION(S)
A replacement for PE and PS, particularly
in situations where more strength is
desired.

TESTING PROTOCOL(S)
Young's modulus, break strength,
elongation at break, glass transition
temperatures (temperature at which
material starts to flow), cross-link
densities, temperature at the maximum
degradation rate.

POLYLACTATE
flax fiber reinforced poly(lactic acid)

MATERIALS ENGINEER
**Jörg Müssig, Bremen College,
University of Applied Science/ISB
Biological Materials**

SUMMARY
Flax fiber is a natural fiber that is taken
from the skin of the stem of the flax
plant. It is stronger than cotton, but with
less elasticity. Flax fiber can be used to
reinforce poly(lactic acid) to increase its
impact, tensile, and shear strengths. Both
components are biodegradable, making
the composite biodegradable.

CURRENT OR INTENDED APPLICATION(S)
Automotive industry, packaging, guide
posts, radar unit housing (doesn't affect
radar like glass fibers do).

TESTING PROTOCOL(S)
Adhesion, interfacial shear strength
(IFFS) as measured by the single fiber
fragmentation test (SFFT), tensile, impact,
etc.

NOTES

1 This is a framework for thinking about "plastics in building" that the author has used in previous public and written discourse on the subject. See "All Plastics in Building," in *Permanent Change: Plastics in Architecture and Engineering*, edited by Michael Bell and Craig Buckley (New York: Princeton Architectural Press, 2014).

2 Another transect is implicit in this statement, though it is internal to individual corporations. It is one that tracks the commercial development of individual building products, and the associated research to formulate the right polymer in order to form the right product.

3 Harold J. Rosen. *Progressive Architecture*. 1960. "Plastics Permeate Specifications Sections," 206.

4 Armand G. Winfield, "The Plastics in Building Professional Activity Group of the International Society of Plastics Engineers, Inc.," in *Intersociety Reports on Plastics in Building Activities* (Washington, DC: NAS-NRC, 1962), 5.

5 Ibid.

6 Ibid.

7 *The State and Columbia Record*, Sunday, September 10, 1961.

8 Armand G. Winfield, "The Plastics in Building Professional Activity Group of the International Society of Plastics Engineers, Inc.," in *Intersociety Reports on Plastics in Building Activities* (Washington, DC: NAS-NRC, 1962), 8.

9 Z.S. Makowski, "Plastics Abroad," in *Plastics in Building*, ed. Irving Skeist (New York: Reinhold Publishing Corporation, 1966), 34–37.

10 R.M. Davies, *Plastics in Building Construction* (London: Blackie & Son LTD, 1965), 38.

11 The Plastics Institute, *Plastics in Building Structures: Conference Supplement No. 1 to the Plastics Institute Transactions and Journal* (Oxford: Pergamon Press, 1965).

12 A transect for translucent and opaque sheets, panels, and sandwich panels was tagged in the data set, though uncertainty about image copyright prevented its publication. Products are found documented as early as 1940. For some compelling photographic evidence of early translucent panel products see *House & Home*. 1956. "Look How Many Ways You Can Now Use … Plastics!" and *House & Home*. 1954. "New Products: Plastics for Building."

13 Albert G.H. Dietz's record of service on the NAS NRC may be tracked through the publication *National Research Council of the National Academy of Sciences Organization and Members*, an annual publication that identifies the various boards and topical subgroups composing those boards. We find here, for instance, that in 1951 the "Committee on Plastics and Elastomers" was under the Advisory Board on Quartermaster Research and Development. We find Dietz's involvement appearing as early as 1953 on the "Committee for Fabrics for Body Armor," which we might presume relates to composites. Dietz eventually transitions to committees related to plastics in building and construction. His involvement may be tracked until 1971.

14 Russell B. Akin, "The Plastics in Building Committee of the Manufacturing Chemists' Association," in *Intersociety Reports on Plastics in Building Activities* (Washington, DC: NAS-NRC, 1962), 26.

15 Albert G.H. Dietz, *Materials for Construction: Wood, Plastics, Fabrics* (New York: D. Van Nostrand and Company, 1949), 203.

16   Types of plastics included: acrylic, allyl (cast), cellulose, nylon (molding), polyethylene (molding), polystyrene (molding), polytetrafluoroethylene (yes, Teflon), polyvinyl butyral, vinyl chloride (and copolymer), vinylidene chloride molding, silicone rubber, polyester, phenol formaldehyde, melamine formaldehyde (molding), and urea formaldehyde (molding).

17   Albert G.H. Dietz, *Materials for Construction: Wood, Plastics, Fabrics* (New York: D. Van Nostrand and Company, 1949), fold out after page 320.

18   Ibid., xii.

19   Albert G.H. Dietz, "Chapter 9: Design Theory of Reinforced Plastics," in *Fiberglas Reinforced Plastics*, ed. Ralph H. Sonneborn (New York: Reinhold Publishing Corporation, 1954), 175–206.

20   Albert G.H. Dietz, *Plastics for Architects and Builders* (Cambridge, MA: MIT Press, 1969), 1. On the acknowledgment page Dietz notes that colleague Marvin Goody, Dupont's Russell B. Akin, and Executive Director of the AIA William Scheick reviewed the manuscript.

21   F.J. Rarig, *Progressive Architecture.* 1970. "Plastics and the Building Codes," 51, 96–99. Rarig is acting as the Secretary and Legal Counsel for Rohm & Haas Company. The result of the decision to refer to plastics as "plastics," especially in the context of the building code, is that we refer to classes of plastics such as "light-transmitting plastics" and "foamed plastics."

22   Albert G.H. Dietz, "The Plastics Laboratory at the Massachusetts Institute of Technology," in *Intersociety Reports on Plastics in Building Activities* (Washington, DC: NAS-NRC, 1962), 8.

23   The material properties in this collection are documented to account for different specifications of one material and sometimes these data can be contradictory. The data do not represent one manufacturer's product; rather, they are intended to be viewed as general properties to help readers understand the range of performance available for one "type" of polymer or elastomer.

24   Reinhard A. Sulzbach and Robert Hartwimmer. 1981. "Process for the Preparation of Aqueous, Colloidal Dispersions of Copolymers of the Tetrafluoroethylene/Ethylene Type." US Patent 4,338,237, filed June 22, 1981 and issued July 6, 1982.

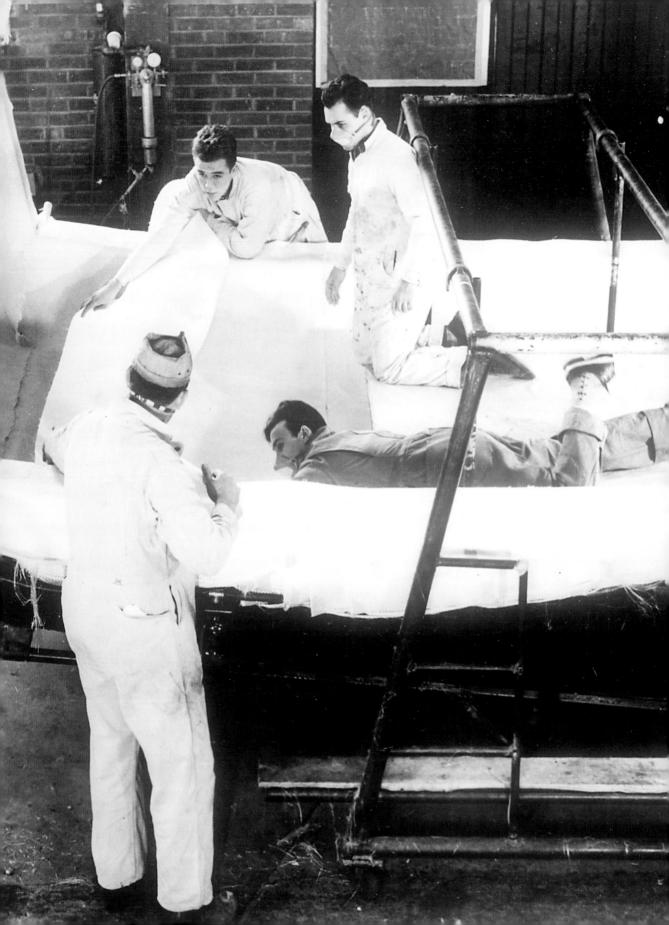

CHAPTER 04

ALL-PLASTICS

"All-plastics" prototypes, 1928–1973, indexed to a list of potential plastics for architecture

The conceptual position "all-plastics" manifested in the form of prototypes for houses, holiday cabins, and disaster relief shelters. Prototypes are indexed against the list of potential plastics found for use in architecture. Revealed is the repeated working of glass fiber reinforced polyester (composites) and polyurethane foam. Their use belies the "all-plastics" challenge to make a thing from the least number of parts possible in the form of stressed skins. Revealed also are the individual houses that deploy a broad palette of plastics, such as the 1956 All-Plastics House, or any one of the NAHB houses. This belies the "all-plastics" challenge to use as many plastics or building products made from plastics as possible. Both of these challenges are possible due to plastics' transmutability, or capacity to change from one form to another, and also polymer chemistries' customizability – or capacity to synthesize a select number of raw materials into diversely functioning materials for molding.

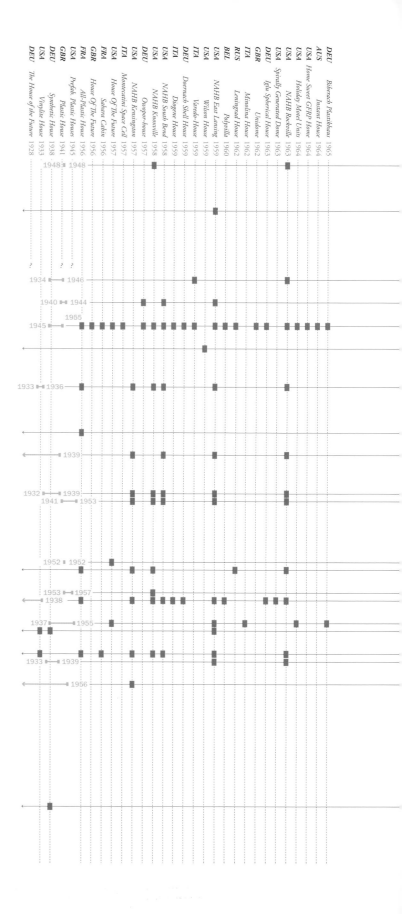

Plastics Found

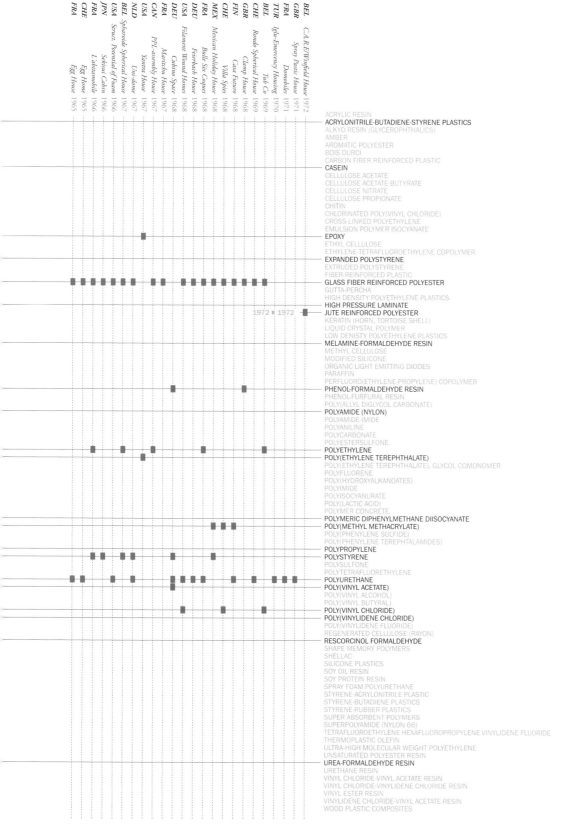

ALL. PLASTICS.

Dissecting the origins of "all-plastics," the opposing pole of "plastics in building," and a literal conceptual position to be taken up when working plastics, brings us directly to the diagnosis "monomaterialmania." This diagnosis finds its basis in the psychological term "monomania," which is the obsession with one thought or one idea. Yet this terminological collage provides an initial way of thinking about one material, plastics, and its ability to do everything. Aligning the word "material" more closely with the prefix "mono" gives us one material, a single material, a single material that can do everything. And everything in the context of architecture may mean structure, space, skin, form, aesthetics, or performance. One material is everything, or one material cures everything.

All. Plastics. Panacea or provocation?

When we take on the conceptual position "all-plastics," we challenge our design intentions with plastics as this position contrasts one where we might assemble differently functional materials across layers. For instance, the invention of a plastics building envelope, a task faced by "all-plastics" house authors, could have required a simple but generative game: Can one material mediate between all environmental flows as one single multi-functional plastics layer? Or is such a construct more rightly two material layers attributed differing functions but working together synergistically? Or three layers, four, five, six, or more where the attributes of each material comprising a layer is understood to provide a specific function, but also understood to be strategically juxtaposed to adjacent material layers?

1954, On working out an all-plastics construction logic

With the emergence of plastics comes searching for single forms that integrate multiple functions.

MISS GRAYBOFF:

ARCHITECTURAL FORUM

I have a question about glazing and also one about sky lighting. I have noticed that, with few exceptions, standard glazing techniques that have been developed for glass are used. Would it be possible in skylights to mold an integral flange on a skylight to eliminate the metal so that it could be directly flashed to a roof? And in the glazing with polyester panel, wouldn't it be possible to work up details that could be sent out to the architect showing the application directly to rough framing or to masonry?

MR. CROUCH:

TECHNICAL DIRECTOR, ILLUMINATING ENGINEERING SOCIETY

That's a long question. The thought is, can we develop the product with flanges and with accessory arrangements that will provide easy usefulness of the materials? Did I capture the thought of it?

MISS GRAYBOFF:

Well, more than just easy application. Make the material work to full advantage, make the plastic work as its own framing, if possible, rather than using metal framing that has to be developed to support it.

DR. PIERSON:

ROHM & HAAS CO.

I would like to point out that this whole development started with self-framing. It would be quite simple to form a dome that would be entirely self-flanging to eliminate most of the metal contact. But there are certain good fire insurance reasons for not doing that. That is why we put metal in the place where a minimum of metal is used to provide fire-proofing around the edge. Also it somewhat simplifies the attachment to the other roofing materials. John, do you want to comment?[1,2]

ALL-PLASTICS, THE FIRST CHALLENGE

Stating that a house is "all-plastics" is not the same as stating that a house is "mostly plastics." The term "all-plastics" is literal and applicable precisely because plastics are transmutable, or capable of changing from one nature or substance to another form or condition. The phrase "all-plastics" is dependent upon plastics' inherent form-assuming capacity. For instance, a washing machine tub, previously assembled from 32 parts, may be assembled from two parts thanks to plastics transmutability; or capacity to change state from liquid to solid and seamlessly fuse geometrical trajectories. This does not mean that the new two-part tub will perform the same as the 32-part tub, but that two-part tubs are possible.[3] An "all-plastics" anything – house or washing machine tub – might belie a challenge: Make that thing from the least number of parts possible. Make that house a single shell.

A monocoque, one shell, or single shell is also termed "stressed skin construction." Literally all of the stresses acting on such a skin – tension, compression, shear and torsion – are transferred through one thin doubly-curved surface. Here the prefix "mono" is at work again. A stressed skin may achieve such mechanical performance when it is a combination of two materials – when it is a composite – an elusive but seductive material state where both materials cease to exist, forming a third other material with properties that alone neither would muster. Wood veneers, paper, and glass fibers, any one of these plus the proper amounts of plastic resin, when combined, have the potential to achieve composite material status. Veneers, paper sheets, and fibers are considered tension-handling bits and will do a lot of work when properly arrayed, one next to, or one on top of each other, and combined with a resinous material. The proper portioning of resin, binding the tensioning bits together, allows loads to be transferred from one fiber to the other.

A stressed glass fiber reinforced polyester (GFRP) skin in contrast to, say, column, beam, and truss construction, where loads are transferred through members at right angles to each other, relies on the work-of-fracture, or the literal force it would take to remove a tension bit (a fiber) from its bonded state. A stressed skin in which two GRFP sheets are held apart from each other by a core – solid foam or honeycombed paper – creates a super sandwich where bonding between the facing sheets and core

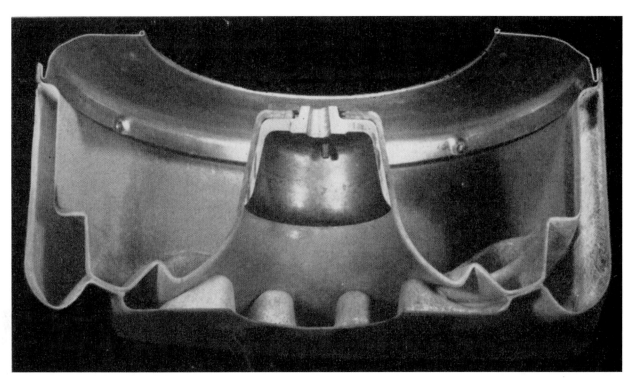

Fiberglass washing machine tub,
c.1950.

facilitates structural performance. In theory, a stressed skin is thinner and lighter and requires less material. Such construction logic was perfected with synthetic thermosetting adhesives in resinous form of the phenolic or formaldehyde family – phenol and resorcinol. These resins were used to adhere wood veneers in strips and sheets to form World War II bomber fuselage technology. While the opaque resins were the first, nearly concurrent with the perfection of fuselage forming, the translucent/transparent resins, polyesters in particular, were used to bind woven glass fibers into housings for radar equipment, body armor, and boats. Fiber reinforced plastics transferred into the commercial sector on a large scale, a simulacra for architecture, in the form of bath tubs, storage tanks, truck trailers, automobile underbodies, motor boats, and small sailing craft. And research continued on such large-scale applications as rocket boosters and rocket nozzles.[4]

When *Architectural Forum* suggests the potential to transfer resin and wood-ply composite technology to the logic of buildings in its June 1940 article "Plastics in Building," and thus foreshadow the conceptual poles "plastics in building" and "all-plastics," we may observe that they based such conjecture on very large performance-specific structures. The collage of photos not only includes a bomber's fuselage mold, it also includes parts – the aircraft's floor and door casing – both formed with the same technology.[5] Dr. Albert G.H. Dietz, in his book *Materials of Construction: Wood, Plastics, Fabrics* implies the same transference, and includes photographs of the bomber, its molded plywood aircraft ducts, and the roof of a station wagon. *Fiberglas Reinforced Plastics*, authored by Ralph H. Sonneborn of Owens-Corning Fiberglas Corporation and published in 1954, evidences many of the large-scale examples noted above and includes a chapter by Dietz titled "Design Theory of Reinforced Plastics." Irrespective of the architectural context associated with Dr. Dietz, Sonneborn simply notes the production of translucent corrugated fiber reinforced plastics construction panels for replacement of windows and skylights in industrial buildings, Quonset huts, homes, awnings, and porch coverings.[6] In the mid 1950s, when teams in the US and teams in France took up the "all-plastics" challenge – to make a house a single shell – they could proceed on the basis of established practices with composites and their numerical characterization as they have previously been implicated in the engineering of highly specific large-scale objects.

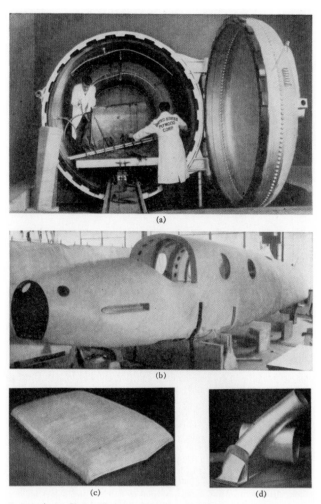

FIG. 10-12. (a) Placing Blanket-Enclosed Assemblage in Autoclave Preparatory to Curing under Steam Pressure. (b) Molded Plywood Fuselage. (c) Molded Plywood Station Wagon Roof. (d) Molded Plywood Aircraft Ducts. (*Courtesy United States Plywood Corporation.*)

Molded plywood single shell component,
from Dietz's *Materials of Construction*.

ALL-PLASTICS, THE SECOND CHALLENGE

Conversely, the phrase "all-plastics" might refer to another challenge altogether, one equally dependent on plastics' transmutability. "All-plastics" might also belie the challenge: Make that house from as many plastics products as possible. Plastics products – doorknobs, wall base, and floor tile – are dependent on plastics' capacity to assume a form like another material. An "all-plastics" house might be assembled from as many "all-plastics" products as possible. Such an approach invites the potential to exhibit what plastics can do – display the diversity of their application. To understand the impetus for such a position, we might consider nearly the

"All-plastics" interior domestic image, circa 1940s, from Post-War Buildings Studies No. 3, Plastics.

first such attempt at an "all-plastics" house named the "Vinylite House." It was positioned on the interior of the Hall of Science at the 1933 Chicago World's Fair. Its purpose was to demonstrate the potential use of plastics, to amalgamate nascent plastic building products – tiles, wall coverings, light fixture lenses, and structural insulated panels – into a compellingly domestic and plastic mis-en-scene. It was described in the press as "A full size bungalow made of entirely chemical materials," and dubbed "the house that chemistry built."[7]

Given plastics' indecipherability, such didactic attempts persist throughout the record. The Vinylite House's modern-day corollary might be said to be General Electric's Plastic House. However, in 1990 it contained only 30 percent plastics. Its originator at GE stated to *Popular Science* in 1988, prior to its construction, "This project's no stunt. It won't result in an 'all-plastic house of the future.' Plastics will be used only where they make sense functionally and economically."[8] Still, the house was established to demonstrate GE's plastics products, albeit as a proxy for a laboratory which allowed for switching in and out of said products as modules. The images of the house provided in the March 1990 issue of *Architecture* in "Plastics for the People" are strikingly reminiscent of those provided by *Architectural Record* in 1933 for the Vinylite House. The toilet, the shower, the relationship between floor, wall, and baseboard are all pictured. The mis-en-scene approach to these houses may be taken up generatively, as instructive toward taking up the challenge to create really "new" uses for plastics by acknowledging them for what they are known to be – building products made from plastics capable of permeating all systems of construction.

ALL-PLASTICS, SYSTEMATIZATION

This collection of "all-plastics" house prototypes suggests that the monocoque logic found purposeful in World War II composites technology should and can be transferred to domestic architecture, along with the factory production of houses. The first and most refined approach toward realizing the potential of glass fiber reinforced plastics was ultimately embodied in the Monsanto House of the Future. This project began development in 1954 through a research program established by the Monsanto Chemical Company at MIT for the express purpose of researching plastics as a building material. The iconic image of this house is summarized as four wings cantilevered to a central column. Each wing would be engineered in what can only be described as a single shell nested within a single shell, the space between shells allowing for the integration of insulation, mechanical air delivery, and return. Though, Ionel Scheins' All-Plastics House would be the first built – dating to 1956 – and was based on a semi-monocoque approach where curving fiber reinforced plastic shells, part wall and part roof, were attached to an internal fiber reinforced plastics frame.

But there are other ways of "stressing" surfaces, ways that involve the layering of materials, ways implicitly predicted by the Vinylite House of 1933 and proposals made separately by Kennedy and Kaiser who, in 1941 and 1945 respectively, asserted that stressed skin rectangular panels are possible with plastics and may be easily factory fabricated, thus supporting the mass production of housing. Where others including Cesare Pea differed from these predecessors was in the assertion that folding or molding panels could make them more rigid and, in some cases, more specific to their intended use. Pea's Montecatini Space Cell, 1957, was one of the earliest to panelize and fold FRP surfaces separated by foam fill, and to search for the right number of connections between panels. Projects such as the Leningrad House of 1962, Biberach Plastickhaus of 1965, and the Feierbach House of 1968 amply demonstrate this strategy. Further, stressed shell structures could be panelized, where the joints between panels might require various strategies for reinforcing to result in the whole structure. This strategy was employed by several "holiday house" products such as Uni-Dome of 1967, Bulle Six Coques, and Futuro. Each one of these paired the factory fabrication of lightweight curved GFRP panel kits with logistical packing know-how for shipment and on-site erection in far-away places.

This collection also suggests that the construction of stressed skins can be accomplished in ways that are independent of GFRP shells or sandwich panels. In situ whole-house foaming systems can be found by Bayer in the form of relief housing deployed both in Turkey and Peru and by Dow in a system for fusing strips of extruded polystyrene foam that rely on spiral generation to form a dome. Plastics properties paired with stressed skin logics can also yield novel construction processes as suggested by Philo Farnsworth III in the Yantra House, and Archigram in the Spray Plastic House, where Farnsworth depends on pressurization of an interior to "bind" a structure together, and Archigram depends on dissolving foam formwork to – voila! – reveal a GFRP structure.

ALL-PLASTICS, RESEARCH

Sponsored programs of research were initiated for both "all-plastics" approaches. In addition to the research program at MIT, sponsored by the Monsanto Chemical Company and resulting in the Monsanto House of the Future, two others from the collection may be identified. One was sponsored by the US National Association of Home Builders (NAHB), resulting in the NAHB's Research House program, and the other was sponsored by the US Department of State, resulting in the University of Michigan's Architectural Research Laboratory's (ARL) Structural Potential of Foam Plastics for Housing in Underdeveloped Areas.

Each research program was sustained over six years or more and produced a number of visible and built works. Curiously, they are divided between two paradigms – the US NAHB's is more closely affiliated with a "mis-en-scene" paradigm, and the ARL's more closely affiliated with a "monocoque" paradigm. The NAHB's Research House program, initiated in 1957 (the same year as the installation of the Monsanto House of the Future in Anaheim, CA), would produce five houses in six years, across various climate zones in order to demonstrate plastics use and facilitate industry, regulatory, and public comprehension of plastics in building. The designation of "research house" by the NAHB and associated research foundation meant that the house would be developed with the consultation of manufacturers; it would be constructed by a contractor, and sold on the open market. Analysis of plastics performance per system occurred throughout all stages – design, construction, and inhabitation. These houses demonstrated, first, the installation steps and, second, the performance of discrete "systems," such as structural insulated panels, vapor barriers, coatings and paints, perimeter EPS foam board, plastics piping for supply and waste, interior trim, hinges, cabinetry, etc.[9] In contrast, the ARL's program sought to quantify the mechanical properties of foam plastics – spray foam polyurethane as it was formed into a variety of structural logics. The ARL built successive prototypes, documenting both the construction and testing process, and quantifying the results.

Sponsored programs of research may also be found that seek to apply "all-plastics" to housing – post-war, post-natural disaster, and housing development. The ARL's program in part was motivated by and addressed housing shortages by exploring these technologies. Bayer

AG's development of its Iglu House spiral generation system was a direct response to searching for a system to rapidly create housing post-disaster. Armand Winfield, who previously organized the exhibition *Plastics, A New Dimension in Building* with the Society of the Plastics Engineers (SPE) in 1961, and generally tracked activities with plastics throughout his career, would summarize the Bayer AG efforts and others including his own at the SPE National Technical Conference in 1972. His summary relays events from late in the preceding year when the United Nations Industrial Development Organization (UNIDO) took up the subject of low-cost housing and plastics with 25 architects, biochemists, engineers, and government officials.

ALL-PLASTICS, A PHRASE AND CONCEPTUAL POSITION IN CIRCULATION

Given two "challenges" which might frame one's approach to an "all-plastics" architecture, varied approaches toward systematization, and programs of research, the accumulation of journal articles, conference proceedings, books, and pamphlets suggest that determining the feasibility and desirability of an "all-plastics" architecture, regardless of the approach taken, figured early into discussing how we should use plastics, both publicly and privately. For instance, point number 85 of the report *On Plastics and Building*, the pamphlet published in 1944 by the British Federation of Plastics, upon assessing the use of plastics for rebuilding after the war, addresses "all-plastics" thusly:

> 85. All-Plastics Buildings. Complete structures for exhibition purposes have been built more or less exclusively of plastics. In an American example, walls and doors were made by moulding vinyl resin over fireproofed paper pulpbord, the walls being formed in 2-ft. panels held in position by steel rods. The floor tiles were moulded from a vinyl resin moulding powder and the skirting and ceiling mouldings were extruded sections. A "synthetic house" was exhibited at the Building Exhibition in Frankfurt in 1938. The walls were stated to be of light-weight blast-furnace slag concrete blocks jointed with urea-formaldehyde resin, there flooring of another resin not specifically described; the tiles and timber were of laminated plastics and the plumbing of plastics. But there is a world of difference between an exhibition model, designed to attract attention regardless of cost or practicability, and a house intended for permanent use. While many

of the features described as having been exhibited were doubtless of practical interest, the designers would probably be the last to wish to convey the impression that all were suitable for immediate application to building practice.[10]

Another more publicly and professionally targeted use of the phrase "all-plastics" can be found in a 1945 advertisement published in *Architectural Forum*. The Celanese Corporation of America, with the tag line "Touch Comfort is an important quality of Lumarith plastics," makes a case for warming up the bathroom environment or the chill of ceramic tile with Lumarith accessories: toilet seat covers, switch plates, towel bars,

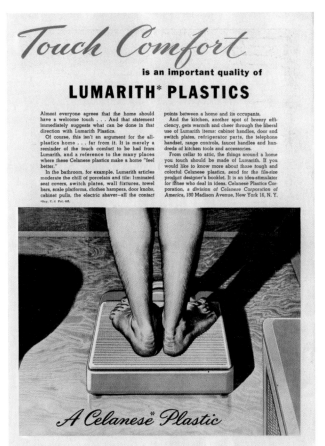

Advertisement, Lumarith plastics, Celanese Corporation appearing in *Architectural Forum*, 1945.

doorknobs, all that is handled and touched.[11] While they argue for the application of plastics to these products, which were once materially bound otherwise, they make an exception to their proliferation thusly: "Almost everyone agrees that the home should have a welcome touch … And that statement immediately suggests what can be done in that direction with Lumarith Plastics. Of course, this isn't an argument for the all plastic home … far from it."[12]

Any one of these statements could be in response to the fact that between the years of 1928 and 1972 one can find 50 or more "all-plastics" houses which involved several countries, including the United States, France, England, Italy, Germany, Russia, Bulgaria, and Sweden. Those endeavoring to fabricate an "all-plastics" house faced the sometimes insurmountable task of forming thermally treatable and flowing materials into structural units, forming plastic joints and connections, and finishing plastic surfaces.[13] Rather than molding plastic into structural shapes, many regarded plastics as colorful, translucent, cost-effective materials capable of being factory fabricated into very thin and structurally continuous shells or sheets with a high strength-to-weight ratio. GFRPs (glass fiber reinforced polyester or plastics) were largely the material of choice for many of these proposals, but also acrylics, HPs (high-pressure laminate) and PVCs (polyvinyl chlorides) were explored alongside a range of foam types.

Serial review of these prototyping efforts may be found published, and some extensively, in the originating data set of 200 plus articles from popular architectural press, and may also be found in conference proceedings and books from the *Plastics in Building* collection. Serial review may likewise be found in Arthur Quarmby's *The Plastics Architect* from 1974, the one book from this period that attempts to summarize the potential relationship between architecture and plastics. Significant serial review, a two-page list with hand-drawn thumbnails of 69 houses, is found in the April 1970 issue of *AD*, under the title "Plastics Buildings," the editors of which chose to republish it from the November 1969 issue of *Architektur und Wohnformen*. A Rosetta stone of sorts, this list clearly indicates that the collection provided herein is by no means comprehensive, and also indicates that such manageable prototyping efforts were tracked and treated separately from serial review of short- and long-span structural concepts for plastics found through authors like Z.S. Makowski.

Such incessant serial review of accomplished prototypes indicates that these efforts were tracked and represented to us as evidence of a newly emerged regime of fabrication techniques, structural paradigms, and forms. Early journal articles collecting palettes of building products under the conceptual position "plastics in building" were joined in the 1960s with technical reviews on how to work and detail plastics into whole architectures representative of the use state "all-plastics." Of these, *Casabella*'s "Designing with Plastics," a reoccurring article appearing across multiple volumes in 1967, is the most comprehensive – we could go on collecting. What comes to the fore in the total cumulative record of journal articles collected from popular architectural press, and implied by the selected collection of prototypes, is how nearly normal an "all-plastics" architecture appeared up until 1972 – and it was an appearance made possible through prototyping.

"ALL-PLASTICS" HOUSES, 1928–1972

This collection of 50 plus "all-plastics" prototypes – limited to houses, holiday cabins, and disaster relief shelters – contains works with plastics searching for new forms, new logics, new techniques, alongside those seeking normalization paths for building products made from plastics, and those implementing prefabrication schemes based on plastics. Some will want to affiliate these "all-plastics" houses with the search for construction logic, a monocoque, a single stressed skin, or an insulated stressed skin, requiring the literal input of energy and know-how to work plastics resin binders and glass fibers. And some will want to affiliate these "all-plastics" houses with the search for plastics' usefulness, described and sold as a cheap, lightweight, durable alternative to other materials. Each schema may be found amply represented in this collection, and likely embodied by the same house along with other assertions culled from this collection:

An all-plastics house is not possible, nor is it practical.

An all-plastics house is inevitable.

An all-plastics house redefines architecture and structural paradigms.

An all-plastics house is a factory-built house, thus combined with the dream of prefabrication.

An all-plastics house is lightweight, deployable, and the basis for disaster relief.

An all-plastics house demonstrates plastics products.

An all-plastics house provides cost-effective housing.

An all-plastics house indicts architecture to define practices for research.

Etc.

1928
Ideal Home, House of the Future
R.A. Duncan, ARIBA and S. Rowland Pierce
Ideal Home Exhibition
London, England

CONSTRUCTION LOGIC
A stainless steel frame filled with a plastic representing material which was described by
the *Daily Mail* as a "thin, horn-like, impervious substance" proposed in multiple colors and
patterns. The presentation of the material was totalizing – it formed interior and exterior
walls and floors – a provocation matched with the house's allusions to ships and cars,
implicitly promising prefabrication and mechanization on a grand scale. It is known as
the first House of the Future exhibited at what was to become a long-standing *Daily Mail*
tradition.

PLASTICS FOUND
Materials unknown.

IN PRINT
Ideal Home, vol. XVII, March 1928, pp. 240–241
The Daily Mail, advertisement "Daily Mail Ideal Home Exhibition" February 18, 1928.
Deborah S. Ryan. *The Ideal Home through the 20th Century*, London: Hazar Publishing, (1997),
    55–56.

APPLIED SCIENCE EXHIBITS . . . ground floor of the Hall of Science

VINYLITE HOUSE

We have seen in other exhibits the tremendous changes which have been brought about by the Age of Alloys. Now the world is at the threshold of what may be an equally important advance—the Age of Plastics.

A Preview of the Age of Plastics

Union Carbide and Carbon Corporation has pioneered experiments with synthetic molding compounds, made from basic materials similar chemically to acetylene gas. The history of vinyl resins goes back to 1838, when a French chemist, Regnault, first created them. Today, vinyl resin castings, as heavy as 150 pounds each, have been successfully produced by Union Carbide engineers.

To demonstrate some of the possible uses of Vinylite the Corporation has constructed a house made largely of this material, across the corridor to the north of the Corporation's other Applied Science Exhibits. It consists of a living-room, kitchen, and bathroom.

Colorful

As you enter you walk on Vinylite tiles — alternately green and yellow in the living-room, black and gray in the kitchen, coral and blue in the bathroom. The walls are of large flat plates of Vinylite. The doorknobs, electric switch plates and the porcelain-like lacquer of the refrigerator are of the same material. Even the doors and windows are Vinylite-molded. It is possible to make Vinylite as transparent as glass, though in this case the window panes have been made translucent rather than transparent.

In the kitchen, a beautiful cabinet is surfaced entirely of Vinylite. About the only articles in the house which do not consist of this amazing material are the plumbing fixtures, the gas range, the bathtub, and such incidentals as upholstered furniture and draperies.

In the living room, the walls, colorful floor tiles, frosted windows and lighting panels, and many decorative accessories are made of Vinylite

Acids from fruits or other foods won't stain this kitchen, nor will hard knocks chip the refrigerator and kitchen cabinet

In the bathroom the uses for Vinylite range from toothpaste and shaving cream tube caps to towel-racks, and include toothbrush handles and hand-rails on the bathtub.

As an added element of interest a Pyrofax cabinet, supplying gas to the kitchen, is installed in the courtyard.

A Versatile Material

Vinylite is truly a versatile compound. It is a plastic material which can be molded into strong panels for walls or rolled into thin sheets almost as transparent as glass. It can be spread over wood and metal in the form of hard washable lacquers. It can be shaped into innumerable articles of

Even in the courtyard the flagstones have been designed with Vinylite floor tiles. The shingles, too, are Vinylite composition

everyday use — toothbrush handles, cigarette boxes, tumblers, trays. Many of these have been placed before your eyes in the Vinylite house. Get acquainted with them now for in a few years perhaps it may be possible to order a factory-made Vinylite home which will be delivered in convenient sections and erected ready for you to move into within a few days.

Vinylite naturally has many other uses. Today long playing flexible phonograph records are made of it because it is nearly unbreakable and because it does not shrink or warp under varying weather conditions. This latter is important because shrinkage or warpage would disturb the delicate sound track and distort the tone.

Applied Science brochure featuring the Vinylite House.

CASE STUDY
1933
THE VINYLITE HOUSE

Sponsored by the Carbide and Carbon Chemicals Corporation
and the John B. Pierce Foundation
Hall of Science, *Century of Progress Exhibition*
Chicago, Illinois

The Vinylite House typifies the murky relationship between emergent materials, normalization routes for those materials, and acts of prognostication. It can be considered in multiple contexts: Its industrial "parent" was the Carbide and Carbon Chemicals Corporation (CCCC); its site, the Hall of Science at the 1933 *Century of Progress Exhibition* in Chicago, Illinois, was organized by the National Research Council (NRC); and arguably its true neighbors, "future houses," were hundreds of yards away as part of the fair's *Homes of Tomorrow* exhibition. Just three rooms – a bath, a kitchen, and a living-room, basic spatial ingredients – were offered for installation as an "experimental research project."[14]

Vinylite, a thermoplastic vinyl resin produced by CCCC since 1927, was applicable in small consumer-oriented products – ash trays, cigarette boxes, and water tumblers. Vinylite's translucent, opaque, dyed, and pigmented versions were available as sheets, molding powders and coatings for metal and wood. The house deployed these materials, polyvinyl acetate (PVAC), and polyvinyl chloride (PVC) copolymers, as molded wall panels, molded doors and windows, and floor tiles, replacing wood and metal versions with vinyl ones – green, yellow, black, gray, coral, blue, and translucent white. The house, at a scale unprecedented for plastic materials, still emphasized touch; a doorknob or drawer pull – vinyl legitimized in residential intimacy.

At the bidding of the NRC, the Hall of Science was organized according to "branch of science" rather than "country of origin," a noted departure for this World's Fair.[15] The chemistry branch claimed the house as well as other plastic products. In this context, the house would recast future living with chemical rather than formal or spatial provocation. *Scientific American*, with the October 1933 article titled "Synthetic Houses," described it as "a dwelling that came out of a test tube," and provides an exterior image, referring to it formally as a bungalow.[16]

Architectural Record, in one last bid to claim affiliation to the house, published it with frontispiece fanfare. "New Housing Designs and Construction Systems," a compilation by Theodore Larson in the journal's January 1934 issue, identifies the house's wall panels as "factory-fabricated sectional wall panels of molded Vinylite." A wall section through the system reveals each wall panel's "insulating and deadening core" of "fire-proofed paper pulp board."[17] This 3" assembly claimed to provide better thermal performance than a 16" clay masonry/air space/lath and plaster assembly, trending building systems' thick-to-thin shift, and foreshadowing plastics' developmental route.

In addition to the Vinylite House, Larson compiled 22 proposals exploring efficient affordable housing; three are the *Century of Progress Exhibition*'s "Homes of Tomorrow," the Stran-Steel House, Design for Living, and the House of the Future. The house's appropriation by Larson is significant: He places the house in an architectural rather than chemical context and wittingly provides what the Hall of Science could not – the Vinylite House immediately juxtaposed to its "future" neighbors. In hindsight the house managed to portend a future, a vinyl future, more exacting than any other.

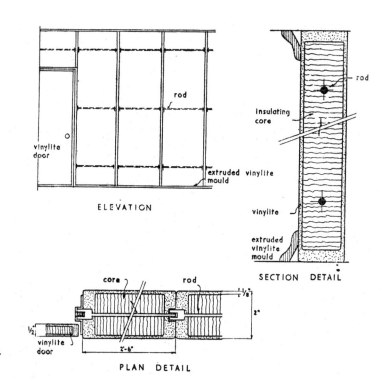

Vinylite House,
wall panel
construction logic.

PLASTICS FOUND
PVAC   Polyvinyl acetate
PVC   Polyvinyl chloride

IN PRINT
"Synthetic Houses," *Scientific American* 149 (4) (October 1933): 180.
C. Theodore Larson. "New Housing Designs and Construction Systems," *The Architectural Record* 75 (1934): 3–35.
British Plastics Federation, *Plastics, Post-War Building Studies No. 3*, London: HMSO (1944), 20.
Joseph B. Singer. *Plastics in Building*, London: The Architectural Press (1952), 26–27.

1938
Synthetic House
Sponsored by I.G. Farben Industrie
German Building Exhibition
Frankfurt, Germany

CONSTRUCTION LOGIC
Walls adopted cues from masonry construction. Stone facsimiles were made from a
mixture of blast furnace and urea formaldehyde. "Mortar" was likewise achieved using urea
formaldehyde. But the approach here was to demonstrate the use of plastics throughout,
hence flooring is described as made from "synthetic resins," as are "insulating materials."
Interior finishes such as tiles and furniture are described as laminated plastics and laminated
wood. PVC pipe, commercially known in Germany by the brand name "Igolit," was used to
demonstrate the plumbing system.

PLASTICS FOUND

UF	Urea formaldehyde	"Mortar" between "stones"
	Synthetic resins	Floors, insulating materials
	Laminated plastics	Tiles
	Laminated wood	Furniture
PVC	Polyvinyl chloride (Igolit)	Plumbing

IN PRINT
Joseph B. Singer, *Plastics in Building*, London: The Architectural Press (1952), 27.
British Plastics Federation, *Plastics, Post-War Building Studies No. 3*, London: HMSO (1944), 20.

1941
Plastic House, unbuilt
T. Warnett Kennedy and Sam Bunton
Building Plastics Research Corporation
Glasgow, Scotland

CONSTRUCTION LOGIC
"Plastic House" was planned as a government-funded Post-World War II experiment in
mass-produced housing based on available plastics. In reference to the Post-War Planning
Committee of the British Plastics Federation, Kennedy argued that mass production was
the only fabrication method by which housing demand could be met and that the post-
war plastics industry must find a solution. Kennedy describes the house as thoroughly
"all-plastics," a statement inclusive of its structural members – "stanchions, beams, purlins,
bracers" – as well as exterior and interior walls, floor, windows and window frames, doors and
door frames, roofing membrane and stairs. Kennedy's 1941 account of the project published
in *British Plastics and Moulded Products* implied that testing of certain components was
complete. Ultimately the production scheme remained unrealized.

PLASTICS FOUND
Material unknown, though listed as "resinous."

IN PRINT
T. Warnett Kennedy, "The First All-Plastics House", *British Plastics and Moulded Products*
(October 1941): 138.
Joseph B. Singer, *Plastics in Building*, London: The Architectural Press (1952), 28.

Collection:
"All-plastics"
houses

Henry J. Kaiser Company's
Prefabricated Plastic House.

CASE STUDY
1945
PREFABRICATED PLASTIC HOUSE, UNBUILT

Henry J. Kaiser Company, Housing Division
Oakland, California

Light, affordable, durable, plastic – the essence of a residential premise put forth in *Prefabricated Plastic Houses*, a report published by the Henry J. Kaiser Company in 1945. "It is recognized that a plastic material capable of being economically moulded or pressed into structural and finished parts for houses would be the ideal type of materials for the mass production of houses and could conceivably displace all existing methods of house construction." A salvo indicative of its context, the post-World War II housing crisis, one million or more homes needed annually, and industry's "can do" attitude.

Kaiser's housing division proposed a venture – plastic materials partnered with prefabrication, formed into a house with requisite landscape, produced as a kit-of-parts, shipped and erected on site. The Henry J. Kaiser Company was seemingly experience-rich in conceiving and producing such large-scale industries, yet implementation was contingent upon the cost of plastic, both its raw material and forming cost, as well as plastics' properties. And, current plastic materials were deemed insufficient: "At the present time, the Kaiser Company is experimenting with a plastic which promises to provide a low-cost plastic, possessing all the essential requirements for the construction of houses. Pending further developments, however, the exact composition and characteristics of this plastic material are being withheld."[18] Regarding this mystery material, the report provides one other detail; experiments with it sought to reduce its specific gravity, thus reducing the cost of transporting house components.

A plastic tongue-and-groove panel, structural and insulated, measuring 3" thick, 10" wide, and as tall as necessary was proposed as the basic prefabricated part for wall and roof applications. Designed as tongue-and-groove and weighing less than 80 lbs, the unit's collapsing of structural and thermal concerns, repeatability, and modularity fit the house's affordability mandate and was conceived to meet the report's "ideal panel" criteria:[19]

1. A lightweight unit containing within its own dimensions structural elements sufficient to take the normal stresses to which a house is subject.
2. Can be readily stored and transported.
3. Can be easily handled at the time of erection.
4. Can be cut, sawed, and nailed.
5. Provides complete heat insulation.
6. Provides essential acoustical values.
7. Is vermin-proof and termite-proof.
8. Is fireproof.
9. Provides a bonding surface for gypsum plaster or Plastite cement or any finishing plaster.
10. Is waterproof.
11. Is inexpensive.

PREFABRICATED PLASTIC HOUSES

HENRY J. KAISER COMPANY
HOUSING DIVISION
OAKLAND, CALIFORNIA
JANUARY, 1945

Henry J. Kaiser's
Prefabricated Plastic Houses,
report cover.

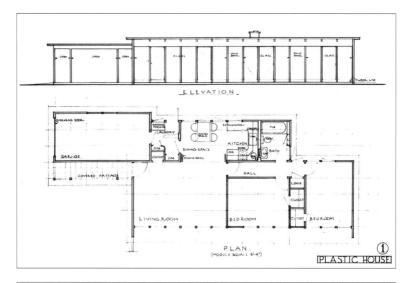

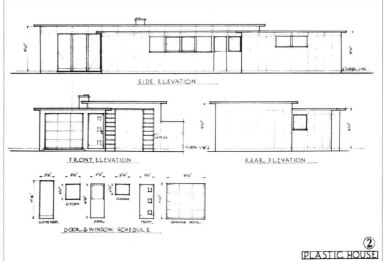

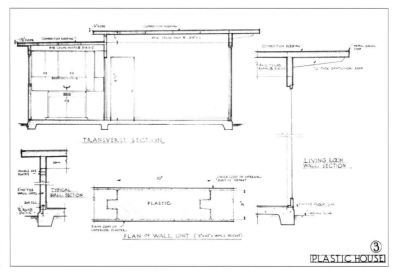

Fabrication documentation
for the Prefabricated
Plastic House.

A proposed construction scenario follows what would now be considered a structural insulated panel system (SIPS): For a wall unit, a 2 × 4 sole plate would be bolted to a concrete foundation; plastic panel units would be nailed to the sole plate and connected at their uppermost edge by a double top plate. The double top plate would serve as the bearing point for roof trusses, transferring their load to the structural plastic panels. Plastic panel units would, likewise, span from joist to joist, forming the house's flat roof and finished ceiling.

Yet, the Prefabricated Plastic House's interior and exterior were not finished in plastic; plastics are not offered as perceptible or tactile. The exterior is finished in "plastite," a cementitious layer applied over plastic panel units, concealing panel joints. The interior floors are finished in linoleum and wood, and the interior walls are finished in plaster. The only divergence away from common taste is formal, rather than material. The house toes the "modernist box" line; an exception noted in the proposal but justified as "easily mass-produced."

The Kaiser Company speculated on plastics' structural value and potential structural optimization in service of prefabrication. Plastics and prefabrication, a material and a manufacturing methodology, remain a seriously unfulfilled but essential pairing.

PLASTICS FOUND
Materials unknown.

IN PRINT
Housing Division of the Henry J. Kaiser Company. "Report on Prefabricated Plastic Houses" (January 1945).

CASE STUDY
1956
ALL-PLASTIC HOUSE

Ionel Schein, Yves Magnant, and R.A. Coulon
Salon des Arts Menagers (The Household Arts Exhibition)
Sponsored by *Elle*, Salon des Arts Menagers, Charbonnages de France, Houilleres du Nord,
and built in collaboration with Gaz de France and the French Chemical Industry
Paris, France

A whole functioning house completely made of plastics, 1,000 square feet – three bedrooms,
a living room, dining room, kitchen, bath, requisite storage, and mechanical services.
Prosaically named the All-Plastic House; it is considered "the first," or more correctly "the first
built," and it made its debut in 1956 at France's annual *Household Arts Exhibition*.

Ionel Schein, the project's concept originator, with Y. Magnant and R. Coulon, would realize
this house, its structural systems, floors, walls, and roof, exterior and interior finish, and
mechanical systems, under Schein's all-plastic material directive: Deploy as many plastics
as possible. The structural system's photographic documentation during fabrication would
come to characterize the house as the first all-fiber reinforced plastic (FRP) house.

Black-and-white photographic documentation, however, obscures a diverse plastic palette
including acrylic transparent/translucent surfaces and furniture, vinyl carpets, vinyl textiles,
nylon textiles, and melamine door panels and sinks – all of which came in colors appointed
by the project's color consultant Antoine Fasani.

In plan, the house was a circle, a more rationalized form of Schein's early ever-curving
sketches.[20] A circle cut like a pie into eight slices or wedges; three extended outward as
bedrooms. Each wedge was a module, conceived individually as a whole structural unit and
connected to its neighbor.

Given the structural system's unprecedented architectural application of FRP, it appears that
the design team sought to optimize the number of pieces comprising the house into the
smallest number of manageable "wholes." Slice the house into four wedges? The house's
components could have been too large and too heavy to manage. Slice the house into sixteen
wedges? The house's joints and connections would be too numerous. Eight may have seemed
just right to Schein's team, which sought to test strategies for prefabrication as well as mass
production. But eight wedges, it seems, would serve merely to regulate structural lines.

Ralph H. Sonneborn, who published his book *Fiberglas Reinforced Plastics* two years prior to
the All-Plastic House's installation, coinciding with ten years of fiberglass production, would
advise the following:

> The greatest success of FRP can be laid to the successful integration of many parts
> into one unit. A classic example is that of a washing machine tub where 32 metal
> parts were replaced with two FRP moldings. This practice can give: less fastening, less
> inspection, less tooling, less part design, less fabrication, less molding, less weight …
> Also, additional strength and rigidity are obtained by using curved sections.[21]

FACING PAGE

All-Plastics House, on exhibition:
(top) exterior; (bottom) interior.

Sonneborn refers to the monocoque, the single shell, a structural paradigm worked out through the World War II airplane industry. Single shell FRP constructions appear throughout Sonneborn's manual including Henry J. Kaiser's Darien sports car, several boat hulls, a radome, and several smaller household and personal items. By 1955, the year Schein proposed the All-Plastic House, FRP practices were fully defined: its resins, fibers, and methods of manufacture including contact molding, vacuum bag molding, vacuum injection molding, and other techniques.

In retrospect, it is conceivable that the design team did not have to do what it ultimately did do – eschew the pursuit of the "single shell" and redefine each module with "frame and fill" logic. Each wedge, individually, became one-eighth floor frame and one-eighth wall frame. A crew of 40 would lay-up successive glass fiber and resin layers to form these full frames into integrated column, beam, and brace units. Roof and wall panels were laid up in a similar manner and most closely resembled shell construction. The floor panels were plastic-impregnated honeycomb sandwiches, an exception to the all-FRP structure. The black-and-white photography taken by Jean Bouvry, the staff photographer for Charbonnages de France, embody the energy expended to finish parts, heave them into place, and troubleshoot misalignments between numerous joints and connections.

The house was more on the order of 50 plus parts – a kit-of-parts, or set of components, organized around its central but concealed specter, one FRP column doubling as a downspout. Two prefabricated FRP units, a bathroom and kitchen, more directly resembling the monocoque paradigm, were installed in the house after frame assembly. After the exhibition, the All-Plastic House was disassembled and reassembled 14 times before permanent installation at the headquarters of Charbonnages de France.

Architecture Aujourd'hui would publish a preview, in January of 1956, a month prior to its debut in Paris. Just five months after its debut, *Architectural Review*'s Bruce Martin would chronicle the house in an article titled "How Should We Use Plastics?," proposing to temper the all-plastic agenda: "The all-plastic house is a valuable experiment, but could bring about an unbalanced environment. Plastic components must be treated as valuable additions to our stock of building parts, but not as replacements and substitutes for all of them."[22] The house would be published for several years, seemingly showing a surge of interest after the successful and sustained debut of Monsanto's House of the Future.

 The following year, Schein, Magnant, and Coulon would prototype the mobile hotel container and propose the mobile library container – both projects fully formed as a single shell, monocoque, structural and spatial solutions. Yet, ten years after the All-Plastic House, an unexpected prologue appears. *Art and Architecture* published what they claimed to be an unsolicited essay authored by Schein and titled "The Phenomenology of Research." It is a full-formed rant against architecture and its legitimization by current modes and practices of research. The house is never mentioned – but like its concealed central column, certainly remains a specter clouding Schein's trajectory.

FACING PAGE

**All-Plastics House:
(row 1) primary structural frame with roof and floor infill
(row 2, left) GFRP molding, laying up fiberglass
(row 2, middle) demolding
(row 2, right) molding the screen wall at the house entrance
(row 3, left) infilling floor panels
(row 3, middle) infilling roof panels
(row 3, right) concealed central column and primary downspout**

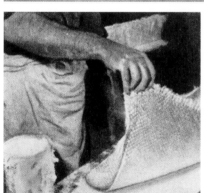

All-Plastics House, post-finishing of exterior wall.

PLASTICS FOUND

PMMA	Polymethyl methacrylate	Transparent and translucent surfaces
PMMA	Acrylic resins	Seat coverings
PE	Polyethylene	Piping, electrical insulation, household utensils
GFRP	Polyester resin	Composite binder for structural walls, floor joists, and roof
PS	Polystyrene	Telephone and household utensils
	Superpolyanides	Textiles
PF	Phenolic plastics	Household appliances
	Glycero phthalies	Paints
PVC	Polyvinyl chloride	Carpet, electrical insulation, household accessories
MF	Melamine resins	Color panels, sink

IN PRINT

R. Coulon, Y. Magnant and I. Schein, "Wohnhaus," *Bauen und Wohnen* (July 1959): 236–239.

"Ganz-Plastik-Haus auf der Ausstellung Arts Menagers 1956 in Paris," *Bauen und Wohnen* 11 (February 1957): 56–60.

"Mobile Hotelkabine," *Bauen und Wohnen* 11 (February 1957): 60.

"La premiere maison tout en plastiques," *Architecture Francaise* 173–174 (January 1957): 44–48.

Bruce Martin, "How Should We Use Plastics?" *Architectural Review* (August 1956): 134, 136, 138.

Lionel Schein, "Una casa costruita totalmente in plastica," *Domus* (May 1956): 15–18.

"La premiere maison tout en plastiques," *Architecture Francaise* 173–174 (January 1957): 44–48.

1956
House of the Future
Alison and Peter Smithson
Ideal Home Exhibition
London, England

CONSTRUCTION LOGIC
A tableau for living replete with walls made from GFRPs which appeared as continuous uniform surfaces, integrating voids for storage, negotiating turns with curves, thus eliminating from the eye mechanical joints and fastening. Several types of chairs demonstrated stressed skin, single shell logic.

PLASTICS FOUND

GFRP	Polyester resin	Walls, furniture
PMMA	Polymethyl methacrylate	Furniture
PA	Polyamide (nylon)	Clothes worn by inhabitants
	Laminated plastics	Freestanding furniture and cabinets

IN PRINT
Deborah S. Ryan. *The Ideal Home through the 20th Century*, London: Hazar Publishing (1997), 112–116.

1956
Sahara Cabin
Societe Spair
Douai, France

CONSTRUCTION LOGIC
The cabin, developed for "research purposes" was a stressed skin insulated structure. The number of parts or components and panelization strategy is unknown, as are the deployment methods.

PLASTICS FOUND

GFRP	Polyester resin	Structural skins
PVC	Polyvinyl chloride	Foam between GFRP skins

IN PRINT
Listed in the compilation "Plastic Buildings," *AD* (April 1970): 167–168.

The Monsanto House of the Future.

CASE STUDY
1957
THE MONSANTO HOUSE OF THE FUTURE

Richard Hamilton and Marvin Goody, Massachusetts Institute of Technology
Dr. Albert G.H. Dietz, Structural Engineers
Sponsored by Monsanto Chemical Corporation and Massachusetts Institute of Technology
Anaheim, California

Does a structural from exist that is unique to plastics? The team at MIT, Richard Hamilton, Marvin Goody, and Albert G.H. Dietz, defined a research program on the subject of plastics in building – and proceeded to search for a way to use plastics to the fullest extent possible, correctly and with a high degree of quality. Dr. Dietz's direct and numerical understanding of plastics and composites was integral to an approach that was about what plastics are, as much as it was about what they were not. Dietz, presenting the engineering aspects of the house at the second meeting of the Plastics Study Group at MIT, stated directly: "All the way through the attempt has been made to use plastics as plastics and not as replacement for other materials. Other materials will be used where it is plainly indicated that plastics are not the materials for the job. On the other hand, the analysis has been made in such a way as to use plastics if possible. If they can do the job, plastics will be used in this house."[23] Ultimately, the team focused on engineering a stressed skin U-shape made from GFRPs and insulated with urethane foam. Dietz described the U-shape as a "croquet-wicket shaped affair," and the team would pursue characterizing its attributes as it interacted with all sorts of phenomena – dead loads, live loads, sun, water, and shade.

The stressed skin U-shape cantilevered and arrayed as wings from a central square concrete column – two U-shapes per side. The construction logic was direct – a U-shape must connect once to another U-shape and once to the central column. Sixteen parts and sixteen points of connection per part. The house, in its final form, appears cushioned. This is because the U-shapes, which were really hyperbolic parabolids, were formed to increase structural spanning capacity. Prior to manufacture, the U-shapes were prototyped and put through a series of tests: loading and effects of wind, heat, and cold, and temperature variation.

Plastics, or in this case, polyester resin, expands considerably with heat. Given the thermal asymmetries of a cantilevered U-shape – the top of the "U" would be exposed to sun, the bottom of the U in constant shade – the team would have to rightly determine where this expansion would be greatest on the top side of the U-shape. And they would need to calculate the difference between the GFRP exterior skin's temperature, which they estimated would reach 170 °F, and the GFRP interior skin's temperature, which they estimated would stay at 70 °F. The presence of a tree casting shade would likewise throw off the uniform expansion and contraction of each plastic shell. The joints, then, the gasketing and sealing, are all in service of these cantilevered U-shapes doing what they were intended to do: quickly define space without column or panel and rightly expand and contract.

Addressing the BRI in 1963, W. Allen Cleneay of the Monsanto Chemical Corporation provides a brief report on six years of use and over 6,000,000 visitors. Fitting the conference theme, his comments are directed to the performance of the house – the tracking of U shape deflection, and the maintenance and wear of the exposed FRP skins. His overall conclusion is commentary on the feasibility of an "all-plastics" architecture:

> It is possible to draw three significant conclusions from testing work done as part of this project.
>
> These are:
>
> 1. It is feasible to design and construct large structures made from plastics materials which will perform their engineering functions in a satisfactory manner.
>
> 2. The mechanical properties of plastics materials can be defined by the same engineering concepts as are applied to standard materials of construction.
>
> 3. The engineering design of structures made from plastics materials can be accomplished by the same engineering principles as are applied to structures made of standard materials of construction.[24]

PLASTICS FOUND

GFRP	Polyester resin	Structural "U-bent" skins
PUR	Urethane foam	Sprayed insulation between skins
PF	Phenolic resin	Binder in floor panel with paper honeycomb core
PMMA	Polymethyl methacrylate	Windows and light diffuser in kitchen ceiling, interior movable louvers in bedroom.

IN PRINT (SELECTED)

"Experimental house in plastics," *Arts and Architecture* 72(1955): 20, 21, 35.

Hamilton und Goody, Architekten, R.P. Whittier, E.D. Schopach, M.F. Gigliotto, Ingenieure, "Monsanto-Haus." *Bauen und Wohnen* (July 1959): 240–242.

Marvin Goody and Richard Hamilton. "The Plastic House of the Future," *Industrial Design* (August 1957): 50–57.

"House of the Future," *The Architect and Building News* (October 9, 1957): 480–485.

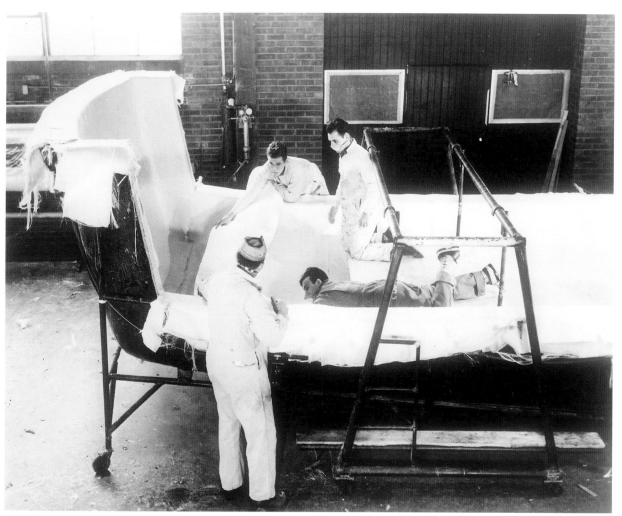

GFRP lay-up of U-shape.

Trial attachment of U-shape.

Stress test of U-shape.

The Monsanto House of the Future, on-site construction.

ALL-PLASTICS

Collection:
"All-plastics"
houses

The Monsanto House of the Future, interior.

1957
Montecatini Space Cell
Cesare Pea
Milan Exhibition (Triennale di Milano)
Milan, Italy

CONSTRUCTION LOGIC
A living unit, 4.8 × 4.8 × 2.7 meters assembled from a structural panel consisting of phenol-impregnated paper honeycomb skinned with GFRP panels. The living unit could be joined to other self-similar boxes, forming an entire house.

PLASTICS FOUND

GFRP	Glass fiber reinforced polyester resin	Stressed skin panel, wall, roof, and floor
PF	Phenol formaldehyde	Adhesive, stressed skin panel

IN PRINT
"Casette 'prestampate,'" *Domus* (September 1957): 4–5.
Z.S. Makowski. "The Structural Applications of Plastics," *Plastics in Building Construction*, edited by R.M. Davies, London: Blackie & Son Limited (1965), 57.

1957
Research House – Kensington
National Association of Home Builders (NAHB) Research Foundation
Kensington, Maryland, USA

CONSTRUCTION LOGIC
The first house built in a multi-year, multi-house research project, initiated to demonstrate installation and performance of plastics building products. This house, based on normative wood frame techniques, was finished outside and inside with plastics where their use was technically and commercially viable.

PLASTICS FOUND

	Resorcinol	Structural adhesives
	Alkyd primer, acrylic top coat	Exterior finish, paint
	Urethane	Exterior caulking
	Alkyd	Interior paints and coatings
PET	Polyethylene terephthalate	Interior films and sheeting
PVC	Polyvinyl chloride	Interior fabric, flooring
PA	Polyamide	Interior rugs, door handles, lock sets, valves, shower head
MF	Melamine-formaldehyde resin	Laminate for interior cabinetry
PMMA	Polymethyl methacrylate	Bathtub and shower enclosure, lighting
PE	Polyethylene	Vapor barrier, valves
PS	Polystyrene	Insulation
	Phenolic	Foamed-in-place insulation

IN PRINT
"Chapter 20: NAHB Research Houses Demonstrate Plastics," in *Plastics in Building*, edited by Irving Skeist, New York: Reinhold Publishing Corporation, 1966.

1957
Owopor-house
Interbau (Industrial Exhibition)
Berlin, Germany

CONSTRUCTION LOGIC

A structural insulated panel assembly, 2" thick consisting of "Styropor®," or EPS foam faced with GFRP.

PLASTICS FOUND

EPS	Expanded polystyrene	Insulating core
GFRP	Polyester resin	Binder in skins

IN PRINT

Z.S. Makowski. "The Structural Applications of Plastics," *Plastics in Building Construction*, edited by R.M. Davies, London: Blackie & Son Limited (1965): 59.

1958
Research House – Knoxville
National Association of Home Builders (NAHB) Research Foundation
Knoxville, Tennessee, USA

CONSTRUCTION LOGIC

A house, based on normative wood frame techniques, was finished outside and inside using plastics where technically and commercially viable per system. This is the second of five demonstration houses built and analyzed between 1957 and 1963 as part of the NAHB Research House program.

PLASTICS FOUND

	Alkyd primer, acrylic top coat	Exterior finish, paint
VDF	Vinylidene fluoride	Exterior flashing
	Alkyd	Interior paints and coatings
PET	Polyethylene terephthalate	Interior films and sheeting, gel coat on cabinets
PVC	Polyvinyl chloride	Interior flooring, piping for cold water supply and waste, drain and vent
MF	Melamine-formaldehyde resin	Laminate for interior cabinetry
PMMA	Polymethyl methacrylate	Bathtub and shower enclosure
PE	Polyethylene	Vapor barrier, piping
PS	Polystyrene	Insulation
	Phenolic	Foamed-in-place insulation
ABS	Acrylonitrile-butadiene-styrene	Piping for cold water supply
PP	Polypropylene	Piping for hot water supply
PS	Polystyrene	Drainage field
GFRP	Polyester resin	Plumbing fixtures

IN PRINT

"Chapter 20: NAHB Research Houses Demonstrate Plastics," in *Plastics in Building*, edited by Irving Skeist, New York: Reinhold Publishing Corporation, 1966.

1958
Research House – South Bend
National Association of Home Builders (NAHB) Research Foundation
In association with Koppers Company Inc, and Rensselear Polytechnic Institute
South Bend, Indiana, USA

CONSTRUCTION LOGIC
Structural insulated sandwich panels – an EPS foam core faced with redwood plywood skins
– are the bearing walls for the third of five research houses built by the NAHB. Plastics are
demonstrated throughout and performance is analyzed per the program's mission.

PLASTICS FOUND

EPS	Expanded polystyrene	Foam core of stressed skin panel, load-bearing and non-load-bearing exterior wall applications, and interior partitions
	Urethane	Exterior coating (liquid), caulking
	Butyl	Exterior caulking
VDF	Vinylidene fluoride	Exterior flashing, interior fabrics
	Alkyd	Interior paints and coatings
PET	Polyethylene terephthalate	Interior films and sheeting, gel coat on cabinets
PVC	Polyvinyl chloride	Interior sheeting, flooring, lighting
PA	Polyamide	Interior rugs
MF	Melamine-formaldehyde resin	Laminate for interior cabinetry
PS	Polystyrene (high impact)	Cabinet drawers
PE	Polyethylene	Vapor barrier
GFRP	Polyester resin	Plumbing fixtures

IN PRINT
"Chapter 20: NAHB Research Houses Demonstrate Plastics," in *Plastics in Building*, edited by
Irving Skeist. New York: Reinhold Publishing Corporation, 1966.

1959
Diogene House
Turin, Italy

CONSTRUCTION LOGIC
Round in plan and referred to as having "vaulted sandwich shells." The number of parts or
component and panelization strategy is unknown, as are the deployment methods.

PLASTICS FOUND

GFRP	Polyester resin	Exterior structural skins and interior partitions
PS	Polystyrene	Foam between GFRP skins (likely EPS)

IN PRINT
Listed in the compilation "Plastic Buildings," *AD* (April 1970): 167–168.

━━━
1959
Doernach Shell House
Rudolf Doernach
Stuttgart Plastics Exhibition
Stuttgart, Germany

CONSTRUCTION LOGIC
A double curving shell assembled from a plastics foam core covered with aluminum skins on the exterior and GFRP on the interior. Doernach commented at the *Plastics in Building Construction* conference, Battersea College of Technology, September 25, 1964:

> I have even used my own family as guinea pigs to live in a plastics house which I built in 1957 and which was then heated electrically, and competitive in price but rather unusual in shape. This all started at a time when no one in the industry knew what Young's Modulus in a certain foaming system would be. I, personally, became so fascinated about using these new materials that I simply continued working with them and I am running now what you would call a development and research group, working with industry and for industry in co-operation with State materials testing institute.[25]

PLASTICS FOUND

GFRP	Polyester resin	Structural skins
PS	Polystyrene	Foam between GFRP skins

IN PRINT
Z.S. Makowski. "The Structural Applications of Plastics," *Plastics in Building Construction*, edited by R.M. Davies, London: Blackie & Son Limited (1965), 59.

━━━
1959
Varedo-House
Bertolotti
Snia-Viscosa
Milan, Italy

CONSTRUCTION LOGIC
Rectangular in plan and referred to as having "vaulted sandwich shells." The number of parts or component and panelization strategy is unknown, as are the deployment methods.

PLASTICS FOUND

GFRP	Polyester resin	Structural skins
EP	Epoxy	Exterior coating
?	Unknown	Foam between GFRP skins

IN PRINT
Listed in the compilation "Plastic Buildings," *AD* (April 1970): 167–168.

1959
Wilson House
Ralph Wilson Sr.
Wilsonart International
Dallas, Texas

CONSTRUCTION LOGIC
Interior surfacing in multicolored plastic laminate throughout, which served to demonstrate the company's product and to test various new and novel applications.

PLASTICS FOUND
MF   Melamine formaldehyde   Interior surfacing throughout

1959
Research House – East Lansing
National Association of Home Builders (NAHB) Research Foundation
East Lansing, Michigan, USA

CONSTRUCTION LOGIC
Structural insulated sandwich panels – an EPS foam core faced with asbestos cement – are the bearing walls for the fourth of five research houses built by the NAHB. Plastics are demonstrated throughout and performance is analyzed per the program's mission.

PLASTICS FOUND

EPS	Expanded polystyrene	Foam core of stressed skin panel, load-bearing and non-load-bearing exterior wall applications, floor and roof applications and interior partitions
CS	Casein (modified)	Exterior adhesives
	Alkyd and acrylic	Exterior paints and coatings, site applied
	Urethane	Exterior coating on roof panels, shop applied
	Butyl	Exterior caulking
	Alkyd, acrylic	Interior paints and coatings
PVC	Polyvinyl chloride	Interior fabric, flooring tile and sheet, bathtub, trim door faces, duct facing, baseboard, piping
MF	Melamine formaldehyde	Interior paints, laminate for interior cabinetry
PET	Polyethylene terephthalate	Interior films and sheeting, gel coat on cabinets
PUR	Polyurethane (foam)	Core of interior doors
PA	Polyamide	Lock sets, wiring, lighting, plumbing valves, hinges
PS	Polystyrene (high impact)	Cabinet drawers
PE	Polyethylene	Shower enclosure, vapor barrier, piping
PVDC	Polyvinylidene chloride	Piping
GFRP	Polyester resin	Plumbing fixtures

IN PRINT
"Chapter 20: NAHB Research Houses Demonstrate Plastics," in *Plastics in Building*, edited by Irving Skeist, New York: Reinhold Publishing Corporation, 1966.

Wilson House, interior.

—
1960
Polyvilla
Laddyjensky
Generales Leemanns and S.A. Plsascobel, Belgium

CONSTRUCTION LOGIC
Frame and fill structural approach comprising PVC pipe filled with concrete as the primary structure that is subsequently infilled with 50 mm thick stressed skin panels.

PLASTICS FOUND

GFRP	Polyester resins	Stressed skin panel, outer and inner skins
PS	Polystyrene	Foam between GFRP skins
PVC	Polyvinyl chloride	Structural members filled with lightweight concrete

IN PRINT
Listed in the compilation "Plastic Buildings," *AD* (April 1970): 167–168.

—
1962
Leningrad House
Russia

CONSTRUCTION LOGIC
Eight individual GFRP frames, rigidized by folded geometry and seemingly continuous corners, are sequentially connected one to the other to form a self-supporting box with a foam core that sits atop a concrete base.

PLASTICS FOUND

GFRP	Polyester resins	Outer and inner structural skin, bath, sink and stairs
PS	Polystyrene	Foam panels
PMMA	Polymethyl methacyrlate	Windows

IN PRINT
"Plastic House 1962," Pathe Newsreel, Film ID 2639.22, 1962.
Z.S. Makowski. "The Structural Applications of Plastics," *Plastics in Building Construction*, edited by R.M. Davies, London: Blackie & Son Limited (1965), 58.

—
1962
Unidome
English Electric Co., England

CONSTRUCTION LOGIC
Geodesic "radome" system comprising 16 triangular panels proposed as a "weekend" or "holiday" house.

PLASTICS FOUND

GFRP	Polyester resins	Stressed skin panel, outer and inner skins

IN PRINT
Listed in the compilation "Plastic Buildings," *AD* (April 1970): 167–168.

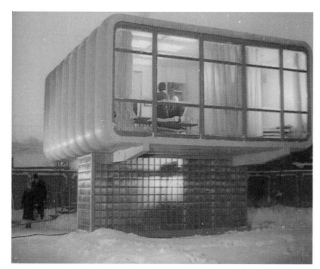

The Leningrad House.

Collection: "All-plastics" houses

1962
Minolina House
Giulio Minoletti
Milan

CONSTRUCTION LOGIC
Structural insulated panel with aluminum facing.

PLASTICS FOUND

PUR	Polyurethane (foam)	Core of stressed skin panel

IN PRINT
Listed in the compilation "Plastic Buildings," *AD* (April 1970): 167–168.

1963
Iglu Spherical House
Joseph Schreyogg & Co.
West Germany

CONSTRUCTION LOGIC
Semi-monocoque molded stressed skin panels insulated and bolted together.

PLASTICS FOUND
Glass fiber reinforced plastic (GFRP)
Polystyrene foam

IN PRINT
Listed in the compilation "Plastic Buildings," AD (April 1970): 167–168.

1963/1966
Spirally Generated Dome
Architectural Research Laboratory, University of Michigan
With Dow Chemical Company
Ann Arbor, Michigan, USA

CONSTRUCTION LOGIC
A dome, 45 feet in diameter, is created by laminating/fusing together 4" thick boards of XPS when fed into a novel machine connected to a centering arm. The dome's completion time was 12 hours and it could be lifted onto its foundation by 30 individuals. The process is credited to Donald R. Wright, who was an engineer with the Dow Chemical Company.

PLASTICS FOUND

XPS	Extruded polystyrene	Shell forming entire dome

IN PRINT
Architectural Research Laboratory, The University of Michigan. "Architectural Research on Structural Potential of Foam Plastics for Housing in Underdeveloped Areas" (May, 1966).
"Spun Plastic Shapes a School," *Progressive Architecture* 48 (July 1967): 156–157.

FACING PAGE

Spirally Generated Dome:
(row 1, left) foundation
(row 1, right) machine laying up foam
(row 2, left) complete prior to cutting
(row 2, right) lifting onto foundation
(row 3, left) cutting the opening
(row 3, right) exterior
(row 4) exterior.

1963
Research House – Rockville
National Association of Home Builders (NAHB) Research Foundation
Rockville, Maryland, USA

CONSTRUCTION LOGIC
Structural insulated sandwich panels – an EPS foam core faced with asbestos cement –
are the bearing walls for the fifth of five research houses built by the NAHB. Plastics are
demonstrated throughout and performance is analyzed per the program's mission.

PLASTICS FOUND

EP	Epoxy	Exterior adhesives, interior grout
	Alkyd and acrylic	Coal tar enamel
	Urethane	Interior coating
	Acrylic	Interior paint
PVF	Polyvinyl fluoride	Exterior film on wall panels
MF	Melamine formaldehyde	Interior paints, laminate for interior cabinetry
PET	Polyethylene terephthalate	Gel coat on cabinets
ABS	Acrylonitrile-butadiene-styrene	Closet doors, waste piping
PVC	Polyvinyl chloride	Windows, trim, baseboard
PS	Polystyrene (high impact)	Door core (foam), cabinet drawers
PE	Polyethylene	Vapor barrier, insulation
PMMA	Polymethyl methacrylate	Lighting (fiber reinforced)
PA	Polyamide	Lock sets, wiring, lighting, plumbing valves, hinges
PVDC	Poly vinylidene chloride	Piping
GFRP	Polyester resin	Plumbing fixtures

IN PRINT
"Chapter 20: NAHB Research Houses Demonstrate Plastics," in *Plastics in Building*, edited by
Irving Skeist, New York: Reinhold Publishing Corporation, 1966.

1964
Holiday Motel Units
Holiday Manufacturing Company
USA

CONSTRUCTION LOGIC
A GFRP shell rigidized with "reinforcement ribs." The number of parts or components and
panelization strategy, as well as the foaming strategy, is unknown, as are the deployment
methods.

PLASTICS FOUND

GFRP	Polyester resin	Outer skin
PUR	Polyurethane (foam)	Core of interior doors
PF	Phenolics	Interior plywood partitions

IN PRINT
Listed in the compilation "Plastic Buildings," *AD* (April 1970): 167–168.

1964

Home Sweet GFRP Home
Goodyear Aerospace Corp.
USA

CONSTRUCTION LOGIC
A GFRP self-supporting shell. The number of parts or components and deployment strategy
is unknown.

PLASTICS FOUND
GFRP   Polyester resin   Outer skin

IN PRINT
Listed in the compilation "Plastic Buildings," *AD* (April 1970): 167–168.

1964

Instant House
Randall, Rober, Waren; Randavel Product Pty.
Australia

CONSTRUCTION LOGIC
Semi-monocoque molded stressed skin panels insulated and bolted together.

PLASTICS FOUND
GFRP   Polyester resin   Outer skin, inner skin not explicitly stated
        Foam (type unknown)   Core

IN PRINT
Listed in the compilation "Plastic Buildings," *AD* (April 1970): 167–168.

1965

Biberach Plastikhaus
Dieter Schmid
Biberach, Germany

CONSTRUCTION LOGIC
GFRP stressed skin panel system attached to a steel structural frame. Wall panels are both
solid units and window units made more rigid by integrating molded geometries. Window
units are very deep and highly articulated, integrating passive thermal strategies such as self-
shading of glass and natural ventilation.

PLASTICS FOUND
GFRP   Polyester resin   Exterior structural skins and interior partitions
PS   Polystyrene   Foam between GFRP skins (likely EPS)
PVC   Polyvinyl chloride   Interior plug at panel joints.

IN PRINT
"Della Germania: una casa in plastic," *Domus* 433 (1965): 16–17.

1965
Egg House
Pascal Hausermann
France

CONSTRUCTION LOGIC
Molded GFRP insulated panels, joined together to form a "bubble shape." The number of parts or bubble panelization strategy is unknown, as are the deployment methods.

PLASTICS FOUND

| GFRP | Polyester resin | Outer skin and inner skin |
| PUR | Polyurethane | Foam core between skin |

IN PRINT
Listed in the compilation "Plastic Buildings," *AD* (April 1970): 167–168.

1965
Egg Home
Pascal Hausermann
Switzerland

CONSTRUCTION LOGIC
Molded GFRP insulated self-supporting panels to form a "bubble shape." The number of parts or bubble panelization strategy is unknown, but appears to have fewer parts then the "Egg House" of the same year.

PLASTICS FOUND

| GFRP | Polyester resin | Outer skin and inner skin |
| PUR | Polyurethane | Foam core between skin |

IN PRINT
Listed in the compilation "Plastic Buildings," *AD* (April 1970): 167–168.

1966
L'abitamobile
Societe Isolfen
Paris, France

CONSTRUCTION LOGIC
Stressed skin insulated panels noted as self-supporting. The number of parts or components and panelization strategy is unknown, as are the deployment methods.

PLASTICS FOUND

GFRP	Polyester resin	Outer skin and inner skin
PUR	Polyurethane	Foam core between skin

IN PRINT
Listed in the compilation "Plastic Buildings," *AD* (April 1970): 167–168.

1966
Sekisui Cabin
Komatsu Plastic Industry
Japan

CONSTRUCTION LOGIC
A stressed skin insulated structure. The number of parts or components and panelization strategy is unknown, as are the deployment methods.

PLASTICS FOUND

GFRP	Polyester resin	Exterior structural skins and interior partitions
PS	Polystyrene	Foam between GFRP skins (could be extruded or expanded)

IN PRINT
Masanori Kanai and Kaoru Maeda. "Part C: Japan," in *Plastics in Building*, edited by Irving Skeist, New York: Reinhold Publishing Corporation (1966), 391–396.

Fabrication, anticlastic umbrella shade.

CASE STUDY
1966
STRUCTURAL POTENTIAL OF FOAM PLASTICS
FOR HOUSING IN UNDERDEVELOPED AREAS

Stephen C.A. Paraskevopoulos, Project Director
Architectural Research Laboratory
The University of Michigan
Ann Arbor, Michigan, USA

Searching for the structural potential of foam plastics was an all-inclusive research program at the University of Michigan's Architectural Research Laboratory – one which sought to apply structural theory, foamed plastics, and a range of techniques for working them to the problem of housing. The program originated in 1962, was sponsored by the US Department of State, and dared to explore a range of foam forms – shells, folded plates, and planar structures – aligned with the various construction techniques of generating a dome spirally with foam, spraying it, paneling it, forming it into flexible but rigid systems, and filament winding around it.

Report cover.

Clearly stated research objectives framed the overall investigation, as the research team recognized from the outset that new attributes and applications were being sought for foam, mostly the polyurethane spray foam variety, a material that was not so stiff, prone to creep, puncture, and easily destroyed. But it is equally lightweight and versatile for shop and field applications. Research objective number five listed in the final report dating from 1966 states "5. To develop information on the physical properties of cellular plastics which are pertinent to their structural use rather than as mere insulation."[26] Such an objective suggests at once a subversive trick – make foam insulation something that it is most decidedly not – or a challenge to double up the performance of foam.

Over several years the team took on a broad range of structural prototypes, as evidenced by the resultant research taxonomy. But they also worked with a range of partnering technologies, such as Dow's spirally generated dome apparatus and Plydom's folded deployable plate structures.

PLASTICS FOUND

GFRP	Polyester resin	Exterior structural skins and interior partitions
PUR	Polyurethane foam	Foam between GFRP skins (could be extruded or expanded)

IN PRINT

Architectural Research Laboratory, University of Michigan. "Architectural Research on Structural Potential of Foam Plastics for Housing in Underdeveloped Areas" (May, 1966).
"The Structural Use of Foam Plastics," *Arts and Architecture* (August 1966): 10–19.
Armand G. Winfield. "Uninhibited Campus Research Opens Portals to New Plastics in Building Concepts," in *Technical Papers, Regional Technical Conference, Plastics in Building*, Society of Plastics Engineers (October 2–3, 1969): 32–48.
"Plastics the Next Decade," *Progressive Architecture* (October 1970): 104.

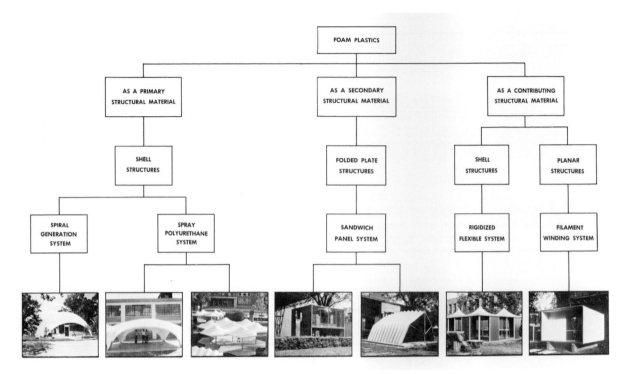

ARL report overview
(page 4.21) and foam
systems taxonomy.

Fabrication, anticlastic
umbrella shade.

FACING PAGE

Deployment sequence for Plydom's
sandwich panel system.

1967
Spheroid Spherical House
Guy de Moreau
Belgium

CONSTRUCTION LOGIC
Listed as seven panels, but the total number of parts or components and panelization
strategy is unknown, as are the deployment methods.

PLASTICS FOUND
Unknown, but likely PUR, polyurethane spray foam.

IN PRINT
"Die Spheroide Raumzelle," *Werk* (June 1968): 366.

1967
Uni-Dome
de Vries
Holland

CONSTRUCTION LOGIC
Stressed skin insulated panels formed into a curving shell, monocoque or semi-monocoque,
with reinforced joints.

PLASTICS FOUND
| GFRP | Polyester resin | Outer skin and inner skin |
| PUR | Polyurethane | Foam core between skins |

IN PRINT
Listed in the compilation "Plastic Buildings," *AD* (April 1970): 167–168.

Uni-Dome.

1967
Yantra House (See-Through Shell House)
Philo Farnsworth
USA

CONSTRUCTION LOGIC
Sixty identical units, proposed as filament wound or molded GFRP, are held in continuous tension in the form of a sphere. Units, in groups of five, aggregate to form 12 uniform circles on the surface of the sphere. The circles are filled with PET film, the interior is pressurized, and the PET forms perhaps a lens shape or a noticeable bulge. Simultaneously, cables connecting the aggregated units together are tensioned, which has the effect of binding the structure into a whole. As a final step, some modules in the sphere are filed with spray foam.

PLASTICS FOUND

GFRP	Polyester resin	Exterior structural skins and interior partitions
PET	Polyethylene terephthalate	Film disks
EP	Epoxy	Adhesive
PUR	Polyurethane	Foam

IN PRINT
"Plastics: Four Steps to the Future," *Progressive Architecture* (October 1970): 74.

Yantra House.

1967
PPL – Assembly House
Protective Plastics Ltd.
Canada

CONSTRUCTION LOGIC
Structural insulated panels for roof and wall applications.

PLASTICS FOUND

GFRP	Polyester resin	Outer skin
PUR	Polyurethane (foam)	Core of interior doors

IN PRINT
Listed in the compilation "Plastic Buildings," *AD* (April 1970): 167–168.

1967
Maritchu House
France

CONSTRUCTION LOGIC
Structural insulated panel with wood facing as the inner skin.

PLASTICS FOUND

GFRP	Polyester resin	Outer skin
PUR	Polyurethane (foam)	Core of interior doors

IN PRINT
Listed in the compilation "Plastic Buildings," *AD* (April 1970): 167–168.

1968
Cubino Space
Doernach System Forschung; Apprich Kg
Germany

CONSTRUCTION LOGIC
Molded foam panels coated with plaster, forming a rectangular box. Number of panel connections between panels is unknown.

PLASTICS FOUND

PVA	Polyvinyl alcohol	Coating over plaster
PS	Polystyrene	Foam core between skins; or
PF	Phenol formaldehyde	Foam core between skins; or
PUR	Polyurethane	Foam core between skins

IN PRINT
Listed in the compilation "Plastic Buildings," *AD* (April 1970): 167–168.

1968
Filament Wound Homes
University of Michigan & Airojet Corp.
USA

CONSTRUCTION LOGIC
A whole room, 7′ 10″ × 10′ 10″ × 16′ 2″, is filament wound – a continuous pattern of glass filament, bonded together by resin, wound around a permanent steel frame mandrel. The steel frame is filled in with rigid polyurethane boards faced with hardboard.

PLASTICS FOUND

	Polyester resin	Binder for continuous filaments
PU	Polyurethane	Foam boards faced with paper, "mold" for wound filament

IN PRINT
Architectural Research Laboratory, University of Michigan. "Architectural Research on Structural Potential of Foam Plastics for Housing in Underdeveloped Areas" (May, 1966).
"The Structural Use of Foam Plastics," *Arts and Architecture* (August 1966): 10–19.
Armand G. Winfield. "Uninhibited Campus Research Opens Portals to New Plastics in Building Concepts," in *Technical Papers, Regional Technical Conference, Plastics in Building*, Society of Plastics Engineers (October 2–3, 1969): 32–48.
"Plastics the Next Decade," *Progressive Architecture* (October 1970): 101.
Rudolph Deanin, Douglas Yuu, and Jere R. Anderson. "New Design Concepts for Plastics in Housing," *Technical Papers, Regional Conference, Plastics in Building*, Society of Plastics Engineers (October 2–3, 1969): 32–48.

Filament Wound Homes:
(top left) mandrel
(top middle) starting to wind
(top right) continuing to wind
(bottom left) off Mandrel, on truck
(bottom middle + right)
transportation from factory to site.

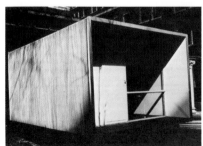

1968
Feierbach House
Feierbach & A Streiter; Wolfgang Feierbach Altenstadt
Germany

CONSTRUCTION LOGIC
Structural insulated panelized construction consisting of molded GFRP plastic skins
filled with EPS foam.

PLASTICS FOUND

GFRP	Polyester resin	Exterior structural skins and interior partitions
PS	Polystyrene	Foam between GFRP skins (likely EPS)

IN PRINT
Albert G.H. Dietz. "Plastics the Next Decade," *Progressive Architecture* (October 1970):
    101.

Feierbach House.

1968
Bulle Six Coques (the "six-shell" bubble)
Jean Maneval
France

CONSTRUCTION LOGIC
Six semi-monocoque shells which nest for transport from the factory; once on site they attach to a hexagonal frame, one per side. The shells connect to each other at their seams via bolts.

PLASTICS FOUND
GFRP   Polyester resin   Exterior structural skins and interior partitions
SPF   Polyurethane spray foam   Interior

IN PRINT
"Pre-magasin Prisunic und Ferienhaus," *Werk* (June 1968): 360–361.

Bulle Six Coques.

1968
Mexican Holiday House
J. Jose; Diaz Infante
Mexico

CONSTRUCTION LOGIC
Folded plates of stressed skin sandwich panels. Deployment methods remain unknown.

PLASTICS FOUND
GFRP	Polyester resin	Outer skin and inner skin
PUR	Polyurethane	Foam core between skins
PMMA	Polymethyl methacrylate	Windows

IN PRINT
Listed in the compilation "Plastic Buildings," *AD* (April 1970): 167–168.

1968
Clamp House
J. Dartford
Mickleover Ltd
Bakelite Company
Great Britain

CONSTRUCTION LOGIC
Expandable folded plate system.

PLASTICS FOUND
GFRP	Polyester resin	Outer skin and inner skin.
PF	Phenol formaldehyde	Foam core between skins.

IN PRINT
Listed in the compilation "Plastic Buildings," *AD* (April 1970): 167–168.

1968
Villa Spies
Staffan Berglund
Toro, Sweden

CONSTRUCTION LOGIC
20 stressed skin wedges form a single domed roof which covers roughly 2000 square feet.

PLASTICS FOUND
GFRP   Polyester resin   Outer skin and inner skin
PUR   Polyurethane   Foam core between skins
PMMA   Polymethyl methacrylate   Windows

IN PRINT
"Experimental Plastic House 4," *Progressive Architecture* (October 1970): 78–79.

1968
Futuro
Matti Suuronen
Finland

CONSTRUCTION LOGIC
Monocoque ellipsoid formed from 16 stressed skin shell segments.

PLASTICS FOUND
GFRP   Polyester resin   Outer skin and inner skin
PUR   Polyurethane   Foam core between skins
PMMA   Polymethyl methacrylate   Windows

IN PRINT
Listed in the compilation "Plastic Buildings," *AD* (April 1970): 167–168.

1969
Rondo Spherical House
Casoni & Casoni
Switzerland

CONSTRUCTION LOGIC
Stressed skin insulated panels formed into curving shell.

PLASTICS FOUND
GFRP   Polyester resin   Outer skin and inner skin
PUR   Polyurethane   Foam core between skins

IN PRINT
Listed in the compilation "Plastic Buildings," *AD* (April 1970): 167–168.

FACING PAGE
Futuro.

1969
Tub Co
Professor Patfoort
Belgium

CONSTRUCTION LOGIC
Rectangular and whole stressed skin room unit.

PLASTICS FOUND

GFRP	Polyester resin	Outer skin and inner skin
PE	Polyethylene	Tubing to heat or cool

IN PRINT
Listed in the compilation "Plastic Buildings," *AD* (April 1970): 167–168.

1970
Iglu – Emergency Housing
Bayer AG
German Red Cross
Turkey and Peru

CONSTRUCTION LOGIC
A lightweight polyurethane foam dome is generated on a turntable, in situ, and over a pneumatically inflated mold. A nozzle attached to a gantry suspended over the mold sprays polyurethane foam as the turntable spins. The resultant dome is lightweight and can be lifted by as little as 12 individuals. Post-finishing includes cutting out doors and windows, infilling doors with tarps and windows with acrylic lenses, and interior and exterior painting.

Bayer AG developed this rapidly deployable system as relief housing in the event of natural disasters. In March 1970 Bayer and the German Red Cross provided housing relief to the residents of Gediz where a 7.2 magnitude earthquake devastated the town. Two months later the system was deployed in Peru after a 7.9 magnitude earthquake devastated the regions of Ancash and La Libertad.

SPF	Polyurethane spray foam	Interior
PVC	Polyvinyl chloride	Pneumatically inflated mold

IN PRINT
Armand Winfield, "UNIDO Report," *Proceedings of the SPE National Technical Conference*,
    November 8–10, 1972.
"Bayer-Iglus im Katastropheneinsatz." Article details are unknown.
Bayer AG and the German Red Cross, *The Door of the Minaret No Longer Looks to Mecca*, film,
    1970.

Bayer AG, Iglu Emergency Housing
deployed in Peru and Turkey.

1970, Gediz, Turkey

Teams from Bayer AG and German Red Cross deploy Iglu Emergency Housing in the aftermath of a 7.2 earthquake. The rapid deployment and construction logic replete with turntable, gantry for foam mixing head, materials, and post processing steps are captured on film in The Door of the Minaret No Longer Looks to Mecca.

ALL-PLASTICS

Collection:
"All-plastics"
houses

1971
Domobiles
Pascal Hausermann
France

CONSTRUCTION LOGIC
Single shell of spray foam applied.

PLASTICS FOUND
PUR   Polyurethane   Foam

IN PRINT
Listed in the compilation "Plastic Buildings," *AD* (April 1970): 167–168.

Domobiles.

1971
Spray Plastic House
Archigram
Great Britain

CONSTRUCTION LOGIC

A process of constructing aggregating lumps of double curved non-uniform surfaces is proposed. A very large EPS block is dug out or carved on the interior to form any number of conjoined curving rooms (akin to a "burrow"). The rooms are then sprayed with GFRP. The remaining EPS (formwork) is discarded/dissolved, thus exposing the GFRP structure below.

PLASTICS FOUND

| EPS | Expanded polystyrene | Formwork |
| GFRP | Polyester | Resultant shell |

IN PRINT

See the Archigram Archival Project.

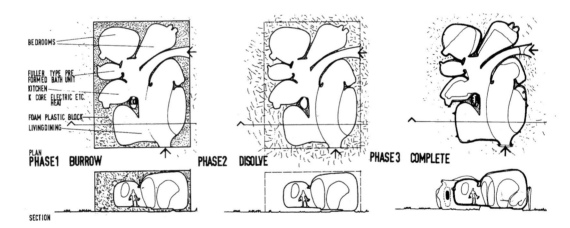

Spray Plastic House, three phases of fabrication.

CARE/Winfield/Bangladesh House.

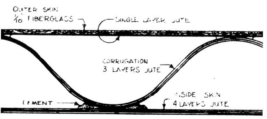

Panel detail.

CASE STUDY
1972
THE CARE/WINFIELD/BANGLADESH HOUSE

Armand Winfield
Winfield Incorporated
Calverton, Long Island and West Babylon, New York

The CARE/Winfield/Bangladesh House documentation evidences an engineering research process engaged; material experimentation; two phases of work; two separately prototyped housing systems; and tests performed on each system. The house was commissioned by CARE, the organization now known as Cooperative Organization for Relief Everywhere. It was commissioned as low-cost, rapidly producible housing for Bangladesh's Ganges River Delta, which suffered massive casualties from cyclone Bohla in November 1970.

Armand Winfield, a frequently published, respected, and active member of the plastics community, and in early 1972 the president of Winfield Incorporated, accepted CARE's commission and responded with a house that offered no critical architectural position or aesthetic posture. Rather, its agenda was found in CARE's mandate; the house must withstand 150 mph winds; cost less than $300; be produced by unskilled or semi-skilled labor en masse at the rate of 100 houses per day; and use jute, a natural fiber integral to the culture and economy of the Bengali people *in association with plastic materials or resins*. The project originated with a composite construction logic requiring knowledge of and experience with combining fiber and resin in ratio to ensure optimal structural capacity.[27]

Winfield's team rationalized that the mechanical properties of jute reinforced polyester (JRP) could be compared to glass fiber reinforced polyester (GFRP), or GFRP's "physicals" could serve as a benchmark by which to judge the structural performance of JRP.[28] This was a rationalization supported by existing research; B.S. Benjamin included GFRP *and* JRP in his book *Structural Design with Plastics* in 1969, notes existing research with JRP, and describes jute and hybrid composites and their benefits beyond JRP composites.[29] Winfield's research started with JRP/GFRP combinations and presupposed a whole-house (monocoque) compositing technique requiring the manufacture and prepping of very large molds, and hand lay-up and rolling of successive layers of woven fiber and polyester or epoxy resin.

Experimentation ensued. Test panels produced during phase-one experimentation note two individual control specimens – a test panel composed of one layer of resin-soaked jute, and a test panel comprised of one layer of resin and glass fiber. Subsequent test panels proceeded to build up layers and increase structural capacity: "one jute layer/one resin and glass layer"; "three jute layers/two resin and glass layers"; "four jute layers/three resin and glass layers." Winfield stopped this round of experimentation when mechanical tests confirmed that jute fiber's capacity to absorb resin decreased glass fiber's effectiveness; the resin coating intended for individual glass fibers was unavailable and work of fracture was decreased.[30]

The team's next round of experiments focused on all-jute-fiber composites, countering their tendency to absorb resin with the addition of fillers – calcium carbonate for one – and the selection of a 22 × 22 thread count, double sheared and calendared jute weave.[31] The house's final structural solution, a stressed skin assembly, had an inner skin, corrugated core, and outer skin and was composed of four layers of JRP (inner), three layers JRP (core), and two layers JRP/GFRP (outer). The final material assembly's form was dependent on the relationship between natural fiber and plastic resin, but also on the form of corrugation and sandwich, totalizing structural strategies.

Phase one house prototyping resulted in a 10' × 20' house, assembled from two 10' × 10' monocoque units, the seam of which created the house's one interior partition. The construction sequencing notes the build-up of the inner skin over wooden molds, the attachment of a separately fabricated corrugated core, the draping of jute over corrugations, and spraying/lay-up of jute and glass fibers to create the final outer skin. The foundation was an integral system; stressed skin units extended 18" below grade and turned out 12" perpendicular to the exterior wall.

A whole house, delivered to Calverton, Long Island, was installed. A pit was dug; the house dropped in it; and the pit refilled around its exterior and on its interior. A Navy A-6A "Intruder" jet targeted the house with winds exceeding 170 mph, and water was pumped at 750 gallons per minute to simulate cyclone conditions. The CARE/Bangladesh house was in residence adjacent to this airport taxiway for the following 18 years.

A second phase of research was engaged which presaged concerns for cost, weight, and transportability, called into question the monocoque duo, introduced a panel logic, and by default a multi-jointed assembly. Phase one's two-to-one/part-to-whole relationship in this phase quickly became nine-to-one and finally eighteen-to-one, as the monocoque structure was re-rationalized into a sandwich panel system. The final prototype erected in West Babylon, New York included a kit of 18 roof and wall panel parts, and connector pieces for joining wall panel to wall panel; roof to wall panel; center partition to wall panel; foundation edge to foundation strap; and trimming window and door seams.

Capitulation to panelization may have been less than optimal to Winfield, especially in light of the fact that Armand Winfield would, for a similar project of 1975 – the UNIDO/Madras/ Winfield house – develop and deploy a monocoque housing system produced by an oxen-powered filament-winding machine.[32]

PLASTICS FOUND

JRP	Jute reinforced polyester	Solid and corrugated wall and roof sheets
GFRP	Polyester	Solid sheet
PP	Polypropylene	Foundation netting
	Elastomeric urethane	Coating, final exterior coating (second prototype only)

CARE/Winfield/Bangladesh House,
testing wind resistance at
Calverton, Long Island.

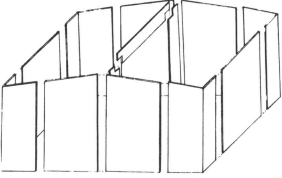

CARE, panel and part logic.

NOTES

1 Building Research Institute, *Plastics in Building* (Washington, DC: NAS-NRC, 1955), 44.

2 The "all-plastics" position taken by Marylin Graboff is exhibited in her patented invention: Marylin Grayboff. 1959. Light-Transmitting Structural Panel," US Patent 3,046,617, filed January 23, 1959 and issued July 31, 1963.

3 Ralph H. Sonneborn, *Fiberglas Reinforced Plastics* (New York: Reinhold Publishing Corporation, 1954), 142.

4 Albert G.H. Dietz notes a large rocket nozzle of carbon–graphite–silica fibers and phenolic resin as measuring 19 feet high and 19 feet in diameter in *Composite Materials: 1965 Edgar Marburg Lecture* (Philadelphia, PA: ASTM, 1965), 12–15.

5 *The Architectural Forum.* 1940. "Plastics in Building," 415.

6 Fiberglass reinforced plastics and translucent corrugated and sandwich panel products were collected throughout the aggregated data set, appearing as early as 1940, but introduced as building products in the mid 1950s. Here, Dietz also references such a building product.

7 *Scientific American.* 1933. "Synthetic Houses," 149 (4): 180.

8 Al Lees. 1988. "Are You Ready for a Plastic House?" *Popular Science*, 48.

9 For a thorough discussion of the NAHB Research House program, see John M. King "Chapter 20, NAHB Research Houses Demonstrate Plastics," in *Plastics in Building*, edited by Irving Skeist (New York: Reinhold Publishing Corporation, 1966), 418–443.

10 British Plastics Federation, *Plastics, Post-War Building Studies No. 3* (London: HMSO, 1944), 20.

11 Lumarith Plastics are moulding compounds made from cellulose acetate or ethyl cellulose. See Celanese Plastics Corporation, *Lumarith Cellulosic Molding Materials, Celanese Plastics; A Handbook for the Layman, as well as the Expert, on the Injection and Extrusion Molding of Lumarith Thermoplastics* (New York: Celanese Plastics Corporation, 1945), 8.

12 The Celanese Corporation of America. 1945. *Architectural Forum*, 229.

13 Working plastics and the challenges associated with forming them into parts are demonstrated through some of the photographic documentation presented in this chapter. For instance, see the images associated with the fabrication of the Schien, Magnant, and Coulon All-Plastics House, of 1956.

14 C. Theodore Larson, comp. *Architectural Record*. 1934. "New Housing Designs and Construction Systems," 75: 1.

15 Cheryl Ganz, *The 1933 Chicago World's Fair: A Century of Progress* (Urbana, IL: University of Illinois Press, 2008).

16 *Scientific American.* 1933. "Synthetic Houses," 149 (4): 180. See summary by Ganz starting on page 65 titled "National Research Council and Science Exhibits."

17 C. Theodore Larson, comp. *Architectural Record*. 1934. "New Housing Designs and Construction Systems," 75: 36.

18 Housing Division of the Henry J. Kaiser Company. 1945. "Report on Prefabricated Plastic Houses," Henry J. Kaiser Company, 1.

19 Ibid., 2–3.

20 See the transformation of the All-Plastic House floor plan in *Bauen und Wohnen*. 1957. "Ganz-Plastik-Haus auf der Ausstellung Arts Menagers 1956 in Paris," 11: 57.

21 Ralph H. Sonneborn, *Fiberglas Reinforced Plastics* (New York: Reinhold Publishing Corporation, 1954), 142.

22 Bruce Martin. 1956. "How Should We Use Plastics?" *Architectural Review*, 138.

23 Building Research Institute, *Plastics Study Group of the Building Research Institute, Report of a Meeting at the Massachusetts Institute of Technology* (Washington, DC: NAS-NRC, 1956), 105.

24 W. Allen Cleneay. "The Building Owner's View: Plastics in Experimental Buildings," in *Performance of Plastics in Building* (Washington, DC: Building Research Institute Inc., 1963), 116.

25 R.M. Davies, *Plastics in Building Construction* (London: Blackie & Son LTD, 1965), 140–141.

26 Architectural Research Laboratory, University of Michigan, *Structural Potential of Plastics for Foam Housing in Underdeveloped Areas* (Ann Arbor, MI: Architectural Research Laboratory, 1966), 4.1.

27 Armand G. Winfield and Barbara L. Winfield, "Major Breakthrough in Low Cost Plastics Housing Using Jute Reinforced Polyesters: The CARE/Winfield/Bangladesh House," in *Proceedings of the 29th Annual Technical Conference, 1974* (Washington, DC: The Society of the Plastics Industry, Inc., 1974), Section 7-A, 1.

28 Ibid., 2.

29 B.S. Benjamin. *Structural Design with Plastics* (New York: Van Nostrand Reinhold Publishing Company, 1969), 63.

30 Armand G. Winfield and Barbara L. Winfield, "Major Breakthrough in Low Cost Plastics Housing Using Jute Reinforced Polyesters: The CARE/Winfiedl/Bangladesh House," in *Proceedings of the 29th Annual Technical Conference, 1974* (Washington, DC: The Society of the Plastics Industry, Inc., 1974), Section 7-A, 1, 4.

31 Ibid., 1.

32 National Plastics Center and Museum. "Biography of Armand G. Winfield," (no date).

CHAPTER 05

WHY WE USE PLASTICS THE WAY THAT WE DO

Plastics found, architectural prototypes, 2000–2013

A collection of 23 architectural projects constructed between 2000 and 2013 which work plastics into transparent, translucent, and opaque whole architectures are found. They are representative of a range of constructed logics – multilayered interior and exterior wall assemblies, multifunctional envelopes, single-layer and pneumatically tensioned roof and wall membranes, and deployable and demountable whole pavilions. The palette of plastics found is broad and inclusive of provocateurs such as super absorbent polymers (SAPs) and biodegradable PETs.

One hundred or more projects from this time period could be collected that similarly work plastics. In such a collection we would likely find that plastic membranes dominate, mostly made from ETFE, worked in the form of pneumatically tensioned multi-layered cushions such as those found in the Kingsdale School by DRMM Architects (2004), or single-layered tensioned membranes such as those found in the Unilever Building by Behnisch Architects (2009).[1] We would also find transparent and translucent cellular sheets of polycarbonate (and acrylic) dominate, forming entire building envelopes such as those found in the Laban Dance Centre by Herzog & De Meuron (2002). The plastics ETFE and PC would be revealed to be worked pervasively, and not GFRP as forecasted by the substantial prototyping efforts occurring between 1956 and 1972.

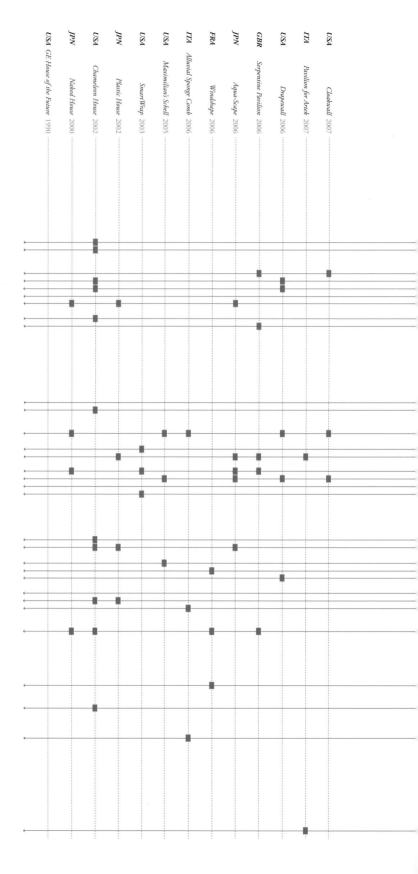

USA *GE House of the Future* 1990
JPN *Naked House* 2000
USA *Chameleon House* 2002
JPN *Plastic House* 2002
USA *SmartWrap* 2003
USA *Maximilian's Schell* 2005
ITA *Alluvial Sponge Comb* 2006
FRA *Windshape* 2006
JPN *Aqua-Scape* 2006
GBR *Serpentine Pavilion* 2006
USA *Drapewall* 2006
ITA *Pavilion for Artek* 2007
USA *Cloakwall* 2007

Plastics Found

Timeline chart. Columns (left to right):

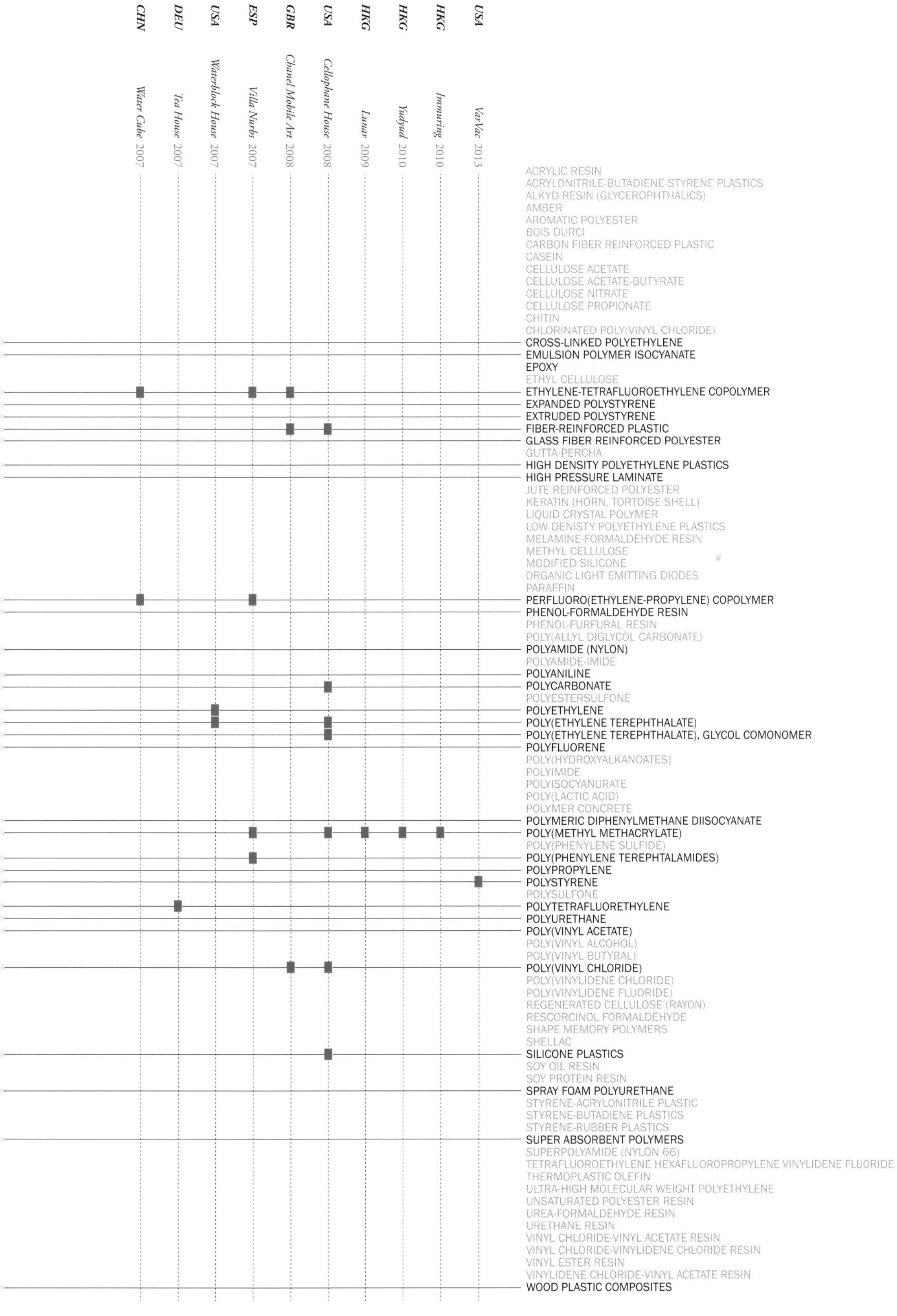

- CHN — Water Cube 2007
- DEU — Tea House 2007
- USA — Waterblock House 2007
- ESP — Villa Nurbs 2007
- GBR — Chanel Mobile Art 2008
- USA — Cellophane House 2008
- HKG — Lunar 2009
- HKG — Yadyud 2010
- HKG — Inmutring 2010
- USA — VarVac 2013

Material rows:

ACRYLIC RESIN
ACRYLONITRILE-BUTADIENE-STYRENE PLASTICS
ALKYD RESIN (GLYCEROPHTHALICS)
AMBER
AROMATIC POLYESTER
BOIS DURCI
CARBON FIBER REINFORCED PLASTIC
CASEIN
CELLULOSE ACETATE
CELLULOSE ACETATE-BUTYRATE
CELLULOSE NITRATE
CELLULOSE PROPIONATE
CHITIN
CHLORINATED POLY(VINYL CHLORIDE)
CROSS-LINKED POLYETHYLENE
EMULSION POLYMER ISOCYANATE
EPOXY
ETHYL CELLULOSE
ETHYLENE-TETRAFLUOROETHYLENE COPOLYMER
EXPANDED POLYSTYRENE
EXTRUDED POLYSTYRENE
FIBER-REINFORCED PLASTIC
GLASS FIBER REINFORCED POLYESTER
GUTTA-PERCHA
HIGH DENSITY POLYETHYLENE PLASTICS
HIGH PRESSURE LAMINATE
JUTE REINFORCED POLYESTER
KERATIN (HORN, TORTOISE SHELL)
LIQUID CRYSTAL POLYMER
LOW DENISTY POLYETHYLENE PLASTICS
MELAMINE-FORMALDEHYDE RESIN
METHYL CELLULOSE
MODIFIED SILICONE
ORGANIC LIGHT EMITTING DIODES
PARAFFIN
PERFLUORO(ETHYLENE-PROPYLENE) COPOLYMER
PHENOL-FORMALDEHYDE RESIN
PHENOL-FURFURAL RESIN
POLY(ALLYL DIGLYCOL CARBONATE)
POLYAMIDE (NYLON)
POLYAMIDE-IMIDE
POLYANILINE
POLYCARBONATE
POLYESTERSULFONE
POLYETHYLENE
POLY(ETHYLENE TEREPHTHALATE)
POLY(ETHYLENE TEREPHTHALATE), GLYCOL COMONOMER
POLYFLUORENE
POLY(HYDROXYALKANOATES)
POLYIMIDE
POLYISOCYANURATE
POLY(LACTIC ACID)
POLYMER CONCRETE
POLYMERIC DIPHENYLMETHANE DIISOCYANATE
POLY(METHYL METHACRYLATE)
POLY(PHENYLENE SULFIDE)
POLY(PHENYLENE TEREPHTALAMIDES)
POLYPROPYLENE
POLYSTYRENE
POLYSULFONE
POLYTETRAFLUOROETHYLENE
POLYURETHANE
POLY(VINYL ACETATE)
POLY(VINYL ALCOHOL)
POLY(VINYL BUTYRAL)
POLY(VINYL CHLORIDE)
POLY(VINYLIDENE CHLORIDE)
POLY(VINYLIDENE FLUORIDE)
REGENERATED CELLULOSE (RAYON)
RESCORCINOL FORMALDEHYDE
SHAPE MEMORY POLYMERS
SHELLAC
SILICONE PLASTICS
SOY OIL RESIN
SOY PROTEIN RESIN
SPRAY FOAM POLYURETHANE
STYRENE-ACRYLONITRILE PLASTIC
STYRENE-BUTADIENE PLASTICS
STYRENE-RUBBER PLASTICS
SUPER ABSORBENT POLYMERS
SUPERPOLYAMIDE (NYLON 66)
TETRAFLUOROETHYLENE HEXAFLUOROPROPYLENE VINYLIDENE FLUORIDE
THERMOPLASTIC OLEFIN
ULTRA-HIGH MOLECULAR WEIGHT POLYETHYLENE
UNSATURATED POLYESTER RESIN
UREA-FORMALDEHYDE RESIN
URETHANE RESIN
VINYL CHLORIDE-VINYL ACETATE RESIN
VINYL CHLORIDE-VINYLIDENE CHLORIDE RESIN
VINYL ESTER RESIN
VINYLIDENE CHLORIDE-VINYL ACETATE RESIN
WOOD PLASTIC COMPOSITES

PLASTICS NOW

It is the emergence of projects in the early 2000s, such as the Naked House by Shigeru Ban (2000), Plastic House by Kengo Kuma (2002), and SmartWrap™ by KieranTimberlake (2003), that permits us, in the present, to ask, "Why do we use plastics the way that we do?" Our literal and surficial comprehension of plastics' total and expansive role in these and other projects, when contrasted with level-headed consciousness of our everyday practice with building products made from plastics – we source, select, and specify them; combined with unexamined attitudes towards them – "plastics are (a, the, in our) future," "plastics are not substitute materials," and "plastics are difficult to decipher" – brings the question "Why do we use plastics the way that we do?" roaring to the fore. We might, consciously or unconsciously, hold on to an "all-plastics" or "all-plasticity" conceptual position as we, more than likely, practice from a "plastics in building" one. But here and now we should make one modification: "Plastics in building" is no longer a "conceptual position" to be taken up and worked toward. As building products made from plastics were normalized, as we worked them into so many bits – backer rod, rug underlayment, and skylights – used them and became assured of their durability, "plastics in building" became, as so many early journal articles and books predicted, and as the US NAS-NRC BRI Plastics Study Group aspired to, a given state, an assured state for any building – a fact, not a process. So, to modify, we practice from the given state "plastics in building," and the practices of sourcing, selecting, and specifying products – of taking up the position "customer" in the building products supply chain – assists our engagement of these materials, as they perform a broad range of functional roles in buildings. When an "all-plastics" proposition is willed into existence – which again, for present-day projects might be a surficial reading – we marvel at the resident tenacity to work these materials this way. A broad palette of building products made from plastics coupled with the tenacity to work them indicates that "describing plastics" continues – their testing and retesting is a perpetual state. A "describing transect" could have been found for each one of our differently functional 90-plus polymer chemistries affiliated with architectural production. From date of invention to present day, we could have tracked their individual formulation, testing, building use case, retesting, reformulation, new use, etc. as they were formed and transformed for building application.[2] Such a timeline might very well have been the ultimate manifestation of the "plastics in building" conceptual position.

If we accept the position that these projects, with such expansive and totalizing systems made from plastics, present another, alternate approach, then in light of the evidentiary set collected herein we must ask: What relationship do these projects have to this aggregated, albeit fragmented, history of plastics and architecture? Why fast-forward to the year 2000?

The condition placed on examining such present-day projects, and why they are presented here alongside this evidentiary set, is that they allow us to see the figural "gap" in the record of experimentation. The record of whole, architectural experimentation with plastics – short- and long-span structures, holiday cabins, relief shelters, and prefabricated houses – as well as the discourse with the plastics industry, inclusive of chemists and manufacturers, appears to peak in the late 1960s early 1970s, and dwindle to naught in the mid to late 1970s. One could surmise that the gap in the experimentation record, between projects then and those appearing in the early 2000s, represents maturation of the building products supply chain.[3] Perhaps the answer to the question "How should we use plastics?" became known and codified. However, this answer alone does not satisfy us. We still utter those three phrases. This gap appears abruptly, as if there was some agreement to make it.

Collections of projects then and now are quite literally separated, cut off from each other, and the source of separation appears to be geopolitical and judicial events that restructured what we may have assumed would be a linear history. It seemed to be a forgone conclusion that an all-GFRP shell or foam-cored GFRP molded sandwich panel, or sprayed in situ polyurethane foam domes, were nearly upon us along with the building products to support making them. The convergence of events in and around the year 1973 formed this history into a nonlinear one, irrefutably altering the relationship between actors in this community and deciding how plastics should and could be used in architecture.

PLASTICS IN 1973

Several items found in our data set from 1973 establish the scene. Early in the year the *Architects Journal* publishes serial articles on GFRP projects built mostly in the UK. Its March, April, and May issues compile upwards of 100 photographs of projects demonstrating use – molded exterior panels on single- and multistory buildings, and short-span folded plate structures.[4] *Progressive Architecture* publishes "Plastic Structures go High-Rise," in which author Armand G. Winfield reviews research on PVC membranes, multi-story columnar forms that deploy floor plates vertically when pressurized, and are made structurally sound through continuous pressurization, though he indicates that the "perfect skin" material has yet to be found.[5] *The Plastics Architect*, Arthur Quarmby's comprehensive book on the subject, is compiled. It documents working plastics over a 20-year period into enclosures, components, sculptures, and utopian ideals, conveying the total body of work through photographic documentation and line drawing.[6] A hint of misunderstanding, technical in nature, makes its way into popular architectural press. In its May 1973 issue, *House and Garden* publishes "Foam: The Controversial New Building Material." The article proceeds to answer for the homeowner questions regarding the use of polyurethane spray foam such as "I have seen houses built of foam before, but are they sound?" and "Are there other dangers such as flammability?"

The foundation entrenched in our building codes is the assurance of life safety – the affirmed safe and quick exit from a building in the event of a fire.[7] Contributing to this is the form of exit and the apportioning of building materials because their amount and exposure constitute a potential fuel load. Are materials flammable? Combustible? How quickly and rapidly do they burn? When burning, how much smoke is produced? What are the characteristics of the gases and particulates contained in this smoke? Based on our cumulative understanding of such characteristics, how should we use plastics? Knowing the burning behaviors of plastics is a technical challenge taken up very early in the aggregated data set – refer back to the account given by Rarig in 1970 when describing the use of acrylics in building.[8, 9] Knowing how something burns is a fundamental technical challenge for any emerging material technology.

Just weeks prior to this article appearing in *House and Garden*, researchers, building code officials, and industry representatives gathered "to confront the fire–research problem directly, and to set a course for future research."[10] The year 1973 is the year that the US Federal Trade Commission (US FTC) sued 26 plastics manufacturers, ASTM, and the Society of the Plastics industry on the basis that several tests, such as ASTM D1692, which permitted plastics to be designated as "self-extinguishing" or "non-burning," misrepresented the burning characteristics of cellular or foam plastics.[11] A "test piece," a sample of a specified area and thickness, when burned horizontally in a testing chamber, did not correctly approximate the burning behavior of the same material when applied in situ to, for instance, a six-sided inhabitable room. The behavior in situ, observed through the occurrence of actual fires, was unequivocally diametric to the behavior observed in the testing apparatus.[12] This called into question 20 years of accumulated knowledge on the tests applied to plastics, knowledge of the burning characteristics of plastics which formed the basis for determining how we should use and detail plastics, and formed the basis for designations given to building products which were already used and applied in buildings. Further implicated here is scale of use, but not in the tectonic sense evoked by Frederick McGarry when he identified one difficulty as the "transition between the little things and big, structural things." The pervasiveness of plastics use, the amount present and their contiguousness is a type of fuel load that presents a real threat to life safety. Nothing is more contiguous than an "all-plastics" stressed skin shell. Nothing is more contiguous than an "all-plastics" polyurethane spray foam dome.

R. Brady Williamson, then an associate professor of engineering science at UC Berkeley, who discovered the discrepancy between the tested and actual combustion characteristics for some types of plastics, who would serve as the US FTC's technical consultant during negotiations with the plastics industry, and who would be "pivotal" in defining the terms of settlement with the plastics industry, presents at this gathering an overview of a five-year research program funded by the US NSF, planned to holistically address fire safety for buildings.[13] His goal is not only to determine useful and accurate information for architects; it is the design process itself. He states that the most important goal is "the search for better ways to utilize the kind of information developed in the engineering part of the project in the architectural-design process."[14] Williamson's address and others would indicate a "first principles" approach to the subject, meaning testing apparatuses were to be rethought, products of pyrolysis – smoke and toxic fumes – scrutinized, and methods for scrutinizing regularized.[15] The very behavior of fire must be known anew – especially as it comes in contact with plastics, which are really hundreds of different materials with the potential to "permeate" the entire system of a building.

The terms of the settlement, decided on November 4, 1974, which are published in the US FTC order titled "The Society of the Plastics Industry, Inc. Et Al," directly address plastics' indecipherable terminological state, requiring collective industries to "cease and desist from using, publishing, or disseminating" such terms as "non-burning," "self-extinguishing," and "non-combustible" as specifically related to foam plastics made from polystyrene and polyurethane.[16] The settlement terms include the formation of a five-year "research program," to be managed by a nine-person Products Research Committee (PRC), a research program that would take up this first principles position to work out not only the burning characteristics of plastics, but also the appropriate test design for plastics.[17] The settlement terms also require the disclosure of foam plastics' intractable combustibility. The US FTC chose to talk to us ultimately through the aegis of popular architectural press, ordering that a "notice" be published within trade journals – architectural, building and construction, fire protection, furnishing, etc.[18] Architectural journals listed by name include *Architectural Digest*, *Progressive Architecture*, and *Architectural Record*. Thus, approximately 60 days after the decision date, the Notice was published in the February 1975 issue of *Progressive Architecture*.[19] Appearing on a quarter of the page, it is easily overlooked amidst gridded content. But, in light of this history, it coyly presents itself as a frontispiece for wrestling with how to use plastics in architecture – as much if not more so than the two singular volumes *Progressive Architecture* previously dedicated to the subject.[20]

Appendix B

Important notice regarding the flammability of cellular plastics used in building construction, and low-density cellular plastics used in furniture

The flammability characteristics of cellular plastics used in building construction, and low-density cellular plastics used in furniture are tested under numerous test methods and standards. Included among these are ASTM D-568, 635, 757, 1433, 1692, E-84, 162 and 286; UL 94 and 723; and NFPA 255. The Federal Trade Commission considers that these standards are not accurate indicators of the performance of the tested materials under actual fire conditions, and that they are only valid as a measurement of the performance of such materials under specific, controlled test conditions. The terminology associated with the above tests or standards, such as "non-burning," "self-extinguishing," "non-combustible" or "25 (or any other) flame spread" is not intended to reflect hazards presented by such products under actual fire conditions. Moreover, some hazards associated with numerical flame spread ratings for such products derived from test methods and standards may be significantly greater than those which would be expected of other products with the same numerical rating.

The commission considers that under actual fire conditions, such products, if allowed to remain exposed or unprotected, will under some circumstances produce rapid flame spread, quick flashover, toxic or flammable gases, dense smoke and intense and immediate heat and may present a serous fire hazard. The manufacturer of the particular product to The Society of the Plastics Industry, Inc., should be consulted for instructions for use to minimize the risks that may be involved in the use of these products.

The Federal Trade commission, Washington, D.C. 20580 requests that any representation that is inconsistent with the terms of this Notice be brought to its attention. This Notice is distributed by The Society of the Plastics Industry, Inc., 250 Park Avenue, New York, New York 10017.

The notice is required by the US FTC to be published in trade journals.

For a material class that was already designated as "difficult to decipher," we can speculate that a mischaracterization of this magnitude must have been highly disruptive to experimentation. Contextualize this disruption inside the geopolitical events of 1973, which ultimately led to the October 16 announcement by the Organization of Petroleum Exporting Countries (OPEC) that the price per barrel of crude oil would increase immediately, and that its production would be incrementally cut as retribution against importing countries for supporting Israel in the Yom Kippur War. Crude oil, the hydrocarbon-rich liquid refined into petrochemicals which are the feedstock for plastics, has emerged as a political weapon. We have to go outside of the aggregated data set to find the *New York Times* article "Plastics Industry Hurt by Lack of Raw Materials Made of Oil." It is the third in a series of articles exploring the impacts of the embargo, and reports on the cascading effects throughout the supply chain – plants manufacturing products with plastics and refineries are forced to temporarily shut down or layoff staff. Small-scale manufacturers find it difficult to source competitively priced resins. Large-scale companies which produce monomers and manufacture products, such as DuPont, Dow, Monsanto, and Union Carbide Corporation are forced to watch their allocations closely. Society of the Plastics Industry President Ralph L. Harding Jr. ascribes the word "paradox" to the industry's current situation. "Having reached the status of full membership in the industrial community," he states, "the plastics industry finds itself threatened by limitations on its vitally needed raw material feedstocks."[21] By mid-March of 1974, when the embargo was lifted, the price of crude oil per barrel had quadrupled to nearly $12.00.

The emphasis here is not the oil embargo per se, nor is it the temporary shortage of petrochemical feedstocks to make plastics. Rather, it is the shortage of gasoline, heating fuel, and jet fuel. It is the palpable experience of an energy crisis. For some, 1973 intimately altered their understanding of crude oil specifically and fuel generally as basic needs and individual livelihoods were threatened. In 1979 another oil crisis, hence another energy crisis, ensued. This time it was precipitated by the Iranian revolution, the decreasing production of crude oil by OPEC nations, and the increased cost per barrel, which more than tripled the 1973 figure over a 12-month period. The events of 1973 and 1979 historically appear as crises to us, as extremely sharp and abrupt inclines in the curve of crude oil's cost per barrel over time, especially when contrasted with what follows – the gradual and sharp decline in cost attributed to the period of armed conflict between OPEC nations Iran and Iraq over an eight-year period, which coincides with plastics' vast proliferation. What we can observe from this period of crisis, as we try to understand why we use plastics the way that we do, is that right here in space and time is the potential for our corporate perception of building products made from plastics to be altered. We have indirectly accrued a tacit understanding of crude oil by experiencing our lives, albeit temporarily, without it.

PLASTICS PARADOX

Two seemingly disparate events, one which questioned our capacity to know and hence use plastics, the other which jeopardized our capacity to source plastics, converged and played out over the same six-year period, 1973–1979. To what degree is one or the other, or both combined, responsible for the admitted separation between our "all-plastics" collection and this collection? To what degree is one or the other or both responsible for what appears to be the abrupt stultification of experimentation and discourse with plastics, inclusive of the plastics industry? To what degree is one or the other or both responsible for our present role as "customer" in a linear and rigid building materials supply chain? Does the aggregated data set provide any answers?

Where our capacity to know and hence use plastics is questioned, we might presume that an international community paid very close attention to the allegations of the US FTC and the findings issued through the various research programs of the PRC – as this gap does appear to be an international one. It is likely misleading and too neat to presume that the events of 1973 severed relationships instantly or completely. For instance, the conference proceedings of SPI's Regional Technical Conference held in 1976 titled *Plastics in Building: Present Status and Future Prospects*, does include a presentation by structural engineer B.S. Benjamin titled "Plastics Shelter for Slum Clearance in Poor Countries." Yet, we can observe the following externality: Several of the respondents to this lawsuits are the very companies that supported cross-industry dialogue and discourse

1973 and 1979, Oil Shock

The cost of importing crude oil, the raw materials refined to produce plastics, gasoline, heating oil, and jet fuel, is used as a political weapon, ushering in the experience of an "energy crisis," and the potential for our corporate perception of building products made from plastics to be altered.

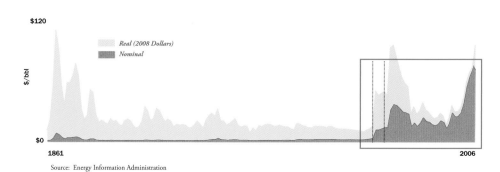

Source: Energy Information Administration

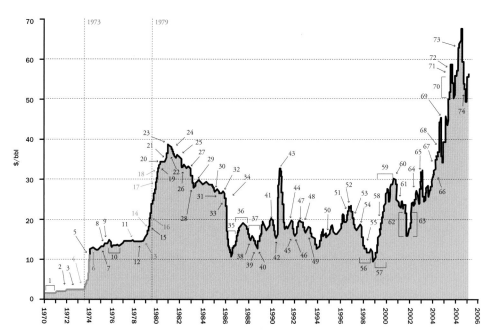

Source: United States Department of Energy

	Official Price of Saudi Light
	Refiner Aquisition Cost of Imported Crude Oil (IRAC)
bbl	*Oil Barrel*
b/d	*Barrels Per Day*
OPEC	*Organization of the Petroleum Exporting Countries*
CO	*Crude Oil*
SPR	*Strategic Petroleum Reserve*

1 OPEC begins to assert power; raises tax rate & posted prices

2 OPEC begins nationalization process; raises prices in response to falling US dollar

3 Negotiations for gradual transfer of ownership of western assets in OPEC countries

4 Oil embargo begins (October 19-20, 1973), price at $3/bbl

5 OPEC freezes posted prices; US begins mandatory oil allocation.

6 Oil embargo ends (March 18, 1974), price nearly $12/bbl

7 Saudis increase tax rates and royalties.

8 US crude oil entitlements program begins.

9 OPEC announces 15% revenue increase effective October 1, 1975.

10 Official Saudi Light price held constant for 1976.

11 Iranian oil production hits a 27-year low.

12 OPEC decides on 14.5% price increase for 1979.

13 Iranian revolution; Shah deposed

14 OPEC raises prices 14.5% on April 1, 1979.

15 US phased price decontrol begins.

16 OPEC raises prices 15%.

17 Iran takes hostages; President Carter halts imports from Iran; Iran cancels US contracts; non-OPEC output hits 17.0m b/d.

18 Saudis raise marker crude price from 19$/bbl to 26$/bbl.

19 US Windfall Profits Tax enacted

20 Kuwait, Iran, and Libya production cuts drop OPEC oil production to 27m b/d.

21 Saudi Light raised to $28/bbl

22 Saudi Light raised to $34/bbl

23 First major fighting in Iran–Iraq War

24 President Reagan abolishes remaining price and allocation controls.

25 Spot prices dominate official OPEC prices.

26 US boycotts Libyan crude; OPEC plans 18m b/d output.

27 Syria cuts off Iraqi pipeline.

28 Libya initiates discounts; non-OPEC output reaches 20 mb/d; OPEC output drops to 15m b/d.

29 OPEC cuts prices by $5/bbl; agrees to 17.5m b/d output – January 1983

30 Norway, United Kingdom, and Nigeria cut prices.

31 OPEC accord cuts Saudi Light price to $28/bbl.

32 OPEC output falls to 13.7m b/d.

33 Saudis link to spot price and begin to raise output – June 1985

34 OPEC output reaches 18m b/d.

35 Wide use of netback pricing

36 Wide use of fixed prices

37 Wide use of formula pricing

38 OPEC/Non-OPEC meeting failure

39 OPEC production accord; Fulmar/Brent production outages in the North Sea

40 Exxon's Valdez tanker spills 11m gal of CO.

41 OPEC raises production ceiling to 19.5m b/d – June 1989

42 Iraq invades Kuwait.

43 Operation Desert Storm begins; 17.3m barrels of SPR CO sales is awarded.

44 Persian Gulf war ends.

45 Dissolution of Soviet Union; Last Kuwaiti oil fire is extinguished on November 6, 1991

46 UN sanctions threatened against Libya

47 Saudi Arabia agrees to support OPEC price increase.

48 OPEC production reaches 25.3m b/d, the highest in over a decade.

49 Kuwait boosts production by 560,000 b/d in defiance of OPEC quota.

50 Nigerian oil workers' strike

51 Extremely cold weather in the US and Europe

52 US launches cruise missile attacks into southern Iraq.

53 Iraq begins exporting oil under UN SCR 986.

54 Prices and tensions rise as Iraq refuses to allow UN weapons inspectors into "sensitive" sites.

55 OPEC raises its production ceiling by 2.5m b/d to 27.5m b/d - the first increase in 4 yrs.

56 World oil supply increases by 2.25m b/d in 1997, the largest annual increase since 1988.

57 Oil prices continue to plummet; increased production from Iraq, no growth in Asian oil demand due to the Asian economic crisis and increases in world oil inventories following two unusually warm winters

58 OPEC pledges additional production cuts to about 4.3m b/d.

59 Oil prices triple between January 1999 and September 2000 due to strong world oil demand, OPEC oil production cutbacks, weather and low oil stock levels.

60 President Clinton authorizes the release of 30m barrels of oil from the SPR over 30 days to bolster oil supplies for heating.

61 Recession in the US; oil prices fall due to weak world demand and OPEC overproduction

62 Oil prices decline sharply following September 11, 2001 terrorist attacks on the US, largely on increased fears of a sharper worldwide economic downturn. Prices then increase on oil production cuts by OPEC and non-OPEC at the beginning of 2002; plus unrest in the Middle East and possibility of renewed conflict with Iraq.

63 OPEC oil production cuts, unrest in Venezuela, and rising tension in the Middle East contribute to a significant increase in oil prices between January and June.

64 Strike in Venezuela, concern over possible military conflict in Iraq, and cold winter all contribute to sharp decline in US oil inventories - cause oil prices to escalate further at the end of the year.

65 Continued unrest in Venezuela and oil traders' anticipation of imminent military action in Iraq cause prices to rise in January and February, 2003.

66 Military action commences in Iraq on March 19, 2003. Iraqi oil fields are not destroyed as had been feared. Prices fall.

67 OPEC delegates agree to lower the cartel's output ceiling by 1m b/d, to 23.5m b/d, effective April 2004.

68 OPEC agrees to raise its CO production target by 500,000 barrels (2% of current OPEC production) by August 1—in an effort to moderate high crude oil prices.

69 Hurricane Ivan damages energy infrastructure in the Gulf of Mexico and interrupts oil and natural gas supplies to the US. 1.7m barrels of oil in the form of a loan are released from the SPR.

70 Continuing oil supply disruptions in Iraq and Nigeria, as well as strong energy demand, raise prices.

71 Hurricanes Cindy, Dennis, Katrina, and Rita disrupt oil supply in the Gulf of Mexico.

72 In response to the hurricanes, US DoE provides emergency loans of 9.8m barrels and sells 11 m barrels of oil from the SPR.

73 Militant attacks in Nigeria shut in more than 600,000 b/d of oil production beginning in February 2006.

74 OPEC members agree to cut the organization's crude oil output by 1.2m b/d effective November 1, 2006. In December, the group agrees to cut output by a further 500,000 b/d effective February 2007.

whose leaders and engineering representatives participated in the Plastics Study Group or Society of Plastics Engineers, or Society of Plastics Industry alongside the design community. Herein listed are the US companies such as Monsanto, Dow, Rohm & Haas Company, and Union Carbide Corporation.[22] Did the events of the 1970s irreversibly sever productive cross-industry discourse?

One article from the aggregated data set is directed toward the future relationship between architecture and plastics. To appropriately contextualize this article, we need to go back to SPI President Harding's statements in the *New York Times* and affix them as a waypoint. Note that by November 1973, manufacturing sectors, or "use sectors" of the plastics industry, of which building and construction is one, were considered financially mature. Also note that Harding makes these statements regarding the present energy crisis amidst controversy in one use sector, building and construction, where technical maturity is presently but separately questioned. The word that Harding is said to have ascribed to the plastics industry situation during the first oil crisis of 1973, "paradox," is the same word that would be implied roughly two years later when the plastics industry, represented by SPI, confronts architects in the journal *Progressive Architecture* with industry-based truisms that should, once and for all, quench the implicit 35-plus years of debate on how architects should use plastics.

"Pandora's Plastic Box," published in September of 1975, begins by admitting that plastics are difficult to decipher and maintains this stance throughout the article, but simultaneously leverages plastics indecipherably by discouraging architects from playing "amateur chemical engineer," preferring to ascribe to us one highly nuanced role: "Architecture is more concerned with the design of the *configuration* of standard building components than with original design for these components."[23] With our role firmly defined in the supply chain – henceforth we will receive products made from plastics to be "configured" in a building – we are then issued the final decree on working toward the conceptual position "all-plastics": "The SPI emphatically states that an all-plastic house is *not* an industry goal. There are situations for which plastics are most sensible, and those which are not."[24] The severing of experimentation firmly accomplished, the SPI then addresses the need for a handbook on plastics, delivering the bad news to us that it's just not going to happen.

The plastics industry, with its numerous materials differently attributed and its fragmented manufacturing base, does not possess a "single authoritative source of information" like the American Iron and Steel Institute (AISI). Instead, they maintain that we must rely on third parties for information – the same third parties who "still bear the scars of spectacular fires involving plastic foam."[25] Before continuing with these directives, the SPI must address the blame for these incidents. "They [the fires] were an accumulation of aggravations: poor building industry communications, optimistic readings of test data, and over-zealous end users." They continue by adding, "Trite as this sounds, not enough questions were asked by end users then. In the opinion of SPI, not enough are asked now." Implying acknowledgment of the paradox in this statement – architects need information but there is no single authority for information – they cite the numerical approach of Albert G.H. Dietz as the basis for moving forward, as well as continued research and continued work by code-reviewing authorities. The SPI concludes by observing:

> Paradoxically, a major problem for plastics is that the architect loves them too well. The profession has traditionally been a leader in innovative materials applications. This willingness to experiment with new products has occasionally led to unjustified and sometimes dire extrapolations from approved specifications. A skylight approved for isolated use becomes an entire domed environment, not always with official sanction. The SPI believes that architects who wish to exceed strict, narrow interpretations of product approvals must subject them to an exhaustive analysis with the full cooperation of manufacturers and code administrators. A creative approach is not precluded.[26]

"Pandora's Plastics Box" is a sobering, singular, and significant missive from the plastics industry to us set amidst this period of uncertainty over plastics' correct use and supply of its raw sources. In this article, our relationship to the task of defining and describing plastics is made perfectly clear. The future of the conceptual positions "all-plastics" and "plastics in building" is firmly decided. And though SPI makes no mention of the energy crisis, we are given leave to move forward with doubts in our minds over raw materials sourced to make plastics, namely crude oil, and the impact that burning plastics might have on the environment.[27] The gap in experimentation found between the mid 1970s and the late 1990s/early 2000s might convince us that architects and the plastics industry followed these directives perfectly.

Architecture and plastics, a summation of events

The cumulative record of events. Not all events, but those that have certain implications when answering the question, "Why do we use plastics the way that we do?"

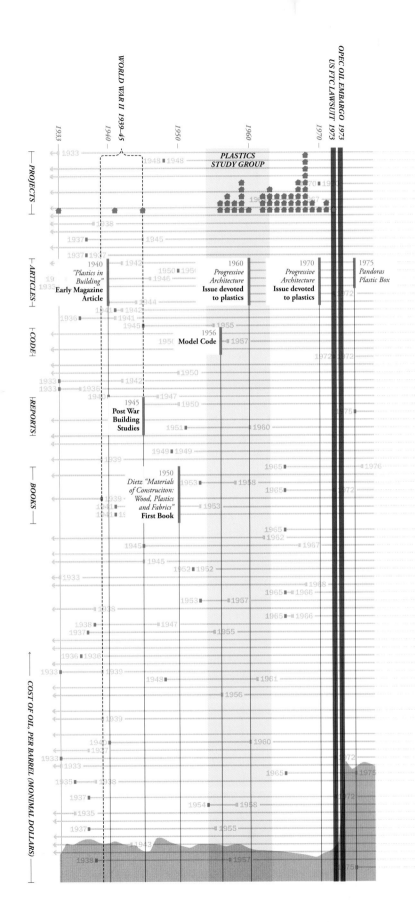

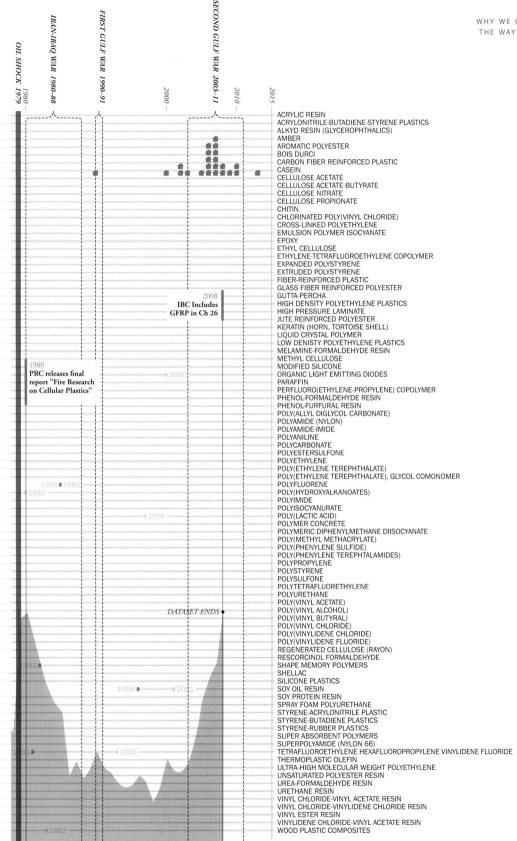

OIL SHOCK 1979

IRAN-IRAQ WAR 1980–88

FIRST GULF WAR 1990–91

SECOND GULF WAR 2003–11

1980
2000
2010
2015

2008
**IBC Includes
GFRP in Ch 26**

1980
**PRC releases final
report "Fire Research
on Cellular Plastics"**

2000

1985 1985
1980

1997

DATASET ENDS

1982

1996 2011

1981

1993

1983

ACRYLIC RESIN
ACRYLONITRILE-BUTADIENE-STYRENE PLASTICS
ALKYD RESIN (GLYCEROPHTHALICS)
AMBER
AROMATIC POLYESTER
BOIS DURCI
CARBON FIBER REINFORCED PLASTIC
CASEIN
CELLULOSE ACETATE
CELLULOSE ACETATE-BUTYRATE
CELLULOSE NITRATE
CELLULOSE PROPIONATE
CHITIN
CHLORINATED POLY(VINYL CHLORIDE)
CROSS-LINKED POLYETHYLENE
EMULSION POLYMER ISOCYANATE
EPOXY
ETHYL CELLULOSE
ETHYLENE-TETRAFLUOROETHYLENE COPOLYMER
EXPANDED POLYSTYRENE
EXTRUDED POLYSTYRENE
FIBER-REINFORCED PLASTIC
GLASS FIBER REINFORCED POLYESTER
GUTTA-PERCHA
HIGH DENSITY POLYETHYLENE PLASTICS
HIGH PRESSURE LAMINATE
JUTE REINFORCED POLYESTER
KERATIN (HORN, TORTOISE SHELL)
LIQUID CRYSTAL POLYMER
LOW DENISTY POLYETHYLENE PLASTICS
MELAMINE-FORMALDEHYDE RESIN
METHYL CELLULOSE
MODIFIED SILICONE
ORGANIC LIGHT EMITTING DIODES
PARAFFIN
PERFLUORO(ETHYLENE-PROPYLENE) COPOLYMER
PHENOL-FORMALDEHYDE RESIN
PHENOL-FURFURAL RESIN
POLY(ALLYL DIGLYCOL CARBONATE)
POLYAMIDE (NYLON)
POLYAMIDE-IMIDE
POLYANILINE
POLYCARBONATE
POLYESTERSULFONE
POLYETHYLENE
POLY(ETHYLENE TEREPHTHALATE)
POLY(ETHYLENE TEREPHTHALATE), GLYCOL COMONOMER
POLYFLUORENE
POLY(HYDROXYALKANOATES)
POLYIMIDE
POLYISOCYANURATE
POLY(LACTIC ACID)
POLYMER CONCRETE
POLYMERIC DIPHENYLMETHANE DIISOCYANATE
POLY(METHYL METHACRYLATE)
POLY(PHENYLENE SULFIDE)
POLY(PHENYLENE TEREPHTALAMIDES)
POLYPROPYLENE
POLYSTYRENE
POLYSULFONE
POLYTETRAFLUOROETHYLENE
POLYURETHANE
POLY(VINYL ACETATE)
POLY(VINYL ALCOHOL)
POLY(VINYL BUTYRAL)
POLY(VINYL CHLORIDE)
POLY(VINYLIDENE CHLORIDE)
POLY(VINYLIDENE FLUORIDE)
REGENERATED CELLULOSE (RAYON)
RESCORCINOL FORMALDEHYDE
SHAPE MEMORY POLYMERS
SHELLAC
SILICONE PLASTICS
SOY OIL RESIN
SOY PROTEIN RESIN
SPRAY FOAM POLYURETHANE
STYRENE-ACRYLONITRILE PLASTIC
STYRENE-BUTADIENE PLASTICS
STYRENE-RUBBER PLASTICS
SUPER ABSORBENT POLYMERS
SUPERPOLYAMIDE (NYLON 66)
TETRAFLUOROETHYLENE HEXAFLUOROPROPYLENE VINYLIDENE FLUORIDE
THERMOPLASTIC OLEFIN
ULTRA-HIGH MOLECULAR WEIGHT POLYETHYLENE
UNSATURATED POLYESTER RESIN
UREA-FORMALDEHYDE RESIN
URETHANE RESIN
VINYL CHLORIDE-VINYL ACETATE RESIN
VINYL CHLORIDE-VINYLIDENE CHLORIDE RESIN
VINYL ESTER RESIN
VINYLIDENE CHLORIDE-VINYL ACETATE RESIN
WOOD PLASTIC COMPOSITES

COLLECTION
PROTOTYPING WITH PLASTICS,
2000–2013

Twenty-three projects comprise a selected collection. Engage it recognizing that it is excised from a much larger speculated collection of projects completed during this time period that work plastics. And, in turn, recognize that any collection is excised from the total body of critical design and architectural work accomplished during a given period. Now ask: Might a selection of twenty-three projects help us answer the question "Why do we use plastics the way that we do?" Do we mean to juxtapose it to the historical recounting that has impressed upon us the near achievement of an "all-plastics" architecture based on integrative stressed GFRP skin configurations?

As a collection isolated from the judicial and geopolitical events recounted above, the projects found herein, built between 2000 and 2013, address diverse material, structural and infrastructural, formal and phenomenal, logistical and performance-based agendas. Materials made from plastics found in each project are listed per project, in the unit by which they are found – sheet, extrusion, film, etc. Tracking plastics through each one of these projects was undertaken less as a search for relevance to an "all-plastics" conceptual position. Rather, it was undertaken as a way to understand access to these units of materials, and the phenomenal and formal wholes possible as evidenced through ample photographic documentation. The use of plastics in each one of these projects is likely attributed to a designer's attitude toward materials, tools, techniques, and form, and may be less attributed to a fascination with plastics per se. Though, for some of these projects, plastics happen to be the recipient of a priori formal designations, for some, form is found by working plastics – though admittedly it is hard to know how to parse this set so finely, and in the end, it may not be interesting to do so. What might be observed is the myriad of construction logics at play – pressurized, layered, laminated, cast, tensioned, folded, petaled, draped, and velcroed ones. Stressed, load-transferring skins seem very far from the minds of the designers represented by this collection – not that they are absent; rather, by working plastics through alternate theoretical discourses, a range of construction logics are found with plastics.

276

WHY WE USE PLASTICS
THE WAY THAT WE DO

Collection:
Prototyping
with plastics

1 →

2000 Naked House

ARCHITECT
Shigeru Ban

LOCATION
Saitama, Japan

PROGRAM
Residence

CONSTRUCTION LOGIC
Translucent plastics, GFRP and PA, "sheathe" a normative
wood frame. On the interior, attachment between sheathing
and frame is accomplished by "hook and loop" adhesives,
rather than mechanical fasteners. Insulation in the cavity
between these layers follows the translucent directive by
being loose PE fill contained in PE bags.

PLASTICS FOUND

GFRP	Polyester	Corrugated sheet	Exterior surface of building envelope, weathering layer, attached to wood studs
PA	Polyamide	Textile	Interior surface of building envelope, attached to wood studs
PA	Polyamide	Adhesive	Velcro®, building envelope, attaches PA textiles to studs
PE	Polyethylene	Insulation	Building envelope, wall insulation
PE	Polyethylene	Film	Sealed bag containing PE insulation attached to wood studs between studs, GFRP corrugated sheet, and PA textile
PVC	Poly(vinyl chloride)	Sheet	Exterior building envelope, cavity

2

3

NAKED HOUSE IMAGES

1 Naked House interior
with PA textile sheathing
2 Disposition of Naked
House interior to rooms
and furniture
3 Naked House at dusk

278

WHY WE USE PLASTICS
THE WAY THAT WE DO

Collection:
Prototyping
with plastics

1 →

2002 Plastic House

ARCHITECT
Kengo Kuma & Associates, Tokyo, Japan

LOCATION
Meguro-Ku, Tokyo Prefecture, Japan

PROGRAM
Residence

CLIENT
Photographer and his mother

TEAM
Kengo Kuma (principal), Hiroshi Nakamura (project)

STRUCTURAL ENGINEER
Kajima Design

BUILDING SERVICES
Kajima Design

HVAC
Koizumi Jyusan

SANITARY/PLUMBING
Koizumi Jyusan

ELECTRIC
Tada Enterprise

PHOTOGRAPHY
Mitsumasa Fujitsuka

CONSTRUCTION LOGIC
Layered wall assemblies of GFRP sheet over PMMA insulation permits translucent solids juxtaposed to expanses of glass. Screens, gratings, and stair treads are meticulously detailed pultruded GFRP assemblies.

PLASTICS FOUND

GFRP	Polyester	Sheet	Exterior building envelope, wall, 4 mm sheet
PMMA	Poly(methyl methacrylate)	Insulation	Exterior building envelope, wall, 10 mm translucent thermal insulation
PC	Polycarbonate	Hardware	Exterior building envelope, wall, bolt connecting GFRP sheet to steel stud
GFRP	Polyester	Profile	Pultruded, bedroom porch screen and terrace rail, 100/22/5 mm rectangular hollow section (RHS)
GFRP	Polyester	Profile	Pultruded, bedroom porch screen, 12/88 mm extruded angle for connecting GFRP RHS to RHS detail
GFRP	Polyester	Profile	Pultruded, bedroom porch floor, 145/16 mm solid section
GFRP	Polyester	Profile	Pultruded, terrace rail, Ø42.7/2 mm support for GFRP railing
GFRP	Polyester	Profile	Pultruded, interior stair tread, 907/257/25 mm grating
PUR	Polyurethane	Coating	Colorless coating on all GFRP parts, pultruded profiles and sheets

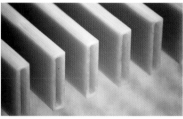

2

3

4

5

PLASTIC HOUSE IMAGES

1   Plastic House exterior with intricately detailed FRP pultrusions and sheets

2–3 Pultruded GFRP profiles

4–5 Plastic House interior and translucent stair made from GFRP profiles

280

WHY WE USE PLASTICS
THE WAY THAT WE DO

Collection:
Prototyping
with plastics

2002 Chameleon House

ARCHITECT
Anderson Anderson

LOCATION
Leelanau Peninsula, Michigan, United States

PROGRAM
Residence

CLIENT
Brondyk Family

CONSTRUCTION LOGIC
Structural insulated panels (SIPs) configured into a tower are
the substrate for cladding layers inclusive of the outermost
transparent and reflective screen made from strips of PMMA.

PLASTICS FOUND

PMMA	Poly(methyl methacrylate)	Sheet	Corrugated, exterior building envelope, screen
EPS	Expanded polystyrene	Insulation	Exterior building envelope, insulation in the structural insulated panels (SIPs) system, 6" and 12" thickness
pMDI	Polymeric diphenylmethane diisocyanate	Adhesive	Exterior building envelope adhesive for oriented strand board (OSB) skins of the SIPs system
PF	Phenol formaldehyde	Adhesive	Exterior building envelope adhesive for OSB skins of the SIPs system
EPI	Emulsion polymer isocyaurate	Adhesive	Exterior building envelope adhesive, OSB-to-EPS bond
PUR	Polyurethane	Adhesive/sealant Adhesive/sealant	Exterior building envelope SIP panel to stud
SPF	Spray polyurethane foam	Sealant	Exterior building envelope, sealant at SIP-to-SIP connections
XPS	Extruded polystyrene	Insulation	Concrete foundation system – perimeter insulation
PVC	Polyvinyl chloride	Piping	Concrete foundation system – perimeter drain n/a
			Silicone acrylic, coating, concrete foundation system – wall
HDPE	High-density polyethylene	Vapor barrier	Floor system, concrete slab, basement floor
PE-X	Cross-linked polyethylene	Piping	Floor system, piping for radiant heating system

1

2

3

4

CHAMELEON HOUSE IMAGES

1–4 SIPs installation process
5   Chameleon House exterior
6–10 Chameleon House PMMA screen effects at various times of day

281

WHY WE USE PLASTICS
THE WAY THAT WE DO

Collection:
Prototyping
with plastics

5

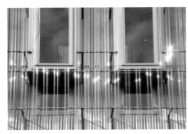
6

7

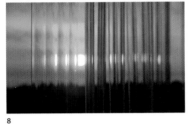
8

9

10

282

WHY WE USE PLASTICS
THE WAY THAT WE DO

Collection:
Prototyping
with plastics

1 →

2003 SmartWrap®

ARCHITECT
KieranTimberlake

LOCATION
Inaugural Solo Exhibition, Cooper-Hewitt
National Design Museum, New York City,
New York, United States

PROGRAM
Pavilion

TEAM
Stephen Kieran, James Timberlake,
Chris Macneal, Jonathon Fallet, Laurent
Hedquist, Christopher Johnstone, Juliet
Lee, Vikas Nagpal, Mark Sanderson,
Richard Seltenrich, Matt Spigelman, Karl
Wallick

STRUCTURAL ENGINEER
CVM Engineers

CONSULTING ENGINEER
Buro Happold

ELECTRICAL ENGINEER
Gabor M. Szakal Consulting Engineers

SKIN FABRICATION
ILC Dover, Inc.

LIGHTING
Sean O'Connor Associates

PRINTING
3M Commercial Graphics

CONSTRUCTION MANAGER
Skanska USA

SKIN TECHNOLOGY CONSULTANT
DuPont

STRUCTURAL ALUMINUM FRAME
Bosch Rexroth Corporation

EXHIBIT LIGHTING
Celestial Lighting

EXHIBIT LIGHTING
ERCO Lighting

2

3

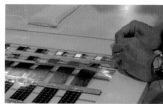

4

5

CONSTRUCTION LOGIC
A thin, translucent/transparent multifunctional film is proposed, based on the emergence of polymer inks and roll-to-roll processing. Integrated functions explored include energy gathering (OPV), energy storage, and light emission (OLED). The substrate may be a range of transparent films but as proposed is PET, which has the advantage of offering a robust recycling infrastructure for end-of-life options.

PLASTICS FOUND

PE	Polyethylene	woven netting	Envelope, 2 layers, 3′ x 12′ x 20mm thick, wove
PE	Polyethylene	woven netting	Envelope, 1 layer, 20mm thick, blue and white
PET	Poly(ethylene terephthalate)	fiber	Envelope, tension string (tennis racket facing)
PMMA	Poly(methyl methacrylate)	plate	Envelope, connectors for tension string network
PC	Polycarbonate	sheet - extruded cells	Envelope, wall and floor
FRP	Glass fiber-reinforced plastic	pultruded profile	Structure, floor

SMARTWRAP™ IMAGES

1–2 CooperHewitt Solos
Exhibition, 2003
3–5 OLED lay-up and testing

284

WHY WE USE PLASTICS
THE WAY THAT WE DO

Collection:
Prototyping
with plastics

2004 Aqua-Scape

Ryumei Fujiki + Fujiki Studio, Kou::Arc, Tokyo, Japan

LOCATION
Echigo-Tsumari Art Triennial, Tokamachi-city, Niigata Prefecture,
Japan

PROGRAM
Portable floating pavilion

CLIENT
Echigo-Tsumari Art Triennal 2006, executive committee, Fram
Kitagawa, Tokyo

TEAM
Ryumei Fujiki (design), Kazuhiro Yokote, Shigemi Shimizu, Kota
Segawa, Akihisa Wakayama, Arata Saito, Takayuki Ishihara,
Masahiro Hoshida, Hirotaka Suzuki, Takaaki Shinohara,
Masahiko Sato, Yota Oyama, Kazunori Nakagawa, Yu Hagioita,
Kanae Kawaguchi, Saori Takenawa, Naoki Sekiguchi, Naohiro
Ogura, Kenta Ochiai, Noriko Yamaguchi, Aki Sakai, Kazunobu
Shimura, Natsuko Takahashi, Tomomi Tsuchiya, Miyako
Harimoto, Takehito Kusanagi, Yoshihito Tanahashi, Itta
Nakamura, Shota Shimizu, Ken-Ichi Onozato, Takuma Ozawa,
Kyoko Fujiwara, Hiroshi Ueda, Yukiko Sato
Lighting consultant: Kyoko Fujiwara

CONSTRUCTION LOGIC
Belts of soft PE netting are woven into an amorphous structural
tube. The tube is post-tensioned with PET string, similar to a
cable net structure, and reinforced with PC at its ends.

PLASTICS FOUND

PE   Polyethylene, woven netting, C-ENG Co. Ltd., envelope,
        two layers, 3′ × 12′ × 20 mm thick, woven

PE   Polyethylene, woven netting, C-ENG Co. Ltd., envelope,
        one layer, 20 mm thick, blue and white

PET   Poly(ethylene terephthalate), fiber, envelope, tension
        string (tennis-racket facing)

PMMA   Poly(methyl methacrylate), plate, envelope, connectors
        for tension string network

PC   Polycarbonate, sheet – extruded cells, envelope, wall
        and floor

FRP   Glass fiber reinforced plastic profile – pultruded, AGC
        Matex Co., structure, floor

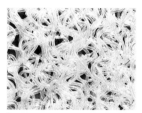

1

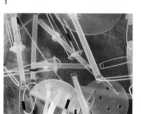

2

3

AQUA-SCAPE IMAGES

1–3   PE netting and PET
        string and PMMA
        connectors
4–9   Launching Aqua-Scape
10–11   Aqua-Scape wall details
12   Inhabiting Aqua-Scape

285

WHY WE USE PLASTICS
THE WAY THAT WE DO

**Collection:
Prototyping
with plastics**

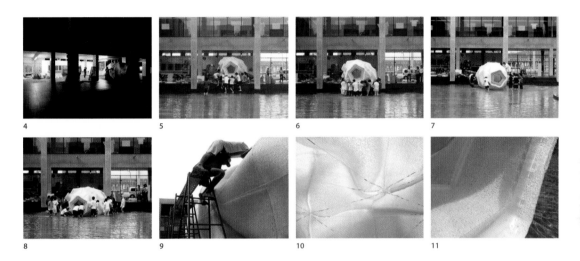

4
5
6
7

8
9
10
11

12

286

WHY WE USE PLASTICS
THE WAY THAT WE DO

Collection:
Prototyping
with plastics

2005 Maximilian's Schell

Ball-Nogues Studio, Los Angeles, California, United States

LOCATION
Materials & Applications, Los Angeles, California, United States

PROGRAM
Shade structure

CLIENT
Materials & Applications

TEAM
Benjamin Ball (principal, design), Gaston Nogues (principal, design), Dewey Ambrosio, Miranda Banks, Freya Bardell, David Bott, Siobhan Burke, Scott Carter, Malachi Conolly, Ben Dean, Jenna Didier, Stephanie Elliot, Rachel Francisco, Rob Fitzgerald, Linda Graveline, Andrew Hardaway, Oliver Hess, Tony Hudgins, Leigh Jerard, Tim Levin, Jonny Lieberman, Brandie Lockett, Kellie Lumb, Alexandra Isaievych, Alex MikoLevine, Fred Moralis, Jim Miller, Phil Miller, Charon Nogues, pAdlAb: Dan Gottlieb & Penny Herscovitch, Harry Pattison, Joanne Pink-Tool, Jeremy Rothe-Kushel, Edward Shelton, Dieter Strolbel, Joe Sturges, Elizabeth Tremante, Hardy Wronskie, and Bryant Yeh.

CONSTRUCTION LOGIC
A tensile matrix of 504 unique PET "petals" where every petal connects to the adjacent petal at three points, forming a whole minimal surface that converges into a vortex. Petal logic lends itself to a sided appearance - petals appear smooth to the exterior, and drape and curl when viewed from the interior.

MEMBRANE ANALYSIS AND ENGINEERING CONSULTANT
Dieter Strobel

STRUCTURAL ENGINEERING CONSULTANTS
David Bott, Hardy Wronske

SOUND
James Lumb

PARAMETRIC MODELING
Benjamin Ball

CURATOR
Jenna Didier, Materials & Applications

1

PLASTICS FOUND

PET	Poly(ethylene terephthalate), film, Mylar®, Dupont™	Petal sheet, sailcloth
PC	Polycarbonate	Rivets, connecting petal to petal
PA	Polyamide	Fiber, nylon, reinforcement in petal
PPTA	Poly(phenylene terephtalamides)	Fiber, Kevlar or Aramid fiber, reinforcement in petal

MAXIMILIAN'S SCHELL IMAGES

1   PET petals from interior
2   Minimal surface from
    exterior

288

WHY WE USE PLASTICS
THE WAY THAT WE DO

Collection:
Prototyping
with plastics

1 →

2006 Alluvial Sponge Comb

Anderson Anderson Architecture,
San Francisco, California, United States

LOCATION
Biennale Gardens, Venice, Italy

PROGRAM
Flood barrier

YEAR
2006

CLIENT
The Venice Biennale

CONSTRUCTION LOGIC
Pleated membranes encase super absorbent polymers (SAPs)
and have the capacity to expand and dam flood waters when
and where necessary.

PLASTICS FOUND

PVC	Poly(vinyl chloride)	Sheet	External membrane, tailored with pleats
PVC	Poly(vinyl chloride)	Sheet	Internal bladder, welded and filled with air
SAP	Super absorbent polymer	Granule	Filling inside bladder (speculative)
PA	Polyamide	Fiber	Providing pressure on the exterior membrane

2

3

4

5

6

7

ALLUVIAL SPONGE COMB IMAGES

1 Inhabiting the Alluvial Sponge
Comb
2–4 Fabrication and testing in
San Francisco
5–7 Final installation in Venice

Collection:
Prototyping
with plastics

2006 Drape Wall/ Drape House

LOCATION
HOMEhouse Project, Weisman Art Museum, University of Minnesota, Minneapolis, Minnesota, United States

PROGRAM
Wall and residence prototype

CLIENT
Weisman Art Museum

TEAM
Blair Satterfield (principal), Marc Swackhamer (principal), Adam Rouse, Pat McGlothlin, Karl Wallick, Susanna Hohmann, Rob Tickle PhD, Dave Hutman, Nick Potts, Antonio Rodriguez, William Dohman, Don Vu, Marcus Martinez

CONSTRUCTION LOGIC
Wall layers are distinctly formed for performance and assembly – the outermost PET "bricks" are lightweight, inexpensive, stackable units, whose deep profile and periodicity permits self-shading and natural ventilation. The innermost PS "bricks" comprise a structural layer and interlock with the outermost. The interior finish layer is at once insulative and made functional with pockets.

PLASTICS FOUND

PET	Poly(ethylene terephthalate)	Sheet	Vacuumed, exterior building envelope, water barrier, high-strength and low-weight exterior bricks, vacuum formed and laser cut, varies in cut design
PS	Polystyrene	Sheet	Vacuumed, exterior building envelope, interlocking structural interior brick, sheets vacuum formed and laser cut, all the same unit
PET	Poly(ethylene terephthalate)		Exterior building envelope, insulator, industrial felt with pockets for storage, often part PET or PA, but can be 100 percent polymer fiber
PA	Polyamide	Prefab unit	Interior cavity seal, zipper, enables felt storage pockets to be operable

DRAPE WALL IMAGES

1	Prototypical assembly, exterior
2	Prototypical assembly, interior
3	Innermost felt finish layer
4–7	Study of unit and bond logic
8–9	Vacuum forming interior and exterior brick modules

Plastics used to prototype possible "unit" systems:

XPS	Polystyrene foam, prefab unit, exterior building envelope, layered sheets to make unit and cut into brick
EPS	Expanded polystyrene, prefab unit, exterior building envelope, CNC-formed brick
PA	Polyamide, prefab unit, exterior building envelope, CNC-formed brick

291

WHY WE USE PLASTICS
THE WAY THAT WE DO

**Collection:
Prototyping
with plastics**

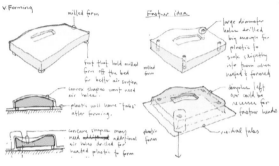

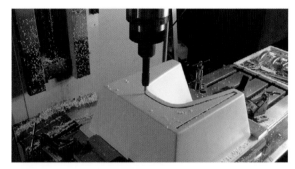

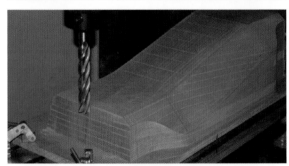

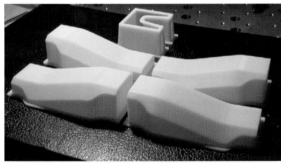

8

9

292

WHY WE USE PLASTICS
THE WAY THAT WE DO

Collection:
Prototyping
with plastics

1 →

2006 Windshape

nArchitects, Brooklyn,
New York, United States

LOCATION
Savannah College of Art and Design (SCAD)
campus, Lacoste, France

PROGRAM
Ephemeral pavilions

YEAR
2006

CLIENT
Savannah College of Art and Design (SCAD)

TEAM
Eric Bunge (partner), Mimi Hoang (partner), Daniela Zimmer
(project architect), Kazuya Katagiri, Takuya Shinoda, Shuji
Suzumori, Jim Bischoff, Michael Gunter, Cindy Hartness, Michael
Porten, Ryan Townsend, Troy Wandzel, with Natalie Bray and
Sarah Walko

FABRICATION
nArchitects and SCAD

CONSTRUCTION LOGIC
Slender tubes of PVC collared by aluminum in groups of three
and shaped through the strategic threading and tensioning of
string to interact with the wind.

PLASTICS FOUND

PVC	Poly(vinyl chloride)	Pipe	Element – flexible tube
PP	Polypropylene	Fiber	Element – flexible fiber connecting tube to tube
SI	Silicone	Adhesive	PVC to "tripod"

2

3

4

5

6

7

8

9

WINDSHAPE IMAGES

1–3 Completed installation of
      Windshape
4–5 PVC pipe preparation
6–7 Installation process
8–9 Complete installation

294

WHY WE USE PLASTICS
THE WAY THAT WE DO

Collection:
Prototyping
with plastics

1 →

2006 Serpentine Gallery Pavilion

Rem Koolhaus, Oma, Rotterdam, Netherlands
Cecil Balmond, Arup, London, England

LOCATION
Kensington Gardens, London, England

PROGRAM
Pavilion

YEAR
2006

CLIENT
Serpentine Gallery Trust, London, England

INTEGRATED DESIGN
Arup

CONSTRUCTION LOGIC
A floating PVC sphere, inflated with helium, may rise or fall over the top of a room encased in PC panels.

PLASTICS FOUND

PC	Polycarbonate	Sheet	Hollow, exterior building envelope, translucent double-layer façade
PC	Polycarbonate	Profile	Extruded, structure solid mullions
ETFE	Ethylene-tetrafluoroethylene copolymer	Film	Interior ceiling, pressurized balloonette window, 0.2 mm thick
PVC	Polyvinyl chloride, coated polyester	Textile	Exterior building envelope, main hall canopy, 2,000 m², inflated with helium and air to 0.07 psi, 8,000 m³ total volume
HDPE	High-density polyethylene	Fiber	Netting to stabilize inflatable
PE	Polyethylene	Sheet	Service, supply pipe reinforced with wire

2

3

4

SERPENTINE IMAGES

1–4 Serpentine Gallery

296

WHY WE USE PLASTICS
THE WAY THAT WE DO

Collection:
Prototyping
with plastics

1 →

2

2007 Water Block House

Kengo Kuma & Associates,
Tokyo, Japan

LOCATION
Home Delivery: Fabricating the Modern Dwelling,
Museum of Modern Art, New York City, New York,
United States

PROGRAM
Wall and residence prototype

CLIENT
Museum of Modern Art

TEAM
Kengo Kuma, Kazuhiko Miyazawa, Shin Ohba, and
Tomoko Sasaki

TECHNICAL
DuPont

LIGHTING
Color Kinetics Japan

CONSTRUCTION LOGIC
An invented unit, a "waterblock," simultaneously
stacks to form a wall or enclosure and stores liquid.
Waterblocks, made of biodegradable PET, support an
end-of-life option.

PLASTICS FOUND

PET	Poly(ethylene terephthalate)	Unit	Biomax® or Apexa® Dupont™, structural wall and building envelope, biodegradable, proposed
PE	Polyethylene	Unit	Structural wall and building envelope, prototype built

WATERBLOCK HOUSE IMAGES

1–2 Waterblock House

298

WHY WE USE PLASTICS
THE WAY THAT WE DO

Collection:
Prototyping
with plastics

1 →

2007 Tea House

Kengo Kuma & Associates, Tokyo, Japan

LOCATION
Museum of Applied Arts, Frankfurt, Germany

PROGRAM
Tea house

CLIENT
Museum of Applied Arts

STRUCTURE ENGINEER
Form TL GmbH, Taiyo Europe GmbH

GENERAL CONSTRUCTOR, BASEMENT
Takenaka Europe GmbH

GENERAL CONSTRUCTOR, MEMBRANE
Cannobio S.p.A.

CONSTRUCTION LOGIC
Two translucent membranes of PTFE separated by
air, but connected, one to the other, by PAT string.
Connections between inner and outer membranes
appear as dimples on the exterior and dots on the
interior.

PLASTICS FOUND

| ePTFE | Expanded polytetrafluoroethylene | Textile | GORE™ Tenara® 3T40, building envelope, two layers, inflatable |
| PAT | Polyester | Fiber | Building envelope, tensile member connecting each layer |

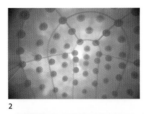

2

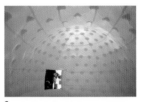

3

4

300

WHY WE USE PLASTICS
THE WAY THAT WE DO

Collection:
Prototyping
with plastics

1 →

2007 Watercube, National Swimming Center

LOCATION
Beijing Olympic Green, Beijing, People's Republic of China

PROGRAM
Swimming center

YEAR
2007

CLIENT
People's Government of Beijing Municipality, Beijing State-owned Assets Management Co., Ltd

TEAM
PTW Architects, Sydney, NSW, Australia: John Bilmon (managing architect, PTW), Chris Bosse (project architect, PTW), John Blanchard (project architect, PTW), Mark Butler (project architect, PTW), Alan Crowe (project architect, PTW), Andrew Frost (project architect, PTW), Michael Lam (project architect, PTW), John Pauline (project architect, PTW), Kurt Wagner (project architect, PTW); *Ove Arup & Partners, Sydney, NSW, Australia*: Tristan Carfrae (design engineer, Arup), Ken Conway (environmental engineer, Arup), Peter McDonald (structural engineer, Arup), Mark Lewis (communications engineer, Arup), Kenneth Ma (building services engineer, Arup), Haico Schepers (building physics, Arup)

CONSTRUCTION
China State Construction & Engineering Corporation – Shenzhen Design Institute (Cscec+Design), Beijing, China

PROJECT MANAGEMENT
Beijing Pake International Engineering Consultancy

EARTHWORK AND FOUNDATIONS
Beijing Mechanical Construction Company

CONSTRUCTION LOGIC
ETFE "bubbles" or pillows under continuous tension through pressurization fill a steel frame. The steel frame and ETFE infill act as a totalizing building envelope.

PLASTICS FOUND

ETFE	Ethylene-tetrafluoroethylene	Copolymer	Exterior building envelope, framed inflated cushions
FEP	Fluorinated ethylene propylene	Ink	Exterior building envelope, printed pattern on pressurized cushions

2

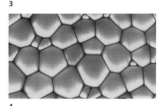

3

4

WATERCUBE IMAGES
1   Bubble effects
2   Watercube bubble-filled interior
3–4 Bubble effects

302

WHY WE USE PLASTICS
THE WAY THAT WE DO

Collection:
Prototyping
with plastics

1 →

2

3

4

2007 Cloak Wall/Cloak House

Houminn Houston, Texas and Minneapolis, Minnesota

LOCATION
Here by Design III: Process and Prototype, the Goldstein Museum
of Design, St. Paul, Minnesota, United States

PROGRAM
Wall and residence prototype

CLIENT
Goldstein Museum Of Design

TEAM
Blair Satterfield (principal), Marc Swackhamer (principal),
Adam Rouse, Pat McGlothlin, Karl Wallick, Susanna Hohmann,
Rob Tickle PhD, Dave Hutman, Nick Potts, Antonio Rodriguez,
William Dohman, Don Vu, Marcus Martinez

CONSTRUCTION LOGIC
Building upon the multi-layered logic of Drape Wall, here
folded metal "bricks" coated in PMMA (automotive) paint which
permits adjustable surface reflectivity are the weathering
layer and the structural layer. The interior finish layer is at
once insulative and made functional with pockets. An ETFE
(prototype as PE) vapor barrier intervenes between these two
layers.

5

PLASTICS FOUND

PMMA	Poly(methyl methacrylate)	Coating, exterior surface, automotive paint with adjustable surface reflectivity due to suspended metallic particles
PA	Polyamide	Profile, structural spacer, separates layers of the system
ETFE	Ethylene-tetrafluoroethylene	Copolymer, film, water vapor barrier/insulation, light-welded together and inflated forming air pockets
PET	Poly(ethylene terephthalate)	Interior building envelope, insulator, industrial felt with pockets for storage, often part PET or PA, but can be 100 percent polymer fiber
PA	Polyamide	Prefab unit, interior cavity seal, zipper, enables felt storage pockets to be operable

Plastics used in the prototyping process:

EPS	Expanded polystyrene	Exterior brick
PE	Polyethylene	Water vapor barrier/insulation

CLOAK WALL IMAGES

1	Prototypical assembly, interior
2	Prototypical assembly, exterior
3–4	Application of PMMA paint
5	Color deployment strategies

304

WHY WE USE PLASTICS
THE WAY THAT WE DO

Collection:
Prototyping
with plastics

1 →

2007 Pavilion For Artek

Shigeru Ban Architects, Tokyo, Japan

LOCATION
Salone Internazionale del Mobile, Triennale Park, Milan, Italy

PROGRAM
Pavilion

CLIENT
Artek (Finnish furniture company) and UPM (Finnish forestry company)

CONSTRUCTION LOGIC
WPC extrusions are rigorously configured into truss elements, arrayed into bays and connected one to the other by similarly configured truss elements. WPC and PC sheathe the frame.

PLASTICS FOUND

WPC	Wood plastic composite	Profile	Extruded, UPM ProFi, structure and exterior cladding, angle made of self-adhesive label materials, layered to create roof and wall
WPC	Wood plastic composite	Profile	Extruded, UPM ProFi, interior flooring, lumber made of self-adhesive label materials
PC	Polycarbonate	Sheet	Corrugated, exterior building envelope, roof and wall

2

3

ARTEK PAVILION IMAGES

1–2 Artek Pavilion
3 Truss detail

306

WHY WE USE PLASTICS
THE WAY THAT WE DO

Collection:
Prototyping
with plastics

1 →

2

2008 Chanel Mobile Art Container

Zaha Hadid Architects, London, England

LOCATION
Hong Kong, Tokyo, New York, Moscow, London,
Paris (traveling)

PROGRAM
Traveling art pavilion

YEAR
2008

CLIENT
Chanel

TEAM
Zaha Hadid (design), Patrik Schumacher
(design), Thomas Vietzke (project architect), Jens
Borstelmann (project architect), Helen Lee, Claudia
Wulf, Erhan Patat, Tetsuya Yamasaki, Daniel Fiser

ENGINEER
Arup

COST/QUANTITY CONSULTANT
David Langdon

CONTRACTOR/TOUR OPERATOR
ES Projects and Bell Lane

FRP MANUFACTURING
Stage One Creative Services Ltd.

CONSTRUCTION LOGIC
A steel frame is clad in 388 unique lightweight FRP
panels, each one arced and sized for handling.

PLASTICS FOUND

FRP	Fiber reinforced plastic	Composite	Exterior building envelope, stressed skin panel
ETFE	Ethylene-tetrafluoroethylene	Copolymer	Foil, exterior building envelope, roof
PVC	Polyvinyl chloride	Film	Exterior building envelope, roof

CHANEL MOBILE ART CONTAINER IMAGES
1   Installing the Art Container in New York
2   Completed Chanel Mobile Art Container

308

WHY WE USE PLASTICS
THE WAY THAT WE DO

Collection:
Prototyping
with plastics

1 →

2008 Villa Nurbs

Cloud 9, Barcelona, Spain

LOCATION
Gerone, Spain

PROGRAM
Residence

CLIENT
Gallego Leon Family

TEAM
Enric Ruiz Geli (principal), Felix Fassbinder (project), Jordi
Fernández Río (project), Agustí Mallol, Manoli Vila (G3), Daniel
Benito Pò, Xavier Badia, Victor Llanos, Miguel Carreiro, Emmanuel
Ruffo, Rosa Duque, André Macedo, Ura Carvalho, Hye Young Yu,
Marta Yebra, Mae Durant, Angelina Pinto, Randall Holl, William
Arbizu, Max Zinnecker, Laia Jutgla, Manel Soler, Megan Kelly-
Sweeney, Alessandra Faticanti, Susanne Bodach, André Brose

ENVIRONMENTAL CONSULTANTS
Estudi Ramon Folch

STRUCTURAL CONSULTANT
Agusti Obiol/Boma S.L., Guillem Baraut, Santos Valladolid

GLAZING
Vicky Colombet, Dominique Haim/Galeria Chanim, Cricursa

CORIAN SKIN
Salvador Vila/IFV

KEVLAR SKIN
TACK Velas

CONSTRUCTION LOGIC
PMMA and PPTA tiles are formed for self shading and arrayed as
cladding on an exterior frame. An encircling of pressurized ETFE
pillows comprise the roof and transmit light into the Villa's interior.

PLASTICS FOUND

ETFE	Ethylene-tetrafluoroethylene	copolymer	Foil, exterior building envelope, roof
FEP	Fluorinated ethylene propylene		Foil ink, exterior building envelope, roof
PMMA	Poly(methyl methacrylate)	Surfacing	Corian®, exterior building envelope, wall
PPTA	Poly(phenylene terephtalamides)	Film	Kevlar, exterior building envelope, wall

2

3

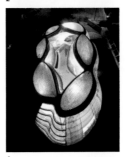

4

5

6

7

8

VILLA NURBS IMAGES

1   PMMA cladding by day
2   PMMA by night
3   Exterior at dusk
4   PMMA by night, top view
5–6 Under construction
7–8 Details of PMMA and PPTA cladding

310

WHY WE USE PLASTICS
THE WAY THAT WE DO

Collection:
Prototyping
with plastics

1 →

2008 Cellophane House®

KieranTimberlake, Philadelphia, Pennsylvania, United States

LOCATION
Home Delivery: Fabricating the Modern Dwelling, the Museum of
Modern Art, New York City, New York, United States

PROGRAM
Residence

YEAR
2008

CLIENT
Museum of Modern Art

TEAM
Stephen Kieran, FAIA (partner), James Timberlake, FAIA
(partner), David Riz, AIA (associate-in-charge), Steven Johns,
AIA (project architect), Chris Macneal, AIA (technical review),
Richard Maimon, AIA, Matthew Krissel, AIA, Andrew Schlatter,
Sarah Savage, Bradley Baer, David Hincher, AIA, Jeremy Leman,
AIA, Alex Gauzza, Bradley Baer, Cesar Querales, David Feaster,
Ryan Meillier, Kate Czembor, AIA, Jose Galarza, Peter Curry,
Dominic Muren, Jason Niebish, Laurent Hedquist, AIA, Casey
Boss, AIA, Rod Bates, Derek Brown, Vincent Calabro, Erin Crowe,
Mark Davis, Billie Faircloth, Trevor Horst, Aaron Knorr, Caleb
Knutson, Marina Rubina, AIA, Paul Worrell, AIA

FABRICATION AND ASSEMBLY CONSULTANTS
Kullman Buildings Corporation, Avi Telyas (president),
Geoff Crossan (project manager)

CONSTRUCTION MANAGER
F.J. Sciame Construction Co., Inc., Joseph Mizzi (president),
Jay Gorman (project manager)

STRUCTURAL ENGINEER
CVM Engineers, Jon Morrison (partner), Vassil Dragonov (project
engineer)

EXTERIOR WALL PANEL FABRICATOR
Universal Services Associates, Inc.

LIGHTING DESIGNER
Arup Lighting, Brian Stacy (senior lighting designer)

ACRYLIC STAIR FABRICATOR
Capital Plastics Company

DISPLAY
Czarnowski

MECHANICAL/ELECTRICAL ENGINEER
Arup, Roger Chang (lead mechanical engineer)

ON-SITE RIGGERS
Craftweld Fabrication Company Inc.
Photography: Albert Vecerka/Esto (assembly), Peter Aaron/Esto
(final)

CONSTRUCTION LOGIC
An aluminum frame, chunked for rapid on-site delivery and rapid
disassembly, is filled with translucent and transparent materials
permitting a pellucid tower. Solid PMMA is configured into the
tower stair; cellular PETG sheets comprise floor decking elements;
the next iteration of SmartWrap® is here as four layers of PET with
an airspace between to trap or vent heat as required.

continued overleaf ↘

Collection:
Prototyping
with plastics

PLASTICS FOUND

PET	Poly(ethylene terephthalate)	Film	Dupont Tejin Films™, exterior building envelope, Next-Generation SmartWrap™ layer 1 weather barrier
PET	Poly(ethylene terephthalate)	Film	Dupont Tejin Films™, exterior building envelope, Next-Generation SmartWrap™ layer 2 with thin-film photovoltaics
PI	Polyimide	Film	Exterior building envelope, substrate for photovoltaics applied to Next-Generation SmartWrap™ on layer 2, 1 mm or 0.025 mm thick
PET	Poly(ethylene terephthalate)	Film	Prestige window film PR70 by 3M™, exterior building envelope, Next-Generation SmartWrap™ layer 3, IR reducing film
PET	Poly(ethylene terephthalate)	Film	Dupont Tejin Films™, exterior building envelope, Next-Generation SmartWrap™ layer 4 interior layer
PC	Polycarbonate	Sheet – extruded	Danpalon®, exterior building envelope, roofing, cellular sheeting integrated with PVs
SI	Silicone	Sheet – flexible	Exterior building envelope, roofing, cap piece
PVC	Polyvinyl chloride	Tube	Exterior transparent downspout
PETG	Poly(ethylene terephthalate) glycol comonomer	Sheet – cellular	3Form® Pep/Stage Quartz, interior floor slab
PETG	Poly(ethylene terephthalate) glycol comonomer	Sheet – solid	3Form® Varia, interior, partitions
PMMA	Poly(methyl methacrylate)	Sheet – solid	Interior, staircase, CNC routed
FRP	Fiber reinforced plastic	Prefabricated unit	Interior, bathroom pod
PMMA	Poly(methyl methacrylate)	Adhesive	3M VHB™, interior/exterior multi-purpose adhesive, PEP to aluminum frame, Varia to stud wall
PMMA	Poly(methyl methacrylate)	Adhesive	3M, padding, grating and aluminum

2

3

4

313

WHY WE USE PLASTICS
THE WAY THAT WE DO

**Collection:
Prototyping
with plastics**

5

6

7

8

9

10

11

12

13

14

CELLOPHANE IMAGES

1	Cellophane House installed
2	Cellophane House interior
3	Cellophane house bathroom module
4–7	On-site installation process
8–9	Stair mock-up and stair installed
10–14	SmartWrap exterior, fabrication and installation

314

WHY WE USE PLASTICS
THE WAY THAT WE DO

Collection:
Prototyping
with plastics

1 →

2008 Lunar House

davidclovers and C.E.B. Reas

CLIENT
Hometta (http://hometta.com)

LOCATION
Typical 50 ft × 100 ft lot with standard setbacks

TYPE
2500 ft^2, three bedrooms, three baths, studio-
residence

STATUS
Construction documentation complete

DESIGN
davidclovers and C.E.B. Reas

DESIGN TEAM
David Erdman, Clover Lee, Casey Reas, Jei Kim,
Juliet Hsieh, Laura Goard, Yvette Herrera, Rathi
Subramanian, Jason Dembski, Damien Hannigan

CONSTRUCTION LOGIC
PMMA solid surfacing is robotically carved and
thermoformed, permitting strategic areas of
translucency and leveraging the thick and thin
effects of the material. Here the scaled model of the
Lunar House is the prototype.

PLASTICS FOUND

| PMMA | Poly(methyl methacrylate) | Surfacing | Corian®, exterior building envelope, wall |

2

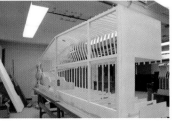

3

4

5

LUNAR HOUSE IMAGES

1   Completed model and
     translucent effects
2   Model, overall view
3–5 Model fabrication process

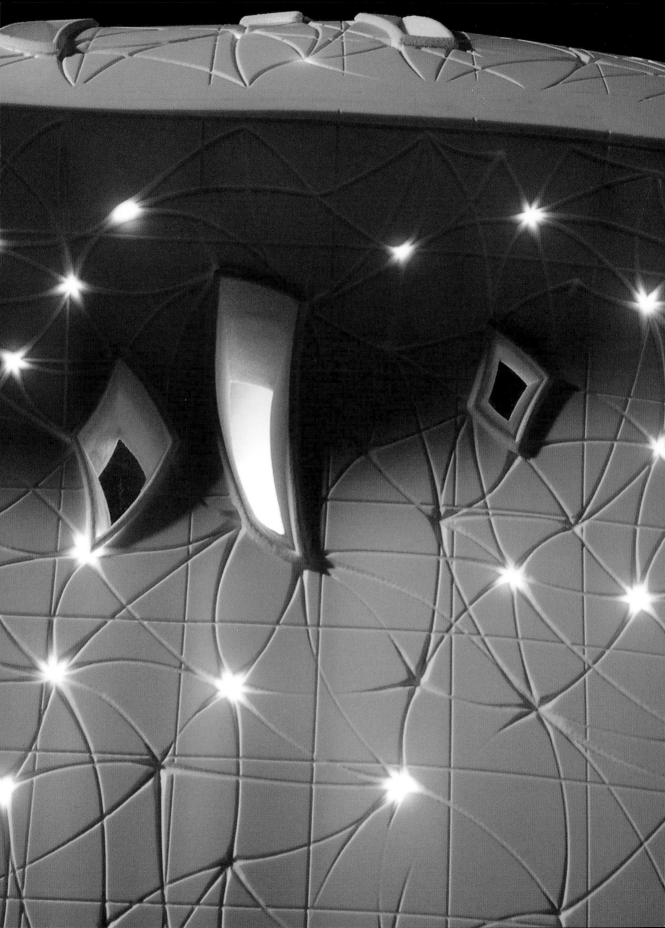

316

WHY WE USE PLASTICS
THE WAY THAT WE DO

Collection:
Prototyping
with plastics

1 →

2009 Yud Yud

DESIGN
davidclovers and C.E.B. Reas

DESIGN TEAM
David Erdman, Clover Lee and Casey
Reas, Fei Mui, Jason Dembski

CLIENT
DuPont China/davidclovers

LOCATION
Wan Chai, Hong Kong

TYPE
Commercial storefront

STATUS
Completed in 2009

CONSTRUCTION LOGIC
The thermoforming, robotic carving
process, and thin/thick effects
explored in the Lunar House are
extended to the full scale fabrication
of Yud Yud, a totalizing storefront
made from PMMA.

PLASTICS FOUND

PMMA	Poly(methyl methacrylate)	Surfacing	Corian®, exterior building envelope, wall

2

3

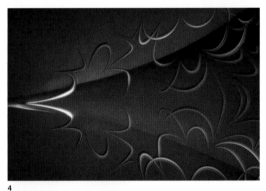

4

5

YUD YUD IMAGES

1   Yud Yud closed
2   Yud Yud open to street
3   Yud Yud installation
4–5 Detail of carved PMMA
     and light-transmitting
     effects

1 →

2010 Immuring

LOCATION
SCIArc, Los Angeles

DAVIDCLOVERS DESIGN TEAM
David Erdman, Clover Lee, Jason Dembski, Shawna Krantz,
Yvette Herrera, Fei Mui

SCIARC STUDENT INSTALLATION TEAM
Shawna Krantz (director); Tristan Brasseur, Kristen George,
Mikhail Gladchenko, Pil-Sun Ham, Soojin Kim, Alice Ying
Leung, Huan Liu, Naureen Meyer, Hyewon Clare Mok, Miguel
Vega

COLLABORATORS
C.E.B. Reas (Los Angeles); DuPont China Ltd.; Speed Top Ltd.
(Hong Kong); E-Grow (Shanghai)

STRUCTURAL ENGINEERING
William Koh and Associates (Los Angeles)

FAÇADE ENGINEERING
Inhabit (Hong Kong)

INSTALLATION CONSTRUCTION SUPERVISION AND SUPPORT
Paul Reynolds of CSB Contractors Inc. (Los Angeles)

LIGHTING
Eco-Green Lighting Inc. (Los Angeles)

FINISHING
Tortoise Industries (Los Angeles)

CLIENT
This research is based upon Lunar House, a 2500 ft² home
designed for Hometta Inc. (Houston, Texas).
This exhibition was made possible with the generous support
of DuPont China Ltd. and Speed Top Ltd. (Hong Kong).

CONSTRUCTION LOGIC
Immuring further extends the scale of thermoforming and
robotic carving demonstrated in Lunar House and Yud Yud,
with the fabrication of larger arrayed units, joining between
units and more pervasive translucent surface effects.

PLASTICS FOUND

PMMA	Poly(methyl methacrylate)	Surfacing	Corian®, exterior building envelope, wall

2

3

4

5

6

IMMURING IMAGES

1 Immuring installed
2–3 Fabrication process
4–5 Installation of
    fiber optics (4) and
    placement of wall
    units (5)
6 Detail of carved PMMA
    and formed void

320

WHY WE USE PLASTICS
THE WAY THAT WE DO

Collection:
Prototyping
with plastics

1 →

2013 VarVac

LOCATION
University of Minnesota, Minneapolis, Minnesota, United States

PROGRAM
Interior acoustics wall

CLIENT
Weisman Art Museum

TEAM
Blair Satterfield (principal), Marc Swackhamer (principal),
Adam Rouse, Pat McGlothlin, Karl Wallick, Susanna Hohmann,
Rob Tickle PhD, Dave Hutman, Nick Potts, Antonio Rodriguez,
William Dohman, Don Vu, Marcus Martinez

Drape Wall is a full-scale wall prototype that presents energy
innovations through new approaches

CONSTRUCTION LOGIC
Vacuum-formed PS panels generated through a custom mold
fill a frame. Planar cutting across PS panels arrays a series of
ovoid openings. Assembled, PS panels lined with PET felt form
an interior surface which absorbs and reflects sound.

PLASTICS FOUND

PS	Polystyrene	Sheet – vacuumed	Exterior building envelope, interlocking structural interior brick, sheets vacuum-formed and laser cut, all the same unit
PET	Poly(ethylene terephthalate)		Exterior building envelope, insulator, industrial felt with pockets for storage, often part PET or PA, but can be 100 percent polymer fiber

2

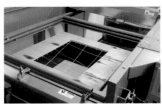

3

4

5

VARVAC IMAGES

1–2 VarVac installed
3 VarVac mold insert at vacuum
former
4 Vacuum formed PS at various
draw heights
5 Post-processing cutting of
vacuum formed PS

NOTES

1   There are several transects missing that others have covered or should cover. A history of inflatable or pressurized structures and a history of plastics structures. These transects, too, will be truncated by the events about to be recounted.

2   Histories for individual polymer chemistries used in architecture was not attempted, but could have been. Transects for materials such as polycarbonate (PC), ethylene tetrafluoroethylene (ETFE), and fiber reinforced polymer (FRP) would have been revealing.

3   This is not to say that experimentation ceased. We do know, for instance, that experimentation with plastic tensioned membranes and inflatables continued. The record ceases, as does the dialogue.

4   *The Architects Journal*. 1973. "Part 1: Glass Fibre Reinforced Plastics for Building Claddings, The Material and Its Uses," "Part 2: Glass Fibre Reinforced Plastics, Translucent GRP," and "Part 3: Glass Fibre Reinforced Plastics for Building Claddings, Pigmented GRP," beginning on pages 690, 817, 1035, respectively.

5   Armand Winfield. *Progressive Architecture*. 1973. "Plastic Structures Go High-Rise," 8: 73.

6   Arthur Quarmby, *Plastics and Architecture* (New York: Praeger, 1974).

7   Life safety is an architect's professional fiduciary responsibility.

8   See Chapter 02 of this book which recounts the development of a building code inclusive of plastics materials which first took the form of "A Model Chapter on Plastics for Inclusion in a Building Code."

9   Refer also to the published papers of Dr. Russell B. Akin of E.I. DuPont de Nemours & Co., Inc. for a thorough pre-1973 discussion of the burning characteristics of plastics and the building code. For instance, see: Russell B. Akin, "Fire Testing and Acceptance of Plastics in Building Codes," in *Technical Papers, Regional Technical Conference, Plastics in Building*, edited by John Hyden (Stamford, CT: Society of Plastics Engineers, 1969), 51–60.

10   Armstrong Cork Company, "To the Reader," in *Symposium: Products of Combustion of (Plastics) Building Materials* (Lancaster, PA: Armstrong Cork Company, 1973), frontispiece.

11   US Federal Trade Commission, "In the Matter of The Society of the Plastics Industry, Inc., et al.," in *Federal Trade Commission Decisions, Findings, Opinions, and Orders July 1, 1974 to December 31, 1974*. Washington, DC: US Government Printing Office, 1975), 1253–1279.

12   Ibid., 1263–1264. See Paragraph 18 for the "diametric" characterization of fire hazards listed in items a–f.

13   Obituary of R. Brady Williamson. *Fire Mater*. 2007; 31: 355–357, published online in Wiley InterScience (www.intersicen.wiley.com) DOI 10.1002/fam.958.

14   R. Brady Williamson, "Fire Safety in Urban Housing: A Description of the NSF-RANN Program at the University of California, Berkeley," in *Symposium: Products of Combustion of (Plastics) Building Materials* (Lancaster, PA: Armstrong Cork Company, 1973), 77.

15   See research findings which took this first-principles approach to fire testing: B.J. Callahan. "Evaluation of the Fire Hazard of Cellular Plastics in Building Construction and the SLRP Concept," in *Technical Papers, Regional Technical Conference, Plastics in Building: Present Status and Future Prospects* (Society of Plastics Engineers Eastern New England Section, 1976), 44–53.

16 For a complete listing of the order see pages 1270–1279 of US Federal Trade Commission, "In the Matter of The Society of the Plastics Industry, Inc., et al.," in *Federal Trade Commission Decisions, Findings, Opinions, and Orders July 1, 1974 to December 31, 1974* (Washington, DC: US Government Printing Office, 1975).

17 For the committee's final report, see the following: Products Research Committee. 1980. *Fire Research on Cellular Plastics: The Final Report of the Products Research Committee*. Washington, DC: PRC.

18 US Federal Trade Commission, "In the Matter of The Society of the Plastics Industry, Inc., et al.," in *Federal Trade Commission Decisions, Findings, Opinions, and Orders July 1, 1974 to December 31, 1974* (Washington, DC: US Government Printing Office, 1975), 1278–1279.

19 See page 92 of *Progressive Architecture*'s February 1975 issue for the requisite quarter-page notice per the FTC order.

20 Here I am referring to the June 1960 and October 1970 issues of *Progressive Architecture*, dedicated solely to the subject of plastics in architecture.

21 Gerd Wilcke, "Plastics Industry Hurt by Lack of Raw Materials Made of Oil," *New York Times*, November 30, 1973.

22 For a list of all "respondent companies," see: US Federal Trade Commission, "In the Matter of The Society of the Plastics Industry, Inc., et al.," in *Federal Trade Commission Decisions, Findings, Opinions, and Orders July 1, 1974 to December 31, 1974* (Washington, DC: US Government Printing Office, 1975), 1253–1257.

23 *Progressive Architecture*. 1975. "Pandora's Plastic Box," 86. Emphasis on word "configuration" is SPI's.

24 Ibid., Emphasis on word "not" is mine.

25 Ibid., 89

26 Ibid., 90

27 Admittedly this context could be broadened. At the US national level in the 1970s, landmark agencies were formed to promote policies on energy, environment, and worker safety. These are the US Environmental Protection Agency (US EPA, 1970), the US Occupational Safety and Health Administration (US OSHA, 1971), and the US Energy Information Administration (US EIA, 1974).

CHAPTER 06

PROFESSING PLASTICS

1957, Amsterdam

The occasion is the World Plastics Exhibition *where all things plastics – their origins, types, brand names, and uses, are displayed didactically and tactically. A tractor is suspended by ribbons of clear plastics film, overtly suggesting that plastics' thinness should not be misconstrued for weakness. Buckets of shimmering granulate are transformed into cups and bowls via various techniques such as blow molding and injection molding. Thin and pliable polystyrene sheet effortlessly transforms into a classical visage via vacuum forming. Witness the material, witness the machinery! Transformation is instant – use instantaneous. Is this how we should use plastics?*

Our inner cultural and corporate monologue is forming: "Plastics take the stage at an international exhibit in Amsterdam. Ingenious alchemy of coal and oil provides the material; ingenious machinery presses and stamps and molds the material into a wide variety of products, articles for household use, as well as tools for industry … and for art too. The horizons of plastic are lengthening and strengthening too, supported by thin strips of it – a tractor. In the world of tomorrow plastics will certainly call a tune." [1]

A series of stills from the film *Modern Alchemy*, Universal International Newsreel, 1957.

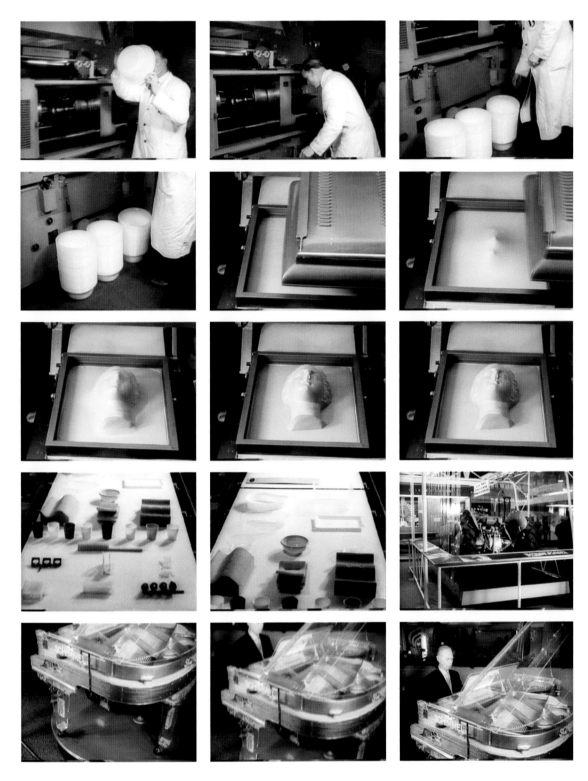

PLASTIC
Roland Barthes

1957, Paris

*Did Roland Barthes attend a
similarly appointed plastics
exhibition? His essay "Plastic,"
published in 1957 amid the
chorus of expositions on myth
and life which comprises the
book* Mythologies, *suggests
that he did. Was he "surprised"
by plastics' customizability,
conjuring the potential for
"infinite transformation"? Did
he sniff out his phrase "nothing
but trajectory" – as inputs and
outputs were both emphasized
and obvious? Did he experience
the heat emanating from the
machinery? Heat coupled with
machine may define plastics as
a "trace of a movement." As he
planned out the myth "Plastic,"
did he hear the refrain of the
popular voiceover?*

In spite of its having Greek shepherds'
names (Polystyrene, Phenoplast, Polyvinyl,
Polyethylene), plastic, of which the products
have just been concentrated in an exhibition,
is an essentially alchemical substance. At the
entrance to the stall, the public waits in a long
line to see accomplished the magical operation
par excellence: the conversion of substance. An
ideally shaped machine, tabulated and oblong
(the right shape to manifest the secret of an
itinerary), effortlessly draws from a heap of
greenish crystals a series of gleaming fluted pin
trays. At one end the raw telluric substance,
and at the other the perfect object; and between
these two extremes, nothing; nothing but a
trajectory, scarcely watched over by a helmeted
employee, half god, half robot.

Thus, more than a substance, plastic is the
very idea of its infinite transformation. As its
vulgar name indicates, it is ubiquity made
visible; moreover, this is the reason why it is
a miraculous substance: a miracle is always a
sudden conversion of nature. Plastic remains
completely impregnated by this astonishment:
it is less an object than a trace of a movement.

And since this movement is here virtually
infinite, transforming the original crystals
into a multitude of increasingly surprising
objects, plastic is, ultimately, a spectacle to
be deciphered: the very spectacle of its end
products. In front of each final shape (valise,
brush, automobile body, toy, fabric, tube, basin,
or paper), the mind unceasingly takes the prim-
itive substance for an enigma. This is because
plastic's quick-change talent is total: it can
form pails as well as jewels. Whence a perpetual
astonishment, the reverie of man at the sight
of the proliferations of substance, detecting the
connections between the singular of its origin
and the plural of its effects. Moreover, this
astonishment is the source of pleasure, since
it is by the scope of transformations that man
measures his power, and since it is precisely
plastic's itinerary which gives him the euphoria
of a prestigious slide through Nature.

But the price to be paid for this success is the
plastic, sublimated as a movement, almost
fails to exist as a substance. Its constitution
is negative: neither hard nor deep, it must
content itself with a neutral substantial quality
despite its utilitarian advantages: *resistance*, a
state which signifies no more than the simple
suspension of yielding. In the poetic order of
major substances, plastic is a disgraced material,
lost between the effusion of rubber and the flat
hardness of metal: it achieves none of the true
productions of the mineral order: foam, fibers,
strata. It is a shaped substance: whatever its final
state, plastic retains a flocculent appearance,
something opaque, creamy and coagulated,
an impotence ever to attain the triumphant
sleekness of nature. But what most betrays it
is its undoing, as its colors, for it seems able
to preserve only the most chemical versions:
of yellow, red, and green it keeps nothing but
the most aggressive state, using them as mere
names, capable of displaying only the concepts
of colors.

The fashion for plastic highlights an evolution
in the myth of the simili. It is commonly
acknowledged that the simili is a historically
bourgeois usage (the earliest vestimentary
"imitation" materials date from the dawn of
capitalism); but till now the simili has always
meant pretension, being part of a world of
appearance, not of usage; it was intended
to reproduce cheaply the rarest substances,
diamonds, silks, feathers, silver, all the luxurious
brilliance of the world. Plastic is in decline, it
is a household material. It is the first magical
material that consents to be prosaic; but it is
precisely because of its prosaic nature that it
triumphs. For the first time, artifice aims for the
common, not for the rare. And thereby nature's
ancestral function has been modified; it is no
longer the Idea, the pure Substance which is to
be regained or imitated; an artificial substance,
more fecund than all the world's deposits, will
replace it, will command the very invention of
the shapes. A luxury object always derives for
the earth, always recalls in a precious way its
mineral or animal origin, the natural theme of
which is merely an actuality. Plastic is entirely
engulfed in its usage: one of these days objects
will be invented merely for the pleasure of using
them. The hierarchy of substances is forthwith
abolished, a single one will replace them all: the
whole world, even life itself, can be plasticized
since, we are told, plastic aortas are beginning
to be manufactured.[2]

COLLECTION
ESSAYS IN RESPONSE TO "PLASTIC"

Step away from this task of aggregating our professional history of plastics – of answering "Why do we use plastics the way that we do?" Rather, let Barthes' bent to coalesce meaning from present experience – from "plastic" – allow you to check your own perceptions of them and form definitive statements about their use and future. Based on where you are right now and how you orient yourself to the pursuit of knowledge – literally what you do – how do you define and describe plastics? Two science writers, two chemists – one who works in the realm of emerging plastics and one who continues to normalize existing plastics – a museum conservationist, a structural engineer, and 13 architectural designers with various philosophical bents – with positions on tools, techniques, making, performance, form, aesthetics, and energy – took up this challenge. The collection of essays follows Barthes and establishes a discourse with Barthes' point of view as much as it critiques it, by contextualizing first-hand accounts of plastics, engaging plastics, and demystifying plastics. Here, there are fewer spectacles and more use and strategic dissection surrounded by individual theoretical or practical points of view. Our contributors may document a focused experience with plastics; translate terminology to the uninitiated; describe virtual plastics or real plastics; portend plastic's future.

An accumulation of voices might yield a starting point from which to dissect plastics' relationship to architecture. Such a starting point might frame one's own series of transects through what has been described as an "unwieldy" data set. Or, conversely, the accumulation of voices might yield a way forward that engages across disciplines. Or furthermore, one might find productive agreements and disagreements within the mix. The results frankly are uncertain – it is an imperfect experiment. However, this collection of essays is reminiscent of the "talking out loud" about plastics (materials) early in their professional public vetting. But while it is mildly reflexive with those series of events, it no way repeats them. If inertia still abounds when it comes to plastics in architecture, it is a mature inertia that respects and recognizes the emergence of disciplines alongside 80-plus years of plastics know-how.

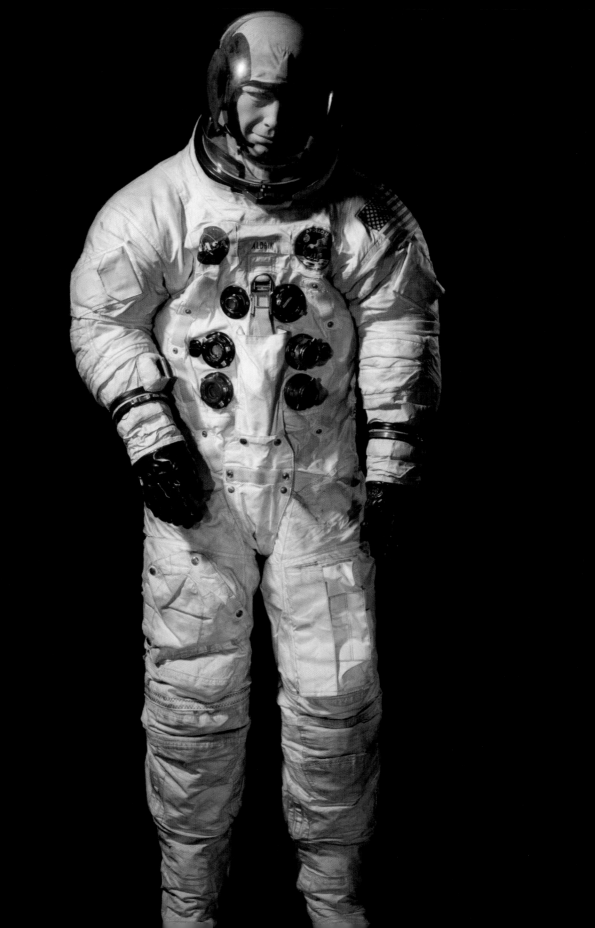

THE PLASTIC PROTEUS
PHILIP BALL

Since the advent of materials we call plastics, every age has reinvented these substances to reflect its own preoccupations. As Roland Barthes pointed out, the first artificial polymers offered a simulacrum of luxury. (Permit here the pedantry of "polymer" in place of the more culturally resonant "plastic." Plastic is really an adjective, a description of mechanical behavior that can apply also to metals and ceramics. Our conventional "plastics" are polymers, materials composed of chains of atoms, generally with backbones of carbon and derived from the hydrocarbons of petroleum oil.) Celluloid, discovered in 1832 and marketed from the 1860s, imitated ivory; Bakelite (1905) pretended to be mahogany; rayon (1924) and nylon (1935) were marketed as faux silk. If you couldn't afford the real thing, these early plastics offered its appearances.

But the utopian plastics of the post-war era in which Barthes wrote had no such pretensions: they celebrated their cheapness, their artificiality, and their Protean nature: they were tinted with garish pigments and injection-molded into smooth, science-fiction contours. They were materials of domestic convenience: non-stick, wipe-clean, waterproof.

Things have moved on. We no longer desire this Sputnik-era democratization of materials. Plastics palled: they flutter in undecaying rags from tree tops, they lodge indecorously in streams and sit unrepentant in landfills. The plastics of the Nixon and Reagan years were more modest, minimalist, even stylish: sleek casings in black, white, and gray, housing ever more pervasive consumer electronics. That was not always sufficient seduction, however: we started to question if plastics were good for us. The manufacture of PVC was found to involve carcinogenic compounds. Additives used to make plastics soft and flexible may also mimic human hormones, disrupting the endocrine system. Some are now banned from children's toys.

And we began to worry about the plastic afterlife: to ponder how these tangles of polymer molecules might be unraveled for re-use, or how they might be made from raw materials other than oil that micro-organisms in the natural environment can chew up and reduce back to non-toxic, invisible matter.

The fact is, however, that "plastics" have found niches far beyond the mundane domesticity that exercised Barthes: they are more mutable, more versatile, more "infinitely transformable" than even he anticipated. They tether oil rigs to the sea floor and carry blood through artificial veins in our bodies. We can make "plastic antibodies," tiny synthetic particles the size of proteins that capture biological molecules. Most tellingly of all, plastics are colonizing the information age. They conduct electrical signals and pulses of data-laden light, they glow in light-emitting diodes, they can be printed like ink into electronic circuits as flexible and almost as cheap as paper. The possibilities trump Dalí: televisions that can be rolled up like magazines, computers that work on T-shirts.

These, perhaps, are the plastics to suit the twenty-first century, woven invisibly into an environment saturated with information, awaiting or even anticipating our commands, changing shape, color, texture at the push of a button. In the end they will become smarter than we are.

PHILIP BALL, PhD
IS A FREELANCE SCIENCE WRITER WORKING IN ENGLAND, THE AUTHOR OF MANY BOOKS INCLUDING *DESIGNING THE MOLECULAR WORLD* AND *MADE TO MEASURE: NEW MATERIALS FOR THE 21ST CENTURY*, AND A CONSULTANT EDITOR FOR *NATURE*, WHERE HE PREVIOUSLY WORKED AS AN EDITOR FOR PHYSICAL SCIENCES.

FACING PAGE

Buzz Aldrin's A7L spacesuit, made of PTFE
(polytetrafluoroethylene), a high-performance plastic.

EVERYWHERE, PLASTICS
JOHN E. FERNÁNDEZ

Plastics are everywhere. In the last century, synthetic polymers were marveled at for their seemingly endless capabilities to *be* almost anything – to *represent* almost any material.[3] Since their development, synthetic polymers have been engineered to *do* almost anything.

Virtuoso imitation characterized early plastics, yet early plastics, such as Bakelite, showed signs of crazing[4] and cracking within just a couple of years of use. Today, high performance drives massive flows of synthetics into every sector of our economy. The latest technical plastics can function under stresses of 110 MPa (polyamide-imides), elongate 800 percent (elastomers), survive temperatures as high as 180° Celsius[5] and act as fire retardants (melamine foams), and resist degradation from UV and concentrated high-intensity radiation (ETFE).[6]

From short-lived packaging to plasticizers for concrete infrastructure meant to last many decades, if not hundreds of years, plastics are everywhere – especially in our cities. We are only now becoming aware of the frenetic dispersion of this wholly synthetic material class into every technical use in our built environment, from sealants, to shims, coatings, rigid composite panels, insulations, fabrics, and sheet materials … and the list goes on and on.[7] And just as plastics first served as inexpensive simulacra of the luxury materials of the nineteenth century – ivory, tortoise shell, gemstones – plastics now accompany the making of a vast new emerging urban future, the material medium serving the new urban appetite.

In fact, we are in the midst of furiously transforming our endowment of fossil crude into the cities of the twenty-first century, through unprecedented energy consumption and petrochemical refinement.

Take India, for example. During the 1990s, plastic consumption – dominated by polyethylene (PE), polypropylene (PP) and polyvinyl chloride (PVC) – grew at a rate twice that of GDP. Per capita Indian synthetic polymer consumption in 2000 was 5 kg (including recycled plastics), compared with 0.8 kg in 1991 – however, still only one-quarter of China's consumption, the world's second largest plastics maker.[8]

So it is no surprise that plastics are everywhere – in innumerable implements and machines in every countryside, village, and city in the world – from the Bulgari watch band to the Vietnamese soup spoon. The proliferation has been so intense for so long that we are no longer in control of it. Consider the fact that 100 million polyethylene bags are discarded every year in Kenya alone and have become the so-called "flower of Africa" (as M. Lacy noted in a *New York Times* article on April 7, 2005), that every ocean has been found to be infested with microscopic particles of the most common of the commodity plastics,[9] that plastics are now among the giants of globally traded commodities.

Uncanny emulation as a primary attribute of plastics has ceded to a pronounced facility to perform – to do almost anything – and therefore, to be everywhere.

JOHN E. FERNÁNDEZ
IS A PROFESSOR AND DIRECTOR OF THE BUILDING TECHNOLOGY PROGRAM IN THE DEPARTMENT OF ARCHITECTURE AT MASSACHUSETTS INSTITUTE OF TECHNOLOGY (MIT). HE IS THE AUTHOR OF *MATERIAL ARCHITECTURE: EMERGENT MATERIALS FOR INNOVATIVE BUILDINGS AND ECOLOGICAL CONSTRUCTION* (OXFORD: ARCHITECTURAL PRESS, 2005).

IM-PLASTIC
MICHELLE ADDINGTON

The normative lexicon of architectural materials privileges the tangible artifact. The primary categories of wood, metals, stone, ceramics, glass, and plastic present and represent the constructive elements and the visible components of design. Wood might be used in structural framing or finished flooring, stone might appear in foundations or countertops. The resulting artifacts are rather limited in comparison to those produced in the larger material world outside of architecture, and as such they are more definite in scope and finite in application.

When a new material enters the scene it does so through the context and categories of our existing lexicon. A material such as a photochromic might be shoehorned into the glass category and thus conceptually constrained to applications in glazing; a material such as shape memory alloy will often be assigned to the metals category, which is perhaps why we see so many attempts by architects to incorporate it into cladding even though its primary use in other fields is for switches. The hegemony of the artifact is so pervasive that these often unprecedented materials are presented as if they are simply additional choices in our traditional palette. Their properties are presented in the same manner as conventional materials, their applications are represented through the typical objects of design. It is as if the nominative supersedes the performative.

The category of plastics is enigmatic within this system of classification. Plastics are often treated as a "universal donor" – materials that can seamlessly substitute for a multitude of other materials used in quotidian applications. Acrylic begets "artificial stone" but also transparent glazing. Nylon may be spun into flowing textiles or rigidly cast into moldings. With the right additives and composites, there is no application that cannot be filled with some form of plastic, there is no visual appearance that cannot be reproduced by a plastic. As such, the term plastic does not readily lead to an image or a specific set of artifacts. We presume that it is formless and featureless until we assign its character.

Paradoxically, the unending formal flexibility of plastics at the macro scale of architectural artifacts results from organizational inflexibility at the micro scale of plastic molecules, particularly those of synthetic polymers. Although polymers are often described as amorphous, they are semi-crystalline in nature. The crystalline structure is not of the three-dimensional matrix that we typically associate with solids, but is instead a one- or two-dimensional linear chain. The chain is inviolate and inflexible, and the length of the chain is an indication of the purity and quality of the polymer. The amorphous nature results not from the molecular chain composition or type, but from how the chains are aggregated. (One of the most common analogic descriptions of polymers is that they resemble a plate of spaghetti – the noodles are the individual chains whereas the mound on the plate results from an interlaced contiguity of noodles.) The formal flexibility that we value so much as architects and designers is almost an ancillary aspect. Yet it is the resultant forms – the artifacts – that we recognize, categorize, and specify.

Rather than thinking about plastics as imitators and substitutes within our conventional palette of materials, could we not think how best to exploit the characteristics that make plastics so unlike all other materials? Fields outside of design that privilege the

performative over the nominitive have capitalized on the morphology of the molecular chain. Drawn filaments are perhaps the purest expression of the chain; thin films are designed by manipulating chain orientation.

The one area in design that has begun to exploit the properties and morphology of polymers is light, which as a sub-micron-scale phenomenon is highly affected by molecular orientation. We are beginning to see a wide range of performative plastic films for color, polarization, and directional control.

The manipulation of light is but a small sliver of the potential available to us if we can exploit the truly unique features enabled by specific molecular organization and uni-directional orientation. By thinking extensively about the potential of the behavior of plastic rather than intensively about its ability to replicate an artifact, we may be able to introduce an unprecedented array of performative materials into quotidian architectural design. The highly engineered materials and systems that are so prevalent today could readily be supplanted by inexpensive, yet highly selective plastics by strategically leveraging specific properties. But it does demand that we radically invert our approach – our lexicon must be rewritten as a matrix of behaviors and results rather than as a list of components and applications.

MICHELLE ADDINGTON
IS EDUCATED AS AN ENGINEER AND ARCHITECT, AND IS CO-AUTHOR OF *SMART MATERIALS AND TECHNOLOGIES IN ARCHITECTURE* AND *EMERGING TECHNOLOGIES*. SHE IS CURRENTLY THE HINES PROFESSOR OF SUSTAINABLE ARCHITECTURAL DESIGN AT THE YALE SCHOOL OF ARCHITECTURE.

FACING PAGE

The unique micro scale of plastics molecular structure found in a nylon filament.

Collection:
Contributed
essay

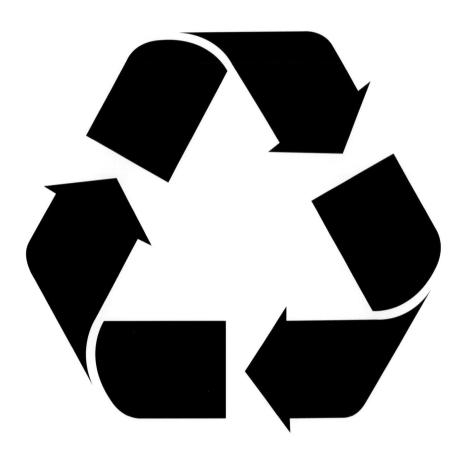

The universal symbol for recycling is a conceptual figure
connoting a general action that may be taken with any material.
Numbers, formed into the bottom of a plastics container, which
amount to the official Resin Identification Code, connote a
specific action for identifiable polymer chemistries.

THE POWER OF PLASTICITY
WILLIAM W. BRAHAM

The recycling numbers on the bottom of plastic containers are too small. And why do they only recycle two or three of them anyway? The simple answer is cost. Some plastics are only "plastic" once and are just "down-cycled" as inert ingredients for new products with much less economic or environmental benefit. The point of recycling is to reuse plastics as a kind of technical "compost" for the industrial system, similar to biological compost in the ecosystem (there are also some "biological" plastics). The ones worth recycling can be made "plastic" again. Put simply, plasticity is the power to be shaped, a power that saves work in manufacturing, but that involves other kinds of costs. Ultimately, all "powers" require energy.

Petrochemical plastics are the organic products of ancient photosynthesis, preserved, concentrated, and transformed by geological processes over millennia. Their stored potential enables petrochemicals to be converted into complex polymers that behave plastically, putting them in the category of other classically valuable building materials, like metals and glass, that can be reformed and recast. It is their plasticity that makes them useful, though conventional accounting overlooks the environmental contributions to that power.

The most comprehensive measure of environmental cost is emergy, a term coined by the systems ecologist Howard Odum to describe the cumulative or embodied energies required to make a particular power or material capacity available. Emergy accounts for the whole chain of energy and material transformations going right back to solar, tidal, and geological processes, the sources of energy in the bio-sphere. In a recent study, Buranakarn estimated the emergy content for common US building materials. Aluminum sheet required 12.7 billion emjoules per gram, float glass required 7.9, and the high-density polyethylene (HDPE, or #2) in plastic lumber required 5.75, as compared with emergy densities of 1 to 2 for bulk materials like wood, brick, and concrete.

In other words, material plasticity requires more energy, making it as valuable as the fruit of any biological process; the analogy to the food chain is reasonably sound. The fruit of the vine, like meat on the hoof, is an environmental product we have learned to cultivate, often forgetting the extra resources required. The power of petrochemical plastics, however, becomes evident with truly plastic recycling. The emergy densities of aluminum or glass are brought down only modestly by recycling, while that of HDPE can be brought into the same range as the bulk materials. Plastic recycling delivers the power of plasticity on an emergy budget, and makes the burning of fossil fuels for heat look even more frivolous.

WILLIAM W. BRAHAM , PHD, FAIA
IS AN ARCHITECT, THE AUTHOR OF *ARCHITECTURE AND ENERGY: PERFORMANCE AND STYLE* AND *RETHINKING TECHNOLOGY: A READER IN ARCHITECTURAL THEORY*, AND CURRENTLY AN ASSOCIATE PROFESSOR OF ARCHITECTURE AND DIRECTOR OF THE MASTER OF ENVIRONMENTAL BUILDING DESIGN AT THE UNIVERSITY OF PENNSYLVANIA.

BRINGING SHAPE-CHANGING PLASTIC TO LIFE
TAT TONG

How does a new plastic come to existence? It can be an act of serendipity, a spark of genius, a result of good fortune, or just the dogged determination of one person. The desire to have something new and better is always the biggest driving force for new invention. Shape-changing plastics hold many promises, ranging from surgical devices to future aircraft structures. More often than not, new plastic emerges through deliberate design and detailed planning that involves various scientific, engineering and economic activities over a long period of time.

Good design is a combination of a well-conceived idea, suitable materials and appropriate manufacturing processes. The design of new shape-changing plastic is built on 20 years of scientific knowledge in shape-memory polymers. The new polymer begins its conception on a drawing board. Polymer chemists, in general, believe a structure–properties relationship exists that allows us to predict the behavior of the polymer once the chemical constituents are defined. In the case of shape-changing plastic, we have to maintain a good balance between its ability to change into a different shape and its inherent tendency to recover its original shape upon activation. After deciding on the desirable performance traits, it is translated into various chemical structures that intuitively have the best chance of success. To the layman, these symbols of chemical structures and equations read just like a foreign language. To a chemist's eyes, they are the art forms of how everything in this world comes into existence. With that, the intellectual groundwork for the birth on a new plastic is laid.

The molecular structure is the blueprint of the intrinsic properties of a polymer, very much like DNA determines the basic appearance and characteristic of who we are. From this perspective, the processing of a polymer is similar to our upbringing. It shapes and forms the polymer into a physical product that gives us the improvement of aesthetic and utility functions that we seek in everyday life.

In the laboratory, the first set of processing conditions is usually created intuitively for the new shape-memory polymer based on experience and knowledge. We have a good candidate shape-changing plastic for further development when the polymer behaves like a rubber band upon heating. The road to a viable new plastic is often long and full of dead ends, albeit many valuable lessons are learned along the way. The hard work goes on until one day all the testing reveals the new plastic has met the specifications set forth by the team of scientists, engineers, and business managers. The activity of making new plastic available to the society is a significant undertaking, both technologically and economically. Once the economic viability is demonstrated, it will be integrated in our life for years to come where shape-changing capability is beneficial. This will continue until the day that its role in the society finally ages and gives way to another new material with better performance.

DR. TAT TONG
IS A CHEMIST AND THE CHIEF SCIENTIST AT CORNERSTONE RESEARCH GROUP IN DAYTON, OHIO, AND IS CURRENTLY SERVING AS A BOARD MEMBER ON THE BOARD OF DIRECTORS AT SPINTECH, LLC, WHICH PROVIDES SHAPE-MEMORY POLYMER TECHNOLOGIES TO SERVE A WIDE VARIETY OF MARKETS.

FACING PAGE

Clyde Beatty, lion tamer, an image suggestive of the role of the chemist with regard to plastics and the Enlightenment-era gestalt on creativity and potential: the world is there for me to wrestle with reason and conquer with science.

Waste Not, an installation by Song Dong at the Museum of
Modern Art, underscores the value exchange that happens
when cheap, everyday plastics become part of a conservator's
carefully tended collection.

PLASTIC MATERIALS: DREAM OR NIGHTMARE?
YVONNE SHASHOUA

Until the late 1970s, plastics were widely believed to be dream materials and to last forever, a belief fueled by the plastics industry.[10] However, degradation of plastic objects in museums is detected from appearance, odor, or feel within 5–25 years of acquisition. Museums aim to preserve objects for the enjoyment and education of the next generation, a minimum of 50 years.

Quackenbos, an industrial chemist, defined the lifetime of a polyvinyl chloride (PVC) film as the time taken to lose 10 per cent of its original weight, because after such loss its performance was no longer acceptable.[11] Industrial plastics are designed to function for a predetermined period. The lifetime of museum objects is reached when they cease to have a recognizable function or significance.[12] In addition to establishing the degradation pathways for plastics in museum objects, it is also necessary to decide how much degradation is acceptable. While yellowing is valued as a sign of maturity in materials such as oil paint, where it is known as patina, the same changes in plastics are deemed unacceptable.[13]

The major causes of degradation of plastics are attributed to physical, chemical, and biological factors. Physical factors may arise from use that is usually prior to collection by museums, interaction with light, heat, or moisture during storage or display, and migration of the anti-aging additives incorporated during manufacture. Chemical causes of degradation comprise reaction of plastics with oxygen, ozone, water, metals, light, and heat. Biological causes of degradation include micro-organisms and fungi. Biological degradation is less common than physical and chemical.

Degradation may occur during two phases in a plastic's lifecycle. During manufacture, plastics are subjected to high temperatures under molding and extruding. During use, plastic is exposed continually to air, moisture, light, and heat, initiating changes in the chemical structures of polymer chains and additives.

Four plastics have been identified as being more vulnerable to degradation than others in museums, namely cellulose nitrate, cellulose acetate, plasticized polyvinyl chloride, and polyurethane foam. Instability of the earliest plastics, cellulose nitrate and acetate, is expected due to their poorly stabilized, experimental formulations and because they are the oldest man-made plastics, dating from the late nineteenth and early twentieth centuries. However, PVC and polyurethanes were first commercially available after World War II and are still used, so their short lifetimes are more difficult to accept.

Once initiated, degradation of plastics cannot be prevented, reversed, or stopped, but only inhibited or slowed. Slowing the rate of degradation is achieved by storing objects in conditions which exclude the main factors causing degradation, particularly oxygen and moisture. Interventive conservation involves adhering broken sections, cleaning, and strengthening. It is poorly developed compared to inhibitive conservation due to the high sensitivity of plastics to cleaning agents, adhesives, and consolidants. There is a high risk of causing irreversible damage to plastics, a nightmare scenario for conservators. However, pressure from professionals who study plastics, the commercial art market, private collectors, and exhibition organizers is accelerating progress in this field.

YVONNE SHASHOUA, PhD
IS A SENIOR RESEARCHER IN THE DEPARTMENT OF CONSERVATION AT THE NATIONAL MUSEUM OF DENMARK AND IS THE AUTHOR OF *CONSERVATION OF PLASTICS: MATERIALS SCIENCE, DEGRADATION AND PRESERVATION* (ELSEVIER, 2008).

A COLLECTIVE APPROACH TO BUILDING FOR THE FUTURE
ANNE WALLIN

I grew up in Casper, Wyoming, with wide open spaces, mountain vistas, lots of antelope, sheep, and cows (and even some people). The field I work in did not exist then, and Anastas and Warner had not developed their 12 principles of green chemistry. Nonetheless, it was clear there are limits – to the earth's capacity; to what watersheds can assimilate; to maintaining our society's cultural and social constructs; to our knowledge of complex systems. And they are all inextricably linked.

To truly understand the earth's limitations, and account for people's need for safe drinking water, adequate food, and affordable shelter, we need to set a new standard for sustainability. We need breakthroughs in new products, and more efficient processes that use fewer resources and alternative feedstocks. This is not a quick fix – we will need to adopt new technologies, change certain behaviors, take more of a lifecycle approach, and consider the total cost of ownership, rather than just the initial cost.[14]

We all have to contribute, to achieve the quality of life we want within the capacity of our planet. As such, architects, designers, specifiers, and builders can: maximize the *efficiency and effectiveness* of space without maximizing the *space*; drive energy-efficiency improvements to increase comfort and reduce climate change impacts; use products, like plastics, to manage moisture, including vapor barriers, flashing tapes, and insulation;[15] utilize new technologies, like vegetative and reflective roofs, to reduce urban heat island effects and photochemical smog; and, most importantly, maximize the use of durable materials. As Robert Lilienfeld and William Rathje say, "We feel good when we fill the recycling bin. In reality, we should feel good when there's no waste to put in it at all!"[16]

However, I would caution that:

1. We need to consider the full lifecycle and get the data. How long you stand in the shower using shampoo is more meaningful than a carbon footprint label on the bottle.

2. As Thomas Friedman said recently, "If you don't have scale in this revolution, you have a hobby."[17] There are limitations to scaling up some technologies and products, like biobased feedstocks, using today's technologies. And scale takes time – it is not realistic to think we'll replace the entire current building stock with more energy-efficient, durable models powered by renewable energy in the next decade.

3. Adding renewable energy to an existing building is a bit like putting a Geo Metro engine in a '57 Chevy. It simply won't perform. For renewable energy to power the world, we will need significantly better insulated buildings.

It took time to create society's current problems, and it will take time, and a collective effort, to solve them. As Vince Lombardi said, "Individual commitment to a group effort – that is what makes a team work, a company work, a society work, a civilization work." Everyone, including you, must be part of the solution.

ANNE WALLIN, PhD
IS A CHEMIST AND THE DIRECTOR OF SUSTAINABLE CHEMISTRY AT THE DOW CHEMICAL COMPANY IN MIDLAND, MICHIGAN.

SPONGEcity:
ADAPTIVE MATERIALITY
LIAT MARGOLIS

Climate change models forecast a simultaneous water scarcity and inundation. Depending on geographical and topographical coordinates, low-lying urbanities are projected to submerge under the rise of sea level. Conversely, in arid zones, sometimes inclusive of lowlands, trends in precipitation indices show a paradox of rainfall – a decrease in overall precipitation, but a spike of intensity for each rain event, resulting in torrents and floods. Access to potable water is projected to further decline due to the increase of temperature, evaporation, and groundwater salinity, compounded further by anthropogenic impacts.

Contemporary design cannot afford to ignore the subject of water, its collection, conveyance, filtration, consumption, and reuse, and likewise, the creative potential in rethinking flood control and water scarcity. What materials and technologies will now shape our cities? What materials can functionally adapt to a continuum of environmental and climatological changes in real-time? And what materials can respond to and self-regulate both floods and drought?

One such material is none other than "diaper technology." Diapers contain a non-woven textile made of super absorbent polymers (SAPs) that are engineered to absorb hundreds of times their own weight in liquid at extremely rapid rates. These super soaking polyacrylate/polyacrylamide copolymers are fabricated into multiple forms such as granules, fibers, and textiles, and have a wide range of applications from personal hygiene products and medical surgery spill-control, to irrigation control for horticulture and agriculture, wire and cable water blocking, and toxic spill clean-up. Engineered to have various filtering and absorptive properties, SAPs can absorb various

salt content, and hydrophobically absorb reactive chemicals, petroleum, and liquids of various viscosities.

Through osmotic pressure the SAPs absorb and release the liquid, which means that, unlike a sponge, they will not leach when applied with pressure. The driving force for the osmotic pressure is typically the higher concentration of sodium or potassium ions in the polymer than in its surrounding environment. Thus, water is drawn in and out of the polymer in an attempt to reach equilibrium. For landscape and agricultural uses, the exceptional absorption capacity is utilized to increase the soil's water-holding capacity by 50–100 percent, reducing irrigation requirements, fertilizer washout, stormwater runoff, and soil erosion. Conversely, when the soil is dry and plants are in need of water, the SAPs provide controlled release of the retained water and fertilizer.

Dubai's astounding island construction projects have been exploring SAP for irrigation control, aiming to cut water consumption by 50 percent, and saving over a million gallons per day in an energy-intensive desalinated irrigation. Considering the world's expanding aridity and endangered water and energy resources, such efficiencies are paramount. The United Nations Convention to Combat Desertification has been cultivating agriculture and aforestation in Iran and Kyrgyzstan using a SAP soil additive in order to prevent soil erosion, improve large swaths of desiccated land, and fight desertification and land degradation. Successful tests in Senegal, Niger, Pakistan, and China have shown water conservation can reach up to 50 percent, while crop yield increase by 25–100 percent.

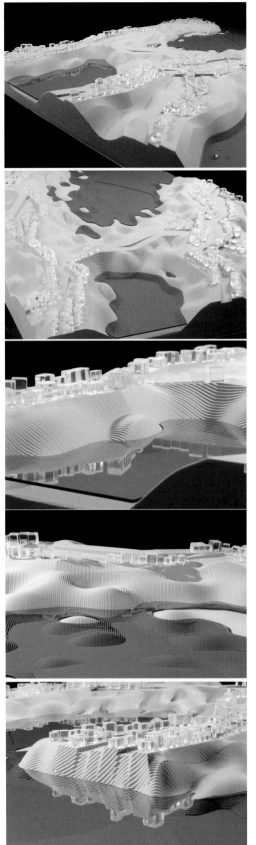

Conceptual models of *SPONGEcity,* where super absorbent polymers (SAPs) may have a pervasive infrastructural role in places below sea level such as the Netherlands and New Orleans.

The same adaptive materiality can attenuate inundation due to rising sea levels or storm events. *SPONGEcity*[18] is a conceptual proposal for the Netherlands and New Orleans, whose urban areas lie below sea level and have been fortified by defensive dyke/levee technologies for centuries. The deployment of the SAPs is intended to provide relief from the detrimental impact of flooding as new water-management urbanism develops. Three-dimensionally woven cell matrixes are envisioned as integrated structures with concrete, soil, and building materials to create a new super soaker infrastructure.

LIAT MARGOLIS
IS ASSISTANT PROFESSOR AT THE UNIVERSITY OF TORONTO, JOHN H. DANIELS FACULTY OF ARCHITECTURE, LANDSCAPE, AND DESIGN. SHE IS DIRECTOR OF THE GREEN ROOF INNOVATION TESTING LABORATORY (GRIT LAB), AND CO-AUTHOR OF *LIVING SYSTEMS: INNOVATIVE MATERIALS FOR LANDSCAPE ARCHITECTURE* AND *OUT OF WATER: DESIGN SOLUTIONS FOR ARID REGIONS*.

POLYMER AWE
IVAN AMATO

I have a bit of a pantheistic tilt, so I sometimes find myself staring at a piece of vinyl or polyethylene detritus on the ground with what another part of me judges as misplaced reverence. Lord knows, these and many other plastics of our materials age have their issues – they're made from petroleum and natural gas and so exacerbate the globe's dependence on these raw materials, and then there's all that litter made of stuff that takes forever to break down.

My pantheistic sensibility derives, in part, from both my student days and my professional life during which I often had to ponder the periodic table of the chemical elements, which, in its 100 or so little boxes, represents the pantry of ingredients in all things that ever were, are, or will be. All things. Planets, pebbles, people, polycarbonate, and everything that doesn't begin with a p.

For most people, the word plastic signifies that class of materials that began showing up in the constructed landscape in the nineteenth century – usually as replacement materials for rare or dear materials like ivory – and that now are ubiquitous. There's plastic in our wallets, in our repaired teeth, and in bottles, wrappings, and other packages of the stuff we buy. When I donate blood, that vital fluid travels from me through a plastic tube into a plastic bag and then from that bag through a tube into a patient whose life might be saved, in part, because of that plastic-enabled transport.

Donating blood can provide a portal to something akin to a religious relationship with plastic. This is where just a small chemical factoid comes in handy. What we think of as plastics are, from a chemical and materials point of view, polymers. Polymers are big, often enormous molecules made of smaller building-block chemicals that link into linear, branched, globular, and ever more complex structures. Blood, although mostly water, is a cornucopia of biological polymers. DNA, which is a rather central component of every red or white blood cell coursing into the blood bag, is a polymer. The many proteins in the blood plasma, among them antibodies and clotting factors, are polymers.

Other tissues are rife with polymers. Muscle fibers are made largely of the proteins actin and myosin. Hair, fingernails, and, if you have them, horns, claws, beaks, hooves, and baleen, are made largely of a protein, a polymer, called keratin. One type of protein; so many shapes and functions. Talk about plasticity! For both natural and synthetic architectures, plastics – polymers, that is – are, to quote Apple's late CEO Steve Jobs, "insanely great."

The logical train from a littered polyethylene terephthalate soda bottle to awe goes this way: that plastic bottle on the ground is made of a synthetic polymer with a chemical kinship to my own DNA and proteins that provide both the architectural instruction and construction material for the body I inhabit and in which I find myself sentient and inclined to ask awe-inspiring questions about the universe.

IVAN AMATO
IS A FREELANCE SCIENCE WRITER AND EDITOR, THE AUTHOR OF
STUFF: THE MATERIALS THE WORLD IS MADE OF AND *SUPER VISION:
A NEW VIEW OF NATURE,* AND FOUNDER AND FACILITATOR OF
DC SCIENCE CAFÉ.

FACING PAGE

A discarded bottle made of polyethylene
terephthalate posturing towards fusion with asphalt.

OVERLEAF

The Beijing National Aquatic Center, called the "Water Cube,"
was built for the 2008 Olympics. Phenomena abound when
light meets a material that permits transmission, reflection,
and diffusion simultaneously.

STRETCHING THE LIMITS:
PLASTICS
WERNER LANG

No other building material has recently stirred a higher interest among architects, engineers, and designers than plastics. The traditional use of linear and planar elements determining the aesthetics of buildings is increasingly challenged by the use of new, carbon-based materials which allow for the creation of any free, user-defined, and ultra-light building skins, structural systems, and buildings.

The constant improvement of existing materials, such as fiber reinforced plastics and the development of new materials, such as fluorocarbon-based polymers like ETFE (ethylene tetrafluoroethylene), have revolutionized construction methods and added new possibilities for aesthetic experimentation.

Taking the current developments in the field of fiber reinforced plastics as an example, it seems as if the technological and aesthetic potential of core-insulated fiberglass elements is almost unlimited, as demonstrated by Zaha Hadid and her design for the Contemporary Art Container in Hong Kong. The amorphous building form appears to be determined by a fluid continuum of space, which is encapsulated by light, prefabricated, core-insulated, lightweight, and durable fiberglass elements. Hadid uses the latest design tools and fabrication technologies to push the aesthetic limits of free-form building to its current apex.

The second, even more revolutionary, development in the field of high-performance building has evolved in highly transparent, ultra-light, very durable, and resilient building skins, such as ETFE films. If compared to glass, these films carry only 1 percent in weight, transmit more light, and easily span distances of up to nine meters with material thicknesses of 0.25 mm and less, as demonstrated by the Watercube for the Beijing National Aquatics Center for the 2008 Olympics. The multi-layered, highly transparent membrane calls for the

reinterpretation of the physical characteristics of architecture, as encapsuled air serves as the main supporting medium for holding the building envelope in tension. The extremely low weight of the façade and roof construction allows for a considerable downsizing of the supporting structure, which creates a lightness in building which had not been seen before.

The current development in the field of plastics seems to be unlimited. PTFE-coated fiberglass membranes for enhanced, high-performance structures and carbon fiber reinforced epoxy sandwich elements are challenging the current limits of the structural and functional performance as well as the aesthetics of buildings.

More importantly, the shift toward a more sustainable approach in building demands highly effective, low-cost and fully recyclable building materials and systems. Enhanced sun protection, heat conservation and storage, electricity production and storage, light transmission and even light emission, improved acoustics, fire resistance, and low-maintenance surfaces are just some of the challenges we are facing today.

Here lies the real future potential of plastics, as we seem to be able to create almost any chemical composition with almost any material property required. Interdisciplinary work and integrated thinking might lead to innovations in the field of plastics for highly functional and effective building skin systems. It is very likely that we will see improved and hitherto unknown material properties emerging in the near future, which will push the use of plastics for future-oriented building beyond the currently known limits. The future of plastics has just begun.

WERNER LANG, PhD
IS AN ARCHITECT, THE CO-AUTHOR OF *IN DETAIL: BUILDING SKINS*, AND A PROFESSOR OF ARCHITECTURE THE TECHNICAL UNIVERSITY OF MUNICH.

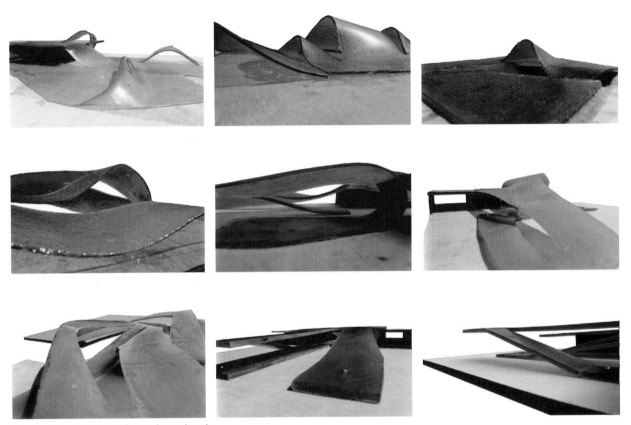

Marc Swackhamer's systematic experiments in resin
allow us to see and feel polymerization – the addition
of monomer to monomer – a rarity in our normative
relationships to plastics.

DON'T MEASURE, JUST CUT (PLASTIC WILL FIX YOUR MISTAKES)
MARC SWACKHAMER

My growth as a designer is proportional to my understanding of one material: plastic. Plastic has been like a cantankerous partner, impressing upon me three principles to which I still adhere: relinquish some control over your work, consider the word craft a verb, and work with people who think differently than you.

I was introduced to plastic through my thesis at Rice University. I studied how varying the thickness and cure time of liquid resin changed its pliability. This resulted in 12 models, each growing more box-like as the resin became less pliable. Through the process, I developed an acute awareness of how the properties of the plastic impacted form. No longer was I in total control. Form was now at the mercy of the plastic. Once I understood this, I found it liberating, and in much of my subsequent work I have sought to identify influences, beyond my intuition, that can impact form.

A few years later I designed a plastic toy shelf for my daughter. Components were digitally cut then shaped by heating the plastic and slumping it over wood forms. Through this process I developed a new understanding of craft: not as a noun, but as a verb. The sequencing of the shelf's assembly and the design of its wood molds involved as much careful planning as the shelf itself. Plastic reframed craft as not just the care with which one constructs an object, but also the care with which one constructs an argument. It actually required less physical crafting than traditional materials, but more planning and strategizing; more crafting of a methodology.

Recently, I designed two experimental wall prototypes, Drape Wall and Cloak Wall, with my partner Blair Satterfield and our firm HouMinn Practice. The walls' modular components were designed, fabricated, and assembled to accomplish all the tasks of a conventional wall. Performance criteria were managed by sophisticated plastics with unique molecular properties. Here, plastic introduced me to a collaborative design process. By necessity, I solicited input from engineers, scientists, and chemists. Plastic allowed me to work with a diverse group of remarkable people and to see the value of divergent perspectives at the design table.

Could I have learned these principles by studying another material? Sure. But plastic somehow resonates with me. It is a mischievous and elusive material. I have found it to be both a limiting and enabling partner; sometimes the glue that fixes my mistakes and sometimes the sand in the ointment that causes them. Plastic elicits in me the same feelings of both frustration and exhilaration that Andy Goldsworthy so concisely described on a cold beach in Nova Scotia in his film *Rivers and Tides*. After a hand-stacked sculpture he had been working on all day collapsed yet again, he said: "This is the fourth collapse today. And each time, I learned a little bit more about the stone. The work grew in proportion to my understanding of the stone. I obviously don't understand it well enough yet."

MARC SWACKHAMER
IS THE HEAD OF THE SCHOOL OF ARCHITECTURE, UNIVERSITY OF MINNESOTA, MINNEAPOLIS, MINNESOTA, AND CO-FOUNDER OF HOUMINN PRACTICE.

PLASTICS BEYOND BARTHES
MICHAEL STACEY

Humankind created plastics before the chemistry of long-chain molecules was understood; invention proceeded knowledge. Polystyrene was discovered by a German apothecary, Eduard Simon, in 1839; however, he did not know what he had discovered! It was not until 1930 that Badische Anilin & Soda-Fabrik (BASF) developed the commercial manufacturing of polystyrene. The first successful plastic, Bakelite, was discovered and patented by Leo H. Baekeland in 1907. Hermann Staudinger was the key scientific pioneer of polymerization and his role was recognized by the award of the Nobel Prize for Chemistry in 1953. In this year Dr. Hermann Schnell of Bayer invented polycarbonate. Dr. Daniel Fox of GE and Dr. Schnell both successfully applied for US patents for polycarbonate in 1955. Arguably it was not until 2003 that this plastic was used to clad a world-class work of architecture, the Laban Dance Centre in London by Herzog and de Meuron.

Plastic – synthetic long-chain polymers – is a material group which ranges from the familiar, possibly the over familiar, expanded polystyrene cup to polyamide turbine blades capable of sustaining around 300 °C for prolonged periods. Plastic has the strange association of being both disposable and difficult to dispose of. Its inherent durability tends to be misused. Polymers can be and should be designed for a specific purpose. Used wisely, reused and recycled. The development of a mature aesthetic for plastic, with some honorable exceptions, has lagged behind the developments in material science. In his 1957 essay, "Plastic," Roland Barthes observed "Plastic is not so much a substance as the notion of infinite remodelling."[19] In part the moldability or formability has cast plastics into an imitative role and its origins were as a substitute for scarce naturally occurring materials. During the 1990s a number of designs and developments indicate the emergence of an independent aesthetic for plastic. In 1999 Jonathan Ive led the design of the iMac for Apple computers. Using transparent and translucent polycarbonate he liberated the personal computer from ill-formed beige boxes and suggested the potency of polymeric skins. The radical fashion designer Hussein Chalayan dramatically demonstrated the materiality and beauty of plastic in his 1999 show, which featured remote-controlled glass fiber reinforced polyester dresses contrasted with the tulle underskirts.

Charles and Ray Eames can be considered the pioneers of a mature esthetic for plastic. In 1948 they entered the Museum of Modern Art's International Competition for Low-Cost Furniture Design with research engineers from UCLA. Initially they considered using stamped steel sheet, based on contemporary automotive technology, but this proved too expensive for low-cost production. Charles and Ray Eames turned to polymer composites. They approached Zenith Plastics of Gardena, California, which had experience of manufacturing fiber reinforced plastic (FRP) radar domes during the war;[20] this collaboration led to the production of one of the first one-piece plastic chairs, which were self-colored and un-upholstered. This Side Chair and its related models formed a key precedent and inspiration for many architects to use FRP. The influential British architect Peter Smithson wrote in 1966 "The Eames chair was like a message of hope from another planet."[21] These chairs inspired many architects, including Renzo Piano, Richard Rogers, and Nicholas Grimshaw. The key quality of this chair, which appears to have been overlooked, was that it was close molded on a hydraulic press with male–female molds producing a high-quality finish on both surfaces. The inventive designers Charles and Ray Eames had pioneered a popular and truly mass-produced item. Hand-laid FRP, a craft-based method of production, tended to dominate the early use of plastic in architecture, leading to problems in quality control and expense as only one fair face is produced.

In 1993 Vitra replaced the glass fiber reinforced polyester shell of the Eames Side Chair with a polypropylene shell – a single thermoformable plastic which can be readily recycled. Initially I mourned the passing of the fine texture imparted by the fibers in the plastic; however, I now realize that this is an indication of the development of plastics and our collective knowledge of this class of materials. It is interesting to note that despite the Monsanto House of the Future, Florida and Smithsons' House of the Future, both from 1956, and projects such as James Stirling's Olivetti Headquarters, Surrey, 1975, it is unreinforced plastics in the form of ETFE, PET, and polycarbonate that have become familiar components in the palette available for the creation of contemporary architecture. And the future? Carbon fiber was invented in Britain by Leslie Philip during 1964. The use of this stiff and durable fiber in a plastic matrix to create new-build architecture appears now to be overdue.

MICHAEL STACEY
IS THE PRINCIPAL OF MICHAEL STACEY ARCHITECTS, THE EDITOR OF *PROTOTYPING ARCHITECTURE*, THE AUTHOR OF *COMPONENT DESIGN*, AND A PROFESSOR WITH A CHAIR IN ARCHITECTURE AT THE UNIVERSITY OF NOTTINGHAM.

THE PLASTICITY OF METASEAMS
TOM WISCOMBE

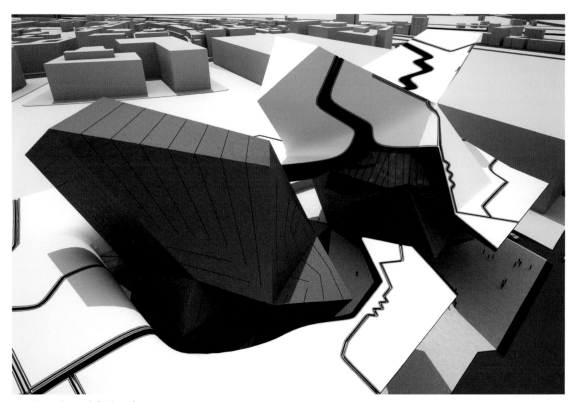

Tom Wiscombe's redefinition of seam as meta-seam,
becoming the basis for a new tectonic theory of
plastics.

Architecture is on the verge of a revolution in
construction, which will likely prove to be as
transformative to our age as plate glass, steel,
and high-strength reinforced concrete were for
Modernism. Polymers and associated composite
materials offer an unprecedented formal plasticity
combined with strength and lightness, forcing a
fundamental reconsideration of twentieth-century
aesthetic and tectonic theory, building system
hierarchies, and project delivery infrastructures.

While polymers have been commercially
available since the 1950s, for instance as seen
in the Monsanto House of the Future built in
Disneyland's Tomorrowland in 1957, it is not until
now that they have become viable for architecture.
The combination of recent technological
advancements, the ability to bid and fabricate
components internationally and transport them
to distant building sites, and the growing capacity
of architectural engineers to analyze surface-
based structures (like their naval and aerospace

counterparts), not to mention the mature market for complex building form stemming from 20 years of digital architectural production, are all now conspiring to create an economy of scale. This new economy is characterized by *polymer-logic* rather than *mineral-logic*; materials are synthetically produced rather than dug up from the earth, components are sedimented or glued together rather than assembled with hardware, and buildings can be constructed in massive, fully integrated chunks rather than stick by stick or brick by brick.

Now that this shift to polymer logics is legitimately underway, it is time for architecture to begin to theorize the consequences. A starting point might be the problem of smoothness, or limitless plasticity. While seamlessness, as in a surfboard, might seem like an obvious consequence for architecture, this is only true if you believe that architecture is a consequence of technology. While we know that there can be no Le Corbusier without reinforced concrete and no Mies without the steel frame, it is also true that those architectures cannot by any means be reduced to outcomes of technological advancement. In addition, it would be naive to think that polymers have no internal limits, and can scale up infinitely – say, from a super-yacht to a high-rise building – and remain seamless. More important, however, is contributing to the long architectural discourse of surface articulation, both tectonic and ornamental, which is independent from material concerns and dead in the middle of aesthetic culture.

The problem with total smoothness in contemporary architecture is that it simultaneously harkens back to Modernism and its efforts to strip off any perceived surface excess, and at the same time, reminds one of the endless unarticulated surfaces of 1990s digital architecture. Both of these would seem to be

retrograde for contemporary architecture. Instead of killing seams and joints, a more interesting approach might be to revel in the new freedom of seams and joints to articulate surfaces in unexpected ways – ways which no longer simply index the beginnings and ends of little pieces of material.

When a seam is released from servitude to a panel – let's call this a *metaseam* – it can begin to interface with building form in a more aggressive, and ontologically equal, manner. Metaseams can be used to create strange scale effects, making a building appear much larger, or much smaller, than it is, possibly even toy-like. They can be used to define super-figuration on mass, such as the mysterious white patches on killer whales, which can create a double- or misreading of the mass itself. Even more aggressive patterns of metaseams might be used in service of a "fake" tectonic system, or better, one which shifts from real to fake and back again through architectural sleight of hand.

Ultimately, considering such a thing as a metaseam in architecture is a way to playfully mark the end of the era of "articulation for free," based on the mineral limits of panels, stones, and bricks. It allows us to speculate on the strange aesthetic and tectonic potentials of the new polymer world.

TOM WISCOMBE
IS AN ARCHITECT, FOUNDER OF TOM WISCOMBE ARCHITECTURE, AND PROFESSOR AT THE SOUTHERN CALIFORNIA INSTITUTE OF ARCHITECTURE.

Artist Lawrence Weiner's intentionally ambiguous
phrase evokes the portion of Blaine Brownell's essay
where he states that the result of using plastics as
an imitator "is none other than the loss of society's
ability to interpret material meaning through
conventional visual or tactile cues."

PLASTIC AMBIVALENCE
BLAINE BROWNELL

As a critical ingredient in products as diverse as appliances, computers, automobiles, and buildings, plastic has come to define our modern existence. In fact, no other material has had such a dramatic influence on contemporary society. Offering the means to defy the natural process of decay, plastic has enabled the expansion of capital and resources in unprecedented fashion, empowering the global distribution of food, the preservation of perishable materials, and protection from the elements.

Yet for all of its benefits, synthetic plastic is steeped in controversy. Its resistance to water and ability to forestall biological processes make it a truly unnatural material, inspiring Thomas Pynchon to consider it "death masquerading as life."[22] Synthetic plastic does not age or develop an endearing patina as other materials do; it refuses to bear the marks of natural cycles that would traditionally encourage human intervention and maintenance. As such, plastic represents a kind of intolerable present – a material perpetuating current realities in the wake of imminent change.

Toyo Ito criticizes this persistent condition in his essay "Architecture in a Simulated City," in which he bemoans the antiseptic homogeneity of the contemporary city – now "covered completely by an empty clarity."[23] Plastic has not only enabled the preservation and diffusion of material wealth, but also encouraged an unrelenting desire for the new. "Although we are surrounded by a variety of goods, we are living in thoroughly homogeneous atmospheres. Our affluence is supported only by a piece of Saran-wrap film."[24]

Plastic's versatility has also allowed it not only to replace other materials, but also to be used to mimic these materials. Wood-grained vinyl siding, fiberglass column capitals, and metallic paint-coated product casings are all examples of plastic employed in disguise as more expensive and fickle materials. This surrogate potential has led to a crisis of material authenticity in the physical world – a condition that Adolf Loos would likely have found more criminal than the use of ornament itself. The result is none other than the loss of society's ability to interpret material meaning through conventional visual or tactile cues.

Recent environmental concerns may offer a chance for plastic to redeem itself. The recognition of fossil fuel limits, coupled with acknowledgment of negative effects caused by plastic-based pervasive pollutants, have compelled plastics manufacturers to consider environmentally healthy substitutes to petroleum-derived polymers. The irony is notable: natural materials are now increasingly used to replace synthetic compounds originally developed to replace natural materials.

The growing presence of plant-based fibers, acids and resins employed instead of petroleum-based content has actually influenced the nature of plastic itself. New bioplastics may be programmed to biodegrade rather than defy natural processes, be easily recycled rather than persist in the waste stream, and possess novel properties such as fire-resistance and shape-memory. Moreover, the types of plant-based substances used can directly influence the appearance and texture of bioplastic. While these developments suggest a powerful change of course, it remains to be seen whether bioplastic will support or challenge humanity's incessant desire for consumption and control.

BLAINE BROWNELL, AIA, LEED
IS A RESEARCHER, THE AUTHOR OF *TRANSMATERIAL: A CATALOG OF MATERIALS THAT REDEFINE OUR PHYSICAL ENVIRONMENT*, THE CREATOR OF TRANSSTUDIO, AND AN ASSOCIATE PROFESSOR AT THE UNIVERSITY OF MINNESOTA SCHOOL OF ARCHITECTURE.

PLASTIC RHEOLOGIES:
FROM THE MOLECULAR TO THE TERRITORIAL
KIEL MOE

Early in the 1967 Mike Nichols' film *The Graduate*, a family friend, Mr. McGuire, pulls the eponymous Ben Braddock aside for a piece of advice:

> "I just want to say one word to you. Just, one word…"
> "Yes sir."
> "Are you listening?"
> "Yes sir, I am."
> "Plastics."
> "Exactly how do you mean?"
> "There's a great future in plastics. Think about it."

Mr. McGuire has just one word for the graduate, yet this word has so many enmeshed social, cultural, ecological, and physical implications. That plastic is a term describing both a range of materials and a range of material behaviors underscores its rheological raison d'être. This rheology emphasizes the relative periods of its various dynamics and molecular states: at one moment it is a fluid state, at another it is a solid under strain, and finally it is a solid of varying suppleness.

While other materials are rheological in similar ways, human technique is the sole generator of this material and its mutations. Its science is social before it is technical. The anthropocentric technics of this class of mutant materials, seemingly infinite in its permutations, signals a sharp contrast with prior material modalities as articulated by thinkers such as Lewis Mumford, Andrei Leroi-Guarhan, Gilles Deleuze, and Manuel de Landa. For the first time the capabilities and culpabilities of a material have become possible solely in the hands of human technique. Given the ubiquity of plastic today, it is the most emblematic material technique of our characteristically rheological times. Twentieth-century human will, perhaps, is not better manifest in anything else in the material world.

But this plastic rheology is not as infinite as Roland Barthes speculated on account of one material property: the majority of plastics do not biodegrade. While green chemistry and promises of recyclability may alter this material ecology in the coming decades, the molecular transmutations and rheology of extant plastics are nonetheless shockingly limited and fixed when compared to the ceaseless dynamics of other forms of matter in the recurrent carbon-based solar-geologic-biologic economy that eternally churns matter over and over through geomorphic activity, UV radiation, weather, erosion, life, and death. There is in fact a future in plastics. It seems that plastic's mutations persist in an altogether unforeseen rheology: a continental-sized viscous vortex of photo-degraded buoyant plastic in the middle of the Pacific Ocean known as the Great Pacific Garbage Patch. This is a new dynamical system lacking familiar qualities of life but that will no doubt spawn novel transformations itself. It is great only in its territorial scale as a swirling monument to the audacity and absurdity of twentieth-century technique. As Barthes noted, this plastic flow does indeed induce "the reverie of man at the sight of the proliferating forms of matter and the connections he detects between the singular of the origin and the plural of its effects." However, this may not necessarily be the miraculous "sudden transformation of nature" Barthes had in mind; but it is something to think about indeed, Mr. McGuire.

KIEL MOE
IS A REGISTERED ARCHITECT AND ASSOCIATE PROFESSOR OF ARCHITECTURE AND ENERGY AT HARVARD GRADUATE SCHOOL OF DESIGN. AT THE GSD, HE IS THE CO-DIRECTOR OF THE MDES PROGRAM AND CO-DIRECTOR OF THE ENERGY, ENVIRONMENTS & DESIGN RESEARCH LAB.

FACING PAGE

A sample taken from the Great Pacific Garbage Patch, a giant accumulation in the North Pacific composed primarily of plastic waste.

Collection:
Contributed
essay

A 3D printer by Fab@Home creators Evan Malone
and Hod Lipson, who in 2006 initiated an
open-source project to make personal fabrication
technology accessible.

PLASTIC – FANTASTIC!
CRISTOBAL CORREA

Its allure has never diminished and the advice once given to Dustin Hoffman's character in *The Graduate* is as relevant today as it was then: plastics.

In the city's architectural studios, you can hear the hum of the 3D printer as it works away, creating the plastic resin model of a starchitect's vision.

Plastic may not be a "noble" building material like the historical ones we frequently use. The modern intention is always to create a uniform, standard and efficient unit for construction, be it wood plank, brick, stone pavers, or the steel I-beam.

Plastic is *none* of these things.

Plastic is formless – the designer controls the shape and has the freedom that comes from a lack of a vernacular vocabulary or of any real intrinsic qualities. This lack of a unified system can maximize the usage of the material, but at the same time requires a more sophisticated descriptive of the shape. This freedom is at once liberating and intimidating in its potential.

Plastic is devoid of quality – the designer enforces her vision by doping plastic with additives or changing the very chemical processes that created it. Plastic is a matrix of possibilities. Make it harder, softer, opaque, transparent, insulating, or conductive.

Plastic is scaleless – from the very small to the very big, use it as a tiny component in a larger piece or as a binder to a larger element. Use it as part of a hybrid piece with other materials.

Plastic is immortal – once we have created it, we can't get rid of it. We must consciously destroy it.

Plastic is organic – as organic a creation as cell differentiation in the biological world. There, from the genetic pool of possibility, a command goes out from the master architect to create the bone, or the skin, or the nerve cell of the individual. In the same way, from the carbon chains of plastic polymers, the designer can create the hard shell, the clear window or the flexible conductor of any architectural creation.

Plastic is noble – through its flexibility as a universal agent. Plastic does not "want" to be anything. It is what you want it to be.

CRISTOBAL CORREA, PE
IS A STRUCTURAL ENGINEER AT BURO HAPPOLD AND A PROFESSOR OF TECHNOLOGY AT PRATT INSTITUTE IN NEW YORK CITY, WHOSE WORK HAS BEEN PUBLISHED IN ENGINEERING JOURNALS AS WELL AS *EXTREME TEXTILES: DESIGNING FOR HIGH PERFORMANCE* AND *30 60 90 05: TEACHING + BUILDING*.

PROFESSING PLASTICS

Collection:
Contributed
essay

ON PLASTICS AND ARCHITECTURE:
OUR PRESENT AND OUR FUTURE
STEPHEN KIERAN AND JAMES TIMBERLAKE

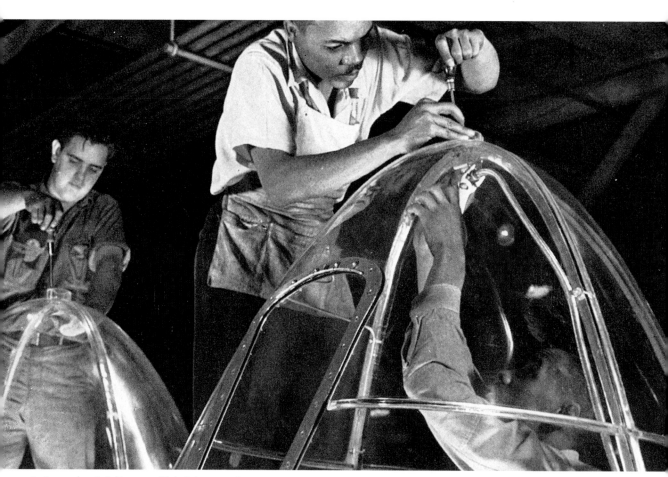

Factory workers in Baltimore prefabricate transparent
plastic noses for aircraft in 1942.

Close your eyes and zoom yourself back 30 or more years. Imagine. Do you remember when we all found ourselves first traveling long distances? Do you remember the airplane interiors from that time? Those interior environments were considerably less plasticized with fewer synthetic surfaces, a greater content of metal, organic material (to form the inside shell and surfaces), and non-synthetic fabrics.

Now, open your eyes. As we sit, 35,000 feet in the air, flying anywhere, in the comfort of an intercontinental jet airplane, we look around at an interior environment nearly entirely synthetic – perhaps a little metal and glass – polyesters and a variety of plastics (PVCs, plastic fibers, and PET among the most predominant by content). Synthetics, and predominantly plastics, form interior walls, bins, flooring, seat binnacles, seat coverings, window interior panels, and ceilings. As we assess these surroundings, nearly the only non-synthetic material we can see, beyond the occupants along with us, is the paper content of the brochures, magazines, and newspapers. This is a plastic and rapidly plasticizing world. We are dependent upon plastic and its various forms for much of what we do and use. In various forms it is light, inexpensive, durable, highly formable, and allows broad creativity in expression.

Why has architecture been far less adventurous and ignorant to this development in the product industry and to progress with the usage of plastics in a comprehensive manner? What is our fear of engaging the interiors and exteriors of our buildings similarly to these products? Why are we where we are with plastics and architecture?

Architects' predilection is to use the "natural," particularly in the last quarter-century of architecture. The "natural" is seen as an extension of craft, of self-making, of control and the absence of control (weathering), whereas plastic is seen as a "non-natural" material, therefore, not organic. Organic, at a present acme, is seen as appropriate, beautiful, and sustainable. Everything else is considered the opposite. Architecture has deeply embraced the ferrous over the faux, the sedimentary and self-finishing over synthetic, and the organic natural over the man-made. Plastic, in its earliest contemporary usage, was considered faux, decorative, and man-made. Therefore, it is considered inappropriate, not beautiful, not sustainable. Wood toys yes, plastic toys no. Plastic is not seen as integral, controllable, able to mark time (again the weathering), or particularly tactile – less human and humanizing than sterile and superficial – inhumane and other worldly.

How do we learn to love something that does not mark time, does not patina? Or is warm to the touch? How do we learn to develop an aesthetic of desire related to plastic?

Look beyond the here and now. The world is upside-down from our earliest architectural training and it is not merely a trend. Sustainability and environmental ethic has caused us to reflect and re-think our norms, our practices, and how we envision our results. Non-petroleum-based plastics have become a normative choice. Plastic recycling, reuse, re-streaming is seen as part of a "natural" process. In the end, the opportunities that plastic holds for architecture, in its myriad, mind-boggling array of applications embracing economies of scale, forms, finishes, lifecycles, and uses offers a way forward beyond "natural" and organic to a new life form – arguably more beautiful, ethical, and sustainable than ripping down forests, mining stone, consuming vast amounts of energy in manufacturing – that, at once, in an artfully man-made, scientifically created product embodies architecture in its making, in its transformation, in its applications.

Plastic IS architecture and architecture IS plastic. So let's use it.

——————————————
STEPHEN KIERAN AND JAMES TIMBERLAKE
ARE PARTNERS AT KIERANTIMBERLAKE, AN INTERNATIONALLY RECOGNIZED ARCHITECTURE FIRM NOTED FOR ITS COMMITMENT TO RESEARCH, INNOVATION, AND INVENTION. THEY HAVE CO-AUTHORED FIVE BOOKS ON ARCHITECTURE, AND THEY CURRENTLY TEACH AT THE UNIVERSITY OF PENNSYLVANIA SCHOOL OF DESIGN.

GEMINI
NERI OXMAN

In his masterful essay Barthes points out the dichotomy between plastic the noun and plastic the adjective. The latter inspires Barthes to qualify plastic as the stuff of alchemy.

Plastic the adjective resonates on deep esthetic and ethical levels when elements of technology, science, philosophy, and the senses are combined to reveal the power of malleability. A power that offers great control over form and formation across spatial and temporal scales and presents unique opportunities to the creator.

The alchemic nature of plastic is at the heart of Gemini, a chaise lounge designed to support the body and quiet the thinking mind. I conceived it originally as an amalgam of an acoustical instrument and a landscape that contains the body as it shifts between functions associated with the absorption of sound and functions associated with the distribution of load.

Gemini is designed as a semi-closed anechoic chamber with curved surfaces and an intricate carpet of globular cells that scatter and absorb sound with increased absorbance around local hollow chambers. This is achieved through the combination of a solid wood milled shell housing and a cellular surface made of sound-absorbing material. The features of the cellular surface are on the order of the wavelength of sound we can hear. They vary in rigidity, opacity, and color to provide structural support, enable corporeal sensation and offer a visual effect at the service of experience that is at its core spiritual. It is the first design to implement Stratasys' Connex3 technology, enabling the use of 44 materials with different pre-set mechanical combinations that contribute to variations in geometrical, structural, and acoustic properties.

Gemini spans multiple scales of the human existence, extending from the warmth of the womb to the stretches of the Gemini zodiac in deep space. It recapitulates a human cosmos: our body – like the Gemini constellation – drifting in space. In this project we explore interactions between pairs: sonic and solar environments, natural and synthetic materials, hard and soft sensations, as well as subtractive and additive fabrication. The design is rooted in the mythical relationship between twins; one is mortal – born of man, the other divine. Made of two material elements, a whole that is bigger than the sum of its parts, like the sun and the moon, like Adam and Eve, the chaise forms a semi-enclosed space surrounding the human with a stimulation-free environment, recapitulating the ultimate quiet of the womb as it echoes our most inner voices. This calming and still experience of being inside the chaise is designed to invoke the prenatal experience of the fetus surrounded by amniotic serenity, an antidote to the stimuli-rich world we live in.

NERI OXMAN
IS AN ARCHITECT, DESIGNER AND ASSOCIATE PROFESSOR OF MEDIA ARTS AND SCIENCES AT THE MIT MEDIA LAB, WHERE SHE FOUNDED AND DIRECTS THE MEDIATED MATTER GROUP.

FACING PAGE

Gemini, designed by Neri Oxman in collaboration with Professor W. Craig Carter (Department of Materials Science and Engineering, MIT). Created for *Vocal Vibrations* (Tod Machover and Neri Oxman), March 28, 2014 to September 29, 2014, Le Laboratoire, Paris. Sponsors: Le Laboratoire (David Edwards, founder) and Stratasys. 3D Printing: Stratasys with Objet500 Connex3 Color, Multi-material 3D Printer. CNC Milling: SITU FABRICATION.

TOWARD PLASTICITY
DAVID ERDMAN AND CLOVER LEE

"Meaningful without signification, progressive but not avant-garde, formed but without abjection, architectural but without hierarchy, plasticity is at the core of the contemporary architectural project."[25]

In "Plastic," Barthes points out the polarizing effect of plastic – it is fascinating, yet threatening; full of promise, yet ethically dubious. Almost half a century later, in *Plasticity at Work*, Lavin identifies the same slippery status of plasticity as the reason why it is important to contemporary architecture. So while ambiguity solicited skepticism in a generation that considered plastic as a purely material condition; ambiguity offers promise in another generation, where plasticity is mined for its all-in-one condition – formal, spatial, experiential, and sensorial. Building on this elusive quality of plasticity, our practice engages plasticity in two distinct ways. First, we work with *mass* to produce effects of plasticity. Second, we cultivate plasticity as an architectural behavior that is simultaneously *received* by and *emanating* from the architecture itself.

Working with mass, we loosen the tether that ties plasticity to material and formal conditions. Understanding mass as a thick substance – as opposed to a solid object or a void between surfaces – allows us to explore plasticity in new dimensions that respond to our contemporary cultural climate, where organizational systems are neither entirely autonomous nor are they enslaved to a singular form. As such, this notion of mass does not adhere to architectural hierarchies, where elements such as structure, surface, or openings are organized and layered to create a larger whole. Here, mass is not only thick, but also absorbent. The infusion of multiple inputs – from contrasting geometries, materials, and construction systems, to light, color,

and texture – produces environments that are moldable both in perception and sensation. Moving between binary conditions such as hardware and software, material and behavior, these environments reside in a state of plastic cohesion.

This state of plastic cohesion is not physical or material, but sensorial. It holds together sensations and behaviors that are multivalent – that which are not only seen, but felt and experienced by both the occupant and the architecture itself. The mass' absorption of lights, sensors, sound systems, servo-motors, and other media shifts the quality of the environment. Together, these different media inputs control the mass' gradient behaviors, such as its changing degrees of opacity, fluidity, or weight. This challenges the notion that architectural behavior is solely registered through the experience of the occupant. Instead we focus on how the architecture and all of its internal logics exude particular sensations. What happens to a building when it is touched by light, water, or wind? How does that shift the quality of the building? Can it vibrate, glow, or liquefy? Can it be soft and luscious?

Embracing instability and elusiveness in producing a density of experiences, plasticity is important to contemporary architecture because it moves beyond the physical realm of a material premise into the sensorial realm of architectural environments. On one hand, plasticity transgresses material and technical constraints in its production; on the other, it transgresses the subject–object divide in its reception. Working with this expanded taxonomy to solicit a more innovative and multidimensional palette of effects, we hope to engage architectural sensation and move one step closer toward plasticity.

FACING PAGE

Michelangelo's *Atlas Slave* statue embodies the "effect of plasticity." The material is meaningless. The form is found in the state of always becoming.

DAVID ERDMAN AND CLOVER LEE
ARE ARCHITECTS, AND COFOUNDERS OF DAVIDCLOVERS IN HONG KONG, WHERE THEY CURRENTLY PRACTICE TOGETHER.

1800

Plastics cited (in response to Mr. Barthes)

In this collection of responsive essays some contributors name plastics by name – PET, PVC, PTFE, etc. When we sum the number of mentions for a specific plastic, might we gain insight into the present mindset for practices with plastics? Though our sample size is admittedly too small to constitute a proper experiment, our accounting does reveal PVC and keratin, a synthetic polymer and a naturally occurring polymer, to receive the greatest number of mentions. This is a fitting pairing as we wrestle with the continuous emergence and working of this material class.

1865

1869

1899

1907

1873

1839

1872

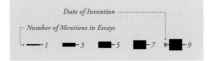

Date of Invention ....

Number of Mentions in Essays

1   3   5   7   9

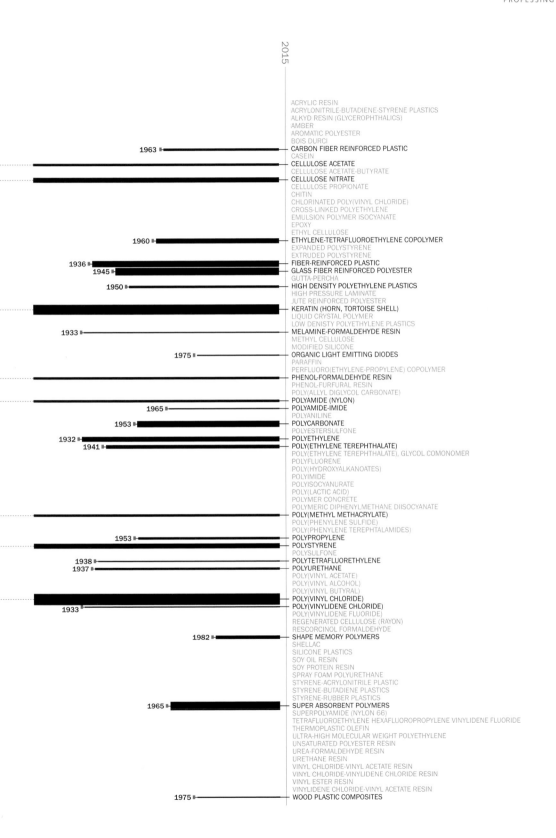

2015

ACRYLIC RESIN
ACRYLONITRILE-BUTADIENE-STYRENE PLASTICS
ALKYD RESIN (GLYCEROPHTHALICS)
AMBER
AROMATIC POLYESTER
BOIS DURCI
1963 CARBON FIBER REINFORCED PLASTIC
CASEIN
CELLULOSE ACETATE
CELLULOSE ACETATE-BUTYRATE
CELLULOSE NITRATE
CELLULOSE PROPIONATE
CHITIN
CHLORINATED POLY(VINYL CHLORIDE)
CROSS-LINKED POLYETHYLENE
EMULSION POLYMER ISOCYANATE
EPOXY
ETHYL CELLULOSE
1960 ETHYLENE-TETRAFLUOROETHYLENE COPOLYMER
EXPANDED POLYSTYRENE
EXTRUDED POLYSTYRENE
1936 FIBER-REINFORCED PLASTIC
1945 GLASS FIBER REINFORCED POLYESTER
GUTTA-PERCHA
1950 HIGH DENSITY POLYETHYLENE PLASTICS
HIGH PRESSURE LAMINATE
JUTE REINFORCED POLYESTER
KERATIN (HORN, TORTOISE SHELL)
LIQUID CRYSTAL POLYMER
LOW DENISTY POLYETHYLENE PLASTICS
1933 MELAMINE-FORMALDEHYDE RESIN
METHYL CELLULOSE
MODIFIED SILICONE
1975 ORGANIC LIGHT EMITTING DIODES
PARAFFIN
PERFLUORO(ETHYLENE-PROPYLENE) COPOLYMER
PHENOL-FORMALDEHYDE RESIN
PHENOL-FURFURAL RESIN
POLY(ALLYL DIGLYCOL CARBONATE)
POLYAMIDE (NYLON)
1965 POLYAMIDE-IMIDE
POLYANILINE
1953 POLYCARBONATE
POLYESTERSULFONE
1932 POLYETHYLENE
1941 POLY(ETHYLENE TEREPHTHALATE)
POLY(ETHYLENE TEREPHTHALATE), GLYCOL COMONOMER
POLYFLUORENE
POLY(HYDROXYALKANOATES)
POLYIMIDE
POLYISOCYANURATE
POLY(LACTIC ACID)
POLYMER CONCRETE
POLYMERIC DIPHENYLMETHANE DIISOCYANATE
POLY(METHYL METHACRYLATE)
POLY(PHENYLENE SULFIDE)
POLY(PHENYLENE TEREPHTALAMIDES)
1953 POLYPROPYLENE
POLYSTYRENE
POLYSULFONE
1938 POLYTETRAFLUORETHYLENE
1937 POLYURETHANE
POLY(VINYL ACETATE)
POLY(VINYL ALCOHOL)
POLY(VINYL BUTYRAL)
POLY(VINYL CHLORIDE)
1933 POLY(VINYLIDENE CHLORIDE)
POLY(VINYLIDENE FLUORIDE)
REGENERATED CELLULOSE (RAYON)
RESCORCINOL FORMALDEHYDE
1982 SHAPE MEMORY POLYMERS
SHELLAC
SILICONE PLASTICS
SOY OIL RESIN
SOY PROTEIN RESIN
SPRAY FOAM POLYURETHANE
STYRENE-ACRYLONITRILE PLASTIC
STYRENE-BUTADIENE PLASTICS
STYRENE-RUBBER PLASTICS
1965 SUPER ABSORBENT POLYMERS
SUPERPOLYAMIDE (NYLON 66)
TETRAFLUOROETHYLENE HEXAFLUOROPROPYLENE VINYLIDENE FLUORIDE
THERMOPLASTIC OLEFIN
ULTRA-HIGH MOLECULAR WEIGHT POLYETHYLENE
UNSATURATED POLYESTER RESIN
UREA-FORMALDEHYDE RESIN
URETHANE RESIN
VINYL CHLORIDE-VINYL ACETATE RESIN
VINYL CHLORIDE-VINYLIDENE CHLORIDE RESIN
VINYL ESTER RESIN
VINYLIDENE CHLORIDE-VINYL ACETATE RESIN
1975 WOOD PLASTIC COMPOSITES

NOTES

1 Voiceover from the Universal International Newsreel titled "Modern Alchemy," 1957.

2 Roland Barthes, *Mythologies* (New York: Hill and Wang, 2012), 193–195. Reprint.

3 Roland Barthes, *Mythologies* (New York: Hill and Wang, 1972), 97–99.

4 Crazing refers to the generation of micro-cracks due to high localized stresses, thermal loading, UV radiation, or chemical exposure. Crazing can easily be discerned as a whitening or "clouding" of the plastic and may lead to yielding of the material.

5 1 MPa = 145 psi: 180 °C ~ 356 °F ~ 450 K.

6 S. Devasahayam, D. J. T. Hill, and J. W. Connell, *High Performance Polymers*. 2005. "Effect of Electron Beam Radiolysis on Mechanical Properties of High Performance Polyimides: A Comparative Study of Transparent Polymer Films," 17 (4): 547–559.

7 John Fernandez, *Material Architecture: Emergent Materials for Innovative Buildings and Ecological Construction* (Oxford: Architectural Press, 2005).

8 N.M. Mutha, M. Patel, and V. Premnath, *Resources Conservation and Recycling*. 2006. "Plastics Materials Flow Analysis for India," 47: 222–244.

9 R.C. Thompson *et al.*, *Science*. 2004. "Lost at Sea: Where is All the Plastic," 304: 838.

10 J. Morgan, "A Survey of Plastics in Historical Collections," Plastics Historical Society and The Conservation Unit of Museums and Galleries Commission, 1994. www.plastiquarian.com/survey/survey.htm

11 H.M. Quackenbos, *Industrial and Engineering Chemistry*. 1954. "Plasticizers in Vinyl Chloride Resins," 46 (6): 1335–1341.

12 S.M. Bradley, "Do Objects Have a Finite Lifetime?" in *Care of Collections*, edited by S. Knell (London: Routledge, 1994), 57.

13 T. Van Oosten, "Here Today, Gone Tomorrow? Problems with Plastics in Contemporary Art," in *Postprints of Modern Art: Who Cares?*, edited by U. Hummelen and D. Sillé (Amsterdam: The Foundation for the Conservation of Modern Art and the Netherlands Institute for Cultural Heritage, 1999), 158–163.

14 In some regions of the US, "insulation would offer the biggest opportunity and could improve heating performance by nearly 30 percent … Although retrofit improvements typically deliver substantial abatement, they cost much more than comparable improvements in new-build shells." *The McKinsey Report*, "Reducing U.S. Greenhouse Gas Emissions: How Much at What Cost?" (December 2007), 39.

15 "The single greatest threat to the durability and long-term performance of the housing stock," Newport Partners, "Building Moisture and Durability Past, Present, and Future" (work prepared for the Department of Housing and Urban Development, October 2004).

16 Robert Lilienfeld and William Rathje, *Use Less Stuff: Environmental Solutions for Who We Really Are* (New York: Ballantine Publishing Group, 1998).

17 Ivy Hughes, "Thomas Friedman offers Michigan Some Green Guidance," *Capital Gains*, www.capitalgainsmedia.com/features/frdmn0237.aspx

18 *SPONGEcity* is a collaborative effort of Claire Agre, Sarah Cohen, Amanda Cox, Natalie DeNormadie, Matthew Gordy, and Liat Margolis. *SPONGEcity* was exhibited at the 2nd International Architecture Biennale: *The Flood*, Rotterdam, May 26 to June 26, 2005.

19 Roland Barthes, Mythologies, Paris, 1957, included in Andrea Deplazes, ed., *Constructing Architecture: Materials, Processes, Structures: a Handbook*, Birkhauser, 2008, 150.

20 Donald Albrecht, "Evolving Forms: A Photographic Essay of Eames Furniture, Prototypes, and Experiments" in *The Work of Charles and Ray Eames: A Legacy of Invention*, edited by Diana Murphy (New York: Harry N. Abrams Inc., 1997), 86.

21 Peter Smithson, Just a few chairs and a house: an essay on the Eames-aesthetic, *Architectural Design*, September 1966, 448.

22 Thomas Pynchon, *Gravity's Rainbow* (New York: Viking Press: 1973).

23 Toyo Ito, *El Croquis*. 1996. "Architecture in a Simulated City," 71: 13ff.

24 Ibid.

25 Sylvia Lavin, "Plasticity at Work," *Mood River* (Columbus, OH: Wexner Center for the Arts, 2002).

PLASTICS AND OUR AGENCY

Imbuing this set of evidence with some agency requires that we begin first with one word – "plastics." We still insist on using one word to describe thousands of materials. Remember, we are said to have wanted "plastics dealt with as plastics and indexed as 'plastics.'"[1] This is a highly suspicious epistemological precondition which births paradoxical constraints – to know "plastics" we determined it best to abandon our intellectual capacity *to know them*. Right here in 1954 originates inertia, born of the term "plastics" and the model code for using plastics in buildings. We practice with this precondition today. Might we proceed by separating rather than continuing to coalesce into one material class? Might we approach each one of these materials as they are – separate and with distinct attributes? Doing so could entirely upend the conceptual positions "all-plastics" and "plastics in building." Actually knowing plastics could allow us to better wrestle with the degree to which we are complicit in working them, to critically engage their ingredients, to work them across their "lifecycle," which is really a practice that pursues the consciousness of time, and to pursue customization of them by engaging their construction logic as it is explicitly connected to the attributes we experience macroscopically.

And … what about those phrases which capture plastics' inertia?

> "Plastics are a/the/in our future."

> "Plastics are not substitute materials."

> "Plastics are difficult to decipher."

They might be restated thusly:

> Plastics are not the future, they just are.

> Plastics are not substitute materials, they just are.

> Plastics are difficult but not impossible to decipher.

The agency we may choose to give any one of the above statements when we purpose ourselves to interact with plastics is a separate mental act. Plastics inertia may be experienced, but never named by us when we unknowingly tread the same technical and formal ground again and again, isolated as we are from real and substantive discourse with materials engineers who customize polymers, and manufacturers who possess the tacit knowledge to work plastics. Our bid of late to collapse design and manufacturing into one numerically controlled step via fused deposition modeling, selective laser sintering, sterolithography, or robotics, with the materials ABS, PC, PA, PEI, PPSF, and SPF is, in light of this history, an interesting guerrilla move that might subvert inaccessible manufacturing regimes.[2]

But, are we to approach plastics in isolation, or in the role of "activist architect"? Is there some other collective arrangement to pursue with industry, some neutral type of ground to be found? A community formed to work out plastics use in architecture, a community composed of chemists, architects, and engineers, from industry and academia. It is there in the record, though it is a fleeting specter. It is there to be found and puzzled over because it seems so very unattainable from our present practice disposition. Perhaps it points to the potential to practice through the aegis of differently knowledged communities, transdisciplinary design communities, rather than through the aegis of professions. Pursuing this might be a radical upending of entrenched practices for both the plastics and the building industry. In so doing we might dispense with those practices that keep us at arm's length from one another.

If there is more agency to this history then it is found when we recognize that the epistemological precondition we created to use plastics, which amounts to the abandonment of knowing a thing because of its complexity, is not limited to our practices with plastics. We may, to our detriment, choose to extend this type of precondition to other materials (remember all materials continuously emerge), but also to climates, ecosystems, thermodynamics, even to technologies, logistics, and forms of governance and control – to several phenomena that normatively fall outside of our professional practice purview. The case of plastics now exposes our innate practice of delimiting an artificial problem-solving boundary for the sake of creating a building. We delimit to exclude or include. We delimit and decipher or mythologize. This power of delimitation is one that we consciously or unconsciously take up when we purpose ourselves to the act of design. How should we use plastics? How should we design with plastics? I dare you to try.

NOTES

1   F.J. Rarig, *Progressive Architecture*. 1970. "Plastics and the Building Codes," 51: 96–99.

2   Yes, a transect on plastics and future plastics for 3D printing could and should be accomplished as well.

BIBLIOGRAPHY

BOOKS REFERENCED, 1990 AND FOLLOWING

Albrecht, Donald. "Evolving Forms: A Photographic Essay of Eames Furniture, Prototypes, and Experiments," in *The work of Charles and Ray Eames: A Legacy of Invention*, edited by Diana Murphy. New York: Harry N. Abrams Inc., 1997.

Ashby, Mike and Kara Johnson. *Materials and Design: The Art and Science of Material Selection in Product Design.* Amsterdam: Elsevier, 2002, 2003 and 2004.

Berge, Bjorn. *The Ecology of Building Materials.* Oxford and Boston, MA: Architectural Press, 2000.

Bradley, S.M. "Do Objects Have a Finite Lifetime?" in *Care of Collections*, edited by S. Knell. London: Routledge, 1994.

Brunner, Paul H. and Helmut Rechberger. *Practical Handbook of Material Flow Analysis.* Boca Raton, FL: CRC/Lewis, 2004.

Burdick, Donald L. and William L. Leffler. *Petrochemicals in Nontechnical Language (4th edition).* Tulsa, OK: PennWell Corporation, 2010. See esp. chapter 5, "Olefin Plants, Ethylene, and Propylene."

Dieste, Eladio. "Architecture and Construction," in Anderson, Stanford, and Eladio Dieste. *Eladio Dieste: Innovation in Structural Art.* New York: Princeton Architectural Press, 2004.

Encyclopedia of Polymer Science and Technology, Volume 1 (3rd edition). Hoboken, NJ: John Wiley & Sons, Inc., 2003.

Fernandez, John. *Material Architecture: Emergent Materials for Innovative Buildings and Ecological Construction.* Oxford: Architectural Press, 2005.

Ganz, Cheryl. *The 1933 Chicago World's Fair: A Century of Progress.* Urbana, IL: University of Illinois Press, 2008.

International Code Council. *International Building Code.* Falls Church, VA: The Council, 2008.

Kaltenbach, Frank, ed. *Translucent Materials: Glass, Plastics, Metals.* Basel: Birkhauser, 2004.

Katz, Sylvia. *Early Plastics.* Buckinghamshire: Shire Publications, 1994.

Koch, Klaus-Michael, ed. *Membrane Structures: Innovative Building with Film and Fabric.* Munich and New York: Prestel, 2004.

Lavin, Sylvia. "Plasticity at Work," in *Mood River*, edited by Jeffrey Kipnis and Annetta Massie. Columbus, Ohio: Wexner Center for the Arts, 2002.

Lilienfeld, Robert and William Rathje. *Use Less Stuff: Environmental Solutions for Who We Really Are.* New York: Ballantine Publishing Group, 1998.

McDonough, William and Michael Braungart. *Cradle to Cradle: Remaking the Way We Make Things.* New York: North Point Press, 2002.

Meikle, Jeffrey L. *American Plastic: A Cultural History.* New Brunswick, NJ: Rutgers University Press, 1997.

Mohanty, Amar K., Manjusri Misra, and Lawrence T. Drzal, eds. *Natural Fibers, Biopolymers, and Biocomposites.* Boca Raton, FL: CRC Press, 2005.

Morris, Peter J.T. *Polymer Pioneers: A Popular History of the Science and Technology of Large Molecules.* Philadelphia, PA: University of Pennsylvania, Beckman Center for the History of Chemistry, 1990.

Museum of Modern Art. *Natural Artifice.* New York: MoMA, 2008.

Odum, Howard T. *Environmental Accounting: EMERGY and Environmental Decision Making.* New York: Wiley, 1996.

Pynchon, Thomas. *Gravity's Rainbow.* New York: Viking Press, 1973.

Rothko, Mark and Christopher Rothko. *The Artist's Reality: Philosophies of Art.* New Haven, CT: Yale University Press, 2004. See esp. the chapter "Plasticity."

Rubin, Irvin I. *Handbook of Plastic Materials and Technology.* New York: Wiley, 1990.

Ryan, Deborah S. *The Ideal Home Through the 20th Century.* London: Hazar Publishing, 1997.

Simmons, H. Leslie. *Olin's Construction: Principles, Material and Methods (8th edition).* New York: John Wiley & Sons, 2007.

Stattmann, Nicola. *Ultra Light Super Strong.* Basel: Birkhäuser, 2003.

Van Oosten, T. "Here Today, Gone Tomorrow? Problems with Plastics in Contemporary Art," in *Postprints of Modern Art: Who Cares?*, edited by U. Hummelen and D. Sillé. Amsterdam: The Foundation for the Conservation of Modern Art and the Netherlands Institute for Cultural Heritage, 1999.

Wool, Richard and Xiuzhi Susan Sun. *Bio-Based Polymers and Composites.* San Diego, CA: Elsevier Academic Press, 2005.

BOOKS REFERENCED, CONSIDERED "HISTORICAL"

Barthes, Roland. *Mythologies.* New York: Hill and Wang, 2012. (First published in French by Editions du Seuil, 1957.)

Benjamin, B.S. *Structural Design with Plastics.* New York: Van Nostrand Reinhold Co., 1969.

Corey, E. Raymond. *The Development of Markets for New Materials: A Study of Building New End-Product Markets for Aluminum, Fibrous Glass, and the Plastics.* Boston, MA: Division of Research, Graduate School of Business Administration, Harvard University, 1960.

Davies, R.M., ed. *Plastics in Building Construction.* London: Blackie & Son Limited, 1965.

Dietz, Albert G.H. *Materials of Construction: Wood, Plastics, Fabrics.* New York: D. Van Nostrand and Company, 1949.

Dietz, Albert G.H. *Plastics for Architects and Builders*. Cambridge, MA: MIT Press, 1969.

Dietz, Albert G.H. *Composite Engineering Laminates*. Cambridge, MA: MIT Press, 1969.

Dubois, J. Harry. *Plastics History U.S.A.* Boston, MA: Cahners Books, 1972.

Engineering Equipment Users Association. *The Use of Plastics Materials in Building, EEUA Handbook No. 31*. London: Constable and Company Ltd., 1973.

Gordon, J.E. *The New Science of Strong Materials or Why You Don't Fall Through the Floor*. Cambridge, MA: Da Capo Press, 1981.

Mactaggart, E.F. and H.H. Chambers. *Plastics and Building*. New York: Philosophical Library, 1955.

Makowski, Z.S. "The Structural Applications of Plastics," in *Plastics in Building Construction*, edited by R.M. Davies. London: Blackie & Son, 1965.

Marshal, Alfred. *Principles of Economics* (3rd edition). London: Macmillan, 1895.

Montella, Ralph. *Plastics in Architecture: A Guide to Acrylic and Polycarbonate*. New York: Marcel Dekker, Inc., 1985.

Museum of Contemporary Crafts of the American Craftsman's Council. *Plastic as Plastic*. New York: under the sponsorship of Hooker Chemical Corporation a subsidiary of Occidental Petroleum Corporation, November 23, 1968–January 12, 1969.

Penn, W.S. *Plastics-in-Building Handbook*. London: Maclaren & Sons, Ltd., 1964.

Quarmby, Arthur. *Plastics and Architecture*. New York: Praeger, 1974.

Reboul, P. and R.G. Bruce Mitchell. *Plastics in the Building Industry*. London: George Newnes Limited, 1968.

Scientific American. *Materials*. San Francisco, CA: W.H. Freeman and Company, 1967.

Seymour, Raymond B., ed. *History of Polymer Science and Technology*. New York: Marcel Dekker, Inc., 1982.

Singer, Joseph B. *Plastics in Building*. London: The Architectural Press, 1952.

Skeist, Irving, ed. *Plastics in Building*. New York: Reinhold Publishing Corporation, 1966. See esp. chapter 3 "Building Codes and Regulations," chapter 19, "Plastics Abroad," and chapter 20, "NAHB Research Houses."

Sonneborn, Ralph H. *Fiberglass Reinforced Plastics*. New York: Reinhold Publishing Corporation, 1954.

JOURNAL ARTICLES, 1933–2008

Alling, Stephen J. "Plastics for Floor and Wall Treatments." *Interior Design and Decoration* (February 1940) 61–64. (Part of "A Portfolio of Addresses at the National Conference on Plastics" sponsored by *Interior Design and Decoration*.)

Altherr, Alfred. "Die Kunststoffe: ihre Zusammensetzung und Formung." *Werk* Vol. 46 (March 1959): 86–91.

Antonelli, Paola. "Mutant Materials: On Plastics and Other Artifacts of Material Culture." *Harvard Design Magazine* (Summer 1998): 47–50.

Architects' Journal. "Technical Study Part 1: Glass Fibre Reinforced Plastics for Building Claddings, the Material and its Uses" (March 21, 1973): 699–706.

Architect's Journal. "Technical Study Part 2: Glass Fibre Reinforced Plastics, Translucent GRP." (April 4, 1973): 817–826.

Architect's Journal. "Technical Study Part 3: Glass Fibre Reinforced Plastics for Building Claddings, Pigmented GRP." (May 2, 1973): 1035–1047.

Architects' Journal. "Exhibitions: Flexible Friends The Plastics Age: From Modernity to Post-modernity." Vol. 191, No. 9 (February 28, 1990): 78–79.

Architectural Design. "Plastic Buildings." Vol. 40, No. 4 (April 1970): 167–618. (Published first in *Architektur und Wohnformen*, November 15, 1969.)

Architectural Forum. "Plastics in Building." (June 1940): 413–417.

Architectural Forum. "Rigging a Roof." Vol. 132, No. 2 (March 1970): 64–69.

Architectural Forum. "Capsules Replace Hospital Rooms." Vol. 132, No. 4 (May 1970): 54–57

Architectural Forum. "Mass Produced in Plastic." Vol. 138, No. 4 (May 1973): 10–11.

Architecture Francaise. "La premiere maison tout en plastiques." Vol. 173–174 (January 1957): 44–48.

Arts and Architecture. "Experimental House in Plastics." Vol. 72 (November 1955): 20–21.

Battle, Guy and Christopher McCarthy. "Multi-Source Synthesis, Atomic Architecture." *Architectural Design* Vol. 65, No. 1–2 (January–February 1995): iii–vii

Bauen und Wohnen. "Ganz-Plastik-Haus auf der Ausstellung Arts Menagers 1956 in Paris." Vol. 11 (February 1957): 57–60.

Bauen und Wohnen. "Mobile Hotelkabine." Vol. 11 (February 1957): 60.

Bauen und Wohnen. "Sandwichplatten aus Kunststoff." Vol. 15 (October 1961): 384–391.

Bigelow, Maurice H. "Coordinating Plastics with Lighting." *Interior Design and Decoration* (February 1940): 52–61. (Part of "A Portfolio of Addresses at the National Conference on Plastics" sponsored by *Interior Design and Decoration*.)

Brooks, Alan Jeremy and Tom Gent. "Plastic Moulding: Architectural Options." *Architects' Journal* Vol. 186, No. 26 (July 1, 1987): 51–55.

Casabella. "Progettare con le materie plastiche, 1 La materie plastiche nell'edilizia." Vol. 1 (March–April 1967): 42–49.

Casabella. "Progettare con le materie plastiche, 2 Il poliestere rinforzato: Stampaggio, stampi, lavorazione." Vol. 1 (March–April 1967): 54–61.

Casabella. "Progettare con le materie plastiche, 3 Metalli. Materie plastiche. Resine poliesteri. Differenze." Vol. 1 (March–April 1967): 22–29.

Charlesby, Arthur. "Even With Small Doses of Irradiation Many Materials Undergo Dramatic Change." *The Architectural Forum* (September 1954): 102–103.

Coulon, R., Y. Magnant, and I. Schein. "Wohnhaus." *Bauen und Wohnen* (July 1959): 236–239.

Dickey, Raymond R. "The New World of Plastics." *The New Pencil Points* 24 (January 1943): 41.

Dietz, Albert G.H. "Potentialities of Plastics in Building." *Architectural Record* (March 1950): 132–137.

Dietz, Albert G.H. "Selecting Plastics for Building Uses." *Architectural Record* (April 1955): 25–231.

Dietz, Albert G.H. "Plastics: The Next Decade." *Progressive Architecture* Vol. 51 (October 1970): 100–109.

Drummond, Josephine H. "Update on Plastic Laminates." *Progressive Architecture* (August 1977): 84.

Domus. "Casette 'Prestampate.'" Vol. 334 (September 1957): 4–5.

Domus. "Della Germania: Una Casa in Plastic." Vol. 433 (October 1965): 16–17.

Domus. "Dal Messico, in fiberglass." Vol. 503 (October 1971): 19.

Ferarra, Anthony. "Architectural Requirements for Roofing Materials." *Journal of the AIA* (December 1957): 478–479.

Fidler, John A. "Glass-Reinforced Plastic Facsimiles in Building Restoration." *APT* Vol. 14 No. 3 (1982): 21–25.

Fire and Materials. "Obituary, R. Brady Williamson." Vol. 31 (2007): 355–357.

Frederick, D. S. "Plastics in the Realm of Furniture." *Interior Design and Decoration* (February 1940): 50–52. (Part of "A Portfolio of Addresses at the National Conference on Plastics" sponsored by *Interior Design and Decoration*.)

George, David H. "GE Plastics Concept House." *Urban Land* Vol. 49, No. 7 (July 1990): 20–21.

Gigliotti, Michael F.X. "Plastics for Interior Walls." *Progressive Architecture* (February 1956): 138–141.

Goody, Marvin and Richard Hamilton. "The Plastic House of the Future." *Industrial Design* (August 1957): 50–57.

Hamilton and Goody, Architekten, R.P. Whittier, E.D. Schopach, M.F. Gigliotto, Ingenieure. "Monsanto-Haus." *Bauen und Wohnen* (July 1959): 240–242.

Haskell, Douglas. "In Architecture, Will Atomic Processes Create a new 'Plastic' Order?" *The Architectural Forum* (September 1954): 100–101.

Hecker, Anne. "PLASTICS: New Piller in Construction?" *AIA Journal* (February 1970): 64–68.

House & Garden. "Prophetic Plastics." Vol. 78, No. 1 (October 1940): 26–31, 72.

House & Garden. "Answers to Your Questions About Foam: The Controversial New Building Material." Vol. 143 (May 1973): 58, 60, 215.

House & Home. "New Products: Plastics for Building." Vol. 14 (February 1954): 158–162.

House & Home. "Look How Many Ways You Can Now Use … Plastic!" Vol. 10 (September 1956): 118–135.

Hughes, Ivy. "Thomas Friedman Offers Michigan Some Green Guidance," *Capital Gains*, www.capitalgainsmedia.com/features/frdmn0237.aspx

Industrial Design. "Why Polyethylene?" Vol. 2 (February 1955): 48–57.

Interior Design and Decoration. "Plastics Utilized in Store Interiors" (February 1940): 31–35.

Ito, Toyo. "Architecture in a Simulated City," *El Croquis* 71, 1996.

Jeska, Simone. "Plastics: Ethereal Materials or Trash Culture?" *Detail* (English edition) Vol. 4 (2008): 342–346.

Journal of the AIA. "BRI Reviews Plastics for Roof Construction: Selected Papers Dealing with Plastics for Roof Construction." (December 1957) 466–473.

Kavanagh, L.B. "Preparing Horn Stock for Combs." *Modern Plastics*, Vol. 1, No. 1 (October 1925): 23, 27–28.

Kennedy, T. Warnett. "The First All-Plastics House." *British Plastics and Moulded Products* (October 1941): 138–139.

Kuczenski, B., & Geyer, R. "Material Flow Analysis of Polyethylene Terephthalate in the US, 1996–2007." *Resources, Conservation and Recycling* Vol. 54, No. 12 (2010): 1161–1169.

Larson, C. Theodore, comp. "New Housing Designs and Construction Systems." *Architectural Record* (January 1934): 1–36.

Lees, Al. "Are You Ready for a Plastic House?" *Popular Science* (August 1988): 47–49, 85.

LeMessurier, William J. "Plastic-Composite Design Cuts Steel Tonnage in Johns-Manville's New Headquarters Building." *Architectural Record* (September 1977): 127–128.

Makowski, Z.S. "Structural Plastics in Europe." *Arts and Architecture* (August 1966): 20–30.

Marshall, Robert F. "Plastics … Practically Speaking." *Architectural Record* (April 1943): 54–59, 86.

Martin, Bruce. "How Should We Use Plastics?" *Architectural Review* (August 1956): 134, 136, 138.

Modern Plastics. "'Plastics': A Definition." (October 1925): 20.

Modern Plastics. "Ideas! Ideas!" (October 1926): 349.

"Monsanto Plastics: 'House of the Future.'" *Architect and Building News* Vol. 212 (1957): 478–485.

Morgan, J. "A Survey of Plastics in Historical Collections." Plastics Historical Society and The Conservation Unit of Museums and Galleries Commission (1994), www.plastiquarian.com/survey/survey.htm

National Plastics Center and Museum. "Biography of Armand G. Winfield," (no date).

Passonneau, Joseph E. "Roof Structures Constructed of Plastic Materials." *Journal of the AIA* (December 1957): 474–477.

Pinto, E.H. and E.R. Pinto. "A Forgotten Plastic." *Country Life* Vol. 113 (April 16, 1963): 1152–1153.

Plastics Catalog Corporation. "Plastics: Characteristics and Applications." *Architectural Record* (June 1944): 103–108.

Progressive Architecture. "Design Data for Acrylic Plastics … Part I." (January 1946): 94–95.

Progressive Architecture. "Acrylic Plastics in Architecture." (June 1949): 78.

Progressive Architecture. "Vinyl Plastics and Resins in Architecture. Vol. 32 (1951): 89–91.

Progressive Architecture "Plastics in Architecture." (June 1960), whole issue.

Progressive Architecture. "Spun Plastic Shapes a School." Vol. 48 (July 1967): 156–157.

Progressive Architecture "Plastics in Architecture." (October, 1970), whole issue.

Progressive Architecture: "Plastics: A Decade of Progress." (October 1970): 65–69.

Progressive Architecture. "Foam home." (May 1971): 7–10.

Progressive Architecture. "One On, One in the Wings." (November 1971): 100–105.

Progressive Architecture. "Important Notice Regarding the Flammability of Cellular Plastics used in Building Construction, and Low Density Cellular Plastics Used in Furniture." (February 1975): 92.

Progressive Architecture. "Pandora's Plastic Box." (September 1975): 86–91.

Progressive Architecture. "High-impact Material." (August 1979): 89–93.

Progressive Architecture. "The Light Heavyweights." (October 1981): 125–133.

Quackenbos, H.M. "Plasticizers in Vinyl Chloride Resins." *Industrial and Engineering Chemistry*, Vol. 46, No. 6 (1954): 1335–1341.

Quarmby, Arthur. "The Design of Structures in Plastic." *Architectural Design* Vol. 31 (November 1961): 518–521.

Rarig, F.J. "Plastics and the Building Codes," *Progressive Architecture* (October 1970): 96–99.

Richardson, H.M. "Research in the Plastics Industry." *Interior Design and Decoration* (February 1940): 68, 74, 76, 78, 80, 82. (Part of "A Portfolio of Addresses at the National Conference on Plastics" sponsored by *Interior Design and Decoration*.)

Rosen, Harold J. "Plastics Permeate Specification Sections." *Progressive Architecture* (October 1960): 206.

Rothenstein, Guy G. "Sprayed-on Vinyl-Plastic Sheeting." *Progressive Architecture* (July 1952): 99–105.

Russell, James S. "What's This Building Made Of?" *Architectural Record* (July 1990): 91–97.

Scheichenbauer, di Mario. "Progettare con le materie plastiche, 4 Le strutture adatte al poliestere rinforzato." *Casabella* Vol. 1 (March–April 1967): 36–43.

Scheichenbauer, di Mario. "Progettare con le materie plastiche, 5 Il progetto dei plastici rinforzati, Accoppiamento con altri materiali." *Casabella* Vol. 1 (March–April 1967): 30–37.

Scheichenbauer, di Mario. "Progettare con le materie plastiche, 6 Resine poliesteri e prefabbricazion." *Casabella* Vol. 1 (March–April 1967): 40–47.

Scheichenbauer, Mario. "Progettare con le materie plastiche, 7 Normazione, collaudi, sviluppi." *Casabella* Vol. 1 (March–April 1967): 24–27.

Schein, Lionel. "Una casa costruita totalmente in plastica." *Domus* (May 1956): 15–18.

Schein, Lionel, Claude Demoulain, Jan Rol, and Jeanine Abraham. "Penthouse Flat and Office, Paris." *Architectural Design* (November 1965): 555–558.

Schein, Lionel. "A Phenomenology of Research." *Arts and Architecture* (August 1966): 31.

Scientific American. "Synthetic Houses." Vol. 149, No. 4 (October 1933): 180.

Smith, Harold DeWitt, "Fabrics: Synthetic and Coated." *Interior Design and Decoration* (February 1940): 64–68. (Part of "A Portfolio of Addresses at the National Conference on Plastics" sponsored by *Interior Design and Decoration*.)

Teague, Walter Dorwin. "Design Principles Applied to Plastics." *Interior Design and Decoration* (February 1940): 44–49. (Part of "A Portfolio of Addresses at the National Conference on Plastics" sponsored by *Interior Design and Decoration*.)

Tetzlaff, Frederick W. and Robert H. Rorke. "Acrylic Plastics in Architecture." *Progressive Architecture* (June 1949): 75–77.

Thompson, R.C., et al. "Lost at Sea: Where is All the Plastic." *Science* 304 (2004): 838.

Walker, Anthony. "Plastics and the Modern House." *Architectural Record*, Vol. 75, No. 1 (January 1996): 72.

Werk. "Die 'Sphéroïde'-Raumzelle." (June 1968): 366.

Werk. "Fensterloser variabler Raumstadt-bau aus Kunststoff- und regulier-baren Glas-Formteilen." (June 1968).

Werk. "Neue Werkstoffe in der bildenden Kunst." (June 1968).

Werk. "Pre-magasin Prisunic und Ferienhaus." (June 1968): 360–361.

Werk. "Spielplatzgerät." (June 1968): 362–363.

"The Wilson House," Wilsonart, www.wilsonart.com/corporate/wilson-house

Wilson, Forrest. "Plastics, Past and Future." *Architecture* (April 1988): 103–108.

Wilson, Forrest. "Plastic for the People." *Architecture* (March 1990): 165–168.

Winfield, Armand G. "Plastic Structures Go High-Rise." *Progressive Architecture* (August 1973): 74–77.

PAPERS PRESENTED AT CONFERENCES AND SYMPOSIA, AND OTHER PAPERS

Akin, Russell. "The Plastics in Building Committee of the Manufacturing Chemists' Association" in *Intersociety Reports on Plastics in Building* Activities, 25–27. Washington, DC: NAS-NRC, 1962.

Akin, Russell. "Building Codes and Durability as Factors in Marketing Plastics for Construction" in *Polymers and Plastics in Construction*, American Chemical Society, A-49–A-54. Washington, DC: American Chemical Society, 1965.

Akin, Russell. "Fire Testing and Acceptance of Plastics in Building Codes" in *Technical Papers, Regional Technical Conference 'Plastics in Building'*, edited by John Hyden, 50–59. Stamford, CT:Society of Plastics Engineers Chicago Section, 1969.

Ambrose, Frank X. "The Building Code Advisory Committee of the Society of the Plastics Industry" in *Intersociety Reports on Plastics in Building* Activities, 38–43. Washington, DC: NAS-NRC, 1962.

Buranakarn, Vorasun. "Evaluation of Recycling and Reuse of Building Materials Using the Emergy Analysis Method." PhD diss., University of Florida, 1998.

Callahan, B.J. "Evaluation of the Fire Hazard of Cellular Plastics in Building Construction and the SLRP Concept" in *Technical Papers, Regional Technical Conference, Plastics in Building: Present Status and Future Prospects*, edited by Rudolph D. Deanin and Stephen Burke Driscoll, 46–53. Stamford, CT: Society of Plastics Engineers Chicago Section, 1969.

Cleneay, Allen W. "The Building Owner's View: Plastics in Experimental Buildings," in *Performance of Plastics in Building*, 115–129. Washington, DC: Building Research Institute Inc., 1963.

Csillaghy, J. "Some Aspects of the Consumption of Plastics in the Building Industry in Europe" in *Polymers and Plastics in Construction*, American Chemical Society, A-145–A-148. Washington, DC: American Chemical Society, 1965.

Dietz, Albert G.H. "Physical and Engineering Properties of Plastics" in *Plastics in Building*, 11–20. Washington, DC: NAS-NRC, 1955.

Dietz, Albert G.H. "Engineering the Monsanto House of the Future" in *Plastics Study Group of the Building Research Institute, Report of a Meeting at the Massachusetts Institute of Technology*, 105–120. Washington, DC: NAS-NRC, 1956.

Dietz, Albert G.H. "The Plastics Laboratory at the Massachusetts Institute of Technology" in *Intersociety Reports on Plastics in Building Activities*, 33–37. Washington, DC: NAS-NRC, 1962.

Dietz, Albert G.H. "Engineering with Plastics" in *Polymers and Plastics in Construction*, A-29–A-36. Washington, DC: American Chemical Society, 1965.

Grove, C.S. Jr. "Proposal for the Compilation of Design Handbook of Plastics in Building" in *Performance of Plastics in Building*. Washington, DC: Building Research Institute, Inc., 1963.

Lien, A.P. "Polymers and Plastics in Construction: A General View" in *Polymers and Plastics in Construction*, A-5–A-17. Washington, DC: American Chemical Society, 1965.

O'Connell, W.J.J., J.B. Williams, G.L. Nelson, and A.L. Bridgman. "Large Scale Fire Tests and Plastics Products" in *Plastics in Building*, edited by Rudolph D. Deanin and Stephen Burke Driscoll, 38–53. Stamford, CT: Society of Plastics Engineers, 1976.

Slater, R.J., M.J. Werkema and E.J. Picucci. "Portable Expandable Shelters" in *Plastics in Building*, edited by John Hyden, 14–23. Stamford, CT: Society of Plastics Engineers, 1969.

Staudinger, Hermann. "Macromolecular Chemistry" in *Nobel Lectures, Chemistry 1942–1962*, 397–419. Amsterdam: Elsevier Publishing Company, 1964.

Williamson, R. Brady. "Fire safety in Urban Housing: A Description of the NSF-RANN Program at the University of California, Berkeley" in *Symposium: Products of Combustion of (Plastics) Building Materials*, 77–81. Lancaster, PA: Armstrong Cork Company, 1973.

Winfield, Armand G. "The Plastics in Building Professional Activity Group of the International Society of Plastics Engineers, Inc." in *Intersociety Reports on Plastics in Building Activities*, 5–10. Washington, DC: NAS-NRC, 1962.

Winfield, Armand G. "Uninhibited Campus Research Opens Portals to New Plastics in Building Concepts" in *Plastics in Building*, edited by John Hyden, 32–49. Stamford, CT: Society of Plastics Engineers, 1969.

Winfield, Armand G. "UNIDO Report" in *Plastics in Building Construction – Realities and Challenges*, 335–362. Stamford, CT: Society of Plastics Engineers, 1972.

Winfield, Armand G. "Major Breakthrough in Low Cost Plastic Housing Using Jute Reinforced Polyesters: The CARE/Winfield/Bangladesh House" in *Proceedings of the 29th Annual Technical Conference*, Section 7-A, 1–11. Washington, DC: The Society of Plastics Industry, 1974.

Wright, Val. "Plastics in Mobile Homes" in *Plastics in Building*, edited by John Hyden, 24–31. Stamford, CT: Society of Plastics Engineers, 1969.

Yuill, Calvin H. "Regulatory Agency Acceptance of Plastics in Building" in *Performance of Plastics in Building*, 51–56. Washington, DC: Building Research Institute, Inc., 1963.

PROCEEDINGS FROM CONFERENCES AND SYMPOSIA, PAMPHLETS AND REPORTS

American Chemical Society. *Polymers and Plastics in Construction*. Washington, DC: American Chemical Society, 1965. (Report of the symposium sponsored by American Chemical Society Division of Petroleum Chemistry, Inc., Atlantic City, New Jersey, September 12–17, 1965).

Architectural Research Laboratory, University of Michigan. *Structural Potential of Foam Plastics for Housing in Underdeveloped Areas*. Ann Arbor, MI: Architectural Research Laboratory, 1966.

Architectural Research Laboratory, University of Michigan. *Research on Potential of Advanced Technology for Housing: A Building System Based on Filament Winding and New Developments in Water and Waste Management*. Ann Arbor, MI: Architectural Research Laboratory, 1968.

Armstrong Cork Company. *Symposium: Products of Combustion of (Plastics) Building Materials*, Lancaster, PA: Armstrong Cork Company, 1973. (Report of symposium sponsored by Armstrong Cork Company, held in Lancaster, Pennsylvania, March, 26–27, 1973).

British Plastics Federation. *Plastics. Post-war Building Studies No. 3*. London: HMSO, 1944.

Building Research Institute. *Plastics in Building*. Washington, DC: NAS-NRC, 1955. (Proceeding of a conference held in Washington, DC, October 27–28, 1954).

Building Research Institute. *Plastics Study Group of the Building Research Institute, Report of the Meeting at the University of Michigan*. Washington, DC: NAS-NRC, 1956. (Report of meeting held in Ann Arbor, MI, November 14–15, 1955).

Building Research Institute. *Plastics Study Group of the Building Research Institute, Report of a Meeting at the Massachusetts Institute of Technology*. Washington, DC: NAS-NRC, 1956. (Second meeting of the PSG, held in Cambridge, MA, July 14–15, 1956).

Building Research Institute. *Plastics Study Group of the Building Research Institute, Report of a Meeting at the Illinois Institute of Technology*. Washington, DC: NAS-NRC, 1957. (Third meeting of the PSG, held in Chicago, IL, December 5–7, 1956).

Building Research Institute. *Plastics Study Group of the Building Research Institute, Report of a Meeting at Washington University*. Washington, DC: NAS-NRC, 1957. (Fourth meeting of the PSG, held in St. Louis, MO, September 17–18, 1957).

Building Research Institute. *Plastics in Building Illumination*. Washington, DC: NAS-NRC, 1958. (Report of the fifth meeting of the BRI PSG held in Houston, TX at the University of Houston, March 5–6, 1958).

Building Research Institute. *Information Requirements for Selection of Plastics for Use in Building*. Washington, DC: NAS-NRC, 1960. (Proceedings of a program conducted as part of the 1960 Spring Conferences of the Building Research Institute, Division of Engineering and Industrial Research).

Building Research Institute. *Intersociety Reports on Plastics in Building Activities*. Washington, DC: NAS-NRC, 1962. (Report of a conference held as part of the 1961 Spring Conference of the Building Research Institute, Division of Engineering and Industrial Research).

Building Research Institute. *Performance of Plastics in Building*. Washington, DC: Building Research Institute, 1963. (Report of a conference held as part of the 1961 Fall Conference of the Building Research Institute, Division of Engineering and Industrial Research).

Davies, R.M., ed. *The Proceedings of a Conference on Plastics in Building Construction*. London: Blackie & Son, 1965. (The proceedings of a conference held at Battersea College of Technology (University of Surrey) on September 24, 1964).

Deanin, Rudolph D. and Driscoll, Stephen Burke, eds. *Plastics in Building*. Stamford, CT: Society of Plastics Engineers, 1976. (Report of the Regional Technical Conference, held in Boston, MA, November 9–10, 1976).

Dietz, Albert G.H. *Composite Materials, Edgar Marburg Lecture*. Philadelphia, PA: ASTM, 1965.

Graduates of the Harvard Graduate School of Business Administration. *Plastics as Building Construction Materials*. Belmont, MA: Structural Plastics Associates, 1960.

Housing Division of the Henry J. Kaiser Company. *Prefabricated Plastic Houses*. Oakland, CA: Henry J. Kaiser Company, 1945.

Hyden, John, ed. *Plastics in Building*. Stamford, CT: Society of Plastics Engineers, 1969. (Report of the Regional Technical Conference, held in Chicago, Illinois, October 2–3, 1969).

McKinsey & Co. *McKinsey Report, The*. "Reducing U.S. Greenhouse Gas Emissions: How Much at What Cost?" December, 2007.

Mobay Chemical Company. *U.S. Plastics in Building and Construction: Marketing Guide & Company Directory*. Stamford, CT: Technomic Publishing Co., Inc., 1965.

Mobay Chemical Company. *U.S. Plastics in Building and Construction: Marketing Guide & Company Directory*. Stamford, CT: Technomic Publishing Co., Inc., 1966.

National Academy of Sciences (US). *Organization and Members: National Research Council*. Washington, DC: NAS-NRC, published annually.

Newport Partners. "Building Moisture and Durability Past, Present, and Future." October, 2004.

Plastics Catalogue Corporation. *Plastics Catalog: The 1945 Encyclopedia of Plastics*. New York: Plastics Catalogue Corporation, 1945.

Plastics Institute, The. *Plastics in Building Structures: Conference Supplement No. 1 to the Plastics Institute Transactions and Journal*. Oxford: Pergamon Press, 1965. (Proceedings of a conference held in London, 14–16 June 1965.)

Products Research Committee. *Fire Research on Cellular Plastics: The Final Report of the Products Research Committee*. Washington, DC: PRC 1980.

Society of the Plastics Industry, Inc. *Facts & Figures of the U.S. Plastics Industry, 1982 edition*. New York: The Society of the Plastics Industry, Inc., 1982.

Society of the Plastics Industry, Inc. *Facts & Figures of the U.S. Plastics Industry, 1988 edition*. Washington, DC: The Society of the Plastics Industry, Inc., 1988.

Society of Plastics Engineers. *Plastics for Architects, Artists, and Interior Designers*. Stamford, CT: Society of Plastics Engineers, 1960.

Society of Plastics Engineers. *Plastics in Building Construction: Realities and Challenges*. Stamford, CT: Society of Plastics Engineers, 1972. (Report of the National Technical Conference, held in Pittsburgh, Pennsylvania, November 8–10, 1972).

US Federal Trade Commission. "In the Matter of The Society of the Plastics Industry, Inc., et al.," *Federal Trade Commission Decisions: Findings, Opinions, and Orders, July 1, 1974 to December 31, 1974*. Washington, DC: US Government Printing Office, 1975.

HANDBOOKS, CODES, AND STANDARDS CONSIDERED "HISTORICAL"

ASTM. *D1600-58 T, Tentative Abbreviations of Terms Relating to Plastics*. Philadelphia, PA: ASTM. 1958.

ASTM. *D1600-64a T, Tentative Abbreviations of Terms Relating to Plastics*. Philadelphia, PA: ASTM, 1964.

ASTM. *D1600-71a, Tentative Abbreviations of Terms Relating to Plastics*. Philadelphia, PA: ASTM, 1971.

ASTM. *D1600-75, Tentative Abbreviations of Terms Relating to Plastics*. Philadelphia, PA: ASTM, 1975.

ASTM. *D1600-86a, Tentative Abbreviations of Terms Relating to Plastics*. Philadelphia, PA: ASTM, 1986.

ASTM. *D1600-91a, Tentative Abbreviations of Terms Relating to Plastics*. Philadelphia, PA: ASTM, 1991.

ASTM. *D1600-08, Tentative Abbreviations of Terms Relating to Plastics*. Philadelphia, PA: ASTM, 2008.

Celanese Plastics Corporation. *Lumarith Cellulosic Molding Materials, Celanese Plastics; A Handbook for the Layman, as well as the Expert, on the Injection and Extrusion Molding of Lumarith Thermoplastics*. New York: Celanese Plastics Corporation, 1945.

Dietz, Albert G.H. "Designing Plastics for Strength" in *Technical Data on Plastics*, 2–6. Washington, DC: Manufacturing Chemists' Association, Inc., 1957.

Manufacturing Chemists' Association, Inc. *Technical Data on Plastics*. Washington, DC: Manufacturing Chemists' Association, Inc., 1957.

United States Department of Labor. OSHA Technical Manual. www.osha.gov/dts/osta/otm/otm_iv/otm_iv_2.html#4, accessed July 23, 2014.

ADVERTISEMENTS

Celanese Corporation of America. *Architectural Forum*. January 1945: 229.

Dow Chemical Company. *Architectural Record*. August 1944: 11.

Dow Chemical Company. *Architectural Forum*. January 1945: 41.

Formica Insulation Company. *Architectural Record*. August 1944: 35.

NEWSPAPERS

"Daily Mail Ideal Home Exhibition." *Daily Mail*, February 18, 1928.

"Building Plastics Display Accents Functional Beauty." *The State and Columbia Record*, September 10, 1961.

Towns, John A. "A 'House of Future' to Showcase Plastics." *New York Times*, January 1, 1989.

Wilcke, Gerd. "Plastics Industry Hurt by Lack of Raw Materials Made of Oil." *New York Times,* November 30, 1973.

FILMS

The Door of the Minaret No Longer Looks to Mecca. Bayer AG and the German Red Cross. 1970. Filmstrip.

Modern Alchemy. Universal International Newsreel. 1957. Filmstrip.

Plastic House 1962. Pathe Newsreel. 1962. Filmstrip.

PATENTS

Grayboff, M. 1959. "Light-Transmitting Structural Panel," US Patent 3,046,617, filed January 23, 1959 and issued July 31, 1963.

Sulzbach, Reinhard A. and Robert Hartwimmer. 1981. "Process for the Preparation of Aqueous, Colloidal Dispersions of Copolymers of the Tetrafluoroethylene/Ethylene Type," US Patent 4,338,237, filed June 22, 1981 and issued July 6, 1982.

PLASTICS TERMINOLOGY

www.acgih.org/TLV

Adewumi, Michael A. and Michel T. Halbouty. "Natural Gas." *AccessScience*. McGraw Hill, 2008. www.accessscience.com/abstract.aspx?id=444800&referURL=http%3a%2f%2fwww.accessscience.com%2fcontent.aspx%3fid%3d444800

American Chemistry Council. "Vinyl Siding Recycling: A How To Guide."

www.americanchemistry.com/s_plastics/doc.asp?SID=6&-DID=6004&CID=1583&VID=178&RTID=0&CIDQS=&Taxono-my=False&specialSearch=False (accessed January 19, 2009).

ASTM. *ASTM D6868-03 Standard Specification for Biodegradable Plastics Used as Coatings on Paper and Other Compostable Substrates*. Conshohocken, PA: ASTM, 2003.

Athena Sustainable Materials Institute. *U.S. LCI Database Project Development Guidelines*. NREL Science and Technology. U.S. Life-Cycle Inventory Database, NREL/SR-33806. February 2004. http://search.nrel.gov/query.html?qp=site%3Awww.nrel.gov+site%3Awww.sst.nrel.gov+site%3Aredc.nrel.gov&qs=&qc=nrel&ws=0&qm=0&st=1&nh=10&lk=1&rf=0&oq=&col=nrel&qt=NREL%2FSR-33806&x=0&y=0

Atlas, Ronald. "Microbial Ecology." *AccessScience*. McGraw Hill. 2008 www.accessscience.com/abstract. aspx?id=422050&referURL=http%3a%2f%2fwww.accessscience. com%2fcontent.aspx%3fid%3d422050

Barlaz, M.A, D.M. Schaefer, and R.K. Ham. "Bacterial Population Development and Chemical Characteristics of Refuse Decomposition in a Simulated Sanitary Landfill." *Applied and Environmental Microbiology* Vol. 55 (1998): 55–65.

Barone, Justin. *New Uses for Animal By-products.* USDA, Research Service. February 2006.

British Plastic Federation. "Construction Sector Analysis." www.bpf.co.uk/Innovation/Construction.aspx (accessed January 19, 2009).

CDC/NIOSH: www.cdc.gov/NIOSH/TOPICS/INDOORENV

Claridge, Elmond L. and Ender Okandan. "Petroleum." *AccessScience*. McGraw Hill 2008. www.accessscience.com/abstract. aspx?id=502600&referURL=http%3a%2f%2fwww.accessscience. com%2fcontent.aspx%3fid%3d502600

Committee D20 on Plastics. "Standard Practice for Marking Plastic Products for Identification in Reuse and Recycling." *ASTM International*, March 2008.

Crelling, J., *et al.* "Coal." *Ullmann's Encyclopedia of Industrial Chemistry*, Wiley-VCH Verlag Gmbh & Co. KGaA, Weinheim, 2006. http:// mrw.interscience.wiley.com/emrw/9783527306732/ueic/article/ a07_153/current/abstract?hd=All,Coal

Damberger, Heinz H. "Coal." *AccessScience*. McGraw Hill, 2008. www.accessscience.com/abstract. aspx?id=143000&referURL=http%3a%2f%2fwww.accessscience. com%2fcontent.aspx%3fid%3d143000

Energy Information Adminstration. "Greenhouse Gases 1987–1994, Glossary." www.eia.doe.gov/oiaf/1605/archive/95report/glossary. html (accessed January 19, 2009).

Field, Joseph H. "Fischer–Tropsch Process." *AccessScience*. McGraw Hill, 2008. www.accessscience.com/abstract. aspx?id=258800&referURL=http%3a%2f%2fwww.accessscience. com%2fcontent.aspx%3fid%3d258800

Gigg, Roy H. "Lipid." *AccessScience*. McGraw Hill, 2008. www.accessscience.com/abstract. aspx?id=385500&referURL=http%3a%2f%2fwww.accessscience. com%2fcontent.aspx%3fid%3d385500

Granta CES Material Selector. Granta Design Limited. Cambridge, UK: 2007 (computer program).

Grewell, David. "Plant Based Plastics and Applications." Midwest Biopolymers and Biocomposites Workshop, April 2008.

Griesbaum, K., *et al.* "Hydrocarbons." *Ullmann's Encyclopedia of Industrial Chemistry*, Wiley-VCH Verlag Gmbh & Co. KGaA, Weinheim, 2005. http://mrw.interscience.wiley.com/ emrw/9783527306732/ueic/article/a13_227/current/ abstract?hd=All,Hydrocarbons

Hassid, William Z. "Polysaccharide." *AccessScience*. McGraw Hill 2008. www.accessscience.com/abstract. aspx?id=536800&referURL=http%3a%2f%2fwww.accessscience. com%2fcontent.aspx%3fid%3d536800

Heinzel, Wolfgang and Verlander, Michael. "Peptide Synthesis." *Ullmann's Encyclopedia of Industrial Chemistry*, Wiley-VCH Verlag Gmbh & Co. KGaA, Weinheim. 2005. http://mrw.interscience. wiley.com/emrw/9783527306732/ueic/article/a19_157/current/ abstract?hd=All,Peptide&hd=All,Synthesis

Hodgson, A., *et al.* "Implementation of VOC Source Reduction Practices in a Manufactured House and in School Classrooms." Lawrence Berkeley National Laboratory, Environmental Energy Technologies Division, Indoor Environment Department and Florida Solar Energy Center, Buildings Research Division, January 2002.

Holt, D.L. *Hydrolytic Processes.* AccessScience McGraw Hill, 2008. www.accessscience.com/abstract. aspx?id=330000&referURL=http%3a%2f%2fwww.accessscience. com%2fcontent.aspx%3fid%3d330000

Ikada, Eiji and Ashida Michio. "Promotion of Photodegradation of Polymers for Plastic Waste Treatment." *Journal of Photopolymer Science and Technology* Vol. 4 (1991): 247–254.

ISO 14040: 2006 *Environmental Management – Life Cycle Assessment – Principles and Framework*. International Organization for Standards, 2006.

Larock, Richard. "Novel Bioplastics and Biocomposites from Agricultural Oils and Co-products." Midwest Biopolymers and Biocomposites Workshop, April 2008. www.biocom.iastate.edu/ workshop/video.html

Lawrence Berkeley Labs. http://eetd.lbl.gov/IEP

London Metals Exchange, Plastic Futures. www.lme.co.uk/plastics/ index.asp (accessed January 19, 2009).

Maddalena, Randy L. "Aldehyde and Other Volatile Organic Chemical Emissions in Four FEMA Temporary Housing Units – Final Report." Lawrence Berkley National Laboratory, November 2008.

Metabolix. "Combined Production of PHA Bio-based Polymer and Biomass Energy." Metabolix Briefing Paper. www.metabolix.com/knowledge/Metabolix_CombinedProductionofPHA.pdf (accessed January 19, 2009).

Metabolix. "Metabolix Announces Results of Life Cycle Assessment for Mirel™ Bioplastic." Press release, October 2007. http://ir.metabolix.com/releasedetail.cfm?ReleaseID=310713

MIT Materials-Science-and-Engineering. *3.051J/20.340J: Materials for Biomedical Applications: Lecture 4 Biomaterials Surfaces: Chemistry Polymer Hydrolysis.* MIT Open Courseware, Spring 2006. http://ocw.mit.edu/OcwWeb/Materials-Science-and-Engineering/3-051JSpring-2006/LectureNotes/index.htm and http://ocw.mit.edu/NR/rdonlyres/Materials-Science-and-Engineering/3–051JSpring-2006/44A540B1-28BA-48F7-AC9A-F3A0F304E77B/0/lecture4.pdf

Narayan, Ramani. "Bioplastics: History, Challenges, and Opportunities." Midwest Biopolymers and Biocomposites Workshop, April 2008. www.biocom.iastate.edu/workshop/video.html

Narayan, Ramani and Charles Pettigrew. "ASTM Standards Help Grow a New Biodegradable Plastics Industry." *ASTM Standarization News* (December 1999): 36–42.

NIBS: http://ieq.nibs.org

NREL US Life-Cycle Inventory Database. www.nrel.gov/lci (accessed January 19, 2009).

OSHA "CFR 29 Health Hazard Definitions (Mandatory) – 1910.1200 App A."

OSHA "Hazard Communication Guidelines": www.osha.gov/Publications/osha3111.html.

OSHA "Recommended Format for Material Safety Data Sheets (MSDSs)": www.osha.gov/dsg/hazcom/msdsformat.html.

OSHA "Standards: Permissible Exposure Limits (PELs)": www.osha.gov/SLTC/pel/standards.html

Plastics Exchange, The. www.theplasticsexchange.com (accessed January 19, 2009).

Rinaudo, Marguerite. "Chitin and Chitosan: Properties and Applications." *Progress in Polymer Science* Vol. 31 (2006): 603–632.

Rinaudo, Marguerite. "Main Properties and Current Applications of Some Polysaccharides as Biomaterials." *Polymer International* Vol. 57 (2008): 397–430.

Sarnafil. Sarnafil Roof Recycling Program. www.sarnafilus.com/index/sustainability_s/recycle.htm (accessed January 19, 2009).

Scientific Applications International Corporation (SAIC). "Life Cycle Assessment: Principles and Practice." US EPA EPA/600/R-06/060, May 2006.

Speight, James G. "Fossil Fuel." *AccessScience.* McGraw Hill, 2008. www.accessscience.com/abstract.aspx?id=270200&referURL=http%3a%2f%2fwww.accessscience.com%2fcontent.aspx%3fid%3d270200

Tuzson, Emily. "Waste Management: Treating Waste as a Renewable Resource." GovEnergy Conference, 2006.

US Department of Energy, Energy Efficiency and Renewable Energy. "Biomass Program." www1.eere.energy.gov/biomass (accessed January 19, 2009).

US DOE. "Office of Fossil Energy." http://fossil.energy.gov (accessed January 19, 2009).

US DOE. "Energy Efficiency and Renewable Energy, Alternative Fuels & Advanced Vehicles Data Center." www.afdc.energy.gov/afdc/fuels/emerging_diesel_process.html (accessed January 19, 2009).

US DOE. "Buildings Energy Data Book." http://buildingsdatabook.eere.energy.gov/TableView.aspx?table=Notes (accessed January 19, 2009).

US EPA. www.epa.gov/iaq (accessed July 24, 2014).

US EPA. "Global Warming – Actions: Agriculture and Forestry." http://yosemite.epa.gov/oar/globalwarming.nsf/content/ActionsAgricultureandForestryBiomassProduction.html?OpenDocument (accessed January 19, 2009).

US EPA "Resource Conservation, Composting Information." www.epa.gov/epawaste/conserve/rrr/composting/basic.htm (accessed January 19, 2009).

US EPA. "Non-Hazardous Waste: Municipal Solid Waste." www.epa.gov/osw/nonhaz/municipal/landfill.htm (accessed January 19, 2009).

USGBC. *LEED 2.2 Materials and Resources.* Washington, DC: USGBC, 2006.

Voragen, A., *et al.* "Polysaccharides." *Ullmann's Encyclopedia of Industrial Chemistry*, Wiley-VCH Verlag Gmbh & Co. KGaA, Weinheim, 2003. http://mrw.interscience.wiley.com/emrw/9783527306732/ueic/article/a21_a25/current/abstract?hd=All,Polysaccharides

Weggen, K., *et al.* "Oil and Gas." *Ullmann's Encyclopedia of Industrial Chemistry*, Wiley-VCH Verlag Gmbh & Co. KGaA, Weinheim, 2005. http://mrw.interscience.wiley.com/emrw/9783527306732/ueic/article/a23_117/current/abstract?hd=All,Oil&hd=All,Gas

Wiles, D.M. and D.J. Carlsson. "Photodegredation." *AccessScience*. McGraw Hill, 2008. www.accessscience.com/abstract. aspx?id=509550&referURL=http%3a%2f%2fwww.accessscience. com%2fcontent.aspx%3fid%3d509550

Williams, R., *et al.* "Solid Waste Conversion: A Review and Database of Current and Emerging Technologies." UC Davis Department of Biological and Agricultural Engineering, December 2003.

DATA ON PLASTICS

ETFE

Moritz, Karsten, and Rainer Barthel. "Building with ETFE Sheeting" in *Translucent Materials: Glass, Plastics, Metals*, edited by Frank Kaltenbach. Basel: Birkhauser, 2004.

Sulzbach, Reinhard A. and Robert Hartwimmer. 1981. Process for the Preparation of Aqueous, Colloidal Dispersions of Copolymers of the Tetrafluoroethylene/Ethylene Type. US Patent 4,338,237, filed June 22, 1981 and issued July 6, 1982.

Vector Foiltec. *ETFE Research and Development*. 2004. www.vector-foiltec.com/resdev.htm

PC

Burger, Edward and Frank Kaltenbach, ed. *Translucent Material: Glass, Synthetic Materials, Metal*. Munich: Birkhäuser, 2004.

GE Structural Products. *Thermoforming LEXAN® Sheet: General Guidelines*.

Harper, Charles A. *Handbook of Plastics, Elastomers & Composites*. New York: McGraw-Hill, 2002.

POLYGAL® Plastic Industries. *Polygal Panels: Mechanical, Thermal and Optical Properties*, brochure.

POLYGAL® Plastic Industries. *Panels Profiles*, brochure.

LDPE

ASTM. *Standard Specification for Flexible, Low Permeance Vapor Retarders for Thermal Insulation*. West Conshohocken, PA.

ASTM. *Standard Test Method for Water Vapor Transmission Rate Through Plastic Film and Sheeting Using a Modulated Infrared Sensor*. West Conshohocken, PA.

Building Science Corporation. *Air Barriers vs. Vapor Barriers*. www.buildingscienceconsulting.com/resources/walls/air_barriers_ vs_vapor_barriers.htm

Rose, William B. "Moisture Control in the Modern Building Envelope: History of the Vapor Barrier in the U.S., 1923–1952" *APT Bulletin*, Vol. 28, No. 4, (1997): 13–19.

US Department of Energy. *A Consumers Guide to Energy Efficiency and Renewable Energy: "Vapor Barriers or Vapor Diffusion Retarders."* www.eere.energy.gov/consumer/your_home/insulation_ airsealing/index.cfm/mytopic=11810

PET/PETG

Ashby, Michael and Kara Johnson. *Materials and Design: The Art and Science of Material Selection in Product Design*. Woburn, MA: Butterworth-Heinemann, 2002.

PMMA

Harper, Charles and Edward Petrie. *Plastics Materials and Processes: A Concise Encyclopedia*. Hoboken: John Wiley & Sons, Inc., 2003.

Siemens, John. *DEGLAS® Corrugated Sheet Installation Instructions*. CYRO, 2002.

XPS

Franklin Associates for the American Plastics Council. *Plastics Energy and Greenhouse Gas Savings Using Rigid Foam Sheathing Applied to Exterior Walls of Single Family Residential housing in the U.S. and Canada – A Case Study*. September 13, 2000.

Pfundstein, Margit, Roland Gellert, Martin Spitzner, and Alexander Rudolphi. *Insulating Materials: Principles, Materials, Applications (Detail Practice)* Basel: Birkhauser, 2008.

SMART POLYMERS, HIGH-PERFORMANCE POLYMERS, BIOPOLYMERS, BIOPOLYMER COMPOSITES

Ball, Philip. *Designing the Molecular World*. Princeton, NJ: Princeton University Press, 1994.

Barone, Justin. "New Uses for Animal By-Products." Presented Thursday, February 16, 2006.

Berglin, Mattias and Paul Gatenholm. "The Nature of Bioadhesive Bonding Between Barnacles and Fouling-Release Silicone Coatings." *Adhesion Science* Vol. 13, No. 6 (1999): 713–727.

Blaiszik, B.J., N.R. Sottos, and S.R. White. "Nanocapsules for Self-Healing Materials." *Composites Science and Technology*, 68 (2008): 978–986.

Blanchet, Graciela B., Yueh-Lin Loo, J.A. Rogers, F. Gao, and C.R. Fincher. "Large Area, High Resolution, Dry Printing of Conducting Polymers for Organic Electronics." *Applied Physics Letters* Vol. 82, No. 3 (2003): 463–465.

Boswell, Clay. "Bioplastics Aren't the Stretch They Once Seemed." *Chemical Market Reporter* Vol. 260, no. 8 (August 20, 2001). FR 15. MasterFILE Premier, EBSCOhost (accessed July 26, 2014).

Brenhouse, Hillary. "A Refuge Made from Refuse." *New York Times*, September 2, 2009.

Capadona, Jeffrey R., Kadhiravan Shanmuganathan, Stephanie Trittschuh, Scott Seidel, Stuart J. Rowan, and Christoph Weder. "Polymer Nanocomposites with Nanowhiskers Isolated from Microcrystalliine Cellulose." *Biomacromolecules* Vol. 10, No. 4 (2009): 712–716.

Devasahayam, S., D.J.T. Hill, and J.W. Connell. "Effect of Electron Beam Radiolysis on Mechanical Properties of High Performance Polyimides: A Comparative Study of Transparent Films," *High Performance Polymers* 17(4): 547–559.

Fahimian, M., D. Adhikari, R. Jayaraman, R.P. Wool, and A. Campanella. "Bio-Composites from Canola Oil Based Resin and Hemp Fibers." *Journal of Biobased Materials and Bioenergy* Vol. 3, No. 1 (2009): 91–99.

Gatenholm, Paul. "Biopolymer Technology." http://nano.nstl.gov.cn/sea/MirrorResources/1345/Gatenholm-E.html (accessed July 26, 2014).

Graupner, Nina, Axel S. Hermann, and Jorg Mussig. "Natural and Man-made Cellulose Fibre-reinforced Poly(Lactic Acid) (PLA) Composites: An Overview About Mechanical Characteristics and Application Areas." *Composites Part A: Applied Science and Manufacturing* 40 (6–7) (2009): 810–821.

Hanlon, Mike. "Self Cleaning Lotus Leaf Imitated In Plastic." www.gizmag.com/go/6729 (accessed July 25, 2014).

Henriksson, Marielle, Lars A. Berglund, Per Isaksson, Tom Lindstrom, and Takashi Nishino. "Cellulose Nanopaper Structures of High Toughness." *Biomacromolecules* Vol. 9, No. 6 (2008): 1579–1585.

Honeywell. "Honeywell Advanced Fibers and Composites." www.honeywell-advancedfibersandcomposites.com (accessed July 26, 2014).

Huang, W.M., B. Yang, L. An, C. Li, and Y.S. Chan. "Water-driven Programmable Polyurethane Shape Memory Polymer: Demonstration and Mechanism," *Applied Phyiscs Letters* Vol. 86 (2005): 1–3.

Kolybaba, M., L.G. Tabil, S. Panigrahi, W.J. Crerar, T. Powell, B. Wang. "Biodegradable Polymers: Past, Present, and Future." ASAE paper, 2003.

Larock, Richard C. "Biopolymers and Composites from Natural Oils" in *Growing the Bioeconomy: Solutions for Sustainability* (a conference held at Iowa State University on December 1, 2009). Presentation.

Larock, Richard C. and Paul W. Gallagher. "Development of Corn/Soy Plastic Composites: Phase II." Department of Chemistry, Iowa State University, IMBA Project 2006–2, progress report.

Lendlein, Andreas. "Shape Memory Polymers: Biodegradable Sutures." Abstracted by AZoM.com, www.azom.com/article. aspx?ArticleID=1542 (accessed July 25, 2014).

Lenz, Robert W. "JTEC Monograph on Biodegradable Polymers and Plastics in Japan: Research, Development, and Applications." International Technology Research Institute, JTEC/WTEC Program, Loyola College in Maryland, March 1995.

Lorenz, J. Bonderer, André R. Studart, and Ludwig J. Gauckler. "Bioinspired Design and Assembly of Platelet Reinforced Polymer Films." *Science New Series*, Vol. 319, No. 5866 (2008): 1069–1073.

Metabolix. "Combined Production of PHA Bio-based Polymers and Biomass Energy" (2008).

Mirel. "Chemical Resistance Technical Bulletin" (2007).

Narayan, Ramani. "Biobased Materials & Biodegradable Plastics 101." Michigan State University, Chemical Engineering and Materials Science. (Undated materials, accessed July 25, 2014).

Narayan, Ramani. "ASTM Standards Help Define and Grow a New Biodegradable Plastics Industry." *ASTM Standardization News* (1999): 36–42.

NatureWorks LLC. "Sourcing Ingeo: Raw Materials." www.natureworksllc.com/The-Ingeo-Journey/Raw-Materials (accessed July 27, 2014).

NatureWorks LLC. "Making Ingeo: Eco-Profile & LCA." www.natureworksllc.com/The-Ingeo-Journey/Eco-Profile-and-LCA. (accessed July 27, 2014).

NatureWorks LLC. "Renewing Ingeo: End-Of-Life Options." www.natureworksllc.com/The-Ingeo-Journey/End-of-Life-Options (accessed July 27, 2014).

NatureWorks LLC. "Innovation Takes Root Conference Report." Planet Hollywood Resort and Casino, Las Vegas, Nevada, September 16–18, 2008.

Physorg.com. "Self Cleaning Lotus Leaf Imitated in Plastic by Using a Femtosecond Laser." (accessed July 25, 2014).

"Plastics Steel": Optically Transparent Plastic Nanocomposites. www.technovelgy.com/ct/Science-Fiction-News. asp?NewsNum=2016, (accessed July 26, 2014).

Ramanathan, T., A.A. Abdala, S. Stankovich, D.A. Dikin, M. Herrera-Alonso, R.D. Piner, D.H.Adamson, J. Liu, R.S. Ruoff, S.T. Nguyen, I. Lhan, A. Aksay, R.K. Prud'homme, and L.C. Brinson. "Functionalized Graphene Sheets for Polymer Nanocomposites," *Nature: Nanotechnology*, Vol 3, No. 6 (2008): 327–331.

Ratner, S., A. Pegoretti, C. Mmigliaresi, A. Weinberg, and G. Marom. "Relaxation Processes and Fatigue Behavior of Crosslinked UHMWPE Fiber Compacts." *Composites Science and Technology* Vol. 65 (2005): 87–94.

Rolex. "Awards for Enterprise: Elsa Zaldivar, Recyclable Homes." www.rolexawards.com/profiles/laureates/elsa_zaldvar/project (accessed July 27, 2014).

Solanyl. "A New Generation of Smart Mateirals." www.solanyl.ca (accessed July 27, 2014).

Somashekar, D. and Richard Joseph. "Chitosanases – Properties and Applications: A Review." *Bioresource Technology* Vol. 55 (1996): 35–45.

Sottos, Nancy, Scott White, and Ian Bond. "Introduction: Self-healing Polymers and Composites." *Journal of the Royal Society* Vol. 4 (2007): 347–348.

Stevens, E.S. *Green Plastics: An Introduction to the New Science of Biodegradable Plastics*. Princeton, NJ: Princeton University Press, 2002.

Toohey, Kathleen S., Nancy R. Sottos, Jennifer A. Lewis, Jeffrey S. Moore, and Scott R. White. "Self-healing Materials with Microvascular Networks." *Nature Materials*. Published online: June 10, 2007; doi: 10.1038/nmat1934.

US Department of Energy, Energy Efficiency, and Renewable Energy. "Production of Polyhydroxyalkanoate Polymers." Biomass Program (June 2006) www.eere.energy.gov/biomass.

Vroman, Isabelle and Tighzert, Lan. "Biodegradable Polymers," *Materials* Vol. 2 (2009): 307–344.

Ward Patrick, G., M. Goff, M. Donner, W. Karminsky, and K.E. O'Connor. "A Two-Step Chemo-biotechnological Conversion of Polystyrene to a Biodegradable Thermoplastic." *Environmental Science & Technology* Vol. 40, No. 7 (2006): 2433–2437.

Wool, Richard P. and Xiuzhi Susan Sun. *Bio-Based Polymers and Composites*. Amsterdam: Elsevier Academic Press, 2005.

Yamada, Munenori, Mizuho Kondo, Ryo Miyasato, Yumiko Naka, Jun-ichi Mamiya, Motoi Kinoshita, Atsushi Shishido, Yanlei Yu, Christopher J. Barrett, and Tomiki Ikeda. "Photomobile Polymer Materials: Various Three-Dimensional Movements." *Journal of Materials Chemistry* Vol. 19, No. 1 (2009): 60–62.

IMAGE, REPRINTS AND HISTORICAL DIALOGUE CREDITS

INDEX